The Morality of
Gay Rights

THE MORALITY
OF
GAY RIGHTS

An Exploration in
Political Philosophy

CARLOS A. BALL

Routledge
Taylor & Francis Group

NEW YORK AND LONDON

Published in 2003 by
Routledge
29 West 35th Street
New York, NY 10001
www.routledge-ny.com

Published in Great Britain by
Routledge
11 New Fetter Lane
London EC4P 4EE
www.routledge.co.uk

Copyright © 2003 by Taylor & Francis Books, Inc.

Routledge is an imprint of the Taylor & Francis Group.
Printed in the United States of America on acid-free paper.

10 9 8 7 6 5 4 3 2 1

Library of Congress Cataloging-in-Publication Data

Ball, Carlos A.
   The morality of gay rights : an exploration in political philosophy / by Carlos A. Ball.
      p. cm.
   Includes bibliographical references and index.
   ISBN 0-415-93140-1 — ISBN 0-415-93141-X (pbk.)
      1. Gay rights—Philosophy. 2. Homosexuality—Moral and ethical aspects.   I. Title.

HQ76.5 .B35 2002
305.9′0664—dc21

                                                          2002069653

*To Richard, and to our sons
Emmanuel and Sebastian*

CONTENTS

Preface   ix

Acknowledgments   xi

Citation Abbreviations   xiii

Introduction
Why Morality?   1

One
Neutral Liberalism   15

1. Rawls's Political Liberalism   17
2. Rawls from a Gay Rights Perspective   22
3. Dworkin's Liberal Equality and Moral Bracketing   30
4. The Later Dworkin: Individual Ethics and the
   Liberal Society   37

Two
Pragmatic Liberalism   41

1. Rorty's Pragmatism   42
2. Rorty from a Gay Rights Perspective   48

3. Posner's Pragmatism and Human Sexuality   58

4. Rational Man as Moral Man   64

Three
Moral Liberalism   75

1. Needs, Capabilities, and the Leading of Full
   Human Lives   77

2. Relationships, Attachments, and Autonomy   91

3. Moral Liberalism and Gay Rights   100

Four
Communitarianism   139

1. Sandellian Values and Communities   141

2. The Role of Community in the Lives of Lesbians
   and Gay Men   145

3. Walzer and Justice   151

4. Internal Social Criticism: Same-Sex Marriage and
   Parenting by Lesbians and Gay Men   155

Five
Postmodernism   171

1. Foucault and Sexual Ethics   174

2. Agency Versus Autonomy in Foucault's Late Writings   185

3. Codes of Conduct and a Gay and Lesbian Sexual Ethic 194

Notes   219

Index   263

PREFACE

The writing of this book began with a single question: Does society have an obligation to recognize and support the relationships and families of lesbians and gay men? The question is an important one given that many of the reform efforts currently underway on behalf of lesbians and gay men, in both legislative and judicial arenas, revolve around it. As I began to think about the question, it seemed to me that some of the principles of political philosophy that for many years have provided the theoretical and justificatory framework for gay rights positions needed to be reconsidered. That framework has been based, in part, on the idea that the state should remain neutral regarding the morality of same-gender sexuality and relationships. The importance attached to neutrality is reflected in the often-heard demands by gay rights proponents that the state refrain from regulating the personal and sexual lives of lesbians and gay men. Paradoxically, however, many lesbians and gay men these days are asking that the state involve itself in their lives by recognizing and supporting their committed relationships and families.

This apparent inconsistency led me to consider whether gay rights supporters have to make specifically moral arguments (as opposed to neutral ones) in order to justify the kinds of state action that many are demanding. If we answer that question in the affirmative, as I believe we should, that raises a series of legitimate concerns about the advisability of incorporating notions of morality and the good into public policy matters associated with same-gender sexuality and relationships, when such notions have in the past contributed immensely to the oppression and marginalization of lesbians and gay men. This book primarily concerns itself with finding the appropriate balance between, on the one hand, incorporating notions of morality and the good into our understandings of the proper role of the state in the regulation of and support for intimate relationships (both sexual and familial) and, on the other hand, protecting the basic rights to autonomy and equality of all individuals, including those whose sexuality is different from the norm.

This book has also been motivated by an additional consideration, one that is less about political philosophy and more personal. Every gay or lesbian person experiences a dissonance between his or her sense of self-worth on the one hand and social norms that deem homosexuality to be intrinsically immoral and perverted on the other. Those of us with a same-gender sexual orientation know from the very core of our beings that our sexuality is neither immoral nor perverted. And yet, in important ways, prevailing liberal norms contribute to rather than mitigate the effects of the dissonance because they encourage us to sidestep rather than directly address the moral objections to our relationships and our lives raised by many opponents of gay rights. This book is, in part, my own (admittedly intellectual) way of quieting that dissonance.

ACKNOWLEDGMENTS

I owe many thanks to individuals and institutions who helped me along the way, and without whose support and assistance this project would not have been possible. At the University of Illinois College of Law, where I work, I have been blessed with thoughtful colleagues and good friends. I thank, in particular, Ellen Deason, Kit Kinports, Andy Leipold, Phil McConnaughay, Janet Murphy, Jim Pfander, Laurie Reynolds, Steve Ross, Elaine Shoben, Nina Tarr, and Cindy Williams. The College of Law provided me with ongoing research support and a sabbatical during which I completed this manuscript. I was fortunate to be able to spend the sabbatical as a guest of the Texas Wesleyan University School of Law, where I was provided with office and library support. I thank both schools for their generosity. Jan Broekman, Don Dripps, David Meyer, David Richards, Mark Strasser, and Marlin Paschal read portions of the manuscript and provided wise and helpful comments. So did participants at law faculty workshops at Ohio State University, Texas Wesleyan University, the University of California at Los Angeles, and the University of Illinois. Andrew Koppelman deserves special mention because he was kind enough to read, in one form or another, almost the entire manuscript. Andy encouraged me to crystalize my ideas and to think about both their metaethical and practical implications; I am deeply indebted to him for that. Chai Feldblum also deserves special mention because she has been an enthusiastic reader and supporter from the beginning. Chai and I seem to be in a minority among academics who write in support of gay rights with our insistence that questions of morality and of gay rights are inextricably linked. It is a minority position that I am proud to share with her. Finally, the person to whom I owe the most is Richard Storrow, who has been a thoughtful reader, a kind friend, and a loving partner. Much of what I think I know about loving and caring for another human being, I have learned from him.

Some sections of chapter 1 appeared previously in "Moral Foundations for a Discourse on Same-Sex Marriage: Looking Beyond Political Liberalism," 85 *Georgetown Law Review* 1871 (1997), while other sections of chapter 1 and some sections of chapter 4 appeared previously in "Communitarianism and Gay Rights," 85 *Cornell Law Re-*

view 443 (2000). I have tried whenever possible in those two chapters, however, to clarify and improve the arguments as presented in the law review articles. Most of chapter 5 appeared previously in "Sexual Ethics and Postmodernism in Gay Rights Philosophy," 80 *North Carolina Law Review* 371 (2002), though I have made changes in organization and length, as well as some in style. I thank the journals for permitting the use of previously published material.

CITATION ABBREVIATIONS

AOC Richard Rorty, *Achieving Our Country: Leftist Thought in Twentieth-Century America* (Cambridge: Harvard University Press, 1998).

ASD Martha C. Nussbaum, "Aristotelian Social Democracy," in *Liberalism and the Good*, eds. R. Bruce Douglass et al. (New York: Routledge, 1990), p. 203.

CIS Richard Rorty, *Contingency, Irony, and Solidarity* (New York: Cambridge University Press, 1989).

DD Michael J. Sandel, *Democracy's Discontent: America in Search of a Public Philosophy* (Cambridge: Harvard University Press, 1996).

ECS Michel Foucault, "The Ethics of the Concern for Self as a Practice of Freedom," in *Ethics: Subjectivity and Truth*, ed. Paul Rabinow (New York: The New Press, 1997), p. 281.

FLE Ronald Dworkin, "Foundations of Liberal Equality," in *Equal Freedom: Selected Tanner Lectures on Human Values*, ed. Stephen Darwall (Ann Arbor: University of Michigan Press, 1995), p. 190.

HFS Martha C. Nussbaum, *Human Functioning and Social Justice: In Defense of Aristotelian Essentialism*, 20 *Political Theory* 202 (1992).

HS1 Michel Foucault, Vol. 1, *The History of Sexuality: An Introduction* (New York: Random House, 1978).

HS2 Michel Foucault, Vol. 2, *The History of Sexuality: The Use of Pleasure* (New York: Random House, 1985).

HS3 Michel Foucault, Vol. 3, *The History of Sexuality: The Care of the Self* (New York: Random House, 1986).

IPR John Rawls, "The Idea of Public Reason Revisited," 64 *University of Chicago Law Review* 765 (1997).

ISC Michael Walzer, *Interpretation and Social Criticism* (Cambridge: Harvard University Press, 1987).

LLJ Michael J. Sandel, *Liberalism and the Limits of Justice* (New York: Cambridge University Press, 1982).

MP Ronald Dworkin, *A Matter of Principle* (Cambridge: Harvard University Press, 1985).

ORT   Richard Rorty, *Objectivity, Relativism, and Truth* (New York: Cambridge University Press, 1991).

PL   John Rawls, *Political Liberalism* (New York: Columbia University Press, 1993).

PLM   Richard A. Posner, *The Problematics of Moral and Legal Theory* (Cambridge: Harvard University Press, 1999).

PSH   Richard Rorty, *Philosophy and Social Hope* (New York: Penguin Books, 1999).

SJ   Michael Walzer, *Spheres of Justice: A Defense of Pluralism and Equality* (New York: Basic Books, 1983).

SR   Richard A. Posner, *Sex and Reason* (Cambridge: Harvard University Press, 1992).

TJ   John Rawls, *A Theory of Justice* (New York: Oxford University Press, 1971).

TP   Richard Rorty, *Truth and Progress* (New York: Cambridge University Press, 1998).

TRS   Ronald Dworkin, *Taking Rights Seriously* (Cambridge: Harvard University Press, 1977).

WHD   Martha C. Nussbaum, *Women and Human Development: The Capabilities Approach* (New York: Cambridge University Press, 2000).

INTRODUCTION

Why Morality?

For most of the history of the gay rights movement in the United States, it has been possible and even advisable for its supporters to avoid engaging questions of morality directly. Arguments based on notions of morality have been used primarily by opponents of gay rights to justify the differential treatment by society of lesbians and gay men. It is the purported immorality of a gay and lesbian sexuality, for example, that justifies in the minds of some denying same-gender couples the right to marry. It is that perceived immorality that also leads some to dismiss the idea of antidiscrimination protection on the basis of sexual orientation as a misguided attribution of "special rights" based on sexual conduct or proclivities. In response to these and other familiar arguments raised by opponents of gay rights about the immorality of gay and lesbian sexuality and relationships, most supporters of gay rights (including political activists and academics) prefer to sidestep moral arguments altogether and instead rely on what are taken to be morally neutral (and largely liberal) arguments based on considerations of privacy, equality, and tolerance.

Political philosophers have a term for this kind of sidestepping: they call it "moral bracketing." Moral bracketing entails the strict separation of moral, philosophical, and religious views (or what philosophers call questions of the good) from considerations of justice (or what philosophers call questions of the right). This book consists principally of arguments in political philosophy against moral bracketing in the context of two issues that are today near the top of the gay rights movement's agenda: same-sex marriage and parenting by lesbians and gay men. The book will argue that there is a proper and positive relationship between morality on the one hand and the formulation, advancement, and justification of gay rights positions in the areas of marriage and parenting on the other.

Although this book is about political philosophy and not history, I want to begin by providing a (very) brief summary of the history of the gay rights movement from the vantage point of moral bracketing. I begin with a little history because the movement, by emphasizing marriage and parenting during the last few years, has entered into areas of social policy where moral bracketing is largely untenable. But that has not always been the case. For most of the movement's history, moral bracketing made a great deal of sense. During the early years of what we today call the gay rights movement, that is, during the pre-Stonewall activism of the 1950s and 1960s, the principal political goal of lesbians and gay men was to reduce the levels of state-promoted oppression. In a society where approximately one million lesbians and gay men were arrested between 1946 and 1961 for engaging in consensual sexual intercourse, as well as for dancing, kissing, and engaging in other open displays of affection,[1] the focus of early activists had, by necessity, to be on protecting lesbians and gay men from the outright coercion and harassment carried out by the state. The best way of accomplishing this goal was by convincing society that the state should not interfere with the private and intimate lives of individuals. The idea of protecting a separate realm of private morality from repressive forces seeking to regulate private conduct on the basis of public morality was understandably appealing to lesbians and gay men as they became active in political and civil rights activities.

The justification for a right to privacy in matters of sexual intimacy was captured famously by the authors of the Wolfenden Committee Report issued in 1957.[2] The report was written by a committee established by the British Parliament to study, among other issues, the possible decriminalization of male homosexual acts. (Britain had never bothered to criminalize female homosexual acts.) In supporting such a decriminalization, the committee noted that "[u]nless a deliberate attempt is to be made by society, acting through the agency of the law, to equate the sphere of crime with that of sin, there must remain a realm of private morality and immorality which is, in brief and crude terms, not the law's business."[3] The report made clear that it did not intend "to condone or encourage private immorality"; rather, it argued that "to emphasize the personal and private nature of moral or immoral conduct is to emphasize the personal and private responsibility of the individual for his own actions."[4] Although the issuance of the Wolfenden Committee Report was barely noticed by the mainstream American press, gay publications "heralded it as a harbinger of a more humane future and a model for American legislators."[5] It was thought by activists at the time that if the state would only leave lesbians and gay men alone, if it could be forced to recognize that they too were entitled to privacy in their personal and intimate lives, then perhaps, at the very least, those who were physically and emotionally attracted to individuals of the same gender could lead quiet and peaceful lives without fear of incarceration or harassment.

The inclination to separate notions of morality from society's response to and regulation of homosexuality, then, has deep historical roots in the life of the gay rights movement. This did not change in any fundamental way in the 1970s and 1980s when gay rights supporters began to formulate equality-based claims to supplement their earlier privacy-based arguments. During this time of increased political activism, the priorities of lesbians and gay men began to shift. They now wanted more from the state than that it simply refrain from repression and harassment; they also sought *protection by* the state, asking that it serve as a civil shield against discrimination.[6] Privacy-based arguments in the context of sexuality by their very nature emphasize the need to leave individuals alone so that they can engage in their chosen forms of sexual intimacy. The equality-based demands made in the 1970s and 1980s, however, were accompanied by a shift toward a focus on the fuller lives of lesbians and gay men, which, like for everybody else, included sex, but also implicated their ability to lead open and forthright lives (as opposed to quiet and closeted ones) without the fear of discrimination or retribution. The focus of the gay rights movement, in other words, was expanded to include not just the demand for the right to be left alone in the private sphere but also for the right to equality in the public one. This led lesbians and gay men to seek the protection against discrimination in employment, housing, and public accommodations provided by the state to other minorities.

To a large extent, so-called morally neutral values such as privacy and equality were well-suited for the attainment of the two principal reform efforts promoted by the gay rights movement through the 1980s: (1) the elimination of the criminal regulation of same-gender sexual conduct in general and sodomy statutes in particular; and (2) the provision by the state of antidiscrimination protection on the basis of sexual orientation. Whether one believes that the state should regulate consensual sexual activity through the criminal law depends on whether one supports the view that the state has a legitimate interest in discouraging conduct that a majority of society considers immoral. Justice Byron White, in upholding the constitutionality of Georgia's sodomy statute in *Bowers v. Hardwick,* answered that question in the affirmative when he argued that the "presumed belief of a majority of the electorate in Georgia that homosexual sodomy is immoral and unacceptable" was not an "inadequate rationale to support" the criminal regulation of same-gender sodomy.[7] Gay rights supporters, on the other hand, have argued that the scope and application of a constitutional right to privacy in matters of sexuality should be determined independently of notions of morality. Thus, law professor Lawrence Tribe, in formulating Michael Hardwick's constitutional challenge to the Georgia statute, argued that the state's efforts to regulate intimate relations conducted in private could not be "defended . . . by 'the mere assertion that the action of the State finds justification in the controversial realm of morals.' Rather, th[e] law can be defended only if it can be shown to serve closely some state objective other than the bald assertion of one possible moral view."[8]

Similarly, gay rights proponents have based arguments in support of the need to protect lesbians and gay men from employment, housing, and public accommodation discrimination on notions of equality and fairness, not on the morality or goodness of same-gender sexuality. Antidiscrimination arguments can comfortably be made within the confines of moral bracketing because it is not necessary to contend that a gay or lesbian sexuality is either moral or good in order to argue that there should be, for example, a federal law prohibiting employment discrimination. All that is needed is to argue that sexual orientation is irrelevant to employment decisions, and that in the same way that heterosexuals are not (or should not) be denied employment opportunities because of their consensual sexual relationships, neither should lesbians and gay men.[9]

Until recently, therefore, it has been possible to justify and advance gay rights positions without having to "neither affirm nor deny the morality of homosexuality."[10] That has changed, however, now that the gay rights movement is seeking societal recognition and support of gay and lesbian relationships and families. Many lesbians and gay men today are no longer asking simply that they be left alone in matters of sexual intimacy (though obviously considerations of privacy remain extremely important). They are also no longer asking simply that their sexual orientation be deemed irrelevant in the allocation of jobs and housing (though obviously protection against discrimination in those areas is vital as well). Rather, lesbians and gay men by the thousands are also stepping forward and insisting that their relationships and families merit societal recognition and support. Neither the establishment of a private sphere of sexual intimacy, even if it were subject to constitutional protection, nor the establishment of a civil shield against discrimination, is sufficient any longer. Now that lesbians and gay men in large numbers are seeking to marry and to become parents, it is no longer possible to avoid normative evaluations about the value, goodness, and implications of same-gender intimate relationships and of families headed by lesbians and gay men.

It is interesting to note, in fact, how the fundamental disagreement in gay rights debates in the United States has in the last decade or so shifted away from an earlier and almost exclusive focus on privacy issues. Many conservative opponents of gay rights today no longer object to the idea that lesbians and gay men have a right "to be left alone" in matters of sexual intimacy. In a television interview a few years ago, for example, the conservative commentator and politician William Bennett (author of the best-selling volume *The Book of Virtues*)[11] acknowledged that "homosexuals should . . . be left alone [since] the value attached [to] leaving people alone is the . . . thing most valued by most people."[12] What Bennett could not countenance was the "validation" of same-gender relationships through a recognition of same-sex marriage. Similarly, while debating the Defense of Marriage Act of 1996, a co-sponsor of the legislation argued on the floor of the Senate that while "most of us agree that everyone should have the right to privacy," the institution of marriage should be limited to a man and a woman.[13] In the same way, John Finnis, one of the leading academic opponents of gay rights, recognizes that it has become generally accepted in Western societies that the state should not criminalize private consensual sexual conduct between adults.[14] It is a different matter altogether, however, for the state "to recognize homosexual 'marriages' or permit the adoption of children by homosexually active people."[15] In those matters, Finnis argues, what is at stake is not a right to privacy but is instead a legitimate state concern with public morality and the common good.

Although I disagree, for reasons that will become clear, with the moral positions of Finnis and other conservative opponents of gay rights, I believe that many if not most of the controversies over homosexuality in our society are at their core *appropriately* moral ones. Even the paradigmatic right to privacy in matters of sexual intimacy, I believe, is most convincingly grounded on a moral conception of the potential for human flourishing that inheres in the exercise of self-determination or autonomy.[16] The public discourse on gay rights, however, does not adequately reflect the moral issues and controversies that are at stake. Conservative opponents of gay rights seem to believe that they have a monopoly on issues of morality; liberal supporters of gay rights are more often than not happy to cede that monopoly, believing (or at least arguing) that issues of morality are irrelevant when determining the appropriate societal responses to homosexuality. Both of these views are in my opinion mistaken, especially when brought to bear on the two issues that will be the main focus of this book: same-sex marriage and parenting by lesbians and gay men.[17] It is my view that, given the kind of recognition and support of gay and lesbian relationships and families that is today being emphasized by the gay rights movement, moral evaluations can no longer be avoided in the formulation, advancement, and justification of at least some gay rights positions. This requires, therefore, a shift in the theoretical foundations that support the more practical aspirations of the movement. The primary goal of this book is to begin the process of thinking about theory in such a way that allows for an incorporation of notions of the good and the valuable into a philosophy of gay rights without compromising or endangering traditional liberal values, such as autonomy and equality, upon which the gay rights movement has relied for several decades now. I hope to explain how it is possible to incorporate notions of morality, as well as the value of community and a substantive conception of sexual ethics, into a theoretical foundation for gay rights positions without abandoning liberalism's basic commitment to ideals of autonomy and equality.

It is important at this early point to distinguish between legal/constitutional arguments for gay rights positions on the one hand and justifications for those positions that are grounded on moral and political philosophy on the other. Although this book will sometimes make references to the former, the main focus will be on the latter. The moral and political philosophy—from neutral liberalism to skeptical pragmatism to relativistic postmodernism—of "leftist" theory in the United States today has one common denominator: a strong reluctance to stake out moral positions that are grounded in universal norms. This reluctance has different rationales: the liberal who promotes state neutrality argues that it is impossible to reach (even basic) agreement on questions of the good; the pragmatist holds that all morality is local and epistemologically indistinguishable from accepted customs and traditions; the postmodernist views morality as nothing more than a reflection of power relations and systems of knowledge. When a gay rights supporter, who is usually a person of the left, therefore, searches for principles that will help him or her understand, explain, and justify gay rights positions, that supporter—whether a liberal-leftist or a progressive-leftist or a radical-leftist—will primarily find theory that is deeply apprehensive about staking out moral positions in the traditional sense; that is, positions based, at least in part, on evaluations as to what is good and bad in human affairs. This book hopes to show that it is both possible and necessary to ground the theoretical underpinnings of at least some gay rights positions in moral assessments regarding what is necessary for individuals to be able to lead full human lives.

I begin in chapter 1 with a critique of the most powerful and influential theory in favor of moral bracketing in contemporary political philosophy, that offered by the neutral liberalism of John Rawls. Rawls's political conception of justice separates the political values that are held in common by citizens in a constitutional regime from the reasonable but incompatible philosophical, moral, and religious doctrines held by those same citizens. For lesbians and gay men facing a society that is at best grudgingly tolerant of, and at worst openly hostile toward, their sexuality and relationships, Rawls offers a political theory that seeks to insulate them from society's moral disapprobation. The liberalism of Rawls, therefore, may appear at first to provide a well-suited theoretical foundation for the pursuit of gay rights goals. Yet, Rawlsian liberalism, by itself, proves incapable of providing a coherent justificatory framework that engages the moral issues that are (and should be) part of the debates over whether society should recognize and support committed same-gender intimate relationships and parenting by lesbians and gay men. Rawlsian liberalism, by insisting on moral bracketing and on defining the right independently of the good, fails to address the normative aspects of these two controversies and is in important ways irrelevant to the ongoing debates. I also in chapter 1 discuss the political philosophy of Ronald Dworkin. Dworkin has in the last few years attempted to formulate a less explicitly neutral kind of liberalism, one that seeks to connect the ethical considerations of liberal citizens with the structure and values of a liberal society. Although Dworkin's theory is in some ways an improvement over Rawls's, it still has limitations, limitations that can only be overcome, as I will argue in chapter 3, by a more explicitly moral form of liberalism.

In chapter 2, I address a conception of liberalism, known as pragmatic liberalism, that, unlike neutral liberalism, is explicitly antiuniversalist and antifoundationalist. In discussing pragmatic liberalism, I explore the writings of Richard Rorty and Richard Posner. I argue that the thin commonalities (such as the sharing of American citizenship and values) that Rorty emphasizes is not particularly helpful (to use Rorty's favored evaluative criterion) in promoting and justifying gay rights positions on marriage and parenting. In order to support many of the claims made on society today by lesbians and gay men, it is necessary to make a more explicitly moral evaluation about exactly that which Rorty argues should be irrelevant to questions of political morality, namely, the characteristics and attributes that define us as human beings. I also in chapter 2 argue that Richard Posner's pragmatist project of articulating and defending a "morally indifferent" conception of sex and its regulation is ultimately unsuccessful. As we will see, Posner's writings on human sexuality raise as many moral questions as they seek to avoid answering.

After criticizing neutral and pragmatic forms of liberalism, in chapter 3—which is the longest chapter in the book—I articulate what I believe to be a more appropriate conception of liberalism, heavily influenced by the writings of Martha Nussbaum, that I call "moral liberalism." Moral liberalism explicitly incorporates notions of the good, in particular what is required so that all individuals may lead lives that are fully human, into discussions of rights and justice without compromising the liberal tenets of autonomy and equality. Moral liberalism is characterized by two main principles. First, it recognizes that human beings share basic needs and capabilities that are indispensable for the leading of full human lives. Second, it rejects the proposition that human beings are inherently individualistic creatures. Instead, it recognizes that we all have a myriad of relationships and attachments that play a crucial role in the exercise of our capacity for self-determination or autonomy. Rather than viewing others primarily as a threat to individual autonomy (as do most forms of liberalism), moral liberalism sees autonomy as emanating largely from our relationships with others. After elaborating on the two main principles of moral liberalism, I explore how they can serve as foundations for compelling moral and political justifications for societal recognition and support of gay and lesbian relationships and families.

In chapter 4, I turn to the communitarian critique of liberalism and to the similarities and differences between communitarianism and moral liberalism. I there explore the writings of two leading communitarian thinkers: Michael Sandel and Michael Walzer. Sandel's work is important because he has been the leading critic of the Rawlsian separation of the right from the good and because he has been an influential proponent of the positive role of community in the lives of individuals. Many lesbians and gay men can attest to Sandel's view that communities can play a crucial function in providing individuals with a sense of identity, self-worth, and empowerment. Sandel's conception of community, however, proves to be too limited because he underestimates both the value of communities of choice and the threats to autonomy and equality that sometimes emanate from the given communities into which we are born.

Michael Walzer's communitarian theory is based on the idea that the most significant and relevant components of moral and social criticism are local—that is—internal to a society's shared traditions. For Walzer, justice inheres in a society's shared understandings of the goods it distributes. In chapter 4, I apply Walzer's theory of internal criticism to the issues of same sex marriage and parenting by lesbians and gay men as a way of exploring its benefits and limitations. The principal benefit of Walzer's theory is that it counsels us against thinking about considerations of justice as being detached from the distinct ways in which particular societies understand the goods (such as marriage and parenting) that they distribute. The limitations become evident when there are unresolvable internal conflicts as to the meanings of the goods as well as when those meanings are oppressive of and harmful to distinct individuals and groups.

I end the book in chapter 5 with a discussion of postmodernism in general, and the writings of Michel Foucault on sexual ethics in particular. Those writings shed further light on two issues discussed earlier in the book. First, they contribute to the discussion of whether it makes sense to think of certain human capabilities, and in particular of a capacity for autonomy, as universal, that is, as shared by all human beings. Second, they help us argue against the prevailing notion held by many opponents of gay rights that they have a monopoly on issues of sexual morality and ethics. In pursuing these themes, I rely on Foucault's less well-known Volumes II and III of *The History of Sexuality* (less well-known, that is, than most of Foucault's other books, including, in particular, Volume I of *The History of Sexuality*) to explore the meaning of a contemporary gay and lesbian sexual ethic. I explain how the legal, medical, and moral decodification of same-gender sexuality that has taken place in the United States in the last forty years has allowed for the emergence of a gay and lesbian sexual ethic defined by values such as openness, mutuality, and pleasure. In doing so, I analogize between the emergence of this sexual ethic and the ethics as practices of freedom in ancient Greece and Rome as identified by Foucault. I argue that a gay and lesbian sexual ethic offers a powerful and appealing alternative to the traditional Christian sexual ethic that makes moral judgments based, in part, on the nature of particular sexual acts. I also explore the role that a capacity for autonomy plays in the development of a gay and lesbian sexual ethic as I seek to find a middle ground between postmodernist and liberal supporters of gay rights.

In my discussions throughout the book of the relationship between morality, ethics, and politics in a philosophy of gay rights, I rely on a form of universalism that considers certain basic needs and capabilities to be constitutive of our humanity. The universalism, which I defend in this book, holds that human beings share certain fundamental attributes that distinguish them from other animals and that impose moral and political obligations on societies. Given the fact that universalism is often associated with essentialism, and that, in turn, no concept engenders a more critical reaction in most gay studies (and feminist) academic circles than essentialism, I want to make it clear at this early point that the universalism of which I speak is different from the kind of essentialism that is at issue in most of the heated debates over whether sexual orientation is an innate or natural characteristic or whether it is instead a social construction. I do not in this book take a position on that issue, which has received considerable (and arguably more than enough) attention elsewhere. Instead, my view is that even if social constructionists are correct that the category of "the homosexual" is created by society, that does not undermine a deeper kind of universality which recognizes that all human beings have certain basic needs and capabilities associated with sexual intimacy. I believe that that shared commonality should be the starting place for moral and political arguments on behalf of lesbians and gay men.

I want to elaborate briefly on the subtleties of social constructionist theory in matters of sexuality so that I am not misunderstood. Those who approach sexuality from a social constructionist perspective can be divided roughly into three groups: soft, moderate, and strict social constructionists. For soft social constructionists, individuals have innate sexual preferences for individuals of one gender or the other (or both), but they express those preferences in different ways according to the norms and influences of different societies. Soft social constructionists, in other words, believe that individuals have a sexual orientation that precedes or is independent of society, though the kinds and meanings of sexual acts that accompany a particular form of sexual orientation will vary greatly across time and place.[18] For moderate social constructionists, on the other hand, the very idea of a same or different gender sexual attraction is socially constructed. Categories such as "homosexuals" and "heterosexuals" (as well as "men" and "women") are both created and given meaning to by society. For moderate social constructionists, therefore, there was no such thing as "a homosexual" until that identity was created through the workings of social norms and disciplines (such as medicine and psychiatry) in the second half of the nineteenth century.[19] For moderate social constructionists, it is society that determines the direction of sexual desire (or object choice) as well as the particular forms in which that desire manifests itself as conduct. Strict social constructionists go one step further and argue that not only is the *direction* of sexual desire socially constructed, but so is the very idea of sexual desire itself.[20] For strict social constructionists, there is *nothing* about sexuality, sex, and the body that can be explained or understood in a general or universal sense because they have no existence or meaning that is independent of the social discourses and power relations that determine and define them.

Given that most contemporary academics in the social sciences and humanities who write on matters of sexuality are social constructionists, my division of them into three broad groups necessarily simplifies the differences and subtleties among them.[21] The point I want to make, however, is that a philosophical position that considers certain needs and capabilities, some of which are associated with sexuality, as shared constitutive characteristics of all human beings is consistent with most social constructionist approaches to sexuality. The position I take in this book that there are universal needs and capabilities shared by all human beings in matters of sexuality only takes issue with strict social constructionism. The kind of universality that I defend rejects the idea that the social construction of sexuality goes all the way down, namely, that there is nothing to our needs and capabilities regarding sexual intimacy that is not socially constructed. To put it differently, we would, I believe, have needs and capabilities for sexual intimacy (however they may be experienced and manifested according to social norms) regardless of when and where we happen to live. Part of that universality can be explained by the materiality of the body; the human body, in other words, has certain needs, characteristics, and limitations that transcend time and place. But the normative value of the universal needs and capabilities associated with human sexuality does not reside in the physical or material or natural facts of the body. Instead, as we will see in chapter 3, it lies in an ethical assessment that it is impossible for anyone, regardless of when and where he or she happens to live, to lead a fully human life in the absence of opportunities to meet basic needs and exercise basic capabilities associated with sexual intimacy. A conception of sexuality that views the directions of sexual desire, as well as how we use our bodies to satisfy sexual needs, as social constructions is not inconsistent with the view that needs and capabilities for sexual intimacy *of some kind* are universal human attributes. It is entirely possible, therefore, to be a soft or moderate social constructionist in matters of sexuality and still agree with the kind of universalism that I defend in this book. Nothing that I say here is meant to support the proposition that distinct sexual orientations, such as the ones that are today common in Western societies, are essential constitutive parts of distinct human beings.

In presenting moral and political arguments in support of societal recognition of gay and lesbian relationships and families based on the needs and capabilities that lesbians and gay men share with all other human beings, I recognize that women, racial minorities, and lesbians and gay men themselves have had good reason in the past to be skeptical of the way in which universalist arguments as to basic human attributes have been framed and defended. To be human has too often been equated with the kinds of characteristics, interests, and priorities associated with being male, white, and heterosexual. When social norms and practices are constructed on top of this slanted and limited view of what it means to be human, those who do not fall under all three categories are vulnerable to stigmatization and marginalization. In the particular context of sexual orientation, I understand and am sympathetic to the skepticism expressed by many scholars of grounding arguments on behalf of lesbians and gay men on what are taken to be constitutive characteristics of human beings. Arguments about human nature—of equating that which is natural (however defined) with that which is moral (and unnatural with immoral)—have, after all, for generations been at the core of moral and political arguments used to justify the oppression of lesbians and gay men. But, in my opinion, the solution to the suffering and oppression that has undoubtedly emanated from homophobic—as well as racist and sexist—understandings of what it means to be human is not to give up altogether on the concept of the human being as a source for normative values and ethical judgments. The better choice is to present and defend a more convincing and nonoppressive conception of what it means to be human and to lead a fully human life. It is important, as the late Peter Cicchino noted, to think about all of this from within "[a] spirit of self-correction, of constant and careful attention to the rich texture and fine detail of human experience, and a profound sensibility to the marginalized and the oppressed."[22] We should not, however, give up entirely on the idea of universal human attributes because in them we find compelling moral and political arguments on behalf of marginalized individuals, including lesbians and gay men.

I also want to distinguish at this early point between moral evaluations aimed at discerning those needs and capabilities that are constitutive of human beings and are necessary for the leading of full human lives on the one hand, and moral *judgments* that criticize individuals for failing to live in certain ways on the other. It is striking, in fact, how many conservatives today find it practically impossible, when addressing issues of morality in general and questions of sexuality in particular, not to criticize and assail the aspirations and relationships of others who choose to live differently from how they live. Although we are, of course, entitled to make moral judgments about the ways in which others conduct their lives, it is a different matter altogether when we seek to incorporate those judgments into public policies. The kind of morality that I advocate in this book is very different from a morality that seeks to instill private virtue (however defined) through public policy. Instead, the morality that I articulate and defend is grounded on individual autonomy and choice in the leading of lives that are fully human. It also speaks of the moral respect that we owe others as human beings, a respect that must be reflected in the actions of public institutions and in the content of public policies.

The morality that I advocate in this book, then, is not about telling people how to live—it is not, for example, about telling people that they need to choose option X (to marry, or to have children, or whatever) in order to lead good or virtuous or moral lives. Instead, it is about acknowledging that many of the opportunities that we have to lead fully human lives are dependent on social conditions and public policies. We have to make sure that those conditions and policies give individuals sufficient opportunities to satisfy their basic human needs and exercise their basic human capabilities.

It is therefore perfectly consistent with the kind of political morality that I will be defending in this book to conclude that it is improper for the state to single out a group of individuals for differential treatment solely because society morally disapproves of their conduct. Efforts by the state to encourage or discourage certain conduct based solely on societal judgments of what is moral or immoral must be distinguished from assessments of those needs and capabilities through which individuals express and realize their humanity and that, as a result, should be promoted and protected through state policies. Those assessments are inherently moral because they call on us to determine what is necessary for individuals to be able to lead fully human lives. But the goal should never be to have individuals behave in certain ways, or to enter into certain relationships, because those are the ones considered morally acceptable by a majority of the society. Instead, the aim should be to create the necessary social conditions that give all individuals the opportunity to lead fully human lives, important elements of which are realized through their intimate relationships with others. Given the diversity and variety of human interests and aspirations, there are correspondingly multiple ways in which individuals can meet and exercise their basic human needs and capabilities in order to lead lives that are fully human. Our principles of political morality must be attuned to and respectful of the existence of that multiplicity, and nothing in this book is intended to suggest otherwise.

As already mentioned, the theoretical and philosophical explorations in this book are necessary because of the new priorities of the gay rights movement. The fact that many lesbians and gay men are seeking societal recognition and support for their relationships and families is what requires us to go back and rethink our theory. We can no longer solely abide by the principles of moral neutrality (or skepticism) that have served as the justificatory bases for gay rights positions for several decades now. Since the focus of this book will be primarily on issues of theory, it is important to emphasize at the outset that theory matters precisely because of the changes that are going on on the ground, namely, the demand by lesbians and gay men that their most intimate relationships, both sexual and familial, be recognized and supported by society.

Given that this book focuses almost exclusively on marriage and parenting, however, a legitimate question can be asked: What about the views and interests of the many lesbians and gay men who are not interested in having their relationships recognized by society or in raising children? It has to be acknowledged that there are some within the gay and lesbian community who are highly critical of the current focus by the gay rights movement on marriage and family. The main concern among these critics is that lesbians and gay men will be assimilated or co-opted into sharing the values of the broader society thus threatening the distinctively liberating potential of same-gender sexuality.[23] A related concern is that those who stay behind and resist the so-called assimilation will be subject to even greater stigma and discrimination as society distinguishes between the "good" gays (i.e., those who are more like heterosexuals) and the "bad" ones.

The need to protect the sexual autonomy of all human beings is one of the reasons why I believe theorizing about gay rights must work within liberalism rather than seek to replace it. The kind of moral liberalism that I defend in chapter 3, like all true forms of liberalism, does not countenance the coercion (or harassment or stigmatization) of individuals based on their consensual sexual conduct regardless of whether that conduct falls inside or outside of relationships that the society considers valuable or good. That much has been a central tenet of liberal theory (though admittedly not always applied in practice) since John Stuart Mill articulated his conception of the harm principle one hundred and fifty years ago. That principle holds that society should not prohibit conduct unless there is a clear and identifiable harm to third parties. Thus, those who today defend and value unfettered sexual freedom—such as, for example, the queer theorist Michael Warner—end up, as a matter of political morality, in essence arguing for no more than the consistent application of the harm principle.[24] I believe, however, that liberal theory must go beyond Mill's harm principle, and other forms of moral minimalisms, if it is to account for the concerns and priorities of those in the gay and lesbian community who value sexual autonomy, at least in part, for the relationships of love and care that it can engender and who have an understandable interest in societal recognition of and support for those relationships. Liberalism, then, must continue to protect the ability of individuals to engage in consensual sexual conduct of their choosing. The more difficult question is how an understanding of liberalism that requires governmental restraint in regulating consensual sexual conduct can also demand that the state recognize and support particular kinds of sexually intimate relationships.

The challenge confronted by a philosophy of gay rights is how to protect and promote the needs and capabilities associated with sexual intimacy of all lesbians and gay men, from those who are interested only in committed relationships to those for whom what is most important is sexual freedom outside of ongoing relationships (and everyone else who falls somewhere in between). This book argues that those needs and capabilities are part of a greater whole, that is, part of the needs and capabilities that all human being share. It is the existence of those commonalities that allow us to make moral evaluations about the way in which a society treats its sexual minorities. A belief in the existence of those commonalities, however, is not inconsistent with the view that different individuals will value and express their basic needs and capabilities associated with sexual intimacy in different ways and that that pluralism should be not only tolerated, but also highly valued. Although I focus in this book on the needs and capabilities that lesbians and gay men share with others, commonalities should not be emphasized to such an extent that we end up disregarding or minimizing important differences. One of the important differences between gays and straights is that the former, because of the oppression that they face, understand the liberationist and self-affirming potential of sex in ways that most heterosexuals—whose sexuality is already privileged by society's norms—do not. Lesbians and gay men have learned to use their same-gender sexuality as a source for both building lives of self-respect and pride and for organizing politically to seek social change. For many heterosexuals, the very idea that one can find pride in one's sexuality and organize politically around it is largely incomprehensible. Lesbians and gay men know, however, that the best way of undermining heterosexist norms that seek to make heterosexuality compulsory is to find strength (both personal and political) in their sexuality.

Another difference that some opponents of gay rights take particular pleasure in accentuating is the view held by a significant number of lesbians and gay men that sexual exclusivity is not a necessary component of a committed sexual relationship. An emphasis on commonalities between gays and straights should never lead the gay and lesbian community to demean or ostracize those of its members who hold views that might be different from the heterosexual mainstream in matters of sexual intimacy. A commitment to pluralism and sexual autonomy, after all, is one of the core values of the gay and lesbian community. At the same time, however, we should not be afraid to emphasize our deeper commonalities with those outside of our community when those commonalities exist because it is through them that we create and foster the conditions for greater understanding and acceptance. The tension, as always, is in finding the appropriate balance between valuing those aspects of ourselves (both as individuals and as members of distinct communities) that make us different from others while recognizing that there are also parts of ourselves that we share with all other human beings. That is an admittedly difficult balance to strike, but one that is certainly worth our while to try.

Let me also address another possible criticism, related to the one already mentioned, of my focusing on what can be categorized as the two principal "assimilationist" goals of the gay rights movement: marriage and parenting. What about the moral and political implications of a more radical and transgressive sexuality—encompassing issues such as cruising or having sex in public places or even intergenerational sex between adults and teenagers—which is frequently promoted by sexual liberationists of all kinds, including some lesbians and gay men? It could be argued that by not discussing these kinds of topics associated with a more transgressive sexuality, I am limiting myself to what can be seen as safer and, to some extent, less controversial subjects. I do not discuss issues such as public or intergenerational sex in this book because I think that gay rights proponents who are interested in promoting these admittedly more transgressive issues already have a well-worn and familiar principle of political morality to support their positions, namely, the Millian/liberal view that counsels against state interference in sexual conduct as long as it is consensual and there is no harm to third parties. Of course, those who are troubled by public or intergenerational sex vehemently disagree with the position that the state should not interfere with the personal autonomy of the individuals involved. But regardless of what one believes is best as a matter of public policy on these specific issues, the theoretical divide is clear and relatively straightforward with one side arguing in favor of sexual autonomy and against state intervention and the other side arguing that sexual autonomy must yield to other considerations (such as, for example, majoritarian standards as to what is acceptable behavior in public). The theoretical divide becomes murkier in the debates over same-sex marriage and parenting by lesbians and gay men because the simple "state interference" versus "no state interference" binary breaks down. In those areas, proponents of gay rights are asking for more than just noninterference by the state; they are also asking for state support and recognition of certain relationships. The traditional Millian/liberal approach of needing to leave individuals alone in order to protect their interests in autonomy and liberty does not by itself impose on society an obligation to recognize and support the intimate relationships of lesbians and gay men. In my opinion, therefore, same-sex marriage and parenting by lesbians and gay men raise more challenging and interesting questions of political philosophy than do the more radical and transgressive issues emphasized by sexual liberationists.

Finally, it is my hope that this book will be of interest to readers who are knowledgeable about contemporary political philosophy, as well as to those who are not. Chapters 1, 2, 4, and 5 contain summaries of the ideas of the principal philosophers and thinkers (Rawls, Dworkin, Rorty, Posner, Sandel, Walzer, and Foucault) discussed therein. The reader who is already familiar with Rawls's conception of political liberalism or with Walzer's theory of internal social criticism or with Foucault's conception of ethics as a care of the self, for example, may want to skip the relevant introductory (and largely descriptive) sections.[25] Those introductory sections are meant to make the ideas of the principal philosophers and thinkers discussed in the book accessible to all readers—regardless of academic background or training—so that they will be better able to understand how the discussions of gay rights issues in each chapter relate to the different theoretical and philosophical positions discussed throughout the book.

ONE

Neutral Liberalism

Liberalism, with its focus on individual rights to freedom, autonomy, and equality, is a natural place to begin a discussion of the intersection of political morality and gay rights. Liberalism, of course, is not monolithic. There are several different ways in which liberalism's prioritization of individual rights can be understood and justified. Utilitarian liberals, for example, are consequentialists in that they value individual rights for their ability to maximize satisfaction or happiness. Deontological liberals, on the other hand, view individual rights as having value in and of themselves regardless of contexts or outcomes. Libertarian liberals prioritize freedom in both political and economic spheres. Egalitarian liberals, on the other hand, argue that economic freedoms must be limited so that the state can implement the necessary redistributive policies that guarantee equality of opportunity (or resources) and a minimum standard of living to all citizens.

The divide within liberalism that I want to emphasize in this book is the one between neutral liberalism and moral liberalism. The principal distinction between the two is that the former eschews questions of the good while holding that a liberal political philosophy should account only for so-called neutral political values such as tolerance and equality. Moral liberalism also highly values principles of tolerance and equality. But moral liberalism is concerned as well with a particular kind of good, namely, the ability of all individuals to lead fully human lives. Neutral liberalism, as we will see, quite comfortably calls for tolerance of consensual same-gender sexual conduct. Neutral liberalism, however, has a more difficult time providing a convincing justification for why society should recognize gay and lesbian relationships as marital relationships. Similarly, many of the values and norms that are part of parenting relate to assessments of the good, and yet under the precepts of neutral liberalism, the good should play no role in the definition of the right. Same-sex marriage and parenting by lesbians and gay men raise fundamental questions about state recognition and support of the good and valuable in human relationships; neutral liberalism is incapable of or uninterested in addressing those questions. A political morality governed by the principles of neutral liberalism was arguably all that was needed during earlier stages of the gay rights movement when the focus was on lessening outright governmental coercion and on winning for lesbians and gay men the same kind of discrimination protection afforded to other minorities. Now that lesbians and gay men have added marriage and family to their list of aspirations, however, neutral liberalism proves to be inadequate. In this chapter, I discuss the limitations, from a gay rights perspective, of neutral liberalism through an exploration of the writings of two of its most influential proponents: John Rawls and Ronald Dworkin.[1]

Before I begin the discussion, I want to address a possible objection with my decision to start an exploration of the intersection of political philosophy and gay rights with liberalism rather than with its alternatives. I begin with liberalism (and three of the five chapters in this book are about liberalism) because I perceive a surprising consensus among those writing on gay issues that the liberal model of individual rights, with its emphasis on freedom, autonomy, and equality, is the best model to protect and promote the interests of lesbians and gay men. In fact, there is a notable disconnect in this regard between theory and practice among some academics writing in this area, especially among queer theorists who are generally skeptical of liberalism because of its emphasis on metanarratives about universal rights. Queer theorists, like all postmodernists, are skeptical of foundational principles and values; they view the promotion of universal norms as problematic because they perceive those norms as benefiting the oppressors rather than the oppressed.

Although postmodernist queer theorists are skeptical of liberal *theory*, many of them remain, at the level of *practice*, focused on a traditional liberal model of individual rights that seeks to protect the freedom, autonomy, and equality of lesbians and gay men. The philosopher and queer theorist Ladelle McWhorter, for example, relies heavily on Michel Foucault's postmodernist writings to critique an essentialist conception of sexual identity as well as foundationalist conceptions of truth and reason.[2] In the end, however, her political approach is a liberal one, namely, to work within the legislative and judicial systems to promote the civil rights of lesbians and gay men.[3] Similarly, Mark Blasius, though defending a Foucauldian interpretation of politics, power, and ethics, nonetheless calls for a recognition of (largely liberal) relational rights enforced through law.[4] By relational rights, Blasius means rights that allow lesbians and gay men to exercise self-determination in their relationships with others. Furthermore, the prominent queer theorist Michael Warner, as already noted, endorses a political morality that is not very different from the liberalism of John Stuart Mill.

Even those who are skeptical of relying on an individual rights model, because they view it as insufficiently radical and transformative of cultural and social norms, often recognize that individual rights can play an important role in the struggle for freedom, autonomy, and equality by lesbians and gay men.[5] As Shane Phelan notes, "[e]ven the most critical of queer theorists returns to rights when needed."[6] Queer theory, then, has not been as skeptical of individual rights as have other leftist academic movements such as critical legal studies and (to a lesser extent) critical race theory. The continued reliance by many queer theorists on an individual rights model may be more a matter of pragmatic necessity than philosophical commitment, but such reliance supports the view that liberal values and priorities remain vital in protecting and promoting the interests and dignity of lesbians and gay men in the United States.[7]

It seems to me, then, that the important divide among those writing on issues of political morality and sexual orientation from a pro-gay rights perspective is not between liberals and nonliberals, but is instead between, on the one hand, those who can be categorized as libertarian liberals who argue that the only obligation of the state is not to interfere with consensual sexual acts and relationships and, on the other hand, those liberals who believe that the state has positive obligations to create the necessary structures and conditions for individuals to be able to exercise, in a meaningful way, their rights to freedom and autonomy associated with physical and emotional intimacy. (Since almost all proponents of gay rights support the enactment of antidiscrimination legislation, which by necessity limits the associational and contractual rights of private parties, almost none of them can be considered pure libertarians. By "libertarian liberals" among gay rights proponents I mean thinkers such as Michael Warner who argue that the state, in matters of sexual intimacy and relationships, should limit itself to noninterference, rather than recognizing and supporting some relationships—such as marital ones—over others.)[8] I will throughout this book be arguing in favor of the proposition that the state has positive obligations to recognize and support good and valuable intimate relationships and concomitantly against the idea that the state *only* has obligations of noninterference vis-à-vis those relationships.

1. RAWLS'S POLITICAL LIBERALISM

John Rawls's conception of a fair and just society, as set forth in his famous book *A Theory of Justice*, is by now well-known. In Rawls's vision, justice is the most important virtue of public institutions, and "a public conception of justice . . . constitut[es] the fundamental charter of a well-ordered human association" (TJ, 5). It is an unwavering commitment to justice that both "establishes the bonds of civic friendship" and appropriately "limits the pursuit of other [public] ends" (TJ, 5). Rawls's model for arriving at fundamental principles of justice is contractarian given that he envisions a group of individuals, acting as representatives of all citizens, negotiating over the content of those principles. Rawls places the representatives in a hypothetical "original position" negotiating behind a "veil of ignorance" that keeps them from knowing their class, natural assets and abilities (such as intelligence and strength), race, and gender (and, presumably, sexual orientation).

Individuals who negotiate behind the veil of ignorance not knowing where they will fall (once the veil is removed) along the range of social and economic hierarchies will, according to Rawls, agree on two principles as the foundations of a just society. "[T]he first requires equality in the assignment of basic rights and duties, while the second holds that social and economic inequalities, for example inequalities of wealth and authority, are just only if they result in compensating benefits for everyone, and in particular for the least advantaged members of society" (TJ, 14–15). The first principle (known as the liberty principle) is one of strict and uncompromising distributive equality and applies to basic liberties such as freedom of speech, assembly, conscience, and thought. Under the second principle (known as the difference principle), inequalities in the distribution of social and economic goods are permissible as long as the inequalities benefit those who are least advantaged. These two principles constitute the core of a liberalism based on justice as fairness because they are the principles that would be chosen by parties who negotiate a social contract under the constraints demanded by considerations of fairness.

There are two other crucial points that Rawls makes in *A Theory of Justice* that complement his original position heuristic. First, Rawls defends a Kantian conception of the self, that is, he views the self as existing prior to and independently of its ends. As Rawls explains, "[i]t is not our aims that primarily reveal our nature but rather the principles that we would acknowledge to govern the background conditions under which these aims are to be formed and the manner in which they are to be pursued" (TJ, 560). The capacity to choose our ends, in other words, is prior to and can be separated from the ends that we actually choose. "[T]he self," Rawls argues, "is prior to the ends which are affirmed by it; even a dominant end must be chosen from among numerous possibilities" (TJ, 560). The conceptual separation of the self from its personal aims and social attachments is consistent with the original position heuristic given that the bargaining parties behind the veil of ignorance have to agree on fundamental principles of justice without knowing which particular choices they will make about how to lead their lives (or with whom) once the veil is lifted.

Second, Rawls argues in *A Theory of Justice* that the right is prior to the good, that is, that fundamental principles of justice are not connected to and are not dependent on any particular theory of what constitutes a good life (TJ, 30–33). Unlike utilitarianism, for example, which links the right to the maximization of the good (defined in terms of maximizing satisfaction or happiness), justice as fairness prioritizes the right over all conceptions of the good. This separation of the right from the good, like the separation of the self from its ends, is consistent with the original position heuristic given that the bargainers in the original position have to agree on fundamental principles of justice without knowing their particular conceptions of the good.

Rawls, however, does not entirely avoid relying on a theory of the good. He defends a "thin" theory that is concerned with the distribution of those items—which he calls primary goods—that all people (regardless of their particular conceptions of the good) rationally want in order to pursue their life plans. These goods include rights and liberties, powers and opportunities, income and wealth, and the social bases of self-respect (TJ, 62–65, 90–95, 440). Rawls distinguishes between his thin theory of the good and thicker theories that are meant to defend particular understandings of what it means to lead a good life. The primary goods, Rawls counsels in his later book *Political Liberalism*, "are clearly not anyone's idea of the basic values of human life and must not be so understood, however essential their possession" (PL, 188).

In *A Theory of Justice*, Rawls envisions a gradual removal of the veil of ignorance as citizens progress from the original position to constitutional, legislative, and administrative stages in the formation of a well-ordered society. There is very little discussion in that book, however, on how it is, exactly, that citizens are supposed to manage their differing conceptions of the good. There is very little, in other words, on how a society can be both well-ordered *and* pluralistic. That is the issue that Rawls addresses directly in *Political Liberalism*. In that book, he continues to defend his original position heuristic and the two principles of justice that emanate from it, as well as the idea that the right is prior to the good. Rawls, however, now argues that his theory of justice is meant to be political and not metaphysical or moral. It is therefore not necessary to defend a particular conception of the self, whether Kantian or otherwise. The priority of the right over the good, he now argues, is not dependent on a philosophical or metaphysical conception of the self (PL, 29–35).

Although Rawls does not in *A Theory of Justice* explicitly address issues of stability, he acknowledges in *Political Liberalism* that one could read the former as concluding that the stability of well-ordered societies results from the voluntary endorsement by their member citizens of a comprehensive philosophical doctrine based on justice as fairness. Rawls now believes that such an explanation for the stability of well-ordered societies is undermined by the descriptive reality that those societies include within them citizens who hold a myriad of reasonable but incompatible philosophical, moral, and religious comprehensive doctrines. Rawls argues that his earlier work underestimated the centrifugal forces that accompany these conflicting doctrines. These forces may, at first, appear to undermine the cohesiveness of a well-ordered society. However, the endorsement by citizens of a *political* conception of justice as fairness, instead of an underlying comprehensive philosophical or moral doctrine, creates the necessary overlapping consensus that provides stability to a well-ordered society. A liberal political conception of justice, then, does not function so as to answer and resolve philosophical or moral disagreements among members of a political community. Instead, a political conception of justice as fairness is only interested in the basic structures and values of a well-ordered society. As Rawls puts it, "[a] political conception is at best but a guiding framework of deliberation and reflection which helps us reach political agreement on at least the constitutional essentials and the basic questions of justice" (PL, 156). In this sense, Rawls's conception of justice is "partial" (as opposed to "comprehensive") because it applies only to the basic political structures and values of particular kinds of political communities, namely, Western democracies. The concern of Rawls's political liberalism, therefore, is how "to work out a conception of political justice for a constitutional democratic regime that the plurality of reasonable doctrines—always a feature of the culture of a free democratic regime—might endorse" (PL, xviii). Although citizens may have incompatible views emanating from their respective comprehensive doctrines, the agreement on a political conception of justice accounts for the stability of well-ordered societies.

Rawls's emphasis on the political nature of his conception of justice leads him to stress the distinction between public reasoning on the one hand and deliberations that are outside of the political process on the other. Rawls defines public reason in a democracy as "the reason of its citizens, of those sharing the status of equal citizenship. The subject of their reason is the good of the public: what the political conception of justice requires of society's basic structure of institutions, and of the purposes and ends they are to serve" (PL, 213). Rawls would limit the public reasoning of government officials, and of citizens engaged in the process of electing those officials, to the political values that underlie reasonable yet incompatible comprehensive doctrines. Political values for Rawls include "toleration and mutual respect, and a sense of fairness and civility" (PL, 122). The constraints apply to political discourse and not to what he calls "background culture"—nonpolitical fora such as "churches and associations of all kinds, and institutions of learning at all levels, especially universities and professional schools, scientific and other societies" (IPR, 768 n.13).

The constraints on public reasoning demanded by Rawls's political liberalism are consistent with the separation of the right from the good that he called for in *A Theory of Justice*. As citizens debate public policy issues within an established constitutional system, Rawls would have them separate political values, which go to the right, from philosophical, moral, and religious values, which go to the good. By making explicit the distinction between a political conception of justice and a philosophical or moral one in *Political Liberalism*, Rawls underscores the neutrality of his conception of liberalism. Unlike Aristotle or Kant or Mill, all of whom, in their very different ways, sought to combine moral philosophy with political morality, Rawls's justice as fairness aims to be morally neutral.

One may inquire, however, why we as citizens would voluntarily abide by the constraints that political liberalism imposes on public reasoning. Why should we not bring to bear our philosophical, moral, and even religious views when addressing issues of justice? We abide by the constraints on public reasoning, Rawls believes, because they are consistent with our own reasonable comprehensive doctrines. Rawls here distinguishes between the "reasonable" and the "rational." The latter is a private virtue that is present when individuals use judgment and deliberation to pursue chosen ends in the manner they think best. Reasonableness, on the other hand, is largely a norm of restraint applicable to individuals whenever they interact with others. Reasonableness for Rawls means nothing more than the idea "that we enter as equals [to] the public world of others and stand ready to propose, or to accept, as the case may be, fair terms of cooperation with them" (PL, 53). By viewing the reasonable in this way, Rawls hopes to strip it of the metaphysical and philosophical baggage that often accompanies the concept of reason. Comprehensive doctrines that do not include within them the rather limited principle (as Rawls sees it) of reasonableness cannot be part of an overlapping consensus shared by most citizens in Western democracies. If the concept of reasonableness is already part of the comprehensive doctrines of most members of Western nations, then most of us accept the constraints on public reasoning imposed by political liberalism because they are a part of, or are at least consistent with, our different comprehensive doctrines.

We also abide by the limitations placed by political liberalism on public reasoning because public institutions must have the ability to exercise power over the lives of individuals when necessary. As citizens explain and justify to each other the use of public power, it is essential that they do so "in terms each could reasonably expect that others might endorse as consistent with their freedom and equality" (PL, 218). To the extent, however, that justifications for the use of public power rely on particular comprehensive philosophical, moral, and religious doctrines, not all citizens will be able to endorse them. "There is no reason why any citizen, or association of citizens, should have the right to use state power to decide constitutional essentials as that person's, or that association's, comprehensive doctrine directs" (PL, 226). By limiting ourselves, when engaging in public reasoning, to arguments based on political values that are part of an overlapping consensus to justify the actions of public institutions, we aim to create and foster a sense of civic reciprocity with those whose comprehensive doctrines are incompatible with our own. This reciprocity, in turn, provides the necessary stability and respect for pluralism that are characteristic of well-ordered societies.

2. RAWLS FROM A GAY RIGHTS PERSPECTIVE

There are three important critiques of Rawlsian liberalism that are particularly relevant to gay rights issues, namely, the ontological, communitarian, and perfectionist critiques. I want to, in this section, introduce all three, though I will only discuss the third in detail here. I will elaborate on the ontological critique in chapter 3 where I discuss moral liberalism and on the communitarian critique in chapter 4 where I discuss, appropriately enough, communitarianism.

ONTOLOGICAL CRITIQUE

The first relevant critique of Rawls for our purposes is that the representatives in the original position, and to a lesser extent the citizens in a constitutional regime who are constrained by the limitations on public reasoning imposed by political liberalism, are stripped of many of the crucial characteristics that are constitutive of who they are. Rawls argues that there are two capabilities that define the moral personhood of citizens: the capability to evaluate which ends to pursue and how to pursue them, and the capability for a sense of justice that allows citizens to assess the fairness of a system of social cooperation (PL, 19). Without in any way minimizing the importance of the capabilities noted by Rawls, however, it is clear that individuals share many other needs and capabilities—such as, for example, the need to be loved and cared for *by* others and the capability to love and care *for* others—that are relevant to many questions of justice, including most gay rights issues, in our society today. If we do not explicitly account for those other needs and capabilities in our theorizing about justice, we ignore at our peril crucial constitutive elements of our humanity (or, as Rawls puts it, of our moral personhood). Failure to recognize needs and capabilities associated with physical and emotional intimacy, to name just one category that is particularly relevant to issues of sexual orientation, will have important limiting repercussions for the way in which we define the right.

I will elaborate on this argument in chapter 3, where I will explain why we need a thicker conception of the self than that suggested by Rawls. As we have seen, Rawls in *Political Liberalism* argues that no particular conception of the self is required to support a *political* conception of justice. But here Rawls gets into some difficulty because if we dispense with the Kantian conception of the self as being prior to its purposes and ends (the conception explicitly adopted by Rawls in *A Theory of Justice*), then why could we not also dispense with the principle that the right must be prior to the good?[9] This is an issue more directly raised by the perfectionist critique of Rawlsian liberalism, which I discuss below.

COMMUNITARIAN CRITIQUE

In the same way that Rawls's conception of liberalism strips individuals, for political purposes, of important needs and capabilities that define them as human, it also fails to appreciate the role of communities in the formulation and understanding by individuals of what is just and right. This communitarian critique and the ontological critique are related since our constitutive needs and capabilities often require interactions and relationships with others for their satisfaction (in the case of needs) and exercise (in the case of capabilities). But the communitarian critique does not depend on ties or connections with others that are constitutive of our humanity per se. Rather, the communitarian argues that there are a myriad of social, religious, familial, and affectional ties that form our identity and character. The self—including the political self—is for communitarians a fully embedded creature; its ties and connections *determine* its sense of right and justice. And yet those ties and connections play no important role in Rawls's theorizing on justice. Communitarians question the separation of the individual from her communities that Rawls's liberalism implies; for communitarians, this separation is artificial, harmful, and descriptively inaccurate. As we will see in chapter 4, the communitarian critique of liberalism is relevant to the lives of lesbians and gay men because communities for them often serve as important sources of identity, support, and empowerment.

PERFECTIONIST CRITIQUE

Another important critique of Rawlsian liberalism—which is often grouped together with the communitarian critique, but which, in order to differentiate from the second critique noted above, I will refer to here as the perfectionist critique—questions the separation of the right from the good. Michael Sandel has been one of the most influential proponents of this critique. Sandel argues that, unlike political liberalism, a perfectionist theory of justice "holds that principles of justice depend for their justification on the moral worth or intrinsic good of the ends they serve. On this view, the case for recognizing a right depends on showing that it honors or advances some important human good."[10] As a perfectionist, Sandel has been quite critical of Rawlsian liberalism's insistence on the need to abide by a strict neutrality on issues of the good. If it is possible to reach reasoned and defensible conclusions on highly disputed questions of the right (in choosing, for example, as Rawls does, justice as fairness over utilitarianism or libertarianism), Sandel asks, why is Rawls so pessimistic about the possibility of reaching reasoned and defensible conclusions on at least *some* questions of the good?[11]

It is likely that if we were to give lesbians and gay men a choice between the neutrality and moral bracketing of Rawlsian liberalism on the one hand and the incorporation of arguments relating to morality and the good into questions of justice as proposed by Sandel on the other, many if not most would at first choose the former. This initial choice is in many ways understandable given that opponents of gay rights regularly use notions of morality to argue against gay rights positions. It is perhaps for this reason that gay rights supporters generally prefer considerations of justice and individual rights that bracket out moral arguments, perhaps believing that they cannot win those arguments in the face of majoritarian opposition.[12] Bracketing out moral arguments would seem to leave conservative opponents of gay rights with few alternatives. If conservatives, in their opposition to gay rights in general and to societal recognition and support of same-sex marriage and parenting by lesbians and gay men in particular, could not refer to the Judeo-Christian moral tradition, or if they could not point to the purported immorality of homosexual conduct, or if they could not rely on so-called traditional or family values, they would be left, in a sense, polemically weakened. The debate would then be conducted with the understanding that freedom, equality, and toleration (all neutral political norms within a Rawlsian framework) are the only permissible values to be considered in a public discourse on gay rights.

One can certainly formulate arguments in favor of same-sex marriage, for example, based on neutral political principles. These by now familiar arguments can be paraphrased as follows: "*All we (lesbians and gay men) are asking is that we be treated equally, and if you (heterosexuals) enjoy the right to marry, so should we. We are not asking that you morally condone our behavior, we are only asking for tolerance and respect*"; or to put it in more explicitly Rawlsian terms, "*We lesbians and gay men are equal citizens in this constitutional regime, and to use moral and religious arguments—which we of course do not endorse—to deny us equal participation in public institutions (such as that of civil marriage) violates the political values of equality and tolerance.*"

In an article that appeared several years after the publication of *Political Liberalism* (and in which he for the first time addresses matters of sexual orientation), Rawls makes these very points (albeit in a more sophisticated way). He argues that issues relating to homosexuality in a well-ordered society can be dealt with exclusively through the political values that constitute its overlapping consensus. Rawls believes that it is possible to address controversial topics involving the family and sexual orientation exclusively through political values that "support and regulate, in an ordered way, the institutions needed to reproduce political society over time" (IPR, 779). Rawls adds, in a highly relevant passage that is worth quoting at some length, that

> [t]his ordered support and regulation rests on political principles and values, since political society is regarded as existing in perpetuity and so as maintaining itself and its institutions and culture over generations. Given this interest, the government would appear to have no interest in the particular form of family life, or of relations among the sexes, *except insofar as that form or those relations in some way affect the orderly reproduction of society over time.* Thus, appeals . . . against same-sex marriages, as [being] within the government's legitimate interest in the family, would reflect religious or comprehensive moral doctrines [and would thus be improper] (IPR, 779, emphasis added).

Although Rawls's constraints on public reasoning undoubtedly favor gay rights positions, a troubling disparity exists between those constraints and the issues that are at stake in the actual debates over gay rights in our society. The debate regarding same-sex marriage, for example, is at its core about whether the state should recognize committed same-gender relationships as being equal to committed opposite-gender relationships. The fundamental disagreement is whether same-gender unions deserve the same amount of social recognition and support as heterosexual unions. This dispute opens up a myriad of normative and moral issues including the value and goodness of committed same-gender sexual relationships for both the individuals involved and for society at large, as well as the issue of whether there is an indispensable connection between marriage and children. When Rawls asks parties on both sides of the debate to limit their public reasoning to the political values and institutions necessary for the "reproduct[ion] of political society over time," he asks that they confine themselves to issues that seem at best tangential to the controversy at hand. This is particularly true given that Rawls wants to exclude from the debate not only moral and philosophical arguments based on religious views, but also secular arguments that citizens make "in terms of comprehensive nonreligious doctrines," even when those arguments are "reflective and critical, publicly intelligible and rational" (IPR, 775, 780).[13] It is not possible, in the end, to make arguments about the value and meaning of marriage in our society solely from the perspective of *political* values and concerns. Rawls's vision of public reasoning, with its demand for strict moral bracketing, is ultimately too thin to support a coherent and convincing argument in favor of same-sex marriage.

Same-sex marriage raises the same concerns with Rawls's constraints on public reasoning that are implicated by his now somewhat famous footnote in *Political Liberalism* that discusses abortion. Rawls argues in that footnote that the permissibility of abortion turns on "three important political values: the due respect for human life, the ordered reproduction of political society over time, including the family in some form, and finally the equality of women as equal citizens." Rawls concludes that "any reasonable balance of these three values will give a woman a duly qualified right to decide whether or not to end her pregnancy during the first trimester" because during that early period "the political value of the equality of women is overriding." A comprehensive doctrine, he adds, which does not recognize such a right, "is to that extent unreasonable" (PL, 243 n.32).

Rawls is not particularly persuasive in his (admittedly brief) discussion of abortion because the weight accorded to his "political values" often depends on moral or religious considerations. For example, the weight assigned to the first value (respect for human life) depends on when a human life begins and that can only be determined according to the moral or religious convictions of the individuals participating in the public debate. As Sandel points out, "if the Catholic Church is right about the moral status of the fetus, if abortion is morally tantamount to murder, then it is not clear why the political values of toleration and women's equality, important though they are, should prevail."[14] In the face of criticism over his footnote on abortion, Rawls, in the introduction to the paperback edition of *Political Liberalism*, states that it was not his intention to argue "for the right to abortion in the first trimester."[15] Instead, he contends that he was simply applying "three political values (of course, there are more) [to] the troubled issue of the right to abortion, to which it might seem improbable that political values could apply at all."[16] It does not seem all that improbable, however, that the political values noted by Rawls apply to the abortion dispute; what does seem improbable is that those values can, on their own and unattached to nonpolitical moral views and understandings, provide the framework for helping citizens express their differing positions on the issue, much less reach some sort of rough consensus. It is, of course, possible to hold (as Rawls does) that all comprehensive doctrines that fail to prioritize liberal political values on the issue of abortion are, from the perspective of justice, unreasonable, but that is a conclusion rather than an argument.

That which applies to abortion applies to same-sex marriage. If same-gender sexual acts are immoral or debasing, as some contend, then it is not clear why society should condone that immorality or debasement by recognizing gay marriages even if there is an overlapping political consensus that tolerance and equality are values to be encouraged and promoted. Although a society, because of constitutional or prudential reasons, may have to tolerate conduct considered by many to be immoral (especially when it takes place in private), it does not follow that it has a corresponding obligation to encourage or reward that conduct. In order to determine, as a political matter, whether same-sex marriages should be recognized, there has to be some discussion of whether committed

same-gender relationships merit societal approval and support. It is difficult, in turn, to engage in that discussion without some normative assessments of the value and goodness of those relationships. A coherent
and effective case for same-sex marriage, then, must "engage rather than
avoid the comprehensive moral and religious doctrines at stake."[17]

Furthermore, asking lesbians and gay men to justify the imposition on
society of an obligation to recognize and support same-sex marriages
only on the basis of the political values required for the society to reproduce itself (in order, presumably, to attain the necessary reciprocity
from opponents of gay rights) is, to say the least, awkward given that
one of the main arguments against same-sex marriage, as we will see in
chapter 3, is that neither two men nor two women can engage in reproductive sexual acts. By limiting the boundaries of public reasoning on
same-sex marriage to the issue of "reproduction," Rawls unintention-
ally joins hands with new natural law thinkers who argue that reproductive sexual acts are a fundamental part of marriage. Although it is true
that Rawls speaks of the reproduction of society and not of individuals
per se, society obviously cannot reproduce unless its members procre-
ate. Rawls is clearly correct that the polity has an interest in reproducing
itself—the issue for us is whether we can limit ourselves to the political
values that inhere in "the orderly reproduction of society over time" in
elaborating a coherent justification for societal recognition of same-sex
marriage.

Lesbians and gay men are arguing that societal recognition of and support for their relationships is not only right and just because it is consistent with political values such as tolerance and respect, but also because
those relationships are expressions of their humanity and of their basic
needs and capabilities for physical and emotional intimacy. To ask lesbians
and gay men to focus only on the former arguments and to disregard the
latter kind is to ask them to set aside their most important convictions
about the value and meaning of their lives and relationships. In the end,
then, Rawls's constraints on public reasoning would not necessarily be
acceptable to many lesbians and gay men.[18] At the same time, the conservative opponents of gay rights are not likely to abide by the limits on
public reasoning that political liberalism demands.[19] In an attempt to separate political values from moral ones, Rawls ends up excluding most of
the real-life participants and their real-life concerns. What remains, as
perfectionist critics of varying political persuasions like to point out,[20] is a
rather sterile account of a debate over policy and rights that has no correspondence to what people on both sides of the debate consider to be
most important. This account asks individuals to separate what they believe is good and valuable in their lives and communities from that which
they, as a matter of public policy, believe is right and just.

What I have been arguing about same-sex marriage also applies to the
issue of parenting by lesbians and gay men. Rawls notes that "[t]he fam-

ily is part of the basic structure of society, since one of its main roles is to
be the basis of the orderly production and reproduction of society and
its culture from one generation to the next" (IPR, 788). Families are important to political liberalism because "[c]itizens must have a sense of
justice and the political virtues that support political and social institutions. The family must ensure the nurturing and development of such
citizens in appropriate numbers to maintain an enduring society" (IPR,
788). Rawls adds, in a statement that is clearly sympathetic to nontraditional families, that "no particular form of the family (monogamous,
heterosexual, or otherwise) is required by a political conception of justice so long as the family is arranged to fulfill these tasks effectively"
(IPR, 788 n.60). Rawls concludes that if gay "rights and duties are consistent with orderly family life and the education of children, they are,
ceteris paribus, fully admissible" (IPR, 788 n.60).

Once again we have an argument that is on its face supportive of lesbians and gay men. But is it enough? Should we limit ourselves, even
while acting as citizens in a democracy, to conceiving of our families primarily in terms of political values? Is it advisable for citizens, as they
work through the issue of whether lesbians and gay men should be allowed and encouraged to become parents, to consider the value of raising and caring for children only from the perspective of the "nurturing
and development" required to instill "a sense of justice and [the] political virtues"? There are many other senses and virtues that are instilled
through the nurturing of and caring for children that should be relevant
to political and policy debates because they are relevant to the raising of
children in ways that gives them the opportunity to become caring, responsible, and fulfilled adults. To limit ourselves, when discussing questions of justice raised by the issue of gay and lesbian parents, to those
matters that support or detract from the transmission of political values
seems as unnecessary as it is unrealistic. It is not that a view of the family
as playing an important role in the way in which the political society and
its institutions reproduce themselves is irrelevant; it clearly is not. It is
just that no moral or political argument about the role and importance
of the family should be limited to that consideration.

Furthermore, it would be nonsensical to argue that issues of morality
should be excluded from debates involving families and children when
morality (broadly defined to include notions of the valuable and the
good) is at the very core of legislative and judicial determinations of
whether particular households (their composition, structure, dynamics,
and processes) are consistent with the best interests of the children involved. To recognize as a policy and legal matter that fidelity, commitment, and loyalty between two adults of the same gender, for example,
can be a contributing factor to the well-being of children is to stake out
a moral position about the value of certain forms of human relationships. Moral arguments relating to the value and goodness of gay and

lesbian families are particularly relevant because the aim of family policy and law is to provide as much stability, continuity, and support for children as possible. In fact, gay and lesbian litigant parents (and their partners) are beginning to win family law cases with some consistency precisely because some courts are recognizing the goodness and value—from the children's perspective—that emanate from committed gay and lesbian relationships.[21] It is impossible to make these kinds of value assessments while remaining neutral on questions of the good in human lives, relationships, and families.

I want to emphasize that my concerns about moral bracketing in the context of same-sex marriage and parenting by lesbians and gay men are not simply based on practical considerations driven by the types of arguments raised by conservative opponents of gay rights. It is not (only) that supporters of gay rights have to make moral arguments because opponents are making them. If it were so, then the position against moral bracketing would simply be a strategic one. But there is more than strategy at stake. As I will argue in more detail in chapter 3, intimate human relationships raise fundamental issues about basic human needs and capabilities, issues that are moral at their core because they are about the attributes and potentialities of individuals, as well as the social conditions and policies meant to account and provide for them, that are necessary for the leading of lives that are fully human. These issues raise crucial questions of political morality as a society goes about deciding how it wants state institutions and policies (including, among many others, those associated with marriage and parenting) to promote and protect basic human needs and capabilities. Rawls's political liberalism, in my opinion, proves too thin to grapple with the core issues at hand.[22] I will argue in Chapter 3 that moral liberalism allows for a fuller (and more accurate) account of the role that love and care play in the lives of both children and adults. It is that fuller account, I believe, that gives moral weight to the argument that gay and lesbian relationships and families should be recognized and supported by society.

Although Rawls's constraints on public reasoning might be at first understandably appealing to supporters of gay rights, those limits are ultimately too convenient; they permit those of us who are liberal supporters of gay rights to emphasize our values, such as tolerance and equality, while characterizing our opponents' values as being beyond the permissible boundaries of public reason because they are based on "comprehensive doctrines." Those of us who support liberal ideals should acknowledge that our vision of a fair and just society is a distinctively moral one rather than hiding behind the facade of neutrality that our opponents justifiably consider hypocritical. We should make it clear (loudly and often) that in the specific context of gay rights, the disagreements between opponents and proponents are not the result of one side raising moral issues while the other seeks to avoid them; rather, the debate is (and should be) about two (admittedly very different) moral perspectives conflicting with one another.

Moral conflict troubles Rawlsian liberals. They will no doubt remind us that we need to protect a well-ordered society from the risk that those conflicts will deteriorate into either despotism or anarchy. It is tolerance and respect for others, they will argue, that accounts for the existence of a well-ordered society to begin with. I do not disagree with that proposition; I just do not see tolerance and respect as neutral values. Instead, I believe they are derived from evaluations (necessarily moral) of the constitutive attributes of human beings, attributes that impose obligations (sometimes of provision and other times of restraint) on society and the state. I will have a lot more to say about this in chapter 3, where I discuss moral liberalism. For now, I hope I have raised at least some doubts about the ability of Rawls's brand of neutral liberalism to provide a sufficient or persuasive justification for the recognition and support by society of gay and lesbian relationships and families.

3. DWORKIN'S LIBERAL EQUALITY AND MORAL BRACKETING

The political theory of Ronald Dworkin can be seen as a bridge between the separation of the right from the good as prescribed by the political liberalism of John Rawls and a moral liberalism that is willing to accept a thicker conception of the good into our understandings of justice and the right. Dworkin has always underscored the importance of equality to a liberal society. The early Dworkin coupled that emphasis with an influential critique of the use of majoritarian morality as a rationale for enacting and enforcing laws. In his more recent writings, Dworkin has argued that an appropriate conception of equality requires the linking of the ethics of individuals on the one hand and the institutions and values of a liberal society on the other. Below I track this progression in Dworkin's work and explore its implications for gay rights debates. Although Dworkin's theory is in some ways an improvement over Rawls's, it still has limitations, limitations that can only be overcome, as I will argue in chapter 3, by a more explicitly moral form of liberalism.

The core of liberalism for Dworkin has always been equality. There are, of course, many differing conceptions of equality. In his earlier writings, Dworkin emphasizes the differences between two such conceptions: one that requires a separation of political decisions from particular understandings of the good and another that holds that it is impossible to treat citizens equally "without a theory of what human beings ought to be" (MP, 191). Dworkin approves of the first conception, calling it the "constitutive political morality" of liberalism (MP, 192). In rejecting the second conception, he argues that a government that chooses among different understandings of the good and then sets policy based on that choice fails to treat citizens equally. Dworkin illustrates this point by using the example of policy decisions made by legislatures to criminalize certain "eccentric sexual practices." These decisions, based on majoritarian views on sexual morality, entail "the domination of one set of *external* preferences, that is, preferences people have about what others shall do or have. The decision invades rather than enforces the right of citizens to be treated as equals" (MP, 196). The liberal strategy, then, should be "to determine those political decisions that are antecedently likely to reflect strong external preferences and to remove those decisions from majoritarian political institutions altogether" (MP, 197).

Dworkin early on specifically wrote about societal regulation of homosexuality as an example of the impermissible use of public policies as extensions of majoritarian morality. In responding to Lord Devlin's famous lectures defending the right of society to use the criminal law as a way of enforcing majoritarian morality, Dworkin argued that the "principles of democracy we follow do not call for the enforcement of the consensus, for the belief that prejudices, personal aversions and rationalizations do not justify restricting another's freedom itself occupies a critical and fundamental position in our popular morality" (TRS, 254). Lord Devlin had argued, in response to the Wolfenden Committee Report's recommendation that consensual same-gender sexual conduct be decriminalized, that the absence of a shared morality leads to the disintegration of society and that legislators therefore have the responsibility to prohibit that which the "reasonable man" considers immoral. Devlin posited that notions of morality that are shared by large members of society act as "invisible bonds" keeping it together.[23] By linking immoral behavior, even if private and consensual, with the possible disintegration of society, Devlin sought to undermine the conceptual separation between private acts and public harm. Whether, in fact, homosexual conduct was immoral was of no import to Devlin; if social norms, as represented by the thinking of the "reasonable man," considered it to be immoral, that was sufficient to justify its criminalization.[24]

Dworkin, on the other hand, argued that it is the job of the legislator to "sift [through the] arguments and positions" that are supposedly part of a community's moral consensus to determine "which are prejudices or rationalizations, which presuppose general principles or theories vast parts of the population could not be supposed to accept" (TRS, 255). An individual's (like a community's) view of homosexuality, Dworkin argued, may be based on "[p]rejudice (resting on the assumption that homosexuals are morally inferior creatures because they are effeminate), rationalization (based on assumptions of fact so unsupported that they challenge the community's own standards of rationality), and personal aversion (representing no conviction but merely blind hate rising from unacknowledged self-suspicion)" (TRS, 254). It is the obligation, Dworkin insisted, of the "conscientious legislator" to "test the credentials of [the] consensus" regarding the morality of homosexuality. Thus, for Dworkin, Lord Devlin's notion that what the "reasonable man" considers to be immoral should be prohibited by law was "shocking and wrong" (TRS, 255).

Dworkin, in criticizing the intrusion of majoritarian moral values into public policy follows in the tradition of John Stuart Mill's harm principle. Mill argued in his famous essay *On Liberty* that "the only purpose for which power can be rightfully exercised over any member of a civilized community, against his will, is to prevent harm to others."[25] Mill's harm principle is usually viewed as a morally neutral one that seeks, in its own way, to separate the right from the good. Mill argued that a person's "own good, either physical or moral," does not justify the exercise of state power; an individual "cannot rightfully be compelled to do or forbear because it will be better for him to do so, because it will make him happier, because, in the opinions of others, to do so would be wise, or even right."[26] Dworkin also wants the "opinions of others" as reflected in external preferences, that is, in preferences for how others should lead their lives, excluded from public policy. His primary interest, however, is not with utilitarian considerations (as was Mill's) but is instead with equality. Dworkin criticizes the incorporation of majoritarian morality into the formulation of public policy because it threatens the equal treatment of individuals by the state. If the state chooses a particular conception of sexual morality, for example, as a way of justifying prohibitions of particular sexual acts, it treats citizens unequally by giving more weight to the sexual morality of some individuals (usually those in the majority) than that of others (usually those in the minority). Dworkin concludes, therefore, that "political decisions about what citizens should be forced to do or prevented from doing must be made on grounds that are neutral among the competing convictions about good and bad lives that different members of the community might hold" (FLE, 225). He adds that when citizens participate in the political processes of a democracy, they should not "even if they are in the majority . . . , forbid anyone to lead the life he wants, or punish him for doing so, just on the ground that they think his ethical convictions are wrong" (FLE, 302).

From a gay rights perspective, this line of reasoning is entirely consistent with that of arguments made in support of the repeal of sodomy statutes. Proponents of sodomy statutes argue that the state can appropriately use its power to discourage "immoral" conduct, whereas opponents avoid such an engagement of morality altogether by arguing that societal notions of morality, in the absence of harm to third parties, cannot justify coercion by the state through the enforcement of the criminal law. Dworkin's approach supports the latter position with an added concern for equality. As Dworkin puts it, "[i]nvasions of liberty—criminal laws prohibiting activities or ways of life some people might wish to take up, for example—are invasions of equality . . . unless they can be justified as necessary to protect an egalitarian distribution of resources and opportunities by providing security of person and property or in some other way. No laws prohibiting activities on grounds of personal morality could pass that test" (FLE, 225).

Dworkin in his writings on the incorporation of morality into public policy and law is mostly concerned with state coercion. It is not clear how Dworkin's criticism of such an incorporation would affect the debate over an issue such as same-sex marriage that does not involve state coercion. One could contend that conservatives today are making arguments in the context of same-sex marriage that are analogous to Lord Devlin's arguments relating to the criminalization of same-gender sexual conduct, that is, that society must protect itself by discouraging relationships and behavior that are considered by most of its members to be inimical to its values. In fact, as we will see in chapter 3, many of the members of Congress who voted for the Defense of Marriage Act adopted a Devlinian position when they argued that recognition of same-sex marriage would constitute a threat to the very survival of society. The statute, from this perspective, is simply an attempt by society to protect itself from what it perceives as a dangerous threat to its most fundamental traditions and norms. A Dworkinian liberal could respond that the introduction of notions of morality into the same-sex marriage debate treats "moral minorities" in an unequal fashion. The Dworkinian could argue, in other words, that when Congress enacted the Defense of Marriage Act, it impermissibly promoted a particular brand of majoritarian morality.

The problem with this Dworkinian critique is that an unwillingness by the state to recognize same-sex marriage, even if grounded in notions of morality, differs qualitatively from a state's use of majoritarian morality to criminalize, for example, same-gender sodomy; the latter, and not the former, involves state coercion that deprives individuals of their liberty. A legislature's refusal to recognize same-sex marriage does not entail, to borrow Dworkin's phrase quoted above, "forbid[ding someone] to lead the life he wants, or punish[ing] him for doing so." Society's refusal to recognize same-sex marriage does not *forbid* lesbians and gay men from leading the lives they think are best for them; instead, it entails withholding societal recognition of and support for their relationships. Even if Dworkin is correct that considerations of majoritarian morality should be kept separate from deliberations as to when to use state coercive power, he has not identified why the same principle should apply when the state sets policies that are neither coercive nor intrusive.

One could argue that Dworkin's use of the word "forbid" is too strong and that by implication it suggests regulation through the use of the criminal law, which is obviously not at issue in the civil regulation of marriage. In order to critique the use of majoritarian morality in both criminal and civil regulations, therefore, it might be advisable to replace the word "forbid" with "restrict," as in "society should not restrict individuals from leading the lives they want" based on an assessment of what constitutes a good life. This broader formulation of the appropriate limits on public action, however, goes too far. Government, including liberal government, regularly sets and enforces policies restricting or providing for the choices of individuals based on distinctions between a good life and a bad one. A broad spectrum of state actions, from prohibiting the use of certain drugs to the promotion of health to requiring a minimum amount of education that is deemed necessary for leading a minimally productive and satisfying life, entail the use of public policies to promote a certain conception of the good. Dworkin's neutral liberalism fails to recognize the ubiquitousness of evaluations of the good engaged in by even the most liberal of states.[27]

A Dworkinian liberal could reply by arguing that even if all liberal societies permit their governments to regulate in order to advance certain understandings of the good associated with issues such as health and education, there is something *different* about intimate associations and relationships, including sexual ones. When choosing to engage in intimate relationships, this argument holds, an individual is entitled to special protection and immunity from a state's (or the majority's) definition of the good. Upon scrutiny, however, a clear distinction between the right and the good fails to materialize even in matters of human sexuality and intimate relationships. When a society prohibits some sexual conduct, even if "only" sexual conduct that is not consensual (or between an adult and a minor regardless of consent), it enforces a definition of sexual morality through its laws. The reasons for the enforcement may be obvious to most and thus not subject to much dispute, but that does not make them any less moral. When a society chooses to regulate sexual conduct, it stakes out a position distinguishing acceptable from unacceptable expressions of sexuality.[28] Since no one, not even the liberals who are most committed to neutrality as a guiding principle for state action, contends that the state should not regulate at least some expressions of sexuality in some ways, it is impossible to avoid, in setting public policy, at least some moral questions pertaining to human sexuality.

The inability of a state (even a liberal one) to remain neutral in matters of sexuality is a principle that conservative opponents of gay rights understand too well, but one that liberal proponents stubbornly resist. If liberals would acknowledge that a conception of sexual morality is always at play whenever sexual conduct is regulated by the state—even if only along the consensual/nonconsensual binary—they would be better able to respond to the familiar and predictable conservative analogies between homosexuality and other forms of relationships such as polygamy. Opponents of gay rights often argue that if society can ban polygamy, why can it not also ban, or at least greatly discourage, same-gender sexual conduct? This argument can be found in the writings of conservative commentators, the speeches of conservative politicians, and even in the opinions of Supreme Court justices.[29] Justice Antonin Scalia in his bitter dissent in *Romer v. Evans* noted that the prohibition against polygamy "involves precisely the effort by the majority of citizens to preserve its views of sexual morality," an effort that is not different from societal discouragement of homosexuality.[30] A liberal relying solely on notions of neutrality cannot satisfactorily respond to this argument (which is why it is a favorite of conservatives). The limitation of spouses to two, like the restriction requiring spouses to be of different genders, is, after all, a restriction on the freedom to marry. Whether these types of limitations should be allowed to trump the freedom at issue requires a normative assessment of the value of the relationships without the limitations, an assessment that most liberals are willing to articulate in banning polygamy—by, for example, pointing out the patriarchy and gender subordination that accompanies polygamous marriages—but not in supporting same-sex marriage. I will in chapter 3 make a positive moral case as to why same-sex relationships are valuable and why, as a result, society should recognize and support them. While I leave the details of the argument for later elaboration, the point for now is that Dworkin's neutral liberalism, like Rawls's, proves inadequate in addressing the substantive moral issues at stake in the debate over same-sex marriage.

Moral considerations also apply to the issue of parenting by lesbians and gay men. Full recognition of the rights of lesbians and gay men in the area of parenting will only come about when there is a recognition that such parenting can be as *good* as heterosexual parenting. In the absence of such an inherently *normative* conclusion, it is unlikely that lesbians and gay men will truly gain *equal* parenting rights. Arguments based on the need to prevent government coercion that is motivated by majoritarian morality do not begin to address the substantive issues associated with what good parenting entails. As with marriage, neutral liberal theory that seeks to bracket out those considerations that attempt to distinguish between good and bad forms of human relationships end up sidestepping the crux of the debate.

This is not to suggest, of course, that once moral arguments relating to the good of gay and lesbian relationships and families are addressed directly rather than avoided, the gay rights positions will necessarily prevail. There is no guarantee that the arguments will prove persuasive to those who maintain an open mind on these issues (and they clearly will not be persuasive to those who are convinced that gay and lesbian relationships are intrinsically immoral). But given that the debate is primarily about which relationships and families deserve the recognition and support of society, the moral questions must be fully engaged.

Gay rights supporters who oppose (on either philosophical or prudential grounds) the purposeful incorporation of notions of morality into gay rights debates may respond that there is no need to so incorporate because a strict, uncompromising, and morally neutral commitment to equality means that lesbians and gay men must be afforded the right to marry and to parent as long as heterosexuals are permitted to do so. In fact, a Dworkinian liberal might argue that the debates over same-sex marriage and parenting by lesbians and gay men are not about the value and goodness of same-gender relationships and families at all but are rather about the full and unconditional equality owed to gay and lesbian citizens. In the context of race, for example, Dworkin argues that "[l]egislation based on racial prejudice is unconstitutional not because any distinction using race is immoral but because any legislation that can be justified only by appealing to the majority's preferences about which of their fellow citizens are worthy of concern and respect, or what sorts of lives their fellow citizens should lead, denies equality" (MP, 68).

The history of racial legislation and practices in this country, however, shows that arguments related to racial equality cannot be disconnected from underlying moral assessments. Equality only has bite as a guiding principle if the two groups whose differential treatment is being critiqued are understood to be similarly situated. If they are not so understood, then that by itself constitutes grounds for denial of equal treatment. The liberal ideal of equality, though obviously a vital component of our constitutional democratic regime, is not, in practice, a free-standing principle. For the principle of equality to have force, for it to change social institutions (whether by dismantling two centuries of segregated schools and public services or expanding the institution of marriage to include two individuals of the same gender), moral arguments must be presented as to why the two groups that are being compared (be they blacks and whites or gays and straights) are indeed *worthy* of equal treatment. This is why a generic, morally neutral argument based on equality and grounded on the idea that if group X is entitled to the benefits and rights provided by social institution Y so should group Z, proves, by itself, unpersuasive in the context of same-sex marriage and parenting by lesbians and gay men. Morally neutral arguments have worked in the context of employment discrimination protection on the basis of sexual orientation in some states (and will also work soon, I believe, at the federal level) because many Americans are coming around to the position that there is not much difference between homosexual and heterosexual *employees*. But we are nowhere near that point in the areas of marriage and parenting where a substantial majority of Americans believe that gays and straights are *not* equally situated. Many Americans insist that there are important differences between a heterosexual parent and one who is lesbian or gay. Similarly, the idea that prohibiting a man from marrying another man or a woman from marrying another woman raises questions of *unjust* inequality is met with either perplexed incredulity or outright anger by many Americans. As I will argue in chapter 3, much of the heavy lifting in gay rights philosophy requires a moral articulation of how and why lesbians and gay men share a commonality with others in those basic human needs and capabilities that are associated with sexual intimacy. Many liberal supporters of gay rights rely on arguments based on equality that assume a form of human commonality that is not made explicit. Neutral liberalism so pervades our thinking that we are overly fearful of delving into those admittedly difficult but nonetheless vital questions relating to what defines us as human and what are the circumstances and conditions required for us to be able to lead full human lives.

In matters of sexuality and intimate relationships, the needs and capabilities of lesbians and gay men are not yet viewed by many as fully human. It is in that perceived moral deficit that much of the resistance to gay and lesbian marriage and parenting resides. An emphasis on equality is appropriate (and crucial) once we are already convinced that the relevant and necessary commonalities exist. We need independent justifications (independent, that is, of equality), however, to decide whether the value of equality is applicable to begin with. The principle of equality does not by itself give us the necessary normative tools through which we can assess whether the requisite commonalities exist.

4. THE LATER DWORKIN: INDIVIDUAL ETHICS AND THE LIBERAL SOCIETY

Although Dworkin's earlier writings rejected the incorporation of moral considerations into political theory, his more recent writings argue that it is possible to connect the ethical concerns of citizens in a liberal society with the political structure and values of that society. In his Tanner lectures on equality, Dworkin seeks to formulate a theory of liberal equality that emanates from the ethical views of liberal citizens. As part of this project, Dworkin aims "to show how liberalism as a political philosophy connects with another part of our intellectual world, our ideas about what a good life is" (FLE, 190).[31] (Dworkin has also argued that judges have no choice but to rely on their views on political morality in deciding hard cases.[32] My interest here, however, is with Dworkin's political philosophy rather than with his theories of jurisprudence.)

In moving away from his earlier pronouncements on the need for strict neutrality on the part of the state, Dworkin has in many ways been responding to perfectionist critics of liberalism. This criticism, which Dworkin deems "formidable," exposes the "ethical and moral schizophrenia" of liberalism: it acknowledges that individuals have personal priorities and preferences on how to lead their lives in what they consider to be a good and ethical manner, but it then asks them to put those priorities and preferences aside when participating in the political process, or as Dworkin puts it, "to check them at the voting-booth door"

(FLE, 202, 207).[33] We all have certain convictions about how to live and how to deal fairly and justly with others in our personal lives. Can it really be true, perfectionists ask, that these convictions are irrelevant when determining the structure and practices of a just society?

Dworkin argues that this critique of liberalism challenges it to address "the apparent conflict between the most fundamental political claims of liberalism, about equality and rights and tolerance, and our most compelling personal convictions about the character of a worthwhile life" (FLE, 202). Dworkin notes two possible responses to this challenge. One is the "discontinuity strategy" suggested by Rawls's contractarianism. Under a contractarian framework, an individual can agree to accept a free-standing political view of liberalism "without subscribing to its principles as his own, just as he can agree to be bound by a contract without accepting that its terms are perfectly fair or even reasonable" (FLE, 204). Dworkin deems Rawls's version of contractarianism brilliant because it improves the traditional contractarian view by insisting that individuals agree to a political conception of justice not for selfish, Hobbesian reasons, but for moral ones. "If a particular political conception of justice would be agreed upon by artificial people in the right circumstances, [Rawls] believes, real people each have a moral reason to accept decisions in accordance with that conception of justice now, even though they have not collectively agreed to do so" (FLE, 213).

For Dworkin, Rawls's discontinuity strategy ultimately proves unsatisfactory, however, because the reasons offered by Rawls in explaining and justifying liberal political action lack a categorical force that goes beyond the fact of agreement. For Dworkin, in other words, it is not enough to argue that the values of a liberal society are correct because those are the ones its citizens agree upon; we also have to explain *why* those values are normatively acceptable.[34] In response to the perfectionist critique of liberalism, therefore, Dworkin prefers his own "continuity strategy" that "tries to construct what we might call a *liberal ethics*—instincts and convictions about the character and ends of human life that seem particularly congenial to liberal political principles" (FLE, 207). Liberal citizens, Dworkin advises, should not view politics as conceptually separate from their ethical values. In fact, it should be just the opposite: Liberal citizens should view politics as an *extension* of their ethics. The challenge, therefore, lies in constructing a link between individual ethics and liberal political values.

According to Dworkin, the best way of linking the ethics of liberal individuals with the institutions and values of a liberal society is through a conception of equality that calls for parity of resources (rather than of welfare or outcome) and that stresses neutrality toward people's choices. Equality of resources insists that the "ideal distribution is achieved only when the resources different people control are equal in the opportunity costs of those resources, that is, the value they would have in the hands of other people" (FLE, 223). Equality of resources is achieved when the "economist's envy test" is satisfied, namely, "equality is perfect when no member of the community envies the total set of resources under the control of any other member" (FLE, 223).[35] As for neutrality, Dworkin notes that "the value of the resources people hold must be fixed by the interaction of individual choices rather than the collective decisions of the majority"; as a result, "the majority has no right to decide what kinds of lives everyone must lead."[36] Dworkin argues that under his model, "justice and ethics merge because whether my life is good depends, among other things, on whether the share of resources available to me is a just share" (FLE, 286). Justice, for Dworkin, "is a parameter of good lives," but it is a parameter that is consistent with people's ethical values and their assumptions about what it means to live a good life (FLE, 299).[37] "Neither of these sets of convictions would be threatened by accepting that living well also means living within the constraints of justice" (FLE, 299). In this way, Dworkin argues, he has completed the link between ethics and justice by suggesting how the ethical values of liberal citizens can be integrated into a liberal conception of justice.

For our purposes, the conceptual link that Dworkin constructs between ethics and justice is important because it seeks to address one of the critiques of Rawlsian liberalism mentioned previously, namely, the strict separation between morality and politics. Dworkin, by recognizing that the ethical considerations of individuals in leading good lives play an important part in determining the institutions and values of a liberal political community and vice versa, is to some extent accepting the relevance of the good in the definition of the right. A truly liberal society that respects equality, according to Dworkin, distributes resources in such a way so as to give everyone the opportunity to lead a good life. As I will discuss in chapter 3, this view is shared by moral liberalism, which is the kind of liberalism that I believe is most compelling and profound. What is missing from Dworkin's account is a more specific exploration of the social conditions that are required for the leading of a good life, including those (of particular interest to us here) relevant to the formation and sustenance of intimate relationships. Part of the problem is that Dworkin has all along grounded his conception of equality on a "vague but powerful idea of human dignity" (TRS, 198). The vagueness in that conception—the unwillingness to provide a thicker understanding of what it means to be human—means that in matters of human intimacy and relationships, Dworkin, even when taking his later writings into account, can offer us only the same important but ultimately limited argument against moral coercion and paternalism on the part of the state. Thus, Dworkin in his Tanner lectures essentially repeats the same criticism of allowing majoritarian morality to be reflected in public policy that he emphasized in his earlier writings.[38] If what Dworkin's more recent writings on equality and ethics means for lesbians and gay men is that the state should avoid using its power to enforce majoritarian notions of morality, then little has been added to his earlier critique of Lord Devlin's political morality. That critique, as we have already seen, is of limited use when we seek to justify the imposition on society of an obligation to recognize and support certain intimate relationships.

Dworkin, in recognizing that liberals can connect their conceptions of the good and the ethical with a political conception of equality and justice, suggests how, in theory at least, it may be possible to incorporate notions relating to the value of same-gender relationships and families into a political framework that remains faithful to liberal ideas. Liberalism, however, needs a fuller account of the needs and capabilities that are constitutive of a fully human life. This account would allow us to explore societal obligations to create the necessary institutions and implement the requisite policies that make it possible for all individuals to meet all of their basic human needs and exercise all of their basic human capabilities. Those obligations entail more than the negative ones required to avoid moral paternalism and the positive obligations required to distribute the primary goods (income, wealth, jobs, health care, and so on) that Dworkin's model of equality of resources concerns itself with. The obligations also require the protection and (just as important) the *promotion* of human relationships centered around love, care, and commitment. I discuss the implications of a fuller account of human needs and capabilities, along with the corresponding greater societal obligations, in chapter 3. Before I do so, however, I want to explore another highly influential form of minimalist liberalism known as pragmatic liberalism.

TWO

Pragmatic Liberalism

John Rawls makes it clear in *Political Liberalism* that his political conception of justice does not include within it an epistemological challenge to the ability of individuals to arrive at truths through the application of their particular comprehensive doctrines as derived from philosophical and moral views. His point is limited to one of political morality, namely, that we should refrain from incorporating notions of truth that emanate from our comprehensive doctrines into a political conception of justice.[1] What Rawls argues, in other words, is that concerns about truth as understood and promoted by comprehensive doctrines should be set aside for purposes of articulating and defending a political (as opposed to metaphysical) theory of justice. He does not contend that the epistemological foundations of truth and reason are either illusory or culture-specific. It is not Rawls's project, therefore, to question foundationalism writ large; instead, he wants foundationalist thinking set aside when determining and effectuating the overlapping consensus of a well-ordered society.

Although Rawls "does not inveigh against the very idea that a comprehensive doctrine might be true," then, he does deem philosophical and moral truths to be outside of the scope of political morality.[2] Ronald Dworkin, on the other hand, is much more explicit in his defense of objective truth in the face of antifoundationalist critiques. In an essay titled "Objectivity and Truth: You'd Better Believe It," Dworkin argues that when antifoundationalists of all stripes claim that there are no right answers to disputed moral questions, they stake out a position that requires no less of a moral judgment than any other.[3] "So, for example, the thesis that there is no right answer to the question whether abortion is wicked is itself a substantive moral claim, which must be judged and evaluated in the same way as any other substantive moral claim."[4] Dworkin adds that "[w]e can't be skeptical, even about values, all the way down."[5]

Dworkin's foundationalism (and Rawls's neutrality on foundationalist issues) stands in sharp contrast to the antifoundationalism of postmodernist and pragmatist philosophy. For postmodernists, understandings of truth, reason, and morality are the effects of hegemonic power relations and systems of knowledge. I will elaborate on postmodernist theory, and its impact on a philosophy of gay rights, in chapter 5 when I discuss Michel Foucault's conception of sexual ethics. I want to in this chapter focus on pragmatic liberalism, and in particular on the writings of two leading contemporary pragmatic thinkers: Richard Rorty and Richard Posner.[6] Both Rorty and Posner abide by a form of moral minimalism not out of a belief in the value of neutrality (as does, for example, Rawls), but out of a skepticism of objective truth and morality. Pragmatists believe that it is possible to reach meaningful and defensible moral conclusions, but those conclusions are by necessity internal to social practices and depend on what is useful and appealing based on local norms, understandings, and needs. Pragmatists such as Rorty and Posner reject the idea that we can reach moral judgments that are universal in nature, that is, that exist—or can be justified—apart from particular societal and cultural values and priorities.

As we will see, there are important differences between Rorty and Posner. Rorty rejects the view that there is an objective reality out there that awaits our discovery; as he sees it, reality is created rather than discovered. Posner, on the other hand, is an empiricist who believes in a reality that is observable and measurable, and that can help us answer disputed moral questions. Despite their important differences, I will argue in this chapter that the normative accounts provided by both Rorty and Posner prove to be too thin when applied to gay rights issues. Rorty's focus on the commonalities that we share as members of a liberal democratic society does not go deep enough into the kinds of human commonalities associated with sexual intimacy that are properly at stake in most of the moral and political debates over gay rights. Posner's attempt to provide us with a conception of sex and its regulation by the state that is grounded in empiricism is neither morally neutral (as he claims) nor sufficient in helping us address some of the more hotly disputed gay rights questions of our time.

1. RORTY'S PRAGMATISM

Richard Rorty is one of the leading and most visible contemporary American philosophers as well as the leading pragmatist thinker of our time. Rorty is part of a long and proud tradition in American pragmatic philosophy, usually thought to have begun with Ralph Waldo Emerson and continued through the work of William James and John Dewey, which eschews metaphysics and the search for truth in favor of problem-solving and results. As Cornel West notes, for pragmatists "philosophy is neither a form of knowledge nor a means to acquire knowledge. Rather philosophy is a mode of cultural critical action that focuses on the ways and means by which human beings have, do, and can overcome obstacles, dispose of predicaments, and settle problematic situations."[7]

It is not possible within the confines of this book on gay rights to provide a detailed account of the rich tradition of American pragmatic philosophy, or of how Rorty's work fits within that tradition. I can, however, provide a summary of Rorty's moral and political philosophy, and then assess it from the perspective of gay rights. Neither discussion is meant to be exhaustive. Rorty at this point in his career has written enough that a comprehensive treatment of his work merits an entire book.[8] A philosophy of gay rights, however, must grapple with the ideas of influential contemporary philosophers such as Rorty. Surprisingly, he has received almost no attention from those writing on issues of sexual orientation.[9]

For Rorty, a philosophical search for first principles is an illusory one. There is for him no neutral or privileged point from which to evaluate moral principles in order to determine whether they are, in fact, first or true. Rorty in this regard divides Western philosophers into two broad groups. On one side are Aristotle, Plato, Descartes, Locke, Kant, and their scores of contemporary followers who believe that we can arrive at objective truths through reason, insight, logic, or observation. On the other side are thinkers such as Nietzsche, Heidegger, Foucault, Sartre, Dewey, and their scores of contemporary followers who believe that there is no such thing as truth, if by it we mean a set of principles or judgments through which we can arrive at objective (and presumably final) moral conclusions. Not surprisingly, Rorty sides with the latter group. Truths for Rorty are created, not discovered or found. He argues from within the pragmatic tradition of James and Dewey that holds that truth is not about moral justification but is instead about what is useful to particular individuals or societies in achieving particular goals given particular contexts.[10] As Rorty puts it, "[t]he purpose of inquiry is to achieve agreement among human beings about what to do, to bring about consensus on the ends to be achieved and the means to be used to achieve those ends" (PSH, xxv). Utility, therefore, is for Rorty a much more apt subject of moral and political discussion than is truth. In fact, utilitarians have it right when they focus on utility; they get it wrong, according to Rorty, only when they limit the relevant utility to pleasure or happiness. Utility is a much more open-ended concept for Rorty, one that we should define expansively based on our many needs and interests.

It is through the lens of utility, for example, that we should evaluate the meaning and role of language. Language is a tool that helps us deal with our environment; language is important because it is *useful* to us in coping with our surroundings. We fool ourselves, Rorty believes, if we think that language allows us to represent an objective reality that sits out there patiently awaiting our description of it. Everything that we describe, we do according to our needs and interests. Instead of focusing on intrinsic or essential characteristics of that which we describe, Rorty urges us to focus on the relationships between the subjects of our descriptions. As he puts it, "there is nothing to be known about anything save its relations to other things" (PSH, 54).

As language goes, so do beliefs. Beliefs are tools that help us define reality according to our needs and priorities—they are not objective concepts that allow us to represent reality accurately. Knowledge for Rorty is not "a matter of getting reality right, but rather [is] a matter of acquiring habits of action for coping with reality" (ORT, 1). We choose our habits depending on what is useful. Beliefs and knowledge, as reflected in our habits, are useful summaries of our generalized intuitions; they are the distillation of our individual and communal experiences that permit us, in an effective and practical way, to deal with changes in our environment. But they are not anything more than that; they do not represent transhistorical or transcendental foundations or truths. As Rorty explains, "to say that a belief is, as far as we know, true, is to say that no alternative belief is, as far as we know, a better habit of acting" (CIS, xxv). This skepticism toward the objectivity of truth applies not only to philosophy, history, and politics, but to science as well. Rorty refuses to privilege scientific knowledge among other forms of knowledge—it has no special or unique relationship to truth that is independent of language and utility (ORT, 35–45).

Furthermore, whereas philosophers who are part of the Platonic and Enlightenment traditions believe that our ability to reason is constitutive of what makes us human (and thus what distinguishes us from other animals), Rorty rejects the idea of an intrinsic human nature. "Since nothing has an intrinsic nature," Rorty notes, "neither do human beings" (PSH, 63). As pragmatism sees it, "humanity is an open-ended notion [and] the word 'human' names a fuzzy but promising project rather than an essence" (PSH, 52). As a result, unconditional and transcultural moral obligations cannot be rooted in universal understandings of what it means to be human. For Rorty, there is nothing to human beings that is outside of or separate from their contingent ties and connections. As he explains, "socialization, and thus historical circumstance, goes all the way down. . . . [T]here is nothing 'beneath' socialization or prior to history which is definatory of the human" (CIS, xiii). The idea that there is an intrinsic human nature that stands apart from our contingencies and particular circumstances is a variation on the idea that there is some force or source, whether divine or secular (such as reason) that constititues a reality that is separate from our understandings of our environment and relationships.

Rorty does at times, however, acknowledge that there are certain characteristics that are unique to humans such as our use of language

(PSH, 63, 74–75; CIS, 73). Yet, as already noted, it is according to him a mistake to view language as having intrinsic characteristics that somehow stand between our subjective assessements and the objective world around us. Instead, "the word 'language' " is simply "a way of abbreviating the kinds of complicated interactions with the rest of the universe which are unique to the higher anthropoids" (PSH, 64). Language is nothing more than a tool that is helpful to us in describing the relationships between objects. Once again the key is utility, rather than truth or correspondence with a reality that is outside of or separate from ourselves and our communities.

In emphasizing utility, Rorty makes it clear that there is no helpful difference between what is right and what is useful. As such, he rejects a stark distinction between morality (unconditional and categorical obligations) and prudence (conditional and hypothetical ones). The difference between the two is simply one of degree; prudence entails "routine and uncontroversial" adjustments to our "non-human and human environments," that can be calibrated largely through our customs and habits (PSH, 73). Those customs and habits, however, only take us so far because sometimes a controversy arises that calls for more than a routine adjustment; it is at that point that we *invent* morality and law. "We invent both when we can no longer just do what comes naturally, when routine is no longer good enough, or when habit and custom no longer suffice" (PSH, 73). Morality, then, is nothing more than a "new and controversial custom" (PSH, 76).

Not surprisingly, Rorty also questions a Kantian/Dworkinian understanding of rights as having universal application or justification. Rorty rejects such a "heroic" view of rights; "[t]o speak of human rights," he argues, is nothing more than "to explain our actions by identifying ourselves with a community of like-minded people" (PSH, 85). Human rights talk is a particular kind of language that permits us to express and apply "culturally influenced intuitions" in a predictable, efficient, and useful way (TP, 171). Human rights, like all other useful concepts, are social constructions.

Rorty also defends the private/public distinction—one that has been much criticized by postmodernist and feminist thinkers—albeit in a different, more complicated way than do most liberals. Rorty sees the private sphere as one of self-creation and aesthetics where every person can be both a poet and an ironist. Rorty means by this that individuals in the private sphere can learn to cope with their contingencies through redescriptions of their lives and through an ironic disposition toward their inability to describe or understand a reality that exists outside of themselves. In the private sphere, the ironist thrives by acknowledging and even flaunting the contingency of her situatedness and therefore of her descriptions (or understandings) of reality and values. In fact, all that the ironist knows for sure is that the only way to critique a description is with a redescription. The ironist, in other words, knows that even what might appear to be final determinations of truthfulness and rightness are always contingent and thus subject to further redescriptions. An ironist, then, is "someone sufficiently historicist and nominalist to have abandoned the idea that [her] central beliefs and desires refer back to something beyond the reach of time and chance" (CIS, xv).

But for Rorty, "[i]rony seems inherently a private matter" (CIS, 87). Irony does not work in the public sphere because when in it the ironist must be cognizant of the fact that repeated efforts to rediscribe the lives of others can be cruel and humiliating. So the Rortian subject in the public sphere trades her irony for a hope that it will be possible to create public institutions and foster public norms that are meant to avoid cruelty and humiliation. It so happens that those institutions and norms already exist: they are the democratic institutions and freedom-based norms of Western liberal societies. Liberalism, through its emphasis on democratic structures and pluralistic values, helps us minimize cruelty and humiliation because it is "dedicated to enlarging itself, to creating an even larger and most variegated *ethnos*" (CIS, 198). What makes liberalism so appealing to Rorty is that it is the only ideology that strives to make the tent bigger, that is, to increase the number of people that it identifies with. Liberalism accomplishes this through its commitment to freedom. Rorty defines freedom in a traditional Millian sense by equating it with rights to be left alone as long as others are not harmed. As he puts it, "[m]y . . . hope . . . is that our culture is gradually coming to be structured around the idea of freedom—of leaving people alone to dream and think and live as they please, so long as they do not hurt other people."[11] Rorty conceives of freedom in a negative sense because for him it is constituted and guaranteed through an absence of force. As Rorty sees it, freedom allows for the exploration of new and better practices and for the exchange of ideas in an atmosphere of tolerance, respect, and solidarity: "A liberal society is one whose ideals can be fulfilled by persuasion rather than force, by reform rather than revolution, by the free and open encounters of present linguistic and other practices with suggestions for new practices" (CIS, 60).

In further defending a separation between private and public spheres, Rorty argues that the lessons that we learn from "ironist theorists" such as Nietzsche, Derrida, and Foucault about the need for self-creation and the value of aesthetics are best applied to our private lives. The work of these thinkers has been "invaluable in our attempt to form a private self-image, but pretty much useless when it comes to politics" (CIS, 83). As Rorty sees it, "[t]he vocabulary of self-creation is necessarily private, unshared, unsuited to argument" (CIS, xiv). On the other hand, "[t]he vocabulary of justice is necessarily public and shared, a medium for argumentative exchange" (CIS, xiv). Because of the irreconcilable differences between these two vocabularies, Rorty argues that it is impossible to hold self-creation (or private perfection) and justice (or human solidarity) in a single vision. Foucault's work, for example, though relevant to issues of self-creation and private autonomy, helps us very little with politics (CIS, 63–65).[12] According to Rorty, Foucault provides us with little guidance on how to build solidarity and strive for a better and more equal society. There is, in other words, no *hope* in Foucault. In the public sphere, then, Rorty trades in the pessimism of Foucault for the liberal optimism and hope of the likes of Whitman and Dewey. In the public sphere, "[w]hat matters for pragmatists is devising ways of diminishing human suffering and increasing human equality, increasing the ability of all human children to start life with an equal chance of happiness" (PSH, xxix).

Rorty is also interested in the ways in which solidarity is attained. What binds societies together, he argues, are shared vocabularies and especially shared hopes. Philosophers are not very good at understanding or promoting hope, but fortunately others, such as novelists and journalists, are. For Rorty, literature in particular plays a crucial role in promoting decency and a greater understanding of those who are different from us, and thus is an important part of the liberal communal *telos* of building solidarity around the shared hope of avoiding cruelty and humiliation. The fiction of Dickens and Robert Wright "gives us details about kinds of suffering being endured by people to whom we had previously not attended," while that of James, Orwell, and Nabokov permit us to understand the "sorts of cruelty we ourselves are capable of, and thereby lets us rediscribe ourselves" (CIS, xvi).

As for how to deal with nonliberals, Rorty urges liberals to respond to their criticisms by putting aside universalist ideals and values and concentrating instead on comparing liberalism to "concrete alternatives" (ORT, 211). He is certain that if individuals were permitted to experience both liberalism and any of its alternatives, most would prefer the former because it allows for a freer and more comfortable life. Thus, Rorty supports a politics of ethnocentrism that defends the values and accomplishments of Western liberal democracies not through the rhetoric of the Enlightenment (of reason, human nature, and universal rights) but by simply pointing out "the practical advantages of liberal institutions in allowing individuals and cultures to get along together without intruding on each other's privacy [and] without meddling with each other's conceptions of the good" (ORT, 209).

The principal political (and economic) alternative to liberalism for most of the twentieth century was, of course, Marxism. Rorty has been consistently and pugnaciously critical of Marxism, even long before the embarrassing collapse of Soviet-style communism. At the level of theory, Rorty groups Marxism with Platonism and Christianity given the former's belief in objective truths as reflected in supposedly universal laws of history. Marxist theory is for Rorty yet another failed attempt at constructing a metanarrative, albeit one based on the inevitable and predictable patterns of history rather than on metaphysics or religion. At the level of practice, Marxism, with its preference for ideological purity over the kind of pragmatic advocacy that can help implement specific programs and policies to protect the weak from the strong, has been a disaster for the American left (AOC, 41–71). Rorty is also quite critical of the non-Marxist, postmodernist academic left for failing to "buil[d] a consensus on the need for specific reforms" (AOC, 15). Rorty is with postmodernists as long as the discussion remains in the realm of philosophy—he is their ally in the fight against essentialism and foundationalism. But Rorty worries that postmodernists (like many of their universalist opponents) have been too concerned with theorizing problems as opposed to solving them. As Rorty sees it, theory is useful only to the extent that it helps us clear some of the philosophical underbrush that remains from the doggedly resilient Enlightenment tradition. But that is about all that can be said for theory; by itself it gets us no closer to developing a practical plan for avoiding cruelty and humiliation.

2. RORTY FROM A GAY RIGHTS PERSPECTIVE

As can be expected for someone who is simultaneously sympathetic to both postmodernism and liberalism, Rorty has been criticized from all sides. Conservatives dismiss him as yet another leftist relativist.[13] The liberal Ronald Dworkin criticizes his emphasis on contingent vocabularies rather than on what is right based on what is just.[14] Those on the nonliberal left find his (partial) appreciation for Derrida and Foucault promising, but they remain largely mystified by his insistence that liberalism offers the best opportunity for constructing a fair and egalitarian society. Rorty is also criticized by leftist nonliberals for defending the private/public distinction and more particularly for being open to redescriptions in the private sphere while rejecting redescriptions (once we have settled on liberalism) in the public sphere.[15]

The question for us is whether Rorty's pragmatic brand of liberalism has much to offer lesbians and gay men. Although Rorty has not written about gay rights at any level of detail, it is quite clear that he is supportive of gay rights causes. In fact, his most recent writings are sprinkled with references to lesbians and gay men. Thus, for example, he notes that "[t]he best single mark of our progress toward a fully fledged human rights culture may be the extent to which we stop interfering with our children's marriage plans because of the national origin, religion, race, or wealth of the intended partner, or because the marriage will be homosexual rather than heterosexual" (PSH, 86).

An opponent of gay rights would likely respond to Rorty by asking "why?," as in why is it a mark of progress that our society is becoming more tolerant of lesbians and gay men? We need to pause for a moment and explore this question. It should not surprise us after the discussion in the previous section that Rorty is not interested in questions of "why?" if they are asked with the expectation of receiving an answer that stands apart from the norms and customs of a particular society. Epistemological and political justifications for Rorty entail nothing more than the giving of reasons, reasons that are determined entirely by local circumstances, understandings, and needs. The only justificatory constraints under which we operate, then, are those formulations that our fellow conversationalists will not allow us to get away with. Even attempts at justifying what may seem obvious, such as why we should not be cruel to each other, cannot be done from a perspective that is outside of our particular social practices and understandings. This means that Rorty believes it is impossible to speak of evils that are intrinsically so because they do violence to universal principles of reason and justice or to some essential characteristic that is constitutive of what it means to be human. Thus, he contends that "the enslavement of one human tribe or race by another or of human females by human males . . . is not an intrinsic evil" (TP, 207). We cannot argue that the Nazis were in the moral wrong, though we can certainly highlight their cruelty.[16] Similarly, we reject patriarchy not because it is intrinsically wrong but because "it is a rejected good, rejected on the basis of the greater good that feminism is presently making imaginable" (TP, 207).

Rorty's faith in the value of internal moral and social criticism finds much in common with the ideas of the communitarian political philosopher Michael Walzer, whose work I discuss in chapter 4. I will there address more specifically the benefits and limitations, for those who are interested in advocating on behalf of lesbians and gay men, of relying solely on a theory of internal criticism. Here I want to focus on the rejection by Rorty of a particular kind of universal justification, namely, that which is grounded on what it means to be human. In the remainder of this section, I make some initial arguments (to be elaborated on in greater detail in the next chapter) as to why it is appropriate to view certain needs and capabilities associated with sexual intimacy as constitutive of what it means to be human. Although there are, of course, other basic needs and capabilities that also define our humanity, those associated with sexuality are for obvious reasons of particular relevance to a discussion of sexual-orientation issues. I also in this section apply Rorty's own evaluative criterion, i.e., usefulness, in assessing pragmatically his categorical rejection of moral and political arguments grounded on a common humanity and seek to show why that rejection, from a gay and lesbian perspective, proves unhelpful.

A discussion of issues of justification and gay rights must begin with the reality that our culture places the burden on lesbians and gay men to justify their inclusion in social institutions and benefits (such as those associated with marriage and parenting). The question of which party has the burden, so to speak, on matters of justification is important because it reminds us that we need to, when discussing issues of political morality, account for power and its corresponding privileges and benefits. Rorty's idea of a liberal utopia—where groups discuss and debate political issues through descriptions and redescriptions in an open and tolerant fashion with the goal of reducing cruelty and humiliation—makes no distinctions among different groups on the basis of power. The groups in power, the ones whose internal descriptions are already largely reflected in what the society takes to be the correct (or best) descriptions, have no need for justification since the status quo *is* their justification. It is those on the outside who have the justificatory burden of showing why the status quo must be changed.

Disparities in power, however, go beyond a simple dichotomy between the outsider and the insider. Marginalized groups, even in liberal democracies, are often placed in the position of having to justify their very existence *as human beings*. In the United States, the humanity of lesbians and gay men is questioned in two principal ways. First, their sexuality is viewed by many as perverse and depraved, often compared to bestiality. Many criminal statutes to this day, for example, equate sodomy with bestiality and other crimes against nature.[17] Similarly, the conservative legal philosopher John Finnis, in a law review article published in 1994, contends that same-gender sexual intimacy is, morally speaking, akin to the "[c]opulation of humans with animals."[18] Reflecting this line of thinking, after the gay college student Matthew Shepard was beaten to death in Laramie, Wyoming, a resident of that town told an interviewer that if his children asked him about the young man's death, he would tell them that homosexuality is wrong because "gay people do . . . what animals do."[19]

The second way in which our culture and norms dehumanize lesbians and gay men is by viewing them only through the prism of sex rather than as full human beings who share a myriad of complex needs and capabilities with others. This form of dehumanization has both moral and political implications. Morally it means that for lesbians and gay men, their sexuality and not the content of their character or their relationships with others or their human aspirations determine who they are in the eyes of society.[20] Politically it means that the resistance to gay rights positions is often driven by, as David Richards puts it, "a dehumanizing obsession with homosexuality solely in terms of a rather bleakly impersonal interpretation of same-gender sex acts . . . [,] an interpretation that deracinates such sex acts from the life of the person that is recognizably human or humane."[21] As a supporter of the Defense of Marriage Act explained approvingly on the floor of Congress, for many Americans homosexuality is about nothing more than lust.[22] It is therefore, as I will argue in greater detail below, a bit too easy and not particularly helpful to tell individuals whose basic humanity has been relentlessly questioned by large segments of society that they need not trouble themselves with a form of justification that depends, in part, on asserting and defending their humanity because, well, it is all hopeless anyway.

The commonalities that Rorty would want us to focus on are those that emanate from our membership in a liberal nation-state. Rorty argues that our commonalities as Americans, properly understood, offer the best justification for the inclusion and tolerance of heretofore marginalized groups. It is more useful, Rorty contends, to emphasize our commonalities as Americans rather than (as many leftist intellectuals have done since the 1960s) emphasize our differences. "To take pride in being black or gay is an entirely reasonable response to the sadistic humiliation to which one has been subjected. But insofar as this pride prevents someone from also taking pride in being an American citizen, from thinking of his or her country as capable of reform, or from being able to join with straights or whites in reformist initiatives, it is a political disaster" (AOC, 100). Rorty argues that only by "mobiliz[ing] what remains of our pride in being Americans" will we be able to achieve and realize the open, tolerant, generous, and caring country that was envisioned by Whitman and Dewey (AOC, 91–92). In an example of what he has in mind, Rorty argues that the "most persuasive way" for an American liberal to react to "the unending hopelessness and misery of the lives of the young blacks in American cities" is to "insist that it is outrageous that an *American* should live without hope" (CIS, 191).

Rorty's concerns about the limitations of focusing almost exclusively on the distinctiveness of minority groups when discussing issues of justice are valid. Rorty is correct that there is room in leftist intellectual thought for a greater emphasis on commonalities. Yet the commonalities that Rorty emphasizes, namely, the common binds and aspirations that we share as *Americans*, prove too thin for two reasons. First, given that Rorty looks forward to the day when "the United States of America . . . yield[s] up sovereignty to what Tennyson called 'the Parliament of Man, the Federation of the World' " (AOC, 3), he is ultimately after a form of inclusiveness and tolerance that will allow individuals to break free of national boundaries and to create bonds of global solidarity. His vision is an "old-fashioned utopian . . . one that leads to a global society of freedom and equal opportunity" (PSH, 236).[23] It is not at all clear, however, how an exclusive focus on what he takes to be distinctive American traditions of hope and progress as represented by Whitman and Dewey would provide for that kind of metainclusivity, unless Rorty were to try to argue (inconsistently with his pragmatist philosophy) that there is something about the ideas of those men that are or should be universal. If only the rest of the world can become more like Americans (and other citizens of Western democracies) is an odd message for someone who purports to be acutely aware of historical and social contingencies. Yet this is precisely what Rorty suggests when he speaks rather hopefully about "the power of the rich European and American democracies to disseminate their customs to other parts of the world" (CIS, 93) and about "the pragmatist attempt to see the history of humanity as the history of the gradual replacement of force by persuasion, the gradual spread of certain virtues typical of the democratic West" (ORT, 216). Even if we were to assume that Rorty is correct to claim that Western democracies have been more adept than other nations at pursuing and implementing ideals of hope, progress, and the avoidance of cruelty and humiliation, we should tread carefully before concluding that those values are exclusive to those cultures in the same way that Amartya Sen has counseled us to be wary of arguments that deem values associated with the Enlightenment tradition, such as freedom and reason, as uniquely Western.[24]

Second, and more important for our purposes, even if we put aside issues relating to a global metainclusivity and focus on moral and political disputes within the United States, it is not at all clear that our commonalities as Americans are enough to address the arguments of those who seek to exclude lesbians and gay men from important social institutions and benefits. As I argue below, Rorty is incorrect when he contends as a categorical matter that arguments based on our narrower commonalities (such as being Americans) are more persuasive (or useful) than those based on our broader commonalities (such as those we share as human beings). This is not to suggest, of course, that the commonalities that we share as Americans, and as citizens of a democracy, are irrelevant or unimportant. In fact, the Supreme Court's ruling in *Romer v. Evans* can be seen as a constitutional recognition of the type of commonality that Rorty emphasizes. (Rorty mentions the case with approval in passing in some of his recent writings (AOC, 53; PSH, 246)). In *Romer*, the Court was appropriately troubled by the attempt of the majority of citizens of one state, through the passage of a constitutional amendment, to deny lesbians and gay men the kind of legal protections that the rest of citizens take for granted "either because they already have them or do not need them."[25] As a result of the constitutional amendment, lesbians and gay men were subjected to a form of legal and civic disability that was not imposed on any other group. Nothing short of a change to the state constitution, lesbians and gay men were told, will earn you the basic protections of laws that are available to all others. The Court could not countenance such an exclusion of a distinct group of individuals from the basic protection of the laws. The amendment, the Court concluded, was "a classification of persons undertaken for its own sake, something the Equal Protection Clause does not permit."[26] *Romer* therefore raises important questions about what it means to be a participant in our democracy and the limits imposed on the state in placing obstacles that deprive citizens of meaningful protection of the laws.

Yet when we speak not of the state and local antidiscrimination laws that were the principal targets of the constitutional amendment at issue in *Romer* but of marriage and parenting, the relevance of a shared *political* community is reduced. As I noted in chapter 1, marriage and parenting implicate interests and values that go beyond those that are relevant to and emanate from the political community. Marriage and parenting raise important questions about who we are as human beings (as opposed to just citizens) and how we relate to those whom we love and care for. Although I will elaborate on these issues in greater detail in the next chapter, I want to here point to another recent judicial opinion to begin to make the argument of how, as Andrew Sullivan puts it, "[t]he denial of marriage to gay people . . . erases them not merely as citizens, but as human beings."[27]

In 1999, the Vermont Supreme Court was asked to rule on the constitutionality of the state's ban against same-sex marriage.[28] The court, in concluding that the state had to provide gay and lesbian couples with the same rights and benefits that it offered to heterosexual married couples, noted the importance of the myriad of legal rights and benefits that attach to the status of marriage. But in elaborating on the scope of the state constitutional provision guaranteeing equality to all citizens, the court went beyond a discussion of the particular legal rights and benefits at stake. Marriage, the court noted, "is a singularly human relationship" and "the essential aspect of the[ ] [plaintiffs'] claim is simply and fundamentally for inclusion in the family of state-sanctioned human relations."[29] The court cited the United States Supreme Court's opinion in *Dred Scott v. Sandford* (the nineteenth-century case that held that African Americans were not citizens eligible for constitutional protections) as a past example "where the law refused to see a human being when it should have."[30] A refusal to recognize committed same-gender relationships through which many lesbians and gay men meet their human needs and exercise their human capabilities associated with physical and emotional intimacy is similarly a failure to recognize their full humanity. The Vermont court could not countenance such a view of lesbians and gay men because the principle of equality as enshrined in the Vermont constitution required it to view them as full human beings. As the court put it, "to acknowledge plaintiffs as Vermonters who seek nothing more, nor less, than legal protection and security for their avowed commitment to an intimate and lasting human relationship is simply, when all is said and done, a recognition of our *common humanity*."[31]

The kinds of broadly shared commonalities underscored by the Vermont court are of particular importance if we follow Rorty's advice and try to build understanding, solidarity, and tolerance through the stories that we tell each other about our lives. Rorty may very well be correct that those values (or, as he would prefer to call them, sentiments) might be more usefully promoted through narratives and literature than through theory. But if that is so, it is important to ask the next question: Why, *as a practical matter*, are narratives and literature useful? Their usefulness derives, I believe, from their ability to encourage readers and listeners to realize and understand the commonalities that they share with those whose lives are being described. As Mario Vargas Llosa notes, as readers of literature, "we understand each other across space and time, and we feel ourselves to be members of the same species because . . . we learn what we share as human beings, what remains common in all of us under the broad range of differences that separate us."[32] If the wealthy white suburbanite reading the autobiography of a black youth living in a deprived urban area (to return to Rorty's example alluded to earlier) did not view the youth as sharing some of her human needs, capabilities, and vulnerabilities, the narrative would not be particularly effective in creating in her an understanding of the importance of being more tolerant toward and concerned with the needs of others. We could say, as Rorty does, that the reader feels a commonality with the impoverished youth as a fellow *American*, but that does not seem correct; rather, the feeling of commonality goes deeper than that because it is generated and driven by a society's (in fact by *any* society's) failure to acknowledge and promote the human potential of a young person. The understanding that a well-to-do American may feel for an oppressed and disadvantaged person in the United States is not significantly different from an understanding of the oppressions and disadvantages experienced by someone living in Sierra Leone or Peru. It is true that the wealthy American may be inclined to first help the American poor as opposed to the Peruvian poor, but we should not equate nationalistic responses with the scope of our empathetic capabilities.[33] We should also not confuse the prioritizing of whom to help based on our familiarity with and greater accountability of national (as opposed to international) redistributive mechanisms with *the reasons* for recognizing and empathizing with the pain and suffering of others.

These same considerations apply to issues raised by sexual orientation. How is it that a straight person who has never felt an attraction for someone of the same gender (and who, in fact, has likely been told repeatedly since a young age that such an attraction is immoral, perverted, and harmful) begin to understand that same-gender sexual intimacy is something not just to be tolerated but also respected and valued? Surely this is not accomplished by emphasizing to the straight person that the gay person is also an *American*. Instead, the heterosexual is reached, at least in part, by encouraging him or her to recognize the humanity of the other.[34] A straight person (or a white person) will only come around to respecting and valuing a gay person (or a black person) fully when the former sees the latter as a complete human being, with the same needs, capabilities, and vulnerabilities. In my opinion, a good part of the progress that the gay rights movement has made in the last few decades is due to the fact that it has been able to get growing numbers of heterosexuals to acknowledge the common human attributes, including needs and capabilities associated with sexual intimacy, that we all share regardless of sexual orientation and that play such an important role in defining us as human. As Leonard Kriegel wrote several decades ago in the context of disability, the privileged only truly see the marginalized when there "is a stripping away of stereotype and symbol and a willingness to accept the humanity of the other, at whatever personal cost."[35]

Rorty argues that the commonalities we may perceive between ourselves and our fellow human beings are simply the result of descriptions and redescriptions that, for example, illustrate to the privileged the living conditions of the marginalized. As he puts it, the "process of coming to see other human beings as 'one of us' rather than as 'them' is a matter of detailed description of what unfamiliar people are like and of redescription of what we ourselves are like" (CIS, xvi). Solidarity for Rorty emanates from particular uses of language that allow us to determine who (we think) we are and what we share with others. It is certainly possible, therefore, to think of gay rights in the way that Rorty views feminism, namely, as a "new way[ ] of speaking" (TP, 223). It is tempting to conceive of gay rights as a language game, that is, to believe that lesbians and gay men (like women and African Americans) *construct* their personhood rather than discover it, and that progress is made when the broader society accepts descriptions that prior to that had only been accepted by the marginalized group. The issue that Rorty glosses over is one of causation: Why is it that the broader community accepts the redescription advanced by the marginalized group? Why is it that at some point the groups who have "invented new moral identities for themselves by getting semantic authority over themselves" succeed in having their language "become part of the language [that] everybody" speaks? (TP, 225). As a practical matter that transition takes place because there is a recognition (often perhaps only a flicker) of shared human needs, capabilities, and vulnerabilities in the other. As Martha Nussbaum argues, compassion for another requires "belief in a common humanity. We do not grasp the significance of suffering" unless we recognize in others "common human limits and vulnerabilities" (HFS, 239, 237). Nussbaum adds that "[t]he recognition of one's own related vulnerability is . . . an important and frequently an indispensable epistemological requirement for compassion in human beings."[36] Although I agree, then, with Rorty that commonalities must be explored and defended, we need to go deeper in our search for those commonalities, certainly deeper than the kinds of nation-based commonalities that Rorty emphasizes.

It is intriguing to note that Rorty himself, despite his strongly antiessentialist views, sometimes speaks of commonalities that all human beings share. As already noted, Rorty believes that the use of language is a distinctive characteristic that separates us from other animals. For

Rorty, language is unique to human beings because we are the only ones, as far as we can tell, who can use it to *describe* things. Rorty also notes that humans have a capacity associated with pain that animals lack, namely, they can feel pain through being humiliated (CIS, 92). In fact, Rorty believes that it is this shared ability to feel humiliated, along with a shared language or vocabulary, that accounts for solidarity among individuals. Furthermore, Rorty notes that the kinds and numbers of relationships that human beings are able to enter into also distinguishes us from other animals. He argues that the pragmatist sees the difference between a human being and other animals as emanating from the former's "much greater flexibility in the boundaries of selfhood, in the sheer quantity of relationships which can go to constitute the human self" (PSH, 81).[37]

These are all, to my mind, crucial concessions because by acknowledging that there are at least three characteristics that distinguish us as humans, the debate shifts from *whether* it is meaningful or useful to speak of common human attributes to *which* are those attributes and *what* are their significance. Rorty believes that because we have to limit ourselves epistemologically to history and interpretation in our search for commonalities, the only commonalities that are meaningful and useful are those we share with other members of our local communities. Rorty associates the search for broader and more universal human attributes with metaphysics rather than with the historicism that he prefers. But as Martha Nussbaum argues persuasively, and as we will return to in the next chapter, it is possible to arrive at human commonalities that are based not on metaphysical principles, or on understandings of our environment and of our fellow human beings that are independent of our interpretations, but on accounts that are rooted in human practices and experiences. As Nussbaum puts it, "the deepest examination of human history and human cognition *from within* [can] still reveal[] a more or less determinate account of the human being, one that divides its essential from its accidental properties" (HFS, 207).[38] We can agree with Rorty, then, that what matters is history and interpretation, but disagree with his categorical position that there are no distinctive human characteristics that run across history and interpretation. Of course, the precise nature of those characteristics are contestable, but contestability is always with us, whether we are discussing our commonalities as Americans or as human beings.

It is interesting to note that both Rorty and Nussbaum are optimistic about our ability to arrive at commonalities, as well as to identify with "the other," through narratives in general and literature in particular.[39] (Surprisingly, neither Rorty nor Nussbaum has written much about the work of the other; neither have the many commentators who have elaborated on their work separately.)[40] The crucial disagreement between them is whether meaningful commonalities are limited to those that emerge from membership in particular communities or societies or whether there are additional commonalities that are deeper, constitutive components of our humanity that transcend time and place. One does not have to partake in Kantian metaphysics in order to recognize (as even Rorty at times appears to do) that human beings, despite the myriad of different ways in which they experience, describe, and rediscribe their lives, are at bottom, creatures who have some common attributes and that those attributes have ethical implications (including, as Rorty notes, determining our obligations not to humiliate and inflict cruelty on others).[41]

A fundamental principle of a philosophy of gay rights must be that gay and lesbian sexuality and relationships are an expression of a common humanity that lesbians and gay men share with everyone else. Despite the best efforts of some opponents of gay rights to dismiss same-gender intimacy as debased and perverted, their arguments are failing to persuade a growing number of people because the opponents have to argue, in the end, that gay and lesbian sexuality and relationships are not, in any recognizable sense, expressions of common needs and capabilities for human intimacy. These arguments are resonating less and less with the vast middle of the American public (i.e., those who are neither committed opponents of gay rights nor gay themselves). Those in that vast middle are increasingly supportive of gay rights positions because they are seeing enough of themselves reflected in the homosexual "other"—not, of course, in the more superficial sense of being attracted to someone of one's own gender, but in the deeper sense that the attraction (whatever its object) is driven by common needs, capabilities, and vulnerabilities that we share, not as Americans, but as human beings.

Another argument that Rorty uses to justify his skepticism of the existence of human commonalities is that oppressors do not think of themselves as humans but as *good* humans. "What is crucial for their sense of who they are," Rorty argues, "is that they are *not* an infidel, *not* a queer, *not* a woman, *not* an untouchable" (TP, 178). Rorty is correct that determined oppressors of lesbians and gay men, among others, may never recognize that the humanity of those whom they seek to oppress is relevant because the issue for them is not whether lesbians and gay men are human beings but whether they are "normal" ones. But the possibility exists that those who are not yet oppressors, especially the young, might not learn to despise and fear lesbians and gay men in the same way. This is more likely to happen if heterosexuals are encouraged to recognize in lesbians and gay men shared needs and capabilities for physical and emotional intimacy. This recognition of commonalities, when it takes place, is the result of observation and interpretation; of seeing and understanding, for example, that the intimate relationship that a parent or a sibling or a close friend might have with someone of the same gender is driven and defined by needs and capabilities for intimacy that are not gay or straight but are part of a broader commonality, one not based on being an American or a Westerner but on being human.

In the end, even if Rorty is justified in his deep epistemological skepticism about the existence of shared human attributes, it is nonetheless inconsistent for him to be so adamantly skeptical of the description or attribution of those traits as a kind of vocabulary. One would think that as a pragmatist, Rorty would be open to the possibility that a vocabulary based on commonly accepted characteristics of human beings could, at least in some circumstances, be *useful* in engendering further solidarity and tolerance among individuals.[42] This is particularly true given that our contemporary discourses on justice and rights in Western societies are often based on what are taken to be universal understandings of those concepts, understandings that view them as applying with equal moral (if not actual) force everywhere.[43] Most Westerners appear to think that the principles of justice and fundamental rights they believe in—broadly speaking, freedom of speech and conscience; rights to privacy, self-determination, and autonomy; the duty of the state to treat similarly those who are similarly situated, and so on—are morally defensible and applicable in all parts of the world. Even if Rorty is correct that such views simply reflect a contingent vocabulary that expresses itself as if it were universal and that has no moral foundation, we need not worry because according to Rorty *no* vocabulary has such a foundation. Rorty's antiessentialism singles out one kind of vocabulary (that which expresses itself through what are taken to be universal understandings) and renders it illegitimate even though he takes great pains otherwise to tell us that no vocabulary is *a priori* (il)legitimate.

There is no place in Rorty's pragmatic liberalism for the kinds of deeper human commonalities that I believe should be part of a philosophy and politics of gay rights. I agree with Martha Nussbaum that we can arrive at those commonalities through historical interpretations and evaluative judgments rather then through *a priori* principles or concepts that stand outside of human experience and interpretation. But, aside from the epistemological issue of how we best determine which are our most relevant commonalities, it is clear that even under Rorty's own rules of the game (i.e., focusing on what is useful), the deeper commonalities, at least some of the time, prove to be more helpful than the thinner ones that he emphasizes as a categorical matter. Even if Rorty is correct that talk of human commonalities is simply another vocabulary without a moral foundation, that vocabulary is one that can be quite useful to lesbians and gay men in attaining greater societal understanding and acceptance.

3. POSNER'S PRAGMATISM AND HUMAN SEXUALITY

Richard Posner is different from the other thinkers (Rawls, Dworkin, and Rorty) whom I have discussed so far because he is not these days primarily an academic (though he is a senior lecturer at the University of Chicago Law School and writes more than most full-time academics). Posner is arguably the most influential and respected federal judge who does not currently sit on the Supreme Court. It was for this reason that when he published a book on sex several years ago called *Sex and Reason* (to go along with his other books on law and economics, the federal courts, jurisprudence, and law and literature),[44] many commentators were intrigued. Posner wrote the book because, as he put it, judges know very little (beyond their personal experiences) about sex and yet are often called on to make important legal decisions relating to sexual intimacy and expression (SR, 1). In *Sex and Reason*, Posner applies empiricism and economic theory to matters of sex and sexuality. He argues that economic theory can serve as an "acid bath" to peel away the ignorance, prejudice, and superstition that have accumulated from the application of moral theories to human sexuality (SR, 437). Posner proposes a "concept of *morally indifferent* sex" that views sexual drives and preferences as largely determined by biological and evolutionary considerations and explains sexual acts as rational responses by individuals to costs and benefits (SR, 85). Posner argues, in other words, that although our sexual preferences are given (and thus out of our control), our sexual conduct is the result of *rational* choices (and thus can be explained and understood without the aid of morality). Similarly, Posner proposes that the regulation of sex be based on empirical observations and predictions of rational behavior without any reliance on moral theories.

Posner has more recently published another book titled *The Problematics of Legal and Moral Theory*, which is his fullest account yet of his conception of pragmatism. In this section, I summarize Posner's brand of pragmatism, noting the areas of overlap with and divergence from Rorty's pragmatism. (As with my discussion of Dworkin, I am more interested in Posner's moral and political philosophy than I am in his positions on jurisprudence and legal adjudication.)[45] I also in this section summarize Posner's pragmatic and empirical account of human sexuality. In the next section, I assess Posner's pragmatism and his so-called morally neutral conception of sex from a gay rights perspective. Posner has written a considerable amount on gay rights issues.[46] Although he deserves credit for attempting to grapple with issues of sexual orientation, his writings end up undermining the very point that he tries to make, namely, that it is possible to discuss human sexuality and its regulation without incorporating notions of morality. Posner's writings on same-gender sexual intimacy, which will be my primary focus, while ostensibly limited to morally neutral forms of pragmatic and economic empiricism, are in reality drenched with moral judgments about the nature of that intimacy. In the end, Posner fails in his attempt to present a conception of human sexuality and its regulation that avoids relying on a distinct *moral* vision.

Posner believes that moral philosophy is largely a waste of time because its penchant for abstract and *a priori* reasoning renders it useless in helping us resolve disputed moral questions.[47] Rorty, as we have seen, argues that there are no foundational principles that can act as objective guideposts in helping us determine what is true and right. Posner is as skeptical as Rorty is about the existence of universal truths. For Posner, morality is local: "I believe that the criteria for pronouncing a moral claim valid are given by the culture in which the claim is advanced rather than by some transcultural ('universal') source of moral values" (PLM, 8). This does not mean that all cultures are morally equal and that we therefore have an obligation to respect the morality of other cultures (a view that Posner rejects as "vulgar relativism"); it does mean that when we say that a practice of another culture is immoral, we can mean nothing more than that it is immoral "by our lights" (PLM, 8).

Like Rorty, Posner argues that our morality depends on our ends. He adds that his brand of empirical pragmatism is concerned with means and not ends. What pragmatists (and economists) can do is tell society that if it is interested in pursuing a particular end or value (freedom, equality, happiness, prosperity, justice, or whatever), "here are policies that will conduce to the goal and here are the costs associated with each" (PLM, 46). The only articulation of ends, or of morality, that Posner is willing to defend is "an *adaptationist* conception" that is, one "in which morality is judged . . . nonmorally . . . by its contribution to the survival, or other ultimate goals, of a society or some group within it" (PLM, 6). It is at first not clear how a "morality" can make judgments "nonmorally" until one understands that, as Posner sees it, the concepts of adaptation and survival allow us to make *functional* judgments (i.e., are a society's practices conducive to its survival?) as opposed to moral judgments (i.e., are a society's practices morally defensible?). Thus, for example, though there are according to Posner (as with Rorty) no universal values that allow us to decide with certainty that the Nazi regime was immoral, we can conclude that its moral code was *ineffective* in achieving its goals because the regime eventually collapsed under the weight of its own failures (PLM, 24–25). The only conclusion that we can reach with certainty is that Nazi morality proved quite poor at adapting and transforming itself in order to survive.

For Posner, there are no convincing answers to moral questions unless they are first reducible to factual inquiries. As he sees it, moral philosophers, unlike scientists and economists, care very little about facts, and thus are in the business of posing useless metaphysical questions for which there are no convincing answers. The principles of moral philosophy upon which we can agree are so general and banal (such as the moral edict "you shall not kill") that they provide no help in settling disputed moral questions (such as those surrounding abortion and the death penalty). Unlike the theorizing of academic moralists, scientific theorizing has proved successful in many areas because science deals mostly with "observable phenomena and 'real' (physically existing) entities" (PLM, 13). It is clear, in fact, that Posner has greater faith than Rorty in the ability of scientific methodologies and vocabularies to represent accurately a reality that exists outside of ourselves. Rorty, as we have seen, is highly skeptical of any claim (scientific or otherwise) that argues for a correspondence between interpretation or language and reality. Posner, on the other hand, believes that science "deal[s] . . . with phenomena that are 'mind independent' " (PLM, 18). But Posner does not stray far from pragmatist orthodoxy because, for him, the success of scientific (as well as economic) theories is not based on their being true, but on the fact that they, unlike moral theories, "help us to predict, understand, and to a limited extent control our physical and social environment" (PLM, 14). The key, then, is usability (or workability) rather than truth.

Although Posner believes that moral philosophy (as opposed to the fields of sociology or anthropology of morals) has little to offer as an academic discipline, his principal goal in *Problematics* is to convince legal academics that moral philosophy has no place in legal adjudication. Thus, instead of relying on abstract principals of moral philosophy in deciding difficult legal questions, such as whether the U.S. Constitution prohibits states from banning abortions, the focus of judges and lawyers should be on trying to determine the practical effects of deciding a case one way as opposed to another. It is empirical investigations, rather than philosophical ones, that can give courts guidance in deciding the hard cases. And legal academics are in a better position to conduct empirical investigations than judges and lawyers, who operate under significant institutional and time constraints. Much to Posner's chagrin, however, legal academics are more interested in philosophical reasoning, and in grand ideas of constitutional theory and interpretation, than they are in empiricism. It is in this light that we should view *Sex and Reason* where Posner the scholar seeks to aid Posner the judge (as well as his colleagues on the bench) with an empirical (and ostensibly morally neutral) description and explanation of human sexuality as well as with a functional (and ostensibly morally neutral) theory of the appropriate level of governmental regulation of it.

In *Sex and Reason*, Posner hopes to bring a "broadly scientific outlook" to the study of sex through the application of economic theory (SR, 4). His approach is both descriptive and normative. On the descriptive side, he seeks to explain the interaction between biology and rational choice theory in accounting for sexual behavior. The sex drive and the *range* of sex acts that any given individual engages in are largely determined by biological considerations, and perhaps also by developmental factors that are mostly fixed at a young age. Posner believes, therefore, that "a person's sexual preference among the possible sexual objects (male, female, or whatever), if costs are the same, is given, not chosen"

(SR, 87). The decision whether to engage in particular sexual acts in particular circumstances, however, is made by individuals by weighing costs and benefits in response to incentives. In this way, sexual agents are not fundamentally different from economic actors, pursuing their preferences rationally and responding to shifting incentives. On the normative side, Posner believes that, on the whole, the state should be agnostic as to people's preferences in matters of sexuality in the same way that it should be in matters of economic preferences. He defends John Stuart Mill's harm principle as the best way of regulating sexual acts: If the conduct does not have third-party effects, that is, if it does not harm others, then the government should refrain from regulation. Here Posner generally follows Mill in arguing that revulsion and indignation by third parties are not by themselves sufficient grounds for state regulation of sex.

For Posner, Mill's libertarianism is a normative theory and not a moral one because it can be applied functionally: We can (usually) determine as an empirical matter whether there are third-party effects arising from sexual conduct and thus we can set the level of state regulation accordingly. There is a compatibility, in other words, between the harm principle (and its distinction between self-regarding and other-regarding conduct) and economic theory. On the other hand, Posner believes that moral theory in matters of sex—whether the conservative kind of Aquinas and the Catholic Church or the neo-Kantian kind of liberal theorists such as Ronald Dworkin—is useless in setting or defending public policy because it is indifferent to empiricism. Moral theories "are irreducible to genuine social interests or practical incentives" and thus contribute little to either our empirical understanding of sexuality or to the normative question of how sexuality should be regulated (SR, 4). Posner the pragmatist, in other words, has no patience for sexual moral theorizing because it lacks an understanding of or appreciation for the facts and consequences of sexual conduct.

Consistent with his pragmatic approach, Posner's discussion of homosexuality in *Sex and Reason* is seemingly empirical and morally neutral. It is largely framed around the following "fact": Alfred Kinsey, in his famous studies of sexuality, rated individuals on a scale of 0 to 6, with a 0 given to those who are exclusively heterosexual and a 6 to those who are exclusively homosexual, with everyone else falling somewhere in between.[48] What this means for Posner is that there are two different kinds of homosexuals: the "real" and the "opportunistic." The former (who get a rating of 6 in Kinsey's scale) prefer men to women, whereas the latter (a Kinsey 4 or 5) "prefer women, but perhaps by virtue of having an unusually strong sex drive, will accept male substitutes in a pinch" (SR, 105). The two types, though often lumped together by society "in an undifferentiated category of 'homosexuals' . . . , are [actually] different from a scientific standpoint" (SR, 105). (Although I prefer to use the term "lesbians and gay men" rather than "homosexual," in discussing

Posner's writings I will use the latter because it is the term that he employs. By "homosexual," Posner means primarily gay men.)[49]

Homosexuals of the "real" variety present an obvious problem for evolutionary theory, though Posner suggests that perhaps they have more time and resources to care for nephews and nieces, thus doing their part for evolutionary adaptation along with every one else (SR, 103). But Posner spends comparatively little time discussing "real" homosexuals; his main interest is "opportunistic" homosexuals because it is their conduct that can be explained in terms of both evolution and economic theory. Posner understands "opportunistic" homosexuality, like other manifestations of what he designates as "deviant" sexuality (such as masturbation, voyeurism, and fetishism), to be an evolutionary safety valve: Men with particularly strong sex drives turn to "deviant" sex when the costs (including search costs) of "normal" sex—defined by Posner as "vaginal intercourse designed either to produce offspring or to reward the male for protecting offspring already produced"—are too high (SR, 98).[50] In fact, the reduced numerical availability of women as sexual partners accounts for most deviant sexual behavior, which is, according to Posner, mostly engaged in by males (SR, 98–99). As Posner sees it, the reduced sexual availability of women is largely the result of biological factors (and some cultural factors such as polygamy that can be seen as cultural manifestations of biological differences between men and women). The different sexual organs of males and females facilitates specialization; men have a much greater capacity for reproduction than women because the former are not incapacitated by pregnancy. Men therefore have on average a higher sex drive than women and tend to be less choosy about their sexual partners. Women, on the other hand, are more concerned with the personal characteristics of their mates and with whether they will contribute to the care of the child that might result from sexual intercourse (SR, 88–98). The reduced sexual availability of women means that men with particularly strong sex drives must seek alternatives. Even in a monogamous society, then, deviant sex will take place because "[u]nless there is instantaneous search and perfect sorting, there will always be some males who lack sex partners. Their condition is analogous to that of the unemployed in a prosperous but not frictionless free-market system" (SR, 99). A focus on empirical considerations of supply and demand and of costs versus benefits, Posner argues, allows us to explain and understand deviant sex much better than does a focus on moral theory.

As for state regulation of same-gender sexual conduct, Posner is quite critical of sodomy statutes when applied to consenting adults. These laws are inconsistent with Mill's harm principle because they regulate private conduct that has no third-party effects other than offending the moral sensibilities of some. In addition, the sodomy statutes that remain in the books go largely unenforced, which suggests that the level of offensiveness is not even that high, or at least that there is a consensus that whatever offense sodomy causes does not outweigh the intrusiveness of police tactics required to enforce the law (SR, 202–09).

Posner, however, distinguishes sodomy statutes from the issue of same-sex marriage. He does not call for state recognition of same-sex marriage because "permitting homosexual marriage would place government in the dishonest position of propagating a false picture of the reality of homosexuals' lives" (SR, 312). It would be a false picture because Posner interprets the empirical data as showing that "[a] pair of men is inherently less likely to form a companionate marriage-type relationship than a man and a woman" (SR, 305). (Posner does not address the issue of whether two women are as likely as heterosexuals to form a "companionate marriage-type relationship," though his premise that women are on average less interested in sex leads him to conclude that lesbian couples have sex less often than do heterosexual couples and male homosexuals (SR, 91)). Although Posner states that a cost-benefit analysis may in the future show that the recognition of same-sex marriage would be advisable, the public hostility toward lesbians and gay men in this country at the present time is so strong that the focus should be on more limited reform efforts such as domestic partnership legislation (SR, 313–14).

Posner also argues that most reasons for excluding lesbians and gay men from the military, such as the risk of blackmail or that "homosexual superior officers may coerce subordinates for sexual favors," are flimsy and weak (SR, 314–16). There is according to Posner, however, one good argument for continuing to exclude lesbians and gay men from the armed forces, namely, that their presence lowers the morale of heterosexual soldiers and thus potentially undermines military effectiveness. Until we have more data, he suggests a compromise: that the military be allowed to continue to exclude lesbians and gay men who want to join while those who are currently serving should be permitted to continue doing so (SR, 316–21).[51]

4. RATIONAL MAN AS MORAL MAN

Posner, like Rorty, incurs the wrath of critics from both the right and the left. There is in *Sex and Reason* more than enough grist for both sides to chew on. Social conservatives criticize his libertarian presumption that most matters associated with sexuality should be left unregulated.[52] On the other side, feminists and gay rights proponents have written blistering criticisms of his understandings and explanations of human sexuality.[53] My main concern here is with Posner's claim that his conception of sex is morally neutral. If Posner is correct that empiricism and what he considers to be a morally neutral functional normativism is all that we need in understanding and regulating human sexuality, then one of the principal arguments that I make in this book, namely, that it is necessary to take into account considerations of morality in determining the appropriate level of societal regulation of and (especially) societal support for sexually intimate relationships, would be seriously undermined. But, alas, Posner is not correct. As I discuss below, neither his normative theory of sex regulation nor the conclusions that he reaches based on his empirical understanding of sex are morally neutral.

Posner wants us to believe that there is a meaningful distinction between his normative theory of sex regulation on the one hand and the regulation prescribed by moral theories on the other. The distinction is not so clear, however. Let us take, for example, the harm principle, which in *Sex and Reason* constitutes the core of Posner's normative theory of governmental regulation of sexual conduct. The harm principle, as understood by Posner, is based, at least in part, on the high value assigned to the exercise of freedom in the pursuit of personal preferences. Martha Nussbaum puts it well when she notes that "[e]ven a strongly libertarian legal theory, such as Posner's, cannot be altogether independent of ethical judgments, as he sometimes seems to suggest. For although in its hands-off way it refuses to pass judgment on practices that many people deem immoral, it does so because of the high worth it ascribes to personal liberty of choice, a central moral value."[54] Although it is possible to defend the harm principle on purely consequentialist grounds (by arguing, for example, that the state should not regulate self-regarding harms because it is likely to punish at the wrong times or in the wrong ways), Posner, like many other liberal and libertarian thinkers, places considerable weight on the *values* of liberty and freedom when he argues that individuals should be permitted to pursue their preferences even at the risk of self-inflicted harm.

Furthermore, Posner does not have a nonmoral argument as to why majoritarian preferences in matters of sex regulation should be disregarded in favor of the harm principle. After all, those are preferences, which, like any others, must be taken into consideration under a utilitarian framework that seeks to account for people's preferences while remaining agnostic as to their content. As Jean Cohen notes, "[u]nless intimate relationships involving sexuality are considered special and important, there is little reason, on utilitarian analysis, to overturn legislated majority preferences on such matters."[55] Indeed, Posner appears conflicted on how to cope with majoritarian preferences in matters of sexuality. He sometimes contends that those preferences should be ignored because they represent nothing more than moralistic prudery. Thus, he argues against the criminal regulation of consensual sex between adults, including between adults of the same gender (SR, 202–09). At other times, however, he argues that majoritarian preferences should be given weight. Thus, he contends that the disapproval by a majority of Americans of same-gender sexual relationships is a sufficient reason to deny the legal recognition of same-sex marriage (SR, 313; PLM, 249–52).

Although Posner in *Sex and Reason* argued that Millian libertarianism in general and the harm principle in particular are the cornerstones of a regulatory regime of sex that is morally indifferent, in *Problematics* he seems to have come around to the view that "even Mill" was a moralist, and that as such, his ideas, as applied to contemporary public policy issues, are of little use. In a short three-page section on Mill, Posner now acknowledges that Mill's harm principle depends on the view that morality should be limited to duties that we owe others, a view that is rejected by those who believe that morality includes within its scope duties that we owe to ourselves (PLM, 64–67). So in *Problematics*, Posner the empiricist eschews "even Mill" the moralist. "How far society should go in shielding self-regarding acts from regulation by law or public opinion," Posner notes, "is a prudential or empirical question that should be answered on the basis of actual conditions in a particular society rather than by defining morality to exclude any concern for such acts" (PLM, 65).

But the harm principle is not the only moral principle that Posner, at least before his short section on Mill in *Problematics*, abides by. He also treats evolution, and human and societal adaptation to change, as a guiding moral principle. Posner admits, as already noted, that his is "an *adaptationist* conception of morality . . . in which morality is judged . . . nonmorally . . . by its contribution to the survival, or other ultimate goals, of a society or some group within it" (PLM, 6). As Ronald Dworkin argues, however, to prioritize adaptation as a normative matter is to view attitudes and inclinations that occur naturally as those that are best, unless factual information tells us otherwise. Dworkin suggests that Posner is a Darwinian pragmatist because he (Posner) argues that we should "put our faith not in our own ability to identify appropriate norms and attitudes, but in nature's ability to do this through natural selection or some analogue to it."[56] The notion that nature knows best, that "natural inclinations must be assumed to be wise," unless empirical information proves to us otherwise "is, at bottom, a substantive and noninstrumentalist moral attitude, because it presupposes that certain kinds of human lives and certain states of human societies are intrinsically superior to others."[57] It could be argued, of course, that the survival that Posner's normative theory focuses on is an instrumentalist goal rather than an intrinsic moral good. The problem is that survival by itself gives us only the broadest outline of what we should aim for. The more interesting and difficult issues implicate not whether we should survive (we should) but *how* we should do so.[58] In answering the latter question, it is impossible to avoid issues of values and morality.

It is not unusual for those who, like Posner, base normative judgments on evolutionary or adaptationist theory to disclaim that they are arguing morally. They are interested, they tell us, not in morality but in the facts (or forces) of nature that can help us better explain and understand human behavior. The difficulty with this position, as Charles Taylor points out, is that "morally neutral" naturalists, after rejecting "all moral ontologies as irrelevant stories," continue to address, along with the rest of us, which human actions are appropriate and how to arrange public policies and social norms accordingly.[59] Evolutionary theory and sociobiology in the hands of a thinker such as Posner, then, simply become another form of moral ontology, which, in a book such as *Sex and Reason*, leave some social institutions (such as heterosexual marriage) unchallenged and lead to the questioning of others (such as same-sex marriage).

Posner's reliance on an adaptationist morality, which holds that what nature calls for is presumptively correct unless factual evidence shows us otherwise, can be seen throughout *Sex and Reason*. It is this moral, non-instrumentalist principle that Posner uses to interpret and give meaning to the empirical data. For example, as noted above, Posner refers several times to the Kinsey scale of sexual orientation that assigns a 0 to exclusive heterosexuals and a 6 to exclusive homosexuals, with everyone else falling somewhere in between. Let us assume for purposes of argument that the Kinsey scale is an accurate representation of sexual preferences in the American population.[60] If all we want to do is *describe* sexual preferences, the Kinsey scale is all that we need, again assuming (as Posner does) that it is accurate. But Posner's project in *Sex and Reason* is not simply a descriptive one; it is also a normative one (though he argues not a *moral* one). Posner takes as a given that those who are a 4 or 5 on the Kinsey scale must prefer women to men (again, Posner writes mostly of male homosexuality), but will engage in homosexual conduct when the costs of heterosexual acts are too high. But why make that assumption? There is nothing in Kinsey's data that requires the interpretation that Posner gives it. It would be just as consistent with Kinsey's data to conclude that those who are a 4 or 5 on the scale are "real" homosexuals who engage in "opportunistic" heterosexual acts when the cost of homosexual activity is too high rather than "real" heterosexuals who are sometimes "opportunistic" in engaging in same-gender sexual conduct.

Posner interprets the data in the way he does because his conception of sexuality is colored by his adaptationist morality; the distinction between "real" and "opportunistic" homosexuals makes sense to him because that is the distinction that evolutionary theory requires. Evolutionary considerations lead Posner to conclude that the number of "real" homosexuals must be the smallest possible because it is difficult to explain their existence from an evolutionary perspective. On the other hand, the existence of "opportunistic" homosexuals is entirely consistent with evolutionary considerations because they are, according to Posner, heterosexuals by orientation who engage in same-gender sexual acts when the cost of opposite-gender sexual acts is too high. Posner is in effect using natural law—albeit in its evolutionary and sociobiological form—

to interpret and give meaning to the Kinsey data on sexual orientation. Posner may or may not be correct in his division of homosexuals into "real" and "opportunistic," but that division, for reasons that I explain below, is decidedly not morally neutral.

Posner may argue that it does not make a difference for his conception of "morally indifferent sex" whether those who are a 4 or 5 on Kinsey's scale are viewed as "opportunistic" heterosexuals or "opportunistic" homosexuals. The results would be the same, he could argue, because we still have individuals whose sexual conduct (though not orientation) is driven by a rational assessment of costs and benefits. But ordering the empirical data as Posner has done *does* make a difference in at least two significant ways. First, it reemphasizes the distinctiveness (which in the context of sexuality is usually translated as the perversity or deviancy) of those who consistently engage in same-gender sexual acts, a distinctiveness that has important implications for the setting of public policy. An example of this phenomenon is the federal statute that calls for the forced separation from the armed forces of a member who "demonstrates a propensity or intent to engage in homosexual acts."[61] Rather conveniently, that same law specifically allows a defense to those whom Posner categorizes as "opportunistic" homosexuals. A member will not be expelled if he or she can demonstrate that the same-gender sexual conduct he or she engaged in "is a departure from the member's usual and customary behavior."[62] In a similar fashion, the New Hampshire Supreme Court, in upholding the constitutionality of a statutory provision (since repealed) that prohibited lesbians and gay men from adopting, ruled that the legislature must have intended to exclude from the scope of the statute those who have in the past (especially while young) engaged in same-gender sexual acts "but who now engage in exclusively heterosexual behavior."[63] The distinction between "real" and "opportunistic" homosexuals, which Posner defends as morally neutral, then, forms the basis for public policies that punish and exclude the former while providing some degree of protection to the latter who, because of unique circumstances (or what Posner would categorize as the shifting of the balance between costs and benefits), strayed from their "natural" inclinations. As Bill Eskridge notes, "[b]y focusing official persecution only on 'real homosexuals,' and not 'normal people' who happen to slip up, the segregation of categories reassures mainstream society of its immunity from . . . bigoted policies, while isolating and ghettoizing the victims of persecution."[64]

The second way in which Posner's interpretation of the empirical data matters is that "opportunistic" homosexuals will *by definition* have few emotional attachments to their same-gender sexual partners because they will quite easily and without much hesitation cease engaging in same-gender sexual activity when the balance of costs and benefits shifts toward making heterosexual intimacy more worth their while. It is reasonable to assume, then, that under Posner's so-called morally neutral empirical approach to human sexuality, "opportunistic" homosexuals will be less interested, when engaging in same-gender sexual conduct, in having that conduct be accompanied by the kinds of emotional and affectional bonds of commitment, loyalty, trust, and love that are likely to make intimate relationships more stable and long-lasting. As a result, under Posner's empirical model, the relationships between "opportunistic" homosexuals (and even those between "opportunistic" and "real" homosexuals) are likely to be fleeting and focused primarily on physical needs. This so-called morally neutral empiricism provides ammunition to those who believe that lesbians and gay men have few human needs and capabilities associated with sexual intimacy that go beyond the orgasm.

And what of "real" homosexuals and their emotional attachments to each other? One would think that for that group—for whom opposite-gender sexual acts carry few benefits or satisfactions—issues of emotional commitment and mutuality would matter. Posner, however, argues that *even* the relationships of real homosexuals are unlikely to be meaningful and long-lasting. Although Posner admits that some "real" homosexuals have established "highly durable" relationships (SR, 306), he believes that there is something intrinsic about homosexuality that makes gay relationships less likely to last than those of heterosexuals. According to Posner, this is not a moral assessment of homosexual relationships but "a proposition about the biology of sex and reproduction" (SR, 305). The quality of homosexual relationships is undermined and threatened by the fact that men as a whole are more interested in multiple sexual partners than on the level and quality of commitment and fidelity in sexual relationships. When we add the fact that same-gender partners cannot both be biologically related to their children and that "[c]hildren are the strongest cement of marriage," Posner "conclude[s] that even in a tolerant society the life prospects of a homosexual—not in every case, of course, but on average—are, especially for the male homosexual, grimmer than those of an otherwise identical heterosexual" (SR, 305, 307). Posner adds that even if all legal disabilities imposed on homosexuals were removed, and even if all heterosexuals became perfectly tolerant of their homosexual peers, it is unlikely that a gay life would cease to be "an unhappy one" (SR, 303).

It is on the one hand surprising, therefore, that for someone who is as ostensibly empirically oriented as Posner is, he does not more fully discuss the empirical literature on the high levels of commitment, quality, and satisfaction of same-gender sexual relationships. That literature, already considerable at the time *Sex and Reason* was published, has become even more extensive since.[65] The growing empirical evidence, however, has not prevented Posner from making the following sweeping statement in his more recent book *Problematics*: "[B]eing homosexual is or at least might rationally be thought a misfortune or disadvantage . . .

if only because homosexuals on average find it much more difficult than heterosexuals to form family units" (PLM, 175). (Ironically, Posner makes this sweeping statement, without empirical support, in the context of defending his position that courts must be more sensitive to empirical data!) On the other hand, it is perhaps not so surprising that Posner downplays or ignores the empirical evidence as to the strength of same-gender relationships because that strength is inconsistent with his adaptationist conception of sexuality. It is difficult to explain or account for the love that a man or a woman feels for another person of the same gender in a sexually intimate relationship when we are assessing (or even explaining) that intimacy from an evolutionary perspective. Posner's adaptationist conception of sexuality is simply one more kind of sexual morality that ends up conceiving of lesbians and gay men as largely sexual creatures, with few needs and capabilities that are independent of the satisfaction of sexual desires. If these are the premises from which he operates—premises purportedly grounded in empiricism—then it becomes quite easy for him to arrive at the normative position that refuses to impose on society an obligation to recognize same-sex marriages.

I want to make it clear that I am not criticizing Posner for incorporating notions of morality into his assessments of human sexuality (though I have, like many before me, taken issue with some of the moral conclusions he does reach). I simply want to make the point that it is difficult not to so incorporate, even for someone who is trying hard to do otherwise. The reality is that issues relating to sexual intimacy raise fundamental questions about who we are and how we treat others. Even if we were to assume *arguendo* that sexual *acts* themselves can be viewed in a morally neutral way, the human *relationships* that often accompany sexual intimacy by their very nature raise moral questions of how individuals should treat each other. As Jean Cohen argues, "sexuality [can] never be norm-free, ethically insignificant, or unregulated, for sexual conduct occurs within intimate relationships and their quality—whether consensual, exploitative, reciprocal, empowering, or debilitating—does matter."[66] This has implications, as I will argue in more detail in the next chapter, for our ideas of political morality because society must grapple with moral considerations when establishing and enforcing laws and policies associated with sexuality, especially those laws and policies that reflect which sexually intimate relationships society chooses to recognize and support.

I also do not want to suggest that there is no value in Posner's call for greater empiricism in discussions relating to the societal regulation of sexual orientation. We could, for example, benefit from a greater attention by policy makers and courts to the empirical studies that, as I will argue in the last sections of chapters 3 and 4, indicate that the sexual orientation of gay and lesbian parents is not inconsistent with the promotion of the best interests of children. But we fool ourselves if we think that all that is needed is to marshal out the empirical data and let it speak for itself. As Posner himself unwittingly shows, how the data relating to sexuality are interpreted matters a great deal, and that interpretation is inevitably colored by moral considerations. Those considerations are not external to the debates; rather, they are necessary components of them.

Again, it is undoubtedly true that a careful empiricism can contribute to debates about homosexuality in our society. But what is largely at issue in gay rights disputes is not so much the facts, but their *interpretation*. If gay rights debates were at their core disputes about empirical issues, one would think that recent studies suggesting that a much smaller percentage of Americans engage in same-gender sexual intimacy or identify themselves as being gay (which are not the same thing) than we thought after the Kinsey studies of the 1940s and 1950s would have had some impact (however slight) on our current gay rights debates (over marriage, gay and lesbian families, gays in the military, and so on).[67] It turns out, however, that it makes *little difference* whether lesbians and gay men, as a strictly empirical matter, constitute 2 percent or 10 percent or 15 percent of the population because the way in which our society problematizes homosexuality makes it inevitable that moral questions will be at the center of assessments and determinations of how society should respond to same-gender intimacy and relationships.

Sexual intimacy exposes our most basic needs, capabilities, and vulnerabilities as human beings. Our sexuality raises important questions about ourselves and who we are, of how we treat others in the pursuit of sexual pleasure, and of how we deal with our own and others' emotional and physical vulnerabilities. None of this means, of course, that all aspects of sex must be morally relevant all the time. To give just one example, the gender of the sexual partners in ancient Greece, as I will explain in chapter 5, was morally *irrelevant*. It did not follow from this, however, that sex raised no questions of morality for the Greeks. Issues of age, class, and sexual roles rather than the gender of the sexual partners took the central moral stage. Given the role that sexual intimacy plays in constituting our sense of selves and our relationships with others, I am skeptical that it is ever possible to think about sex in a completely morally indifferent way. In honor of the localism behind the pragmatism of Rorty and Posner, however, let me instead put it this way: Given the problematization in our society of same-gender sexuality from so many different perspectives and in so many different ways, same-gender sex will continue to raise moral questions for the foreseeable future; it serves no one, including lesbians and gay men, to pretend otherwise. Certainly Posner, by distinguishing between "opportunistic" and "real" homosexuals, by evaluating the nature and implications of homosexuality from the perspective of an adaptationist conception of morality, by arguing in the context of same-sex marriage (though not of sodomy laws) that the perceived moral offensiveness of gay and lesbian relationships is a sufficient rationale not to recognize those marriages, and by suggesting that gay men are intrinsically less capable of experiencing lasting and committed relationships than heterosexuals, has done little to "de-moralize" issues of (same-gender) sexuality. Posner's "acid bath" application of empiricism and economic theory to issues of homosexuality raises as many moral questions as it seeks to avoid answering.

Posner seems to believe that if we can rid our sex talk of Christian morality (as well as of Kantian morality), we will be able to purge that discourse of its moral content. But as Jean Cohen suggests, "[p]erhaps Posner should reread his Foucault."[68] Foucault convincingly demonstrates, as I will explain in more detail in chapter 5, that a *moralistic* Christian discourse on sexuality was replaced in the nineteenth century with a *moralistic* biological, medical, and psychiatric discourse on sexuality that also sought to distinguish between normal and abnormal sex. Posner's book *Sex and Reason* falls neatly within that second moralistic tradition as he seeks to use biological and evolutionary norms to explain "deviant sexuality" and to determine the appropriate level of societal regulation of it.

There is an additional unavoidable moral component to same-gender sexuality that Posner misses altogether, one that implicates notions of integrity. Given the ways in which our society problematizes same-gender sexual intimacy, how lesbians and gay men lead their sexual lives inevitably raises issues of integrity for them because they must, as sexual actors, constantly contend with the disparity between society's negative evaluations of them based on their sexuality and their own assessments of self-worth and self-respect. This is a point that Martha Nussbaum, in a review of *Sex and Reason*, touches on when she discusses E.M. Forster's posthumously published novel *Maurice*.[69] In the novel, set in early twentieth-century England, the two principal characters (Maurice and Clive) are sexually attracted to men. Maurice decides to give up his career, social status, and country in order to be with the man he loves, a man from a much lower social class than he. Clive, on the other hand, represses his feelings for other men, marries a woman (whom he does not love), pursues a successful career in politics, and, above all else, seeks to maintain his social status as determined by the privileges and respect afforded by others. Under Posner's "acid bath" application of economic theory to matters of sexuality, it is Clive who weighed the costs and benefits of same-gender sexual acts and acted rationally. Maurice, on the other hand, acted irrationally to the extent that he ignored the measurable costs associated with his sexuality in favor of leading a life of integrity. As Nussbaum explains,

> [i]t is the novel's point that [Maurice's] intransigence in desire, and [his] recklessness in its expression, are manifestations of integrity, that by pursuing an end that is not even one of Posner's economic ends, but is a kind of self-affirmation and deep self-expression . . . Maurice is living well, and [Clive is] living badly.

Posner's explanatory account could not have predicted [Maurice's] choice, which must on that account be seen as irrational and incomprehensible.[70]

In the end, Posner's account of sexuality fails to consider sufficiently the value and importance of integrity, that is, of living according to one's convictions and commitments to one's sense of self even when doing so is inconsistent with measurable utility.[71] As Katharine Bartlett puts it, Posner's rational sexual actor "does not have an identity, a history, or a set of traditions that would lead her to pursue goals or engage in behaviors so that she can be true to some view she has of herself or her community, for its own sake."[72] Given the way in which society morally problematizes same-gender sexual conduct and relationships, those who engage in them choose to live according to what they believe is true and right despite considerable personal costs. This is why the picture of the rational sexual actor who only weighs costs against benefits seems to miss so much of what is important to lesbians and gay men: it fails to capture the way in which they use their sexuality to construct lives of integrity by being true to "what is most important to them and gives them reasons for living," often at the cost of measurable utility.[73] Posner's account of sex and sexuality, in other words, speaks to Clive's priorities but not to Maurice's.

The four thinkers whom I have discussed so far have different reasons for wanting to separate morality from their respective understandings of liberalism. Rawls does so in order to maintain the functioning of a well-ordered and pluralistic society; Dworkin does so in order to promote the equal treatment by the state of all its citizens; Rorty does so in order to focus on our contingent (as opposed to universal) commonalities; Posner does so in order to replace morality with empiricism and rationality. All of these efforts are in different ways supportive of some gay rights positions, but they are ultimately unsatisfactory for the reasons discussed. We need to consider, therefore, a form of liberalism that allows for the explicit incorporation of morality and the good into debates about justice and rights. It is to an exploration of that kind of liberalism, and to a discussion of what it means to lesbians and gay men, that I turn to next.

THREE

Moral Liberalism

In chapter 1, we saw how neutral forms of liberalism that refuse to incorporate notions of the good into questions of political morality and justice cannot by themselves justify the kind of state recognition and support of their relationships and families that many lesbians and gay men are demanding. In chapter 2, we saw how pragmatic forms of liberalism (Rorty's and Posner's) that are skeptical of universal norms and values and of a moral understanding of human sexuality (Posner's) are also problematic from a gay rights perspective. There is a third kind of liberalism, however, which I will here call moral liberalism, that allows for an explicit consideration of what is necessary for individuals to be able to lead fully human lives into a discussion of political morality. It is this form of liberalism that I believe constitutes the most cogent and persuasive theoretical foundation for the attainment of gay rights goals.

I use the adjective "moral" to modify "liberalism" to emphasize the differences between what I take to be the most appropriate form of liberalism and those kinds that prioritize moral neutrality or skepticism. Moral liberalism is defined by two main principles. First, it recognizes that human beings share basic needs and capabilities, the meeting of which (in the case of needs) and the exercise of which (in the case of capabilities) are indispensable for the leading of full human lives. Traditional liberalism (by which I mean to include both Kantian/Rawlsian and Millian liberalism) has a thin conception of the self and of human nature, viewing both as defined primarily by our capability to reason. Moral liberalism has a thicker conception of the self—and thus a thicker conception of the good—because it recognizes that our ability to reason is one of *several* constitutive capabilities that define our humanity. As moral liberalism sees it, political philosophy must grapple directly with the broader domain of human needs and capabilities associated with the body, emotions, and relationships.

The second main tenet of moral liberalism is related to the first. Traditional liberalism views the self as largely individualistic, unfettered by ties and connections to others that are not freely chosen. For traditional liberalism, the primary role of the state is to protect what is taken to be this natural or pre-existing condition of individual autonomy. Moral liberalism conceives human autonomy differently because it conceives the self differently. Moral liberalism begins with the proposition that we are not inherently individualistic creatures; instead, we all have a myriad of ties and relationships that *play a crucial role in our ability to lead autonomous lives*. Rather than viewing others primarily as a threat to autonomy, moral liberalism sees autonomy as emanating largely from our relationships with and our dependencies on others. For moral liberalism, human relationships and attachments, rather than being relegated to a private sphere that is best left outside of the jurisdiction of political morality, are instead an integral part of that morality because they are an integral part of the way in which individuals lead autonomous lives.

I will, in this chapter, elaborate on the meaning of moral liberalism and explore its implications for a philosophy of gay rights. As we will see, the political morality of moral liberalism, with its emphasis on human needs, capabilities, and relationships, takes us beyond the normative paradigm of traditional liberalism that, in the context of gay rights issues, focuses almost exclusively on principles of noninterference. The fuller conception of the self and of the good held by moral liberalism helps us understand and speak to the moral issues raised by the requests by lesbians and gay men for societal recognition and support of their relationships and families. Instead of relying only on the right to be left alone, or only on the need for the state to remain neutral as to different conceptions of the good, moral liberalism invites us to grapple with the value and goodness of different kinds of human relationships, including gay and lesbian ones.

This last sentence will make many liberals, as well as nonliberal progressives, nervous. They will argue that assessments of the value and good of different relationships are inherently subjective, and when engaged in by the state, potentially dangerous and coercive. I will address this legitimate concern at different points in this chapter. The gist of my response to the objection will be twofold. First, liberal states *already* make distinctions among relationships (e.g., they all recognize, and to different degrees, prioritize marital relationships over other kinds of sexually intimate relationships). As a result, it is difficult to argue as a practical matter that such distinctions are inconsistent with the existence of a liberal state. There is always, of course, much room for disagreement as to *which* relationships the state should prioritize and *how* it should do so—these are, after all, the questions raised by the debate over same-sex marriage—but I will argue that the mere fact that the state makes distinctions among relationships is not by itself improper. Second, the idea that it is permissible and, I will argue, *necessary* for the state to recognize some relationships as being particularly valuable is not inconsistent with the liberal idea that it is individuals who are the best judges of which relationships are most appropriate for them given their life plans and aspirations. I will have a lot more to say about both of these points below.

As will become clear in this chapter (in particular in the discussion of relationships and attachments), moral liberalism is highly influenced by feminist theory. I view moral liberalism as combining liberalism's commitment to autonomy with feminism's concern for relationships and an ethic of care. Moral liberalism also takes the communitarian critique of liberalism seriously, though I will postpone until the next chapter an exploration of that critique and its implications for a philosophy of gay rights.

1. NEEDS, CAPABILITIES, AND THE LEADING OF FULL HUMAN LIVES

Liberal political philosophy places great importance on the status of human beings as rational agents. For traditional liberalism, the ability to reason is *the* distinctive characteristic that distinguishes us from other animals. It is this ability that entitles all human beings to the protection afforded by a host of fundamental rights—from freedom of speech and conscience to rights to privacy—that are meant to protect their ability to decide for themselves which life plans to pursue and how to do so. For John Locke, therefore, the very idea that "man" is a free being "is grounded on his having reason."[1] John Stuart Mill considered the ability to reason to be "the source of everything respectable in man as an intellectual or as a moral being."[2] John Rawls, for his part, argues that persons enjoy two moral powers, both of which are dependent on their ability to reason: a capacity for justice and a capacity to form, revise, and pursue a life plan or a conception of the good (PL, 19).

Critics of liberalism (and of the Enlightenment tradition as represented most influentially by Kant) object to the prioritization that it gives to reason. Postmodernists question using reason as the foundation for a metanarrative that seeks to defend objective standards of truth and morality. For postmodernists, the philosophical endorsement of reason and objectivity is simply one more type of discourse constituted by a particular way of interpreting the world, albeit one that has had much influence among, and provided many benefits to, intellectual and political elites in Western societies. For their part, feminists criticize the way in which "reason" has been understood, despite claims of universality, as primarily a male attribute whereas "emotions" have been viewed (and dismissed) as characteristically female traits. Feminists question, both epistemologically and politically, the dichotomy between reason and emotions (such as loving and caring) arguing that emotions are a helpful and even necessary part of reasoning and the acquisition (or construction) of knowledge as well as an important concern of political morality.[3] As feminists see it, the reason/emotion dualism tracks the body/mind dualism that has been such an important part of Western philosophy since Descartes.[4] The lives and aspirations of women, feminists argue, have been associated with what are taken to be the less valuable or morally significant parts of the dualisms (i.e., the emotions and the body) contributing to the formation and perpetuation of patriarchal societies and norms.

In these philosophical debates about reason and various forms of dualisms, the liberal philosopher Martha Nussbaum stands in a somewhat unique position. Of contemporary American philosophers, I view her as the most eloquent proponent of moral liberalism (which is my term, not hers).[5] She is very much part of the Enlightenment tradition because she acknowledges that the capability to reason is a universal capability that is constitutive of our humanity. She does not, however, limit her definition of what it means to be human to the capability to reason. Instead, as I elaborate below, she views needs and capabilities associated with the body, emotions, and relationships as playing crucial roles in permitting us to lead lives that are recognizably human. She also agrees with the postmodernist critique of the metaphysical components of the Enlightenment tradition and the idea that there is an objective reality out there that awaits our discovery through the application of *a priori* philosophical principles or abstract reasoning. Nussbaum's moral and political philosophy rejects metaphysics in favor of evaluations and interpretations that are internal to human history and experience. At the same time, however, she argues that evaluations and interpretations of people's actual lives can lead us to recognize universal human attributes that run across time and place. As such, she is an outspoken critic of postmodernist philosophy in general and its relativistic manifestations in particular (HFS; WHD, 34–59). Nussbaum's willingness to speak normatively of universal human attributes also sets her apart from many contemporary feminist theorists who view discussions of such attributes with great skepticism because they have too frequently been used to promote patriarchal values and practices.[6] I explore below Nussbaum's moral and political philosophy as a way of articulating what I mean by moral liberalism and how it contrasts with more traditional forms of liberalism such as that of John Rawls.

The priority that traditional liberalism gives to our capacity to reason is reflected in its penchant for viewing the contractual relationship as the paradigmatic relationship for political theory. From a contractarian perspective, rational individuals (whether in a Lockean state of nature or in a Rawlsian original position) come together to bargain and reach agreement as to how best to construct a social order. In the case of Locke, the bargainers rationally agree on the framework of a civil society that protects the life, liberty, and property previously enjoyed in the state of nature. In the case of Rawls, the bargainers rationally agree on the framework of a civil society that protects basic liberties for all and distributes economic and social goods in a way that benefits the least advantaged.

Under neither framework is there an effort to determine what are the needs and capabilities associated with either the body or with the emotions that motivate and define our relationships with others and that are, along with the capacity to reason, constitutive components of our humanity. Rawlsian liberalism is silent on issues relating to the body. Although feminist and postmodernist theorists have viewed the body as a site subject to and defined by political power and social discourses, the traditional liberalism of Rawls has little interest in the body as such.[7] It has nothing to say on either its needs or its political implications. As for human emotions such as love, loyalty, and caring, and the kinds of relationships with others that they engender, Rawlsian liberalism deems them to be matters relating to the good as opposed to the right. For Rawls, as we have seen, discussions of the good must be kept separate from questions of political philosophy that go to issues of the right. For moral liberalism, on the other hand, the satisfaction of the complete panoply of human needs and the exercise of the broad spectrum of human capabilities, including those associated with the body, emotions, and relationships, are crucial for the leading of lives that are fully human. As moral liberalism sees it, the full range of human needs and capabilities raises questions of political morality that must be addressed in our theorizing about justice.

Although Nussbaum in her work has focused more explicitly on capabilities than on needs, she recognizes that it is important to emphasize both. We can define essential needs as those that must be satisfied if human beings are to be able to function at all.[8] Essential needs, in other words, are the bare minimum without which we could not lead a human life; they include the need for nourishment, shelter, and periodic rest. The need for companionship and some interaction with other humans in some capacity is also an essential need. And so is the need for sexual satisfaction. As Nussbaum puts it, "sexual need and desire are features of more or less every human life. It is . . . a most important basis for the recognition of others different from ourselves as human beings" (HFS, 217–18).

The list of essential needs is relatively short because it constitutes a minimum threshold that must be satisfied if one is to be able to lead a life that is recognizably human. But lives can be recognizably human and still be extremely limited. For example, a person who is institutionalized for life against her will and who is provided with food, shelter, and opportunities to rest and to interact with others can be said to lead a life that is recognizably human. But such a life is not a *fully* human life because it is neither a good nor an autonomous one. If we are concerned that individuals be able to lead lives that are not only recognizably human but are also fully human, then we must incorporate into our evaluation notions of capabilities. As the philosopher and economist Amartya Sen argues, capabilities ("What can the person *do*?") are often more relevant to issues of well-being and freedom than are needs ("What can be *done* for the person?").[9] We then must ask the following question: What are the basic capabilities the exercise of which are necessary for the leading of a fully human life?

Before we move to answer that (admittedly big) question, however, it is important to keep in mind that human needs and capabilities come bundled together. For example one of the attributes that makes us human, as I will argue later in this chapter, is the capability to love and care for those who love and care for us. If we focus exclusively on our *capability* to love and care for others, we may neglect the fact that we also *need* to be loved and cared for by others. This may not be the kind of essential need referred to previously, which I defined as a need that must be satisfied in order for humans to function at all. But it is an important or basic need nonetheless, one that must be satisfied if we are to lead fully human lives. Since many of the basic capabilities that are constitutive of our humanity involve other individuals, we must keep in mind that one person's capability often requires consideration of another person's need.

It is also important to note that issues related to basic needs and capabilities by their very nature implicate human vulnerabilities. A failure to satisfy basic needs and to exercise basic capabilities exposes our vulnerabilities as creatures—both as individuals and as a species—who have limited control over our environment. It is crucial, in addressing questions of political morality, to remind ourselves constantly of just how vulnerable we are to deprivation, pain, and suffering. The Lockean conception of the self-reliant man who only needs to be left alone in order to be free disregards and even conceals the kinds of physical, emotional, and material vulnerabilities (and dependencies) that we are all subject to and that are therefore characteristic of our humanity.

Nussbaum in her work addresses all of these issues as she seeks to couple an appreciation for our vulnerabilities as limited and mortal beings with an Aristotelian concern for human flourishing. We must, Nussbaum argues, be concerned, both ethically and politically, with the conditions necessary for the leading of full human lives. She therefore promotes an understanding of society's obligations that is grounded on what she calls a capabilities approach to questions of justice; that is, an approach that focuses on those basic capabilities that all individuals must have the opportunity to exercise if they are to be able to lead lives that are fully human.[10] With that goal in mind, she has through the years devised and refined what she considers to be a list of basic human capabilities.[11] The list has always included the capability to have good health, to be adequately nourished, and to have proper shelter. It has also always included the capability to use the five senses; to imagine, think, and reason; to love and care for others; to control one's body and protect it against abuse by others; to seek opportunities for sexual satisfaction and for choice in matters of reproduction; to live for and with others and to engage in various forms of familial and social interactions; and to laugh, play, and enjoy recreational activities. Nussbaum has also more recently explicitly included in her list the capability to make political choices and to exercise rights to free speech and association, as well as the capabilities to own property, seek employment on an equal basis with others, and be free of unwarranted searches and seizures (WHD, 80). Nussbaum argues that a life that lacks opportunities to exercise all of these basic capabilities cannot be considered a fully human life. As she puts it, the basic capabilities "are not just instrumental to further pursuits: they are held to have value in themselves, in making the life that includes them fully human" (WHD, 74).[12]

The capabilities approach aims to treat each person as an end—it is the capabilities of *each* person that matters. Although families, communities, and states play important roles in providing for capabilities (as well as, more problematically, sometimes *impeding* capabilities), the normative focus of our most important principles of political morality must be on the individual. This focus allows us to make sure that all individuals are moved "across a threshold of capability into circumstances in which they may choose to live and function well" (ASD, 203). It is the individual, in other words, who is the end, whereas the collective entities are the means. The capabilities approach, Nussbaum argues, can provide a foundation for the kinds of core constitutional guarantees that allow individuals to make demands of their governments (WHD, 74–75). She also suggests that it can serve as a conceptual framework for understanding and realizing the goals of international treaties such as the Universal Declaration of Human Rights.[13] But her main practical application of the capabilities approach has been in the area of international development, and in particular, in conceiving of ways to improve the quality of life of women in the developing world. As part of this project, she has immersed herself in the history, traditions, and laws of India with the goal of grounding her capabilities approach not only in the Western culture from which she comes, but also in at least one very important Eastern culture.[14]

The capability to reason plays an important role in Nussbaum's list. She considers practical reasoning to have an architectonic function that supports the other capabilities. It is practical reasoning that allows individuals to choose which other capabilities to exercise and how to do so (WHD, 82). But Nussbaum also believes that our capability to affiliate with others plays an architectonic role in our lives because we exercise most of our capabilities with and through others. As she puts it, "[t]o plan for one's own life without being able to do so in complex forms of discourse, concern, and reciprocity with other human beings is . . . to behave in an incompletely human way" (WHD, 82). (We will, in the next section, explore in more detail the importance of human relationships, attachments, and dependencies in the leading of autonomous lives.) In addition, Nussbaum incorporates into her capabilities approach many capabilities, such as those associated with nutrition, shelter, sex, and the use of the five senses, that have a bodily component to them. Nussbaum rejects the Kantian idea that locates the source of human dignity solely in our capacity to reason and which separates our minds from our bodies; for Nussbaum human dignity resides in both. In formulating basic principles of political morality, therefore, we must acknowledge that there are needs and capabilities associated with the body that must be met and exercised if one is to lead a life that is fully human. To prioritize the mind (and its ability to reason) at the expense of the body is to give an incomplete account of what it means to be human.

The Kantian tradition has also sought to dichotomize reason and emotions. Kantianism views reasoning as constituting one sphere of human attributes and emotions as constituting a distinct (and lesser) other, roughly corresponding to the distinction between the right and the good. The Kantian tradition, upon which much of contemporary liberalism is grounded, conceives of issues of the right in terms of objectivity, reason, and justice while thinking of the good in terms of subjectivity, emotions, and attachments to others. It has been one of Nussbaum's principal philosophical projects to question the dichotomy between reason and emotions.[15] For Nussbaum, an understanding of human emotions (grief, compassion, love, and so on) are essential to an understanding of human reasoning, including ethical reasoning. By arguing that emotions play a crucial role in reasoning, Nussbaum questions the placing of our personal relationships, and the way in which we care for and about those who are closest to us, outside of the jurisdiction of moral and political philosophy.

In sum, Nussbaum, by including in her list of basic human capabilities those that are associated with the body, emotions, and relationships, gives us a fuller and more complete account of human beings than one that isolates reasoning as the only human capability that is of much interest to moral and political philosophy. Moral liberalism believes that this latter conception of human beings is too limited because it overlooks a host of other needs and capabilities that are, in addition to our ability to reason, constitutive of our humanity. These other needs and capabilities must also be accounted for when we are determining the obligations placed on society by considerations of justice.

Nussbaum's project is an explicitly universalist one since it is meant to explain how it is that we "recognize others as human across many divisions of time and place" (HFS, 215). But her conception of what it means to be human is decidedly nonmetaphysical. It is derived not from philosophical principles gleaned through the application of abstract reasoning, but from the interpretation of human history and practices, including the stories we tell each other about our lives and aspirations. It is also not dependent on "facts of human nature," whether physiological or psychological, that are separate from our ethical evaluations of what is necessary for the leading of a full human life. Although there is a biological component to many of our basic needs and capabilities (e.g., our bodies need calories in order to survive), the meaning and value of basic human needs and capabilities are for Nussbaum determined through ethical interpretations and evaluations of human practices, rather than through the discovery of natural or biological principles or facts that are independent of those practices.[16]

The distinction between arriving at universal human attributes through, on the one hand, determining the relevant "facts of nature" and, on the other, through the ethical evaluation of human lives, can be illustrated by using the human capability for language as an example. At its most basic level, the capability to use language has physiological components, both in terms of the mental functions required for its use, as well as other bodily functions (involving the mouth, the hands, and so on) that permit actual communication between individuals. Our ability to use language, therefore, can be seen as a "fact of nature." But the *value* of language does not arise from the shared physiological components that are an admittedly necessary part of its use; instead, its value arises from the universality of a capability that allows human beings to think, reason, dream, communicate, and affiliate through language. As Louise Antony argues, "[t]he ability to communicate is *valuable* [as opposed] to just *useful* [because] it is centrally connected to nearly everything human beings have ever claimed to value about themselves, everything from our capacity for abstract thought . . . to our capacities for social affiliation and cultural creation."[17] The ways in which different individuals think, reason, dream, communicate, and affiliate in different societies are, of course, different, but underlying those differences is a shared capability to build distinctively human lives and cultures partly on the basis of the use of language.

Another way in which the evaluative component of the capabilities approach can be illustrated is by thinking of human attributes that might be universal, but that we could not consider necessary for the leading of a full human life. It can be argued, for example, that a capability for cruelty is part of our "human nature." We have all inflicted and experienced cruelty; some instances of cruelty are devastating and even deadly; others are petty and annoying. Yet in both its small and large manifestations, cruelty seems to be part of the human condition. That universality, however, obviously does not imbue a capability for cruelty with moral significance (in terms of needing to be promoted and protected) except that it reminds us of the shared capability (or vulnerability) to feel the physical and emotional pain that often results from cruelty. The point to emphasize, then, is that a capabilities approach to justice requires assessments of human beings and their lives that are evaluative and ethical rather than simply descriptive of "human nature."

Given that Nussbaum's capabilities approach relies on ethical judgments rather than on metaphysical or natural principles, the conception of the human being that arises from it is open-ended, leaving consider-able room for modification based on experience and interpretation. Nussbaum acknowledges that the composition of her list of basic capa-bilities invites dispute and disagreement. Her intention is not to formu-late a list that constitutes the final word on basic capabilities; instead, the list is meant to be revisable and contestable. Her aim is to convince oth-ers that it is possible to engage in evaluative judgments about basic capa-bilities that are *both* universal and internal to human history—that is—in judgments grounded on universal commonalities that are determined through experience and interpretation rather than through abstraction and metaphysics or empirical descriptions of human nature.

It is also necessary to emphasize the important role that autonomy and choice play in Nussbaum's capabilities approach. That importance is re-flected in the way in which she distinguishes between capabilities and functionings (WHD, 86–96). What matters to the capabilities approach is that societies provide individuals with opportunities to exercise their basic capabilities rather than require or expect them to function in certain ways. Our political institutions, therefore, should focus on making sure that all individuals have opportunities to exercise basic capabilities—that is—opportunities to cross that minimum threshold without which it would be impossible to lead fully human lives. But whether individuals actually cross that threshold, and how they do so, is up to them.

We can use the capabilities associated with sexual intimacy as a way of illustrating the difference between capabilities and functionings. If we were to argue, for example, that the *actual* exercise of our capabilities for sexual intimacy is required in order to lead a full life, then we would have to conclude absurdly that a celibate Catholic priest or a layperson who has chosen to be celibate cannot lead a fully human life.[18] Our con-cern, therefore, should be with the societal conditions that promote or impede the exercise of basic capabilities, not with whether individuals choose to exercise them or with how they do so, as long as others are not harmed. As moral liberalism sees it, the basic capabilities that we all share as human beings impose obligations on society to provide the nec-essary conditions that make their exercise possible. So that, for example, if society were to incarcerate individuals for engaging in consensual sex-ual acts, it would interfere with the exercise of basic human capabilities associated with sexual intimacy. And, as I will argue in much more detail later in this chapter, if society uses the institution of companionate mar-riage as a way of encouraging and supporting individuals in the exercise of their basic capabilities (and in the meeting of their basic needs) associ-ated with sexual intimacy (including the capabilities to love and care for others that often accompany sexual intimacy), but then denies some of its members the opportunity to marry without adequate justification, it would fail to meet its moral obligations to account for all the capabilities of all of its citizens. The important point for now is to note that how individuals decide to exercise their basic capabilities is up to them, as long as others are not harmed. Similarly, whether individuals exercise those capabilities *at all* is also up to them. A focus on capabilities rather than on actual functionings, then, allows us to make antipaternalistic arguments without having to rely on the kind of strict neutrality about questions of the good demanded by Rawlsian or Dworkinian liberalism. It is not for society to tell individuals how to live; it is for society to make sure that individuals have the *opportunity* to lead full human lives.[19]

In some of her earlier writings, Nussbaum criticizes Rawls for his thin conception of the good, limited as it is to the distribution of primary goods (such as wealth and income) rather than focusing on "the totality of the functionings that constitute the good human life" (ASD, 209).[20] She contrasts Rawls's conception of the good with the thick but vague conception of the good as held by the capabilities approach. That conception is "thick" because it is explicitly moral; it engages in an evaluative inquiry that "is concerned with *ends* and with the overall shape and context of the human form of life" (HFS, 215). These concerns take it beyond the "traditional political distributables" such as "money, land, opportunities, and offices" (ASD, 209). In addition to being thick, however, the conception of the good held by the capabilities approach is also deliberately vague because "it admits of much multiple specification in accordance with varied local and personal conceptions" (HFS, 215). In other words, Nussbaum makes clear that capabilities are never experienced in abstract or vague ways; rather, they are always understood in ways that are particular to specific cultural and historical forces. These forces shape not only how the different capabilities are understood, but also the choices that individuals make in light of those understandings. As a result, different societies promote and provide for basic capabilities in different ways. The capabilities approach is flexible enough to account for this cultural pluralism; it does not specify the precise ways through which individuals should be given the opportunity to move across the minimum threshold that allows for the leading of full human lives, so long as whichever ways are chosen are effective and meaningful. By leaving room for individual choice—that is, by emphasizing capabilities over actual functionings—and for the particularities and specifications of different societies, then, Nussbaum seeks to mesh an Aristotelian concern for human flourishing with a liberal concern for diversity, pluralism, and personal freedom. At the same time, by requiring that the means chosen be effective and meaningful in permitting all individuals to lead lives that are fully human, the capabilities approach makes it clear that moral and political evaluations should not be wholly internal to the norms of any particular society, but should also be based on what is required by human commonalities shared across time and place.

Several years after she began articulating her capabilities approach, and at around the time that *Political Liberalism* was published, Nussbaum started describing it in terms of a Rawlsian overlapping consensus that could be agreed upon by individuals with different conceptions of the good.[21] In emphasizing the similarities between her approach and Rawls's political liberalism, Nussbaum now points out that Rawls, from the very beginning, included in his list of primary goods the social bases of self-respect, although he has more recently added freedom of movement and choice of occupation, all of which, according to Nussbaum, tilt Rawls's list in the direction of her capabilities approach.[22] Nussbaum for her part, as noted earlier, has added to her list of basic capabilities ones that are explicitly liberal in a political sense, such as the capability to make political choices and exercise rights to speech and association (WHD, 80).

It seems to me, however, that important differences remain between the substantive content of Nussbaum's and Rawls's respective overlapping consensuses. First, Nussbaum intends for her overlapping consensus to be a universal one, whereas Rawls limits the application of his to well-ordered Western democracies. As such, it is clear that Nussbaum seeks to articulate and defend commonalities that we all share *qua* human beings. The universality of such an approach, grounded as it is on the many different human traits (in addition to the capability to reason) that define our humanity, significantly distinguishes it from Rawls's approach in *Political Liberalism*. Second, Nussbaum has never explicitly categorized her capabilities approach as one that is morally or politically *neutral*, and she would have a hard time defending it as such if she tried. Her approach, for example, holds that affiliation and recreation are constitutive characteristics of a full human life. As such, governments must concern themselves with capabilities associated with affiliation and recreation by making sure that social conditions are conducive to their exercise. Rawls would likely consider issues relating to affiliation and recreation as beyond the jurisdiction of the political. He would likely hold, in other words, that whether affiliation and recreation are necessary for the leading of a fully human life is a matter strictly for individuals and their differing conceptions of the good and should not be of concern to political morality. Although it is possible, as Nussbaum suggests, to describe Rawls's "social bases of self-respect" broadly enough to include a concern for the exercise of the full spectrum of constitutive capabilities that Nussbaum argues define us as human beings, Rawls has never explicitly done so. For Rawls to take such a position, it seems to me, would undermine the kind of neutrality that political liberalism aims for because it would require determinations of what are the necessary prerequisites and conditions for the leading of *good* human lives. Those are precisely the kinds of questions that Rawls's neutral liberalism wants to avoid asking, much less answering.

Nussbaum argues that her capabilities approach, like Rawlsian liberalism, is meant to allow us to make political judgments, regardless of our ethical, religious, and metaphysical views (WHD, 76). She also argues, to clarify her earlier writings, that it "is not grounded in any theory of the human being that goes beneath politics."[23] The important point, however, is that Nussbaum has a much more expansive definition of the *political* than does Rawls. To speak of one's capability for imagination, to use the five senses, and to love and care for others (to pick just three of the basic capabilities on her list) as being relevant to questions of political morality illustrates the much greater jurisdictional ambit that Nussbaum gives to the political. I think Nussbaum's capability approach is correct to define the political as broadly as it does because it is necessary, when theorizing about justice, to take into account the full humanity of individuals as opposed to accounting only for their capability to reason. But in doing so, the capabilities approach distances itself in important ways from the minimalist liberalism of Rawls.

Nussbaum is correct, then, to argue that her capabilities approach can constitute an overlapping consensus, but its substantive content is different from Rawls's. The capabilities approach can serve as a source of agreement for individuals and societies with different conceptions of the good. For example, a Muslim or a Hindu citizen of India might have a different understanding of the kinds of affiliation or recreation that are necessary for the leading of a full life than would, say, an American Christian. Such differences, however, can be accommodated under a capabilities approach because it recognizes that different forms of affiliation and recreation will be valued differently in different societies. And yet, the flexibility of the capabilities approach does not undermine the broader point that the opportunity to engage in some forms of affiliation and recreation (again, to name just two important capabilities) are necessary for the leading of a life that is fully human. If we view the characteristics that make us human broadly enough, we can allow for significant local specification. On the other hand, the basic capabilities as articulated by Nussbaum are not *so* broad that they lose all meaning or utility. Thus, Nussbaum has written eloquently about the specific ways in which a capabilities approach to international development can improve the lives of women in the developing world by offering them greater opportunities to lead lives that are both fulfilling and dignified.

To recapitulate: the kind of liberalism that I believe Nussbaum defends is moral (as opposed to neutral) because it requires us to determine what are the requisite needs and capabilities that must be provided for if a person, regardless of where she lives, is to be able to lead a life that is fully human. Under this conception of liberalism, there must be an ethical assessment of what is required for the leading of a full human life, even if that assessment is purposefully broad enough to aim for universal agreement. But moral liberalism is liberal because it values pluralism and diversity—it recognizes that different societies, as well as different individuals, have different ways of promoting and pursuing basic needs and capabilities. It is also decidedly liberal because it sees the capability to choose as playing a fundamental role in our lives. Moral liberalism, then, has a thicker conception of the good than does Rawlsian liberalism—it goes beyond neutral political values to an evaluation of constitutive human needs and capabilities without which it would be impossible to lead lives that are fully human. But it is not any thicker than that. It does not require that individuals engage in certain conduct, or hold certain beliefs, because that conduct or those beliefs are good (either intrinsically or instrumentally); those decisions are to be made by individuals through the exercise of their capacity for choice or autonomy. Moral liberalism is only concerned with placing individuals in a position where they can make important decisions affecting their lives in a meaningful way. A thicker conception of the good than the one held by moral liberalism—one, in other words, that would require making important choices *for* individuals rather than providing the structure and support necessary for those choices to be made by individuals—would be inconsistent with the exercise of human autonomy.

Moral liberalism, then, recognizes that autonomy plays a fundamental role in the ordering of our lives and in our well-being. The value of autonomy is not just that it allows us to choose a life plan; autonomy (or more precisely, its exercise) allows us to choose to lead full human lives in the myriad of ways in which leading such lives is possible. It is this link between autonomy and the leading of full human lives that imposes on the state both negative and positive obligations. The negative obligations are consistent with the principle that the state should not interfere with the ability of individuals to choose and pursue a life plan. John Stuart Mill's harm principle, which prohibits the state from punishing an individual for actions that do not harm others, is one of the ways in which liberalism has sought to distinguish between appropriate and inappropriate interferences with personal autonomy. For moral liberalism, however, rights to freedom and autonomy are not only about *protecting* individuals from state-sponsored coercion; they are also about *promoting* the conditions necessary for individuals to be able to lead full human lives, which requires their having the opportunity to meet basic needs and exercise basic capabilities according to their own conceptions of the good.

The legal philosopher Joseph Raz argues that there are two components to autonomy. The first component entails a capacity for at least partial self-determination and self-authorship as individuals participate in the fashioning of their destiny through successive decisions made during the course of a lifetime.[24] The second component concerns autonomy as an end state or as an achievement. This second element of autonomy itself has two prerequisites. First, there should be no governmental coercion that interferes with the attainment of autonomy. This is, of course, why we protect negative freedoms. But a lack of governmental coercion, Raz argues, proves insufficient to guarantee an "autonomous life as an achievement."[25] Thus, the second prerequisite for autonomy to be a realizable end state is that the individual must have "a sufficient range of significant options available to him at different stages of his life."[26] We are able to lead autonomous lives, in other words, only to the extent that we are provided with a range of meaningful options from which to choose. This is why moral liberalism's conception of autonomy imposes obligations on society that exceed the (undoubtedly important) protection of negative freedoms; that conception also requires society to create the necessary conditions so that individuals can exercise their capacity for autonomy. What ends up determining whether we actually lead autonomous lives is as much dependent on our environment as constituted by social conditions as it is on us.[27]

Moral liberalism, then, is cognizant of the fact that human beings have certain basic needs that must be satisfied and basic capabilities that must be exercised in order for them to lead lives that are fully human. This requires of the state more than noninterference with people's lives—it also requires that the state provide the conditions necessary for the leading of full human lives. In turn, these conditions implicate more than the traditional subjects of distributive justice (e.g., property and income) because basic needs and capabilities are not only relevant to material well-being but also implicate the conditions necessary for the formation of human relationships and attachments without which, as the second fundamental tenet of moral liberalism holds, the leading of full human lives would be impossible.

Before I turn to a discussion of this second basic principle of moral liberalism, I want to address what is likely to be the main objection to moral liberalism that will be raised by supporters of neutral liberalism. They will argue that when the state involves itself in determining what is required for the leading of a full human life, there is a real danger that it will make decisions that will threaten rather than promote autonomy. Supporters of neutral liberalism will argue that the distinction between a life that is fully human and one that is not is an inherently subjective differentiation based on moral and philosophical views; those kinds of distinctions, it will be argued, should be made by individuals and not by the state. I want to make it clear that moral liberalism does not dispute the proposition that it should be the individual who chooses a life plan and how to pursue it. A state that makes decisions *for* individuals as to what their life plans should be or on how to pursue them does not sufficiently respect the value of autonomy and the corresponding concern for pluralism and diversity that that value demands. It is a different matter altogether, however, to argue that the state cannot create structures and implement policies that are meant to allow individuals to choose to lead full human lives (which, again, for moral liberalism means having the opportunity to meet basic needs and exercise basic capabilities).

If there were no meaningful distinction between a state that decides for individuals how best to lead their lives (which moral liberalism, like all forms of liberalism, holds to be an improper use of state power) and a state that promotes and protects the ability of individuals to choose to lead full human lives (which moral liberalism holds to be a proper use of state power), then no state could recognize marriage (and provide spouses with the many rights and benefits that accompany it) or, for that matter, implement a myriad of other policies (from compulsory education to the promotion of health) intended to promote the leading of full lives, and still abide by the kind of strict neutrality that neutral liberal theory requires. Yet in practice, liberal states are able to stake out a host of normative positions, as reflected in public policies on what constitutes a full human life—such as an educated and healthy one—while somehow abiding by the kind of tolerance and respect for pluralism that liberalism demands. What ends up protecting and providing for freedom and autonomy in liberal states is not the kind of strict neutrality called for by Rawlsian or Dworkinian liberalism but is instead a recognition of and appreciation for those human needs and capabilities that require state provision in some areas and state restraint in others. I agree, then, with neutral liberalism's warning that we should not, as a matter of political morality, prioritize one conception of the good life over another. I believe that it is possible, however, in formulating our basic principles of political philosophy and justice, to agree that there are basic needs and capabilities that are necessary for the leading of full human lives, even while recognizing that there are many different (good) ways in which the leading of such lives is possible.

The moral questions that are inevitably raised by an evaluation of which needs and capabilities are constitutive of full human lives must be distinguished from the kinds of moral judgments that are at issue when we praise or criticize others for the ways in which they lead their lives. It is important, in other words, not to conflate moral determinations of the constitutive needs and capabilities of human beings with moral *judgments* of how particular individuals meet and exercise them. Moral liberalism, as a theory of political morality, wants no part in the latter. Moral liberalism's respect for the autonomy and the dignity of all human beings requires that individuals be able to decide for themselves whether and how to meet their basic needs and exercise their basic capabilities, as long as others are not harmed. In this crucial sense, the priorities of moral liberalism are very different from the kind of strongly perfectionist views of political morality held by new natural law theorists and some communitarians who call on the state to promote certain kinds of behaviors and virtues both personal and civic.[28] For these thinkers, the state has a legitimate interest in strongly discouraging individuals from making decisions that will make it either more difficult or impossible for them to lead virtuous lives (however defined). Moral liberalism sees it very differently because it is concerned only with the social conditions and public policies that are necessary for individuals to be able to meet their basic needs and exercise their basic capabilities. Whether and how individuals decide to do so is up to them.

For those who believe that the state should encourage the leading of virtuous or moral lives and that same-gender sexual intimacy is inconsistent with the leading of those lives, sodomy statutes and antigay constitutional amendments such as the one at issue in *Romer v. Evans*[29] are proper uses of state power. From this perspective, the judgment, presumably shared by a majority of the population, that the sexuality of lesbians and gay men is immoral constitutes a sufficient ground for state policies that seek to discourage same-gender sexual behavior and relationships. Moral liberalism, on the other hand, does not believe that the aim of public policy should be to have individuals behave in certain ways, or to enter into certain relationships, because those are the ones considered morally acceptable by a majority of the society. This is why it is crucial to distinguish between efforts by the state to encourage or discourage certain conduct based solely on societal judgments of what is moral or immoral and an understanding, embraced by moral liberalism, that human beings have certain needs and capabilities through which they express and realize their humanity and that, as a result, should be promoted and protected through state policies.[30] Moral liberalism is concerned only with providing individuals with an adequate range of choices so that they will have the opportunity, if they choose, to satisfy those needs and exercise those capabilities that are constitutive of their humanity.

2. RELATIONSHIPS, ATTACHMENTS, AND AUTONOMY

Moral liberalism is moral because it is concerned with ethical assessments of what is required for individuals to be able to lead full human lives. Neutral liberalism of the Rawlsian kind refuses to broach the subject of what is required to lead a full human life because it considers that to be a subject of morality rather than of (political) justice. Moral liberalism, on the other hand, considers issues of justice to be inextricably linked to the conditions required for individuals to be able to lead full human lives. It is impossible to determine whether a society is just or not without a discussion of whether it both protects and provides for the opportunities of individuals to meet their basic human needs and exercise their basic human capabilities.[31]

One of the most important factors that determine the ability of individuals to lead full human lives is their opportunity to affiliate with others. As already noted, Martha Nussbaum argues that the capability to affiliate with others—like the capability to reason—is an architectonic capability, by which she means that "it organize[s] and suffuse[s] all the others, making their pursuit truly human" (WHD, 82). Our interactions with others, as well as our dependencies on others, are crucial to our ability to lead lives that are fully human. Even the most essential needs (such as those for food and shelter) are difficult to satisfy without the assistance of others. Other needs and capabilities (such as the need to be loved and cared for by others and the capability to love and care for others) by their very nature require affiliations with fellow human beings. Our capability "to live with and toward others, to recognize and show concern for other human beings, to engage in various forms of social interaction" all depend on our relationships with and attachments to others (WHD, 79). It is because our human needs and capabilities inevitably link our lives with those of others that moral liberalism gives affiliations a high normative priority. But as also noted previously, moral liberalism gives the *highest* normative priority to the individual because the needs and capabilities of *each* individual matter. As moral liberalism sees it, our political morality should view individuals as ends for whom certain affiliations serve as important means through which they meet many of their basic needs and exercise many of their basic capabilities. To speak of these affiliations as "means" is not to demean their importance because they play crucial roles in allowing individuals to lead lives that are fully human. By placing the highest normative priority on the individual, moral liberalism clearly distinguishes itself from communitarians and others who argue that collective entities (whether relationships, communities, or societies) have an intrinsic worth that is separate from their individual constitutive members. At the same time, however, moral liberalism seeks to give the collective entities their due by recognizing their importance in providing individuals with the means and support necessary for them to be able to lead full human lives.

The issue that I want to explore in this section is the connection between our affiliations with others, on the one hand, and our ability to lead autonomous lives on the other. This connection is crucial for the political morality of moral liberalism because rather than viewing others primarily as a threat to our autonomy, moral liberalism sees autonomy as emanating largely from our relationships with and our dependencies on others. Human relationships and attachments, therefore, rather than being relegated to a private sphere that is best left outside of the jurisdiction of political morality, are instead an integral part of that morality because they are an integral part of the way in which individuals attain their autonomy. In formulating its conception of autonomy, moral liberalism, as will be clear from the discussion that follows, seeks to take the feminist critique of liberalism seriously. In fact, moral liberalism incorporates many of the philosophical arguments made by feminist theory, in particular its conception of the self and its ethic of care.

Feminists have for a long time been critical of the way in which liberalism has traditionally conceived of individuals as having needs and interests that are, as Alison Jaggar puts it, "separate from if not in opposition to those of other individuals."[32] This view of the self has both epistemological and political implications. As to the former, it suggests that individuals are beings who exist prior to and independently of their connections and ties to others. As to the latter, it suggests that the paramount objective of political structures and norms should be to protect individuals from each other so that they can pursue their interests and meet their needs without interference. Under such a political regime, as Robin West notes, "we come to identify our 'rights'—our most precious political entitlements, and hence our political identity—as rights to individuate and distance or sever ourselves from, rather than rights to safely connect or relate to, our families, intimates, communities, or co-citizens."[33]

To be fair to liberals, especially Kantian/Rawlsian liberals, it should be noted that for them it is the separateness of individuals that justifies the imposition of moral and political obligations to treat others with the respect and dignity that they, as distinct human beings, deserve. The problem is that in emphasizing almost exclusively the separateness of individuals, many liberals have not been sufficiently cognizant of the way in which relationships and attachments define the very interests and needs that individuals seek to pursue and satisfy. For feminist (and communitarian) critics of liberalism, therefore, it makes no sense to think of individuals as existing separate from or prior to their relationships and communities. (I will discuss the communitarian critique of liberalism—and its implications for lesbians and gay men—in the next chapter.) Our political morality, they argue, should reflect the value, importance, and meaning of our connections with and responsibilities toward others.

The traditional liberal response to this line of criticism has been to deny that liberalism ignores relationships and attachments. In fact, the liberal usually argues, it is precisely because our relationships and attachments are so important, that they must, as a political matter, be placed in a distinct (private) sphere that is insulated from societal (public) regulation. (Similarly, because of the importance for individuals of some communities, such as religious ones, it is imperative that they be kept outside of the reach of public regulation.) It is through building a fire wall between the private and the public, it is argued, that we make sure that individuals are free to enter into the relationships that are most important to them. As feminists have been pointing out for a long time, however, the divide between a private and a public sphere does not promote the well-being and autonomy of those who historically have been the subjects of subordination *within* the private sphere. The marital exception to rape laws and the law's historical indifference to domestic violence, to give just two examples, illustrate the ways in which *noninterference* with private relationships can undermine rather than promote both well-being and autonomy.[34] Part of the problem has been that though liberal theory has tended to view all conduct that takes place within the family as self-regarding (and thus as outside of the scope of legitimate public regulation), for the women whose bodies have been abused, whose lives have been demeaned, and whose aspirations have been ignored, internal family practices can be very much other-regarding. Although the intent behind the private/public distinction may be to increase the range of personal choices, which is in and of itself a laudable goal, the distinction in practice has increased the choices of men at the expense of those of women.[35]

Feminists argue, then, that a conception of the self that values its individualism and separateness above all else does not match the descriptive reality or the normative aspirations of most women's lives. An important conceptual breakthrough for feminists took place in the early 1980s when the developmental psychologist Carol Gilligan, in her studies of the ways in which women address moral dilemmas, noticed that women emphasized notions of responsibility and care much more often than did men, who focused instead on considerations of justice and rights. As Gilligan put it, the moral imperative of many "women is an injunction to care, a responsibility to discern and alleviate the 'real and recognizable trouble' of this world."[36] Gilligan and the many feminists who in the last twenty years have elaborated and built on her work defend a morality grounded in *responsibility* that emphasizes connectedness, compromise, and an ethic of care rather than a morality grounded in *rights* that emphasizes the individual, separateness, and conflict.[37] A feminist morality is based on the experiences of women as mothers and caretakers, experiences that have been insufficiently accounted for in liberal theory.

As feminists have sought to articulate the meaning and consequences of a distinct feminist ethic, there have been many disagreements among themselves along the way, including whether such an ethic inappropriately essentializes the differences between men and women,[38] or insufficiently accounts for the distinctive voices of lesbians and women of color,[39] or improperly dichotomizes justice and care.[40] Although these debates within feminism have been extensive and remain largely unresolved, the important point for our purposes is that feminist theory provides us with a moral and political framework that accounts for the high degree of connectedness and responsibility toward others that is an integral part of our lives. Given the prevalence of relationships of care and dependency in human lives (e.g., between a parent and a child, between a child and an elderly parent, between spouses, between friends, and so on), feminists ask, why should the contractarian relationship of parties bargaining at arm's length be the paradigmatic relationship in political theory?[41] The characteristics of a society arising from a Lockean state of nature or a Rawlsian original position, for example, would be different if those who bargain over the social contract care for and feel responsible toward others.[42] Instead of a political morality that emphasizes noninterference and the pursuit of self-interest, there would emerge a political morality that recognizes the importance of connectedness and the meeting of needs through the caring, supporting, and nurturing of others.

The Kantian tradition, which has been so influential in contemporary liberal theory, is skeptical of emotions and personal relationships because it deems them to be inconsistent with ideals of reason, objectivity, and universality.[43] The kind of specific obligations that we owe our families, for example, differ from the kinds of obligations that we owe humanity, most of whom, except for an infinitesimal number, are strangers to us. In fact, the developmental psychologist Lawrence Kohlberg, whose understanding of moral development as grounded in impartiality, justice, and rights (and highly influenced by Rawls) constituted Gilligan's principal target of criticism, responded *to* Gilligan by arguing that her work addressed a separate moral domain, that of personal relationships, from the one he was interested in, that of impartial and universal moral obligations.[44] Kohlberg's response predictably fell back on the same old private/public distinction that, as Marilyn Friedman puts it, deems "the world of personal relationships, of the family and of family ties and loyalties, that is, the traditional world of women [to be] a world of lesser moral interest and importance than the public world of government and of the marketplace, that is, the male-dominated world outside the home."[45] Friedman, among others, has noted how the separation between justice and care is not as stark as Kohlberg (or even Gilligan) believes.[46] This is particularly true if we include within our understanding of justice obligations to meet the basic needs of others and to relieve their suffering.

The relevance of personal relationships in the determination of universal moral obligations is one that has attracted a great deal of interest from philosophers, an interest that can be traced back (at least) to fundamental disagreements between Hume and Kant.[47] The point that I want to emphasize here is the connection between those relationships and autonomy. Some feminists, in critiquing liberalism, have come to see the norm of autonomy as the antithesis of a feminist ethic of connectedness and care.[48] It is important to note, however, that the conception of autonomy that feminists have, with good reason, been skeptical of is one that equates it with atomistic behaviors and norms. It is this conception of autonomy that glorifies the self-reliant and self-made person (read: man) and the social practices and values that are meant to support and protect his independence. It is this view of personal autonomy that has contributed to the subordination and second-class status of women; it is women who have historically been expected to provide the necessary support and care to the "self-made" man, while enjoying neither the time nor the support to pursue their interests and priorities. Women, in turn, have had little recourse for complaint because, under the traditional liberal view, internal family practices and conduct are supposed to be of concern only to the parties involved. But just because the concept of autonomy has in the past been incorrectly viewed by many as a synonym for individualism within a privileged and protected private sphere does not mean that the concept "*properly understood* is male-biased or antifemale."[49]

In fact, liberal feminists have argued that it is precisely individuals' connections with and dependencies on others that permits them to lead autonomous lives. As Jennifer Nedelsky argues, it is "relationships—with parents, teachers, friends, loved ones—that provide the support and guidance necessary for the development and experience of autonomy. . . . [R]elatedness is not, as our tradition teaches, the antithesis of autonomy, but a literal precondition of autonomy, and interdependence a constant component of autonomy."[50] Autonomy, in other words, is not realizable without the ongoing support and care provided by others. The link between connectedness and autonomy, therefore, is a causal rather than a dichotomous one. The exercise of one's autonomy is not primarily a function of being left alone, but is instead primarily a function of being permitted to have certain kinds of relationships with others. (I say "primarily" because, as I argue below, there are obviously certain relationships that interfere with autonomy and where separation and protection from others is necessary.) In this way, liberal feminism offers us a conception of autonomy that is relational as opposed to individualistic; the autonomous person is viewed not as self-reliant or self-sufficient, but rather as being able to lead an autonomous life *through* relationships with others.

In the last section, I noted how the exercise of our capacity for autonomy is very much dependent on our environment. Our capability to lead autonomous lives entails the combination of our internal capacity for self-determination with an environment that provides us with meaningful choices and opportunities to meet basic needs and exercise basic capabilities. A crucial component of that environment is constituted by our relationships of mutual support with and dependence on others.

The link between relationships and attachments, on the one hand, and autonomy on the other, is, in fact, reflected in the Supreme Court's privacy jurisprudence. It is primarily through that jurisprudence that the Court has endeavored to protect the rights to personal autonomy of American citizens. And yet, as Robin West notes, those cases, "liberal rhetoric to the contrary notwithstanding, do not by any stretch protect the isolated liberty right of individuals 'to be left alone.' They [instead] protect the right of individuals to form independent societies of interaction with select others, within which the state will not intrude."[51] Take *Bowers v. Hardwick*, for example. In many ways that case can be viewed as raising the paradigmatic scenario of an individual who wanted to be left alone and where, traditional liberal theory holds, the state in criminalizing consensual sodomy, violated the individual's rights to privacy and autonomy. What gets left out of this analysis, however, is that on the night of Mr. Hardwick's arrest, he did *not* want to be alone. Mr. Hardwick on that night invited another man into his home for the purpose of having sex. What the state interfered with was not his right to be left alone, but the right to connect with another human being (albeit sexually). In fact, the majority in *Bowers* could not bring itself to acknowledge that the case raised the same issues of interactions and associations with others raised by earlier privacy cases—such as the contraception cases—where the state tried unsuccessfully to regulate heterosexual intimacy.[52] Thus, Justice White, in his majority opinion in *Bowers*, concluded flatly and without any qualification that "[n]o connection between family, marriage, or procreation on the one hand and homosexual activity on the other has been demonstrated."[53] Justice Blackmun's dissent, on the other hand, recognized that the right to autonomy and privacy at issue in the case was not just about the right to be left alone, but was also about the way in which "individuals define themselves in a significant way" through their relationships with others, including their sexually intimate relationships.[54] As Blackmun put it, "[o]nly the most willful blindness could obscure the fact that sexual intimacy is a 'sensitive, key relationship of human existence, central to family life, community welfare, and the development of human personality.' "[55]

The right to an abortion is also usually explained as grounded in a fundamental right to privacy and to make important decisions affecting one's body without interference by others. Yet the abortion procedure is not a private act—it must be done (if it is to be done safely) by another who is almost always a stranger. But even more fundamentally than that, the decision of whether to have an abortion is often made by women from within a web of relationships (with families, lovers, spouses) and a sense of responsibility toward others, including, of course, to the fetus (and potential child) itself. As Gilligan found in her study of how women approach the moral dilemmas raised by abortion, it is too simplistic to view the decision to have an abortion as that of a woman exercising a right to be left alone. Instead, relational obligations and constraints frame the moral decision-making process for many women when deciding whether to abort. The decision to have an abortion is usually made from within a context of relationships and connections to others as the choosing woman struggles between her obligations to herself and her obligations toward others.[56] As another study of women who seek abortion services found, decisions to abort often reflect the women's "desire to optimize the quality of their marital and childbearing experiences, and to reduce the risk of physical, psychological, social, and economic disadvantage for themselves and their children."[57] Again, a conception of autonomy that is limited to principles of noninterference and the need to leave individuals alone fails to capture the complexity and interactional components of the issues at stake.

There are admittedly some exceptions to the idea that the exercise of personal autonomy is always framed and determined through relationships with others. In *Stanley v. Georgia*, for example, the Supreme Court recognized the right of an individual to possess pornography in his home (presumably to aid solitary masturbatory fantasies).[58] But cases such as *Stanley* are the exception rather than the rule. Almost all of the important cases that make up the Court's autonomy and privacy jurisprudence consist of circumstances where individuals were seeking to associate with or make important decisions affecting others. Thus, in *Griswold v. Connecticut* and *Eisenstadt v. Baird*, the Court concluded that statutes that prohibited the use of contraceptives were unconstitutional because they either interfered with the rights of married *couples* (*Griswold*) or improperly treated unmarried *couples* unequally (*Baird*).[59] In *Loving v. Virginia* and *Zablocki v. Redhail*, the Court affirmed the rights of heterosexual *couples* to marry.[60] In *Moore v. City of East Cleveland*, the Court upheld the right of *family* members to live together.[61] In *Troxel v. Granville, Pierce v. Society of Sisters*, and *Meyer v. Nebraska*, the Court protected the rights of parents to make important decisions *relating to their children* without interference by the state.[62] The Court itself has noted that constitutional protection for certain personal relationships (marital, parental, familial), "reflects the realization that individuals draw much of their emotional enrichment from close ties with others. Protecting these relationships from unwarranted state interference therefore safeguards the ability independently to define one's identity that is central to any concept of liberty."[63] As the Supreme Court has recognized, then, and as liberal feminists such as Nedelsky and West have argued, we exercise our autonomy primarily through our relationships with others. It is others that provide us with the support, nurture, and care that make leading an autonomous life possible. Milton Regan nicely summarizes this point when he notes that "we are always embedded in a network of relationships with others that is the very basis for our sense of our individuality and our capacity for meaningful choice."[64]

Moral liberalism brings together the lessons learned from a relational understanding of autonomy—an understanding that is possible largely as the result of feminist theory—with the idea that human beings have certain needs and capabilities that are constitutive of their humanity, the meeting and exercise of many of which would be impossible in the absence of relationships with and attachments to others. Moral liberalism recognizes that we both define ourselves and pursue our life goals largely through our affiliations with others. It is through those affiliations that we form a sense of identity and belonging that both nurtures and accounts for our well-being and autonomy. We are as human beings social creatures; we need from others and are capable of providing to others love, affection, companionship, and intimacy. We live our lives, in other words, through the lives of particular others, especially friends, families, spouses, lovers, and children. It is for this reason that "deep personal bonds have an ineluctable moral priority."[65]

The issue of *particular* others is important because we cannot meaningfully think of our most important relationships and attachments in an abstract manner. Intimate relationships have two defining characteristics. First, in an intimate relationship the identity and attributes of the other *matter*. An intimate other is not replaceable by someone else (in the same way, for example, that an other in a commercial relationship or even in a student-teacher relationship is replaceable). In fact, when the intimate other becomes replaceable (as happens in a hopelessly broken marriage), then at that point the relationship ceases to be an intimate one. Second, in an intimate relationship our sense of happiness and fulfillment is linked to that of the other. We care about the life of the intimate other, for its own sake and also for the meaning and purpose that that life gives our own. It is this aspect of intimacy that allows for the unique forms of sharing, commitment, and respect that are characteristic of our closest relationships.[66]

Before concluding this discussion of the roles that relationships and attachments play in promoting human autonomy, I want to emphasize again that moral liberalism's concern for the connectedness and interdependencies of individuals does not mean that it is willing to subserve the interests of the individual to those of others. Our moral and political focus must remain on individuals and their capacity to lead full human lives. Such a focus, however, is not inconsistent with respecting, appreciating, and valuing the ways in which individuals lead full human lives, in part, through loving, supporting, and caring for others. What moral liberalism rejects is the view that human well-being and autonomy can be sufficiently promoted and protected solely through principles of noninterference. At the same time, moral liberalism does not require that individuals give up their priorities and interests in order to serve collective ends. Moral liberalism instead helps us understand that those priorities and interests are often determined and attained through our interactions with others, particularly with those with whom we share our intimate and emotional lives.

Not every relationship, of course, is conducive to the attainment of our well-being and the exercise of our autonomy. Some relationships are exploitative, demeaning, and oppressive and as such interfere with rather than promote the leading of an autonomous life. This has been an issue of particular concern for feminists, for whom it is crucial to distinguish between relationships in women's lives that are healthy, enriching, and supportive from those—usually with abusive husbands or boyfriends—that are not. To argue that all relationships are valuable is too simplistic, in the same way (as we will see in the next chapter) that to argue that participating in community life is per se valuable is itself simplistic and potentially dangerous. Distinctions must be made among relationships (and communities), which is why, once again, we cannot remain neutral as to their value; it is necessary to distinguish between those relationships that are valuable because they are conducive to the leading of full human lives and those that impede the leading of such lives.

3. MORAL LIBERALISM AND GAY RIGHTS

So what does moral liberalism mean for gay rights? Or more specifically, what does a political morality that focuses on needs, capabilities, and the role of relationships and attachments in the leading of full human lives mean for those who are seeking to have the state recognize and support gay and lesbian relationships and families? This is the question that I address in the remainder of this chapter.

It is clear that basic needs and capabilities are implicated in many of our debates over gay rights. Whether we are assessing the scope of the right to engage in sexual intimacy without interference by the state or deciding whether the state should recognize and support gay and lesbian relationships and families, we are in effect determining the societal conditions under which those who are attracted to others of the same gender are allowed and encouraged to meet basic human needs and exercise basic human capabilities associated with sexual intimacy. If we believe lesbians and gay men share commonalities with all other human beings that makes their basic needs and capabilities as morally relevant as those of heterosexuals, then we must be sensitive to the ways in which public policies allow or impede the satisfaction of those needs and the exercise of those capabilities.

The appropriate range of options that the state is morally required to provide its citizens in all public policy matters—including those that implicate intimate relationships (both sexual and familial)—should be determined with the aim of making sure that all citizens are able to meet basic human needs and exercise basic human capabilities. For our purposes, the principal issue becomes whether same-gender sexual conduct, relationships, and families implicate at least some of those needs and capabilities. Many conservative opponents of gay rights argue that they do not because there is something morally wrong with same-gender sexuality. For many conservatives, therefore, the state has an interest in *discouraging* homosexuality as much as is prudentially possible. In fact, conservatives point to the need to discourage homosexuality in just about every gay rights controversy, from the introduction of topics related to sexual orientation in school curricula to having openly gay teachers in schools to permitting lesbians and gay men to serve openly in the military to allowing lesbians and gay men to marry and encouraging them to become parents.

Furthermore, for many conservatives, calls for discrimination protection on the basis of sexual orientation should be rejected because no other group receives legal protection on the basis of "improper" (sexual) conduct. Why would we ever want the state, conservatives argue, to encourage (as opposed to simply permit or tolerate) choices that are bad both for the individuals involved and for society as a whole? I suggest that the framing of the question in this way is not improper. It is a legitimate question under the theoretical model proposed by moral liberalism because it raises the issue of whether, in fact, same-gender sexual conduct, relationships, and families implicate the kinds of basic needs and capabilities that are constitutive of human beings, or whether, as many conservatives argue, they are constitutive of nothing more than bad (or abnormal or immoral or dangerous or harmful) choices on the part of some individuals that are not worthy of moral respect and that justify the differential treatment of them by society. This is a question that must be answered directly rather than sidestepped.

In addressing the subject of whether homosexuality is, in fact, a "bad choice," many supporters of gay rights have taken issue with the second part of the assessment, namely, with whether it is a choice at all. Part of the rationale for this is that many supporters believe (perhaps not unreasonably) that an already hostile society will blame lesbians and gay men less for engaging in conduct that is, in effect, beyond their control. Several scientific studies published in the early 1990s—studies that remain quite controversial today—seem to bolster the position of those who argue that homosexuality is a physiological condition that places it outside of the realm of choice.[67] That position has constitutional implications given that courts (including, at different times, the Supreme Court) have suggested that immutability is relevant in determining whether the actions of the state violate the Constitution's equal protection clause.[68] The state has a less valid justification, the argument goes, to differentiate among citizens based on immutable traits (such as race). Some lower federal courts have denied lesbians and gay men the added protection provided by a heightened judicial scrutiny of government policies that make distinctions on the basis of sexual orientation because they have viewed sexual orientation (or more precisely, homosexuality) as a mutable characteristic.[69]

Ultimately, however, whether homosexuality is a choice is a derivative question of whether it, or more accurately, its manifestation in terms of same-gender sexual conduct, relationships, and families, is "good" or "bad." If it is "bad," then the fact that it is not a choice mitigates its "badness" but does not necessarily turn it into something that society should support or encourage. If same-gender sexual conduct, relationships, and families, however, are good—by which I mean if they are means through which lesbians and gay men meet some basic human needs and exercise some basic human capabilities—then whether one "chooses" to be a lesbian or a gay man would become as irrelevant a question as whether one chooses to be a heterosexual. In addition, it makes more sense to focus on the normative aspect of same-gender sexual conduct, relationships, and families as opposed to whether homosexuality is a choice because even if one's sexual orientation is given and not chosen, what one *does* with that status in terms of one's conduct and relations with others can always be characterized as an issue of choice, which takes us right back to the question of whether the exercise of the choice is good or bad.

Moral liberalism recognizes that a normative evaluation of the connection, if any, between homosexuality and basic human needs and capabilities is required when determining the obligations of the state in this area. To put it differently, moral liberalism recognizes that the *value* of same-gender relationships and families is a legitimate issue of political morality. Although the state, in order to protect the liberty of individuals, must tolerate a broad range of conduct and relationships irrespective of their value as long as others are not harmed, the state must only proactively provide for those choices that are valuable. (Again, moral liberalism does not concern itself with the choices that individuals make, as long as they do not harm others, but with the range of options that is made available to them.) As long as the focus of the gay rights movement was exclusively centered, as it was prior to the 1990s, around the proposition that the state should tolerate same-gender sexual conduct by not criminalizing it and that the state should protect lesbians and gay men from employment and housing discrimination, there was no real need to assess whether gay and lesbian relationships and families were good and valuable. Principles of noninterference, coupled with the advisability of using the state as a civil shield to protect individuals against discrimination, were sufficient justifications for the attainment of the gay rights movement's earlier goals. Now that the movement, however, is asking for recognition and support of gay and lesbian relationships and families, the nature of the justificatory considerations has changed. We must now answer the following question: Are gay and lesbian relationships and families, in general, good and valuable? (I add the qualifier "in general" because not every gay relationship or family will, of course, be good and valuable, just as not every heterosexual one will be either.) The fundamental issue now becomes whether the composition, qualities, and dynamics of gay and lesbian relationships and families are good and valuable or whether conservative opponents of gay rights are correct that those relationships and families are morally problematic and harmful to the individuals involved and to society. If conservatives are correct, then there can be no moral obligation on the part of the state to recognize and support gay and lesbian relationships and families.

Moral liberalism encourages us to view individual rights in their relational or associational context. The right to marry and the right to have and to raise children cannot be understood or justified if we only focus on the rights of individuals to be left alone; instead, those rights implicate the fundamental interests of individuals to have certain kinds of relationships with others. The value, nature, and impact of those relationships are legitimate considerations when the state is deciding whether to recognize and support them rather than to merely tolerate them. If what is sought is simply toleration, then notions of negative freedom and noninterference can serve as sufficient justifications for gay rights positions. But if what is sought is recognition and support, then there has to be an evaluation of the value and impact of the relationships at issue.

In our society, companionate marriage and parenting are two of the principal institutions through which individuals satisfy their basic needs and exercise their basic capabilities associated with physical and emotional intimacy. I address below the issue of whether same-sex marriage and parenting by lesbians and gay men as currently proposed (in the case of marriage) and carried out (in the case of parenting) are good and valuable forms of human associations. Conservatives are correct when they argue that society should only be required to recognize and support (as opposed to merely tolerate) those relationships and forms of human associations that are good and valuable. Where conservative opponents of gay rights err, as I argue below, is in their moral assessments of the value and goodness of gay and lesbian relationships and families.

THE VALUE OF SAME-SEX RELATIONSHIPS AND SAME-SEX MARRIAGE: NEEDS, CAPABILITIES, AND AUTONOMY

In this section, I explain the connection between human needs, capabilities, and autonomy on the one hand and the value of same-sex relationships and marriage on the other. I also in this section address the objections to same-sex marriage made by critics on both the left and the right and argue that both sides are, in their very different ways, insufficiently sensitive to the societal obligations to promote and protect basic human needs and capabilities. Finally, an exploration of the value of same-gender relationships would not be complete without some attention to the consequentialist implications of state recognition of those relationships. I therefore finish this section with a brief discussion of consequentialist arguments both in favor of and against state recognition of same-sex marriage. I leave, for the last section of the chapter, a discussion of the value of parenting by lesbians and gay men.

An exploration of the value of same-gender relationships begins with the basic human needs for sexual satisfaction. As with the capability for language discussed earlier in this chapter, the needs for sexual satisfaction, as well as the corresponding capabilities to satisfy the sexual needs of others, have a physical or bodily component to them. Our bodies in general, and certain organs in particular, are sites of sexual pleasure for ourselves and others. But as with language, what gives sexual needs and capabilities moral value is not the physiological or biological compo nents of sex but is instead the ethical recognition that a life that lacks the opportunity for sexual satisfaction of some kind cannot be a fully human life. It is impossible, in other words, to conceive of a human life as a full one if the holder of that life does not have at least some opportunities for sexual satisfaction. As a result, human needs for sexual satisfaction are in and of themselves worthy of moral respect.

A necessary element of this moral respect is the recognition that, in order for the satisfaction of sexual needs to be meaningful, there must be some correspondence between attraction and sexual acts. In sexual relationships, as in all intimate relationships, the identity and attributes of the other *matter*. In order for sexual activity to satisfy an individual's sexual needs, therefore, he or she must find the sexual partner attractive. Attractiveness can, of course, entail much more than just physical characteristics, but a certain amount of physical attractiveness is necessary for the meaningful satisfaction of sexual needs. The opportunity for sexual activity with a person of a gender to which one is not physically attracted, therefore, is not a meaningful or effective opportunity to satisfy basic human needs for physical intimacy.

The satisfaction of sexual needs often (though obviously not always) involves needs and capabilities associated with the caring for others, a caring that goes beyond the duration of the sexual acts themselves. There are, of course, many different kinds of caring relationships that contain within them a sexual component. These include, but are not limited to, relationships where the primary focus is the physical intimacy and where the caring for the other as an emotional matter is of secondary importance; relationships where the opposite is the case, namely, where the primary focus is the caring for or friendship with the other, with physical intimacy being of secondary importance; and relationships where the emotional and physical intimacy are not easily separable and where the giving and receiving of sexual pleasure goes hand in hand with emotional mutuality and commitment. It is this latter category of relationships that is of particular interest to us here because it is their participants, experience tells us, who are most likely to seek societal recognition of and support for their relationships.

The ability to connect physical intimacy with emotional intimacy (whether in its limited or expansive forms) is one of the distinctive characteristics that make us human. Only humans are able to construct their lives around the unique and powerful emotional intimacy that can accompany physical intimacy. The ability to combine both kinds of intimacies allows human beings to explore their full potential to love and care for another human being. Our needs and capabilities for physical and emotional intimacy, therefore, are constitutive elements of our personhood. It is impossible to separate our lives or identities as human beings from those basic needs and capabilities. It is for this reason that efforts to distinguish between lesbians and gay men as persons, on the one hand, and their needs and capabilities associated with physical and emotional intimacy, on the other, are morally problematic.[70] Lesbians and gay men, like everyone else, pursue and express their humanity, in part, through their intimate relationships, including sexual ones. Lesbians and gay men need and are capable of participating in intimate sexual relationships because they too are human. It is no more possible to separate their needs and capabilities for physical and emotional intimacy from their moral personhood and their identity as human beings than it is to do so for heterosexuals. To attempt to do so is to attempt to quite literally dehumanize lesbians and gay men because it is an effort to strip them of a meaningful and enriching sexuality that helps define them as human beings. If we morally strip lesbians and gay men of their same-gender sexuality, and thus deny that they have needs and capabilities for meaningful physical and emotional intimacy along with everyone else, we fail to recognize them as full human beings.

When lesbians and gay men seek physical and emotional intimacy with others of the same gender, therefore, they are doing nothing more and nothing less than pursuing their human needs and capabilities for sex, care, and affection. The needs and capabilities of lesbians and gay men to love and care for another in a sexually intimate relationship are defining traits of their humanity, and as such merit moral respect. This does not mean that the physical and emotional expression of *a gay and lesbian* sexuality is an intrinsic or essential part of the humanity of lesbians and gay men. It does mean that a sexuality *of some kind* is an intrinsic part of their humanity, a sexuality that for whatever reasons (biological, social, or a combination of the two) entails needs and capabilities for physical and emotional intimacy with someone of the same gender. The morally relevant point is that lesbians and gay men have needs and capabilities for physical and emotional intimacy and that those needs and capabilities—as expressed through their sexuality and their love for and care of others—help define them as human beings. The morally irrelevant point, as I will argue when I address the arguments raised by opponents of same-sex marriage, is that the person at the other end of those needs and capabilities is someone of the same gender.

We begin an analysis of the value of same-gender sexual acts and of the relationships of care and affection that often accompany them, then, with a moral argument, namely, that the sexuality of lesbians and gay men is a constitutive part of their humanity. Through their same-gender sexuality, lesbians and gay men express important characteristics, attributes, and potentialities that allow us to recognize them as human beings and that permit them to lead fully human lives. The next question is one of *political* morality: What must society do about the fact that some of its citizens satisfy their basic human needs and capabilities associated with sexual intimacy with others of the same gender? There is no simple answer to that question because, as noted earlier, sexual intimacy takes place in a variety of contexts. Given that variety, it is permissible for society to treat different expressions of same-gender intimacy differently. When that intimacy is expressed through the satisfaction of physical needs without a caring for the other that extends beyond the duration of sexual acts, then society meets its obligations through restraint and non-interference with those acts. But when the sexual intimacy is more valuable than that—that is—when it implicates not only the satisfaction of physical needs but also the need to be loved and cared for by another and the capability to love and care for another, then the societal obligations go from "mere" noninterference to the creation of the necessary conditions that will promote and protect the ability of individuals to meet those additional needs and exercise those additional capabilities.

The statement in the previous sentence that some forms of sexual intimacy are "more valuable" than others will make many liberals and progressives nervous because it calls for a normative assessment of the value or good of particular kinds of sexually intimate relationships. Moral liberalism, however, does not shy away from arguing that some sexual relationships are more valuable than others: relationships that permit individuals to satisfy a greater number of basic needs and exercise a greater number of basic capabilities are more valuable than those that implicate fewer basic needs and capabilities. This does not mean that sexual acts whose primary, or even sole purpose, is to satisfy physical needs have no value; as I argued at the beginning of this section, they do have value because the need for sexual satisfaction is a basic human need that by itself merits moral respect. It *does* mean that the societal response to sexual conduct that is not part of the meeting of needs and the exercise of capabilities associated with the expression of care for another human being (a caring that goes beyond that which takes place during the sexual acts themselves), can be justifiably different—that is—it can be one of tolerance and restraint, rather than of the kind of recognition and support merited by physical intimacy that is accompanied by ongoing emotional mutuality and commitment.

I want to make it clear at this point that my argument is not that because committed same-gender sexual relationships implicate several basic human needs and capabilities that society therefore has a moral obligation to recognize and support them. It is not so easy, if nothing else because opponents of gay rights will at this point raise their familiar objections that those interested in polygamous or incestuous relationships, for example, could also contend that their relationships should be recognized and supported by society because they also, it could be argued, implicate basic needs and capabilities associated with physical and emotional intimacy. A separate analysis would have to be conducted in the case of those relationships to determine whether they are, in fact, valuable or whether there is something about them—such as the power disparities among their participants and associated issues of gender subordination—that makes them morally problematic. It is one thing to argue that needs and capabilities for physical and emotional intimacy are constitutive of what it means to be a human being and that lesbians and gay men share in those forms of human commonalities, and quite another to contend that those commonalities impose on society *specific* obligations to recognize and support, for example, same-sex marriages. It is not a direct line, in other words, between acknowledging, on the one hand, that basic human needs and capabilities are implicated whenever we discuss issues of sexual intimacy and, on the other, imposing on society an obligation to recognize and support specific kinds of relationships. What *is* required of a society is that it tread with care when basic needs and capabilities are implicated and that it recognize and support those forms of intimate relationships, including sexual and familial ones, that are *good* as defined by its norms and values. This is the way in which moral liberalism seeks to balance the universalism of liberalism with the localism and particularism of pragmatism and communitarianism. We can, for example, agree with Nussbaum that the capability "to live for and with others, to recognize and show concern for other human beings, [and] to engage in various forms of familial and social interaction" (HFS, 222) is a universal human trait while acknowledging that different societies will recognize and value intimate relationships differently.

It is not possible, then, to speak of the right to marry someone of the same gender as a universal right applicable across time and place. It *is* possible to speak of a right to same-sex marriage in a moral sense if it is consistent with the way in which a society allows or encourages its members to meet their basic human needs and capabilities associated with physical and emotional intimacy. There is significant room in the political morality of moral liberalism for local traditions and norms. What a society should not do is stifle (explicitly) or fail to provide (implicitly) mechanisms for the meeting of basic human needs and the exercise of basic human capabilities.

The particular characteristics and benefits of marriage and family vary from society to society. The nuclear family, which to many Westerners seems like the natural unit of familial composition, is not privileged under the analysis suggested here. There are some societies where duties and obligations to more extended family members, or even to close friends, are akin to the duties and obligations that Westerners feel for members of their nuclear families. These are the kinds of local specifications and variations that we find whenever we compare the familial arrangements of different societies.[71] It is not that lesbians and gay men have a universal right to have their relationships and families recognized in the way in which American or Western European law and culture define marriage and family. The point is broader than that, namely, that society has an obligation to provide for all of its citizens' basic needs and capabilities, including those associated with their most intimate relationships. This requires considerably more than just the noncriminalization of sexual acts that are consensual; it also requires the provision of social structures and the implementation of public policies that allow committed intimate relationships to be formed and maintained. The exact nature and composition of those structures and policies will vary by society, but those structures and policies, however designed and formulated, must allow for opportunities to lead full human lives, important aspects of which depend on the ability of individuals to meet the full panoply of needs and exercise the full range of capabilities associated with sexual intimacy.

If we view those needs and capabilities narrowly—for example, simply in terms of our needs to satisfy sexual urges and our capabilities to satisfy the sexual urges of others—then it can be argued that a society meets its obligations to promote and protect basic human needs and capabilities associated with sexual intimacy by simply giving individuals the necessary freedom to connect with potential sexual partners. One can imagine that a perfectly libertarian state, where any consensual sexual relationship is tolerated but where no relationship is recognized or privileged over any other, would satisfy that minimum moral threshold. When we speak of human needs and capabilities associated with sexual intimacy, however, we mean more than just the satisfaction of sexual urges. Since the need to be loved and cared for by others and the capability to love and care for others often (though again, of course, not always) accompanies sexual conduct, there is more at stake for individuals than simply having opportunities for sexual satisfaction. Human relationships do not exist in a social or cultural vacuum; as Joseph Raz puts it, "[m]arriage, friendships, parenthood," among other relationships, "are all molded and patterned by the common culture which determines to a very considerable degree the bounds of possible options available to individuals."[72] It is society, through its norms, policies, and practices that provides the support and conditions that can turn what might otherwise be fleeting sexual encounters or short-term relationships into meaningful, rewarding, and long-lasting relationships.

Moral liberalism is fully cognizant of the role of social institutions and policies in establishing the necessary conditions for the caring for and loving of others from within intimate relationships that are stable and enduring. Moral liberalism, to quote Nussbaum, "is explicitly committed to a prominent place for love and care as important goals of social planning and as major moral abilities" (WHD, 245). Such a commitment means that moral liberalism requires more of society than that it not interfere with the capability of individuals to enter into and remain in what are for them meaningful and life-enhancing committed relationships; it also requires society to provide the necessary support and conditions that make it possible for individuals to love and care for others in long-term intimate relationships in an atmosphere of stability, safety, and continuity. In the context of sexually intimate relationships, the principal way (though, as I will argue, it does not have to be the only way) through which our society seeks to provide the necessary support and conditions is through the institution of companionate marriage. It is primarily through that institution that our society encourages us to construct our lives around love for and commitment to another human being in order to meet the needs and provide for the well-being (emotional, physical, and material) of ourselves and of that other.

(The understanding of marriage that I present here is an admittedly normative and idealized one. The descriptive reality of marriage for many women differs from this understanding given the way in which marital roles in the United States have undermined rather than promoted women's needs and capabilities. As I will argue in more detail later in this chapter, however, a normative and to some extent aspirational understanding of marriage is not inconsistent with a forceful critique of the patriarchal practices that have been improperly promoted and defended through the institution of marriage.)

Through the institution of marriage, society encourages us to be less egoistic, to live for another person at the same time that we live for ourselves. One of the truly magical characteristics of love is that it allows for an expansion of the self. When a person loves another, she begins to see that other as an extension of herself. The object of love does not prioritize the welfare of the subject over her own as much as she sees it as an extension of her welfare.[73] Although this kind of deep affection and commitment can, of course, exist outside of a socially recognized relationship such as the marital one, commitment "may be more comfortably sustained and reciprocating love more easily offered where personal feelings are reinforced and expectations are coordinated by social institutions."[74] Public recognition of relationships also makes it clear that there is an identifiable individual (a "spouse" or a "parent," for example) whose responsibility it is to care for the well-being of another. That public recognition, when it is accompanied by social support and encouragement, makes it more likely that the relevant responsibilities will be met. The structure that marriage provides, and the obligations that it requires, then, can strengthen and make more durable the affectional components of sexual intimacy that are characterized by ongoing commitment and mutuality. The socially recognized marital relationship can provide the structure through which the well-being of the partner becomes inextricably linked to the well-being of the self as "the boundary between self and other becomes blurred."[75] By creating and promoting an institution such as companionate marriage, our society encourages (though, of course, by no means guarantees) the kind of self-expansion that most frequently takes place in committed sexually intimate relationships. This is the potentially enduring value of a relationship such as the marital one; it potentially allows for self-definition and self-expansion through love and commitment for another human being in a relationship whose very purpose is to provide for the satisfaction and exercise of physical and emotional needs and capabilities in the context of long-term reciprocity and mutuality.

Through an institution such as the marital one, an individual's life becomes inextricably linked with that of another so that both individuals to-

gether seek to lead full and autonomous lives. As we saw in the previous section, moral liberalism recognizes that individuals' exercise of autonomy often depends on their ability to enter into and remain in caring relationships in which they receive support, encouragement, and guidance. The marital relationship provides a structure and a means for a form of care that has the potential to be deep and enduring and that allows individuals to make decisions about their lives and futures with the support and assistance of another. The right to marry, then, is not about the right to be left alone or to exercise one's autonomy in the traditional liberal sense of making decisions that affect no one but ourselves. Yes, marriage is about choosing a partner to share one's life and to have that choice recognized and supported by society. But the good and autonomy that is gained through that choice is inseparable from the needs of and concerns for another person. The institution of companionate marriage is the principal way in which our society encourages and provides for that unique sense of satisfaction and intimacy that accompanies the sharing of one's life with another. If we accept that both our well-being and freedom are dependent on the human relationships that make our lives meaningful, purposeful, and worthwhile, then no socially recognized relationship in our culture has the potential for promoting lives with those characteristics as does the marital one (with the possible exception of the parent-child relationship, which I will discuss at the end of this chapter).

It is for these reasons that the traditional liberal position in matters of intimate relationships, summarized by calls to "leave people alone" and to "get the government out of people's bedrooms," proves to be an inadequate justification for the imposition on society of an obligation to recognize and support committed same-gender relationships. Principles of political philosophy that are limited to ideas of neutrality and noninterference on the part of the state do not obligate the recognition and support of *any* relationship. On the other hand, if our political morality is conscious of the role that social institutions and policies play in the ability of individuals to meet basic human needs and exercise basic human capabilities, then we can better understand why that morality demands more of the state than simply the protection of people's choices; it also requires the *provision* of them. The choice to participate in durable and committed long-term sexual relationships is much more likely to be real and meaningful if there are social institutions and policies that support and provide for them.

I want to make it clear that I am not arguing that considerations of governmental toleration and noninterference in matters of sexuality and relationships are peripheral to the promotion and protection of personal autonomy. Clearly, meaningful freedoms on such matters would be impossible if there were police present in people's bedrooms. An absence of governmental coercion and intimidation is necessary if individuals are to enjoy freedom and autonomy in their personal lives. I pay relatively

little attention to that issue in this book because there is strong agreement on that point among proponents of gay rights. Furthermore, as
mentioned in the introduction, even some conservatives who are otherwise skeptical of gay rights positions recognize that lesbians and gay men
are entitled to a right to privacy and to be left alone. The much more interesting and difficult questions have to do with the *affirmative* obligations of the state in matters of intimate relationships. Clearly, as long as
it remains constitutional for the state to criminalize same-gender sexual
ity (as long, in other words, as *Bowers v. Hardwick* remains good law)
and as long, for example, as the police in some parts of the country continue to harass lesbians and gay men while providing them with insufficient protection from the harassment of others, ideals of negative liberty
will and should continue to play a crucial part of gay rights positions and
their moral and political justifications. My point is that those considerations of negative liberty are a necessary but insufficient way of attaining
the kind of full equality and acceptance that many lesbians and gay men
are today asking of society.

I also want to make it clear that I am not suggesting that love and
long-term commitment in sexually intimate relationships are impossible
to achieve in the absence of societal recognition and support. In fact, I
will in chapter 5, when discussing the meaning of a gay and lesbian sexual ethic, explore the ways in which many lesbians and gay men have
constructed strong and durable relationships, friendships, and communities on the basis of care and mutuality largely in the absence of social
structures and support. The fact that many lesbians and gay men have
been able to persevere as best they can in the face of deep social hostility,
however, does not exempt society from its obligations to promote and
protect the basic human needs and capabilities of all of its citizens. Lesbians and gay men know from personal experience the pain, suffering,
and harm that the *absence* of social recognition of their relationships can
inflict on their personal and emotional lives. Our society, by depriving
lesbians and gay men of the opportunity to avail themselves of marriage,
the principal way in which it seeks to protect and promote basic human
needs and capabilities associated with physical and emotional intimacy in
long-term relationships, fails to recognize and provide for the full humanity of lesbians and gay men. Such a failure is immoral.

Finally, I want to emphasize again that I am not arguing that marriage
itself is a basic human need and that it is for that reason that lesbians and
gay men must be allowed to marry. The institution of companionate
marriage is simply that: an institution. It has no moral significance as an
end—instead, it is a means through which many individuals in our society who are in committed relationships satisfy basic needs and exercise
basic capabilities associated with physical and emotional intimacy. What
merits moral attention is not the institution itself, but rather the human
needs and capabilities that it is meant to account for. If we believe that

Egalitarian = asserting — promoting — or married by equality

lesbians and gay men share with heterosexuals distinctive human attributes and potentialities for enduring and enriching commitment, care, and mutuality from within sexually intimate relationships, then they should be granted access to the primary social institution that is meant to nurture and provide for those attributes and potentialities.

There are some, of course, who argue that a gay and lesbian sexuality is inconsistent with an appropriate or acceptable exercise of human sexuality. Before I explain and seek to refute the arguments made by some conservative opponents of same-sex marriage as to why a gay and lesbian sexuality is *not* entitled to moral respect, and thus why the differential treatment by society of gay and lesbian relationships is justified, I want to first address the arguments made by some on the left as to why marriage should be neither a moral nor a political aspiration for lesbians and gay men.

The Left Critique of Same-Sex Marriage. Some feminists and queer theorists are highly skeptical of the institution of marriage in general and of the priority that the gay rights movement has recently given to winning state recognition of same-sex marriage in particular.[76] These critics argue that the institution of marriage should be rejected altogether because it has historically played such a prominent role in the subordination of women. The left critics are also troubled by attempts to privilege distinct forms of intimate relationships because to do so, they argue, inevitably leads to the coercion and stigmatization of those who remain outside of the socially privileged relationships. I address both of these objections below.

There is nothing about the argument that social institutions such as marriage are an important part of promoting commitment, loyalty, and stability in human relationships—and thus a vital component in the ability of individuals to satisfy basic needs and to exercise basic capabilities associated with physical and emotional intimacy—that requires us to accept the way in which those values have been historically promoted in the United States through patriarchal and inegalitarian marital norms. As Cheshire Calhoun notes, what is at stake in the debate over same-sex marriage (as well as in the one over parenting by lesbians and gay men) is not "the right to participate in a traditional form of family life but the right to *define* what counts as a family."[77] Lesbians and gay men have shown that their relationships are more egalitarian and less role-driven than are heterosexual relationships and there is no reason to believe that that will change when they are eventually offered the opportunity to marry.[78] There is no reason to believe, in other words, that lesbians and gay men will adopt the traditional patriarchal and inegalitarian marital norms that feminists and queer theorists justifiably criticize. Furthermore, although same-gender relationships are in general more egalitarian than heterosexual ones, it cannot be disputed that countless heterosexual couples have in the last few decades constructed marriages characterized

Even if this became the new norm, still this will be exactly "gaya" — the norms are quite the others (individual interests) excercised.

Not an argument
No reason to believe they will not

by egalitarianism and respect where both parties are able to lead mutually
fulfilling and satisfying lives.[79] The existence of these marriages, even if
they constitute a minority of heterosexual marriages, belie the idea that
marriage is an inherently patriarchal and inegalitarian institution that
makes it so uniquely tainted that it is beyond the grasp of reform.

The philosopher Claudia Card argues that given the patriarchal history and norms that define marriage as a social institution, to point out
that there is true love and commitment in some heterosexual marriages
is akin to arguing that there was devotion and mutual respect in some
slave-owner relationships.[80] What Card is suggesting, in effect, is that it
is impossible for *any* woman to experience and realize a true mutuality in
a heterosexual marital relationship regardless of how committed she and
her male partner are to each other's needs and vulnerabilities. Although
I agree with the view that marriage in the United States has played a
nefarious role in the subordination of women (an issue to which I will
return when I discuss some of the social consequences that will follow
the recognition by the state of same-sex marriage), I think that Card is
too pessimistic about the ability of heterosexual spouses to create egalitarian relationships defined by mutual love and respect even in the face
of social norms that encourage and support gender inegalitarianism and
subordination within marriage. There is, in fact, a similarity between
Card's argument and the one made by conservative new natural law
philosophers, who, as we will see below, contend that it is impossible for
any lesbian or gay man to experience and realize a true mutuality in a
marital relationship regardless of how committed she or he is to the
partner's needs and vulnerabilities. The critique of same-sex marriage
from the left paints with too broad a brush in arguing that marriage is
inherently patriarchal and inegalitarian in the same way that critics on
the right paint with too broad a brush in arguing that lesbians and gay
men are incapable of enjoying and participating in the kind of mutual
love and care that are supposed to define committed relationships such
as the marital one.

As for the antiprivileging part of the left critique of marriage, I understand the intuition of wanting to avoid the kinds of normative judgments that are required when deciding which intimate relationships to
privilege. On its face, the argument that the state should support and
encourage *all* relationships seems appealing. Why should the state pick
and choose?

In formulating a response to this argument, it is first interesting to
note that the kind of neutrality that some feminists and queer theorists
demand in the area of intimate relationships is one that they reject in almost every other area of social policy. These critics reject arguments of
state neutrality in matters of racial and gender inequality, for example,
because they correctly associate strict neutrality with oppression and the
status quo. In the area of race, strict neutrality means the application of

"color-blind" norms that deem even the most modest affirmative action programs to be unacceptable forms of racial discrimination. In the area of gender, strict neutrality means making sure that the state does not interfere with what is considered to be a private familial sphere, a position that, as I have noted, has contributed immensely to the oppression of women. In the areas of race and gender regulation, in other words, the left critics are quite comfortable with asking for state implementation of a particular moral vision that requires its active participation in eliminating the sources of oppression and in creating the necessary social conditions that will promote the full and unsubordinated equality of racial minorities and women. And yet, when it comes to determining which intimate relationships to privilege, many of the same critics on the left demand a form of strict neutrality from the state that requires it to recognize and support either all or none.

If our moral focus is, as it should be, on the basic needs and capabilities of individuals, then I believe it is appropriate for the state to promote and encourage those intimate relationships, both sexual and familial, that are able to provide for them. It is not unreasonable for the state, which in our society has the responsibility to define who is "married" and who is a "parent," to prioritize intimate relationships where a kind of commitment and mutuality is likely to exist that makes it possible for individuals, through those relationships, to meet several of their basic human needs and exercise several of their basic human capabilities. This does not mean that *only one* kind of relationship or familial arrangement should be privileged; but it does mean that distinctions in these matters are appropriate. One such distinction that may be appropriate is one between polygamous heterosexual relationships and committed same-gender relationships. Whereas the former, at least in this country, have been built around traditional gender roles and a pronounced disparity of power between the partners, committed gay and lesbian relationships, the social science studies tell us, are rather impressively egalitarian. It is more likely, therefore, that the parties in a committed same-gender relationship will be able to meet their basic needs and exercise their basic capabilities associated with physical and emotional intimacy than the parties (in particular, the women) in heterosexual polygamous relationships, at least as traditionally carried out in this country. Although I will leave it to others to criticize (or defend) state recognition of polygamous marriages in more detail,[81] the point I want to emphasize is that these are the kinds of distinctions that in my estimation a state may properly make in deciding which intimate relationships to recognize and support (as opposed to merely tolerate). It is impossible to make these kinds of distinctions if we demand that the state always remain neutral as to the value of different kinds of relationships.

None of this means, however, that the state has to meet its obligations to provide the necessary structures and support for committed relationships through marriage as it has traditionally been conceived, or even for that matter, through marriage exclusively. Civil unions, domestic partnerships, and other forms of relationships where there is likely to be commitment and mutuality also merit state support and recognition because they can also be important vehicles through which individuals meet and express some of their basic human needs and capabilities. The battle in our society is currently over companionate marriage because it is primarily through that institution that our social norms and laws encourage long-term commitment in sexually intimate relationships.

The precise ways in which the state privileges and encourages some relationships over others should always be open to debate; that is, after all, what the same-sex marriage dispute is all about. What should be recognized, however, is that the state has an interest in creating and an obligation to promote the necessary institutions and conditions that encourage long-term commitment and mutuality in intimate relationships. In order to exercise its interests and meet its obligations, the state cannot abide by a kind of strict neutrality that would require it to support equally all intimate relationships. We could, of course, ask that the state not give support to *any* relationship, but that takes us right back to the problem that basic needs and capabilities, including those associated with physical and emotional intimacy, are much more difficult to satisfy and exercise in the absence of institutions and policies that are specifically created for those purposes. Instead of embracing an ideology of strict neutrality (of which feminists and queer theorists are usually highly skeptical), critics on the left would be better served by continuing to contribute to the reform of social institutions and practices associated with the family as they currently exist in order to make them more humane and more inclusive.

A recognition that commitment and mutuality in sexually intimate relationships are valuable because they contribute to the meeting of some human needs and the exercise of some human capabilities, and that the state should therefore seek to privilege relationships characterized by such commitment and mutuality, does not require the adoption of rules and norms that oppress those who decide not to participate in socially privileged relationships. In fact, the best way to address the threat of coercion and stigmatization of those who decide not to participate in socially privileged relationships (however defined) is not by eliminating social institutions that are meant to promote commitment and mutuality in human relationships but is instead to make those institutions more inclusive. Those who decide not to participate in socially privileged relationships (whether marital or otherwise) will then do so on the basis of what they believe is best for them, rather than because they were denied access based on an assumption by others that they are not capable of the kind of commitment and mutuality that the social institutions are meant to promote and protect. It seems to me that most of the stigma associated with nontraditional relationships emanates from that assumption—one that in effect questions the basic humanity of their participants—rather than from any intrinsic characteristic of social institutions such as marriage. A willingness to reach normative evaluations about the good of long-term commitment and mutuality in human relationships must be accompanied by a deep respect for personal autonomy and a recognition that it is ultimately up to individuals to decide how they want to structure and conduct their intimate lives. The idea that the state should promote loyalty, stability, and reciprocity in human relationships is not inconsistent with the idea that individuals are the best judges of what is most appropriate for their personal lives. That is the balance that moral liberalism tries to strike, and one that is consistent with both the recognition by the state of same-sex marriage and with the need for pluralism and diversity in matters of the human heart and the human body.

Critics on the left fear that if same-sex marriages are recognized, the targets of oppressive and normalizing sexual mores will simply change from all lesbians and gay men to those individuals (both straight and gay) who remain unmarried. Although such a concern is legitimate, the empirical evidence on this issue is reassuring. As Bill Eskridge points out, those nations (such as the Netherlands and Denmark) and American states (such as Vermont and Hawaii) that have seriously considered recognizing same-sex marriage, have as part of that process recognized different kinds of relationships that are not marital (such as domestic partnerships, reciprocal beneficiaries, and civil unions).[82] When political communities have taken the debate over same-sex marriage seriously, in other words, the result has not been to continue dividing the population into two neat and distinct categories (the married and the unmarried), but has been instead to recognize new kinds of relationships with varying degrees of rights and responsibilities. The availability of these new kinds of legally recognized relationships—which is the result of gay rights activism as well as the changing cohabiting patterns of heterosexuals—should be particularly welcomed by those who are most concerned about the oppressive and gender-subordinating history of traditional marriage.

Having raised the issue of alternatives to marriage, I want to address briefly the particular option offered by civil unions. That alternative has become a reality at least in Vermont, where the legislature, under orders from the state Supreme Court,[83] recently created the new institution of civil unions. Although lesbians and gay men are still not permitted to marry in Vermont, and though they are not eligible to receive the myriad of federal benefits (ranging from social security payments to tax breaks) that Vermont married couples are entitled to receive, the institution of civil unions provides those lesbians and gay men who join it with all of the rights and benefits (as well as obligations) that the state of Vermont provides to (or requires of) married couples.

This is just another way of allowing for benefits to gays + les. since the "term" marriage is still withheld

If society has a moral obligation to provide the necessary institutions and policies that make it possible for all human beings (including lesbians and gay men) to meet their basic needs and exercise their basic capabilities (including those associated with emotional and physical intimacy), the issue for us then becomes whether that obligation is satisfied through an alternative institution such as civil unions as opposed to through the recognition of same-sex marriage. I think it is still too early to answer that question with any certainty because we do not yet know what the meaning and impact of civil unions will be in our society. On the one hand, there are some who argue that civil unions are inadequate because there remains a two-tiered system whereby society continues to exclude lesbians and gay men from the most privileged form of socially recognized intimate relationships, namely, the marital one.[84] On the other hand, there are some who argue that civil unions are an appealing way for lesbians and gay men to enjoy the same legal benefits that heterosexual married couples enjoy while retaining the egalitarianism and distinctiveness of gay relationships.[85] From the perspective of moral liberalism, there is no obligation to recognize a particular institution such as same-sex marriage as long as the necessary social structures and conditions exist that provide for the meeting of basic needs and the exercise of basic capabilities associated with physical and emotional intimacy. If civil unions end up providing the necessary structure, security, and permanence for committed same-gender intimate relationships without stigmatizing or demeaning those relationships, then civil unions will be an acceptable alternative. Time will tell.

The Right Critique of Same-Sex Marriage. If some feminists and queer theorists on the left are skeptical of attempts to privilege particular kinds of intimate relationships by deeming them marital, many on the right believe that it is the immorality or abnormality of a gay and lesbian sexuality that makes lesbians and gay men ineligible to participate in socially privileged relationships such as the marital one. When asked whether the love, commitment, respect, and affection that a man feels for another man or a woman feels for another woman in a sexually intimate relationship can be as valuable, self-expanding, and other-regarding as it can be for heterosexuals, many opponents of same-sex marriage insist that it cannot. The legal philosopher John Finnis, for example, argues that same-gender sexual acts are not "a humanly appropriate use of sexual capacities."[86] He adds that to recognize and support same-gender intimate relationships "is to endorse an important falsehood about what is good for human persons."[87]

As some conservatives see it, then, when lesbians and gay men say that they love and are committed to their same-gender partners, or, for that matter, that they are capable of providing their children with a care that is both loving and healthy, it may appear as if they are doing nothing more than expressing their humanity, but what they are doing, really, is dressing up their abnormal and harmful behavior in the trappings of marital and parental responsibility. It is in this way that lesbians and gay men are denied the opportunity to share in those institutions (such as marriage and parenthood) that are meant to provide and account for the needs and capabilities of individuals to share their physical and emotional intimate lives with others. In this section, I address the moral objections to same-gender sexual intimacy, objections that translate into opposition to state recognition of same-sex marriage on moral grounds. I leave until the next section a discussion of some of the consequentialist objections to same-sex marriage that are based on the effects of such a recognition on society.

The philosophers who these days are presenting the most forceful moral objections to same-gender sexual intimacy are the new natural law theorists. Finnis is the most prominent among them. He believes that there are certain forms of basic goods that are always part of human flourishing. Finnis defines basic goods as those that are not reducible to the pursuit of other goods. Basic goods for Finnis are self-evidently good rather than being so in an empirical, historical, or demonstrable way.[88] For Finnis, the value in the choices and pursuits available to us is determined by their ability to help us realize the basic goods. He identifies the following as basic goods: life, knowledge, play, aesthetic experience, sociability (or friendship), practical reasoning, and religion.[89] Finnis has also at times written of (heterosexual) marriage as a basic good; it is in that context that he discusses the immorality of all same-gender sexual conduct.[90] Although Finnis has never explicitly connected his list of basic goods to a comprehensive theory of political morality, it is clear that he believes the state has an obligation to promote the attainment of basic goods and to discourage practices that make their realization less likely.

Before discussing Finnis's understanding of same-gender sexual acts and the ways in which they are, according to him, incompatible with marriage as a basic good, I want to first note the differences between the idea of human flourishing as held by moral liberalism and that of new natural law (NNL). A supporter of the kind of neutral liberalism discussed in chapter 1 or of the form of pragmatic liberalism explored in chapter 2 may be tempted to dismiss moral liberalism as a somewhat sanitized version of NNL. The liberal critic of moral liberalism may point to Finnis's ideas as an example of how an incorporation of notions of human flourishing into considerations of political morality can quickly disintegrate into illiberal ideas and practices. That is why, the liberal critic may argue, we need to abide by the minimalistic neutral liberalism of John Rawls or the minimalistic skeptical liberalism of Richard Rorty.

It is true that both moral liberalism and NNL speak in terms of human flourishing. It is also correct that human flourishing has political ramifications for both perspectives that translate into positive and negative state obligations. The scope of and justification for those obligations, however, are very different. Moral liberalism, as explained earlier, places the highest normative priority on the individual. It is the needs and capabilities of each individual that matter; the role of the state is to create the conditions that make it possible for all individuals to satisfy their basic needs and exercise their basic capabilities. How individuals choose to do so (or even *whether* they choose to do so) is no business of the state as long as others are not harmed in the process. This is a very different theory of state action from the one advanced by NNL, which holds that the state has an obligation to promote a particular kind of (virtuous) life, namely, that which is consistent with the pursuit of the basic goods. New natural law is concerned with *actual* functionings as opposed to opportunities to function. Moral liberalism holds that the state meets its obligations as long as the necessary opportunities are made available for individuals to lead fully human lives in the myriad of ways in which leading such lives is possible. For NNL, opportunities are meaningless unless individuals actually behave in certain ways, namely, in ways that are consistent with the basic goods. The goal for NNL, then, is the promotion of a particular form of living, one that treats the basic goods as synonymous with virtue and the good (or best possible) life. Moral liberalism, on the other hand, does not believe that the state should be in the business of "making men moral" and considers such promotion as antithetical to personal autonomy.[91] The state meets its moral obligations engendered by the potential for flourishing that human beings share when it provides its citizens with opportunities to meet basic human needs and exercise basic human capabilities. It would be inconsistent with the tenets of moral liberalism, therefore, to view the institution of marriage as having an intrinsic value (as proponents of NNL argue) that is independent of the human needs and capabilities that that institution is meant to foster and promote.

New natural law, with its "self-evident" truths about the intrinsic value and characteristics of marriage (as I will discuss), conceives of marriage as a natural institution rather than a socially constructed one. For NNL proponents, as well as for many other conservatives, when the state protects and promotes heterosexual marriage (and the nuclear family) it is simply recognizing that which exists prior to society and thus is in essential ways pre-political.[92] We can, in fact, think of NNL as being at the other end of the spectrum from postmodernist theory, which, as we will see in chapter 5, holds that everything that is of philosophical or moral interest is socially constructed. For postmodernists, not only are institutions such as marriage socially constructed, but so are the individuals who participate in them. There is for postmodernists no parts of individuals that can be separated in any meaningful or understandable way from social networks of power, knowledge, and discourse. Moral liberalism stands between these two poles. It argues that there are some needs and capabilities of human beings that transcend society-specific contexts and that are thus recognizable, even as they are manifested in particular and distinct ways, through time and place. On the other hand, moral liberalism believes that institutions that nurture and provide for those shared human traits are socially constructed means subject to local variation and specifications. What is "pre-political," then, what merits universal moral respect, are the attributes that define us as human. Institutions such as marriage are simply tools through which society allows, encourages, and promotes the expression of our humanity. As a social institution, marriage should be as subject to criticism, revision, and, when appropriate, expansion as any other institution. The moral focus of conservative opponents of same-sex marriage is, in the end, misplaced. Their focus is on the purported intrinsic goodness of a social institution as currently defined rather than on the human attributes and potentialities that that institution is meant to account for.

Another important difference between moral liberalism and NNL is that the former, as I have discussed, finds moral value not in *a priori* principles or truths but in the basic needs and capabilities of human beings as determined through interpretation of human history and experience. Moral liberalism requires us, for example, to pay attention to the stories told by lesbians and gay men about their intimate lives to see if we can glean similarities between those experiences and the ones of heterosexuals. Are there common needs and capabilities between homosexuals and heterosexuals in matters of physical and emotional intimacy? Is it possible to speak of commonalities in human sexual relationships that transcend both membership in particular societies and the gender of the parties? What do people's real lives tell us about those commonalities? The kind of universalism that moral liberalism seeks, in other words, is one that is internal to human experience. For NNL, on the other hand, the basic goods that are essential for human flourishing are considered to be self-evident, arrived at through a form of practical reasoning that is independent of descriptions and interpretations of actual human experiences. This epistemological difference between moral liberalism and NNL is crucial because, as I argue below, only by closing itself off from the experiences of real human beings can NNL arrive at the conclusion that it is impossible for same-gender couples to attain a level of mutuality through their sexual intimacy that is real and meaningful.

Now that I have explained the important differences between moral liberalism and NNL, I turn to a discussion of how the latter understands the intrinsic value of marriage and the corresponding intrinsic immorality of same-gender sexual relationships. Finnis in his scholarship seeks to show that all same-gender sexual acts, regardless of context or of the (self-perceived) mutuality between the partners, are immoral. For Finnis, only sexual intimacy that takes place within the institution of heterosexual marriage is morally acceptable. As he puts it, "[g]enital intercourse between spouses enables them to actualize and experience (and in that sense express) their marriage itself, as a single reality with two blessings (children and mutual affection). Non-marital intercourse, especially but not only homosexual, has no such point and therefore is unacceptable."[93] Finnis's argument, then, is that: (1) marital union is only available where children and real mutuality are possible; (2) same-gender sexual acts can neither lead to children nor to the attainment of real mutuality between the partners; (3) same-gender sexual acts, therefore, are not about attaining the goods associated with marriage but are instead about using the human body instrumentally in order to experience physical pleasure.[94] This use of the human body is immoral because it is done for its own sake rather than to actualize or experience a real human good. Finnis's conclusion about the intrinsic immorality of all same-gender sexual acts has political implications: Because those acts are only about the pursuit of pleasure, they are a form of vice that the state is entitled to discourage. The state should not recognize or privilege relationships that are about nothing more than the pursuit of pleasure.

The first difficulty that Finnis's moral argument faces has to do with children. There was a time when raising children distinguished long-term heterosexual relationships from same-gender ones. But children these days can be part of a committed same-gender union in a myriad of ways, with adoption, the use of donated sperm by a lesbian couple, and the reliance on a surrogate mother by a gay male couple serving as the most obvious examples. The fact that thousands upon thousands of gay and lesbian couples in the United States are either currently raising children together or are planning to do so in the near future means that the children/no children distinction no longer categorically distinguishes gay from straight committed relationships, a problem (for conservatives) that is likely to become even more evident in the future. The moral priority for Finnis, however, lies not in whether two individuals are raising a child together, but on whether the two individuals *through their sexual acts* have created (or, as we will see below, have the *potential* for creating) a child. Much of the moral opposition to same-sex marriage is grounded in the inability of lesbians and gay men to create a new human being through their sexual acts, which undermines what for many is an essential connection between marriage and reproduction. In fact, the ability to reproduce appeals instinctually to NNL proponents because it would seem to be *the* criterion that distinguishes the sexual intimacy they condone (uncontracepted penile-vaginal intercourse) from the kind they condemn (e.g., sodomy).

As we have understood for several centuries since at least the writings of David Hume, attempts to make moral arguments about what *ought to be* based on what *is*—arguments that philosophers call naturalistic fallacies—are doomed from the start.[95] The mere fact, for example, that anthropologists and historians tell us that same-gender sex can be found in just about every known culture does not by itself render that sex moral or valuable. Similarly, *the fact* that many men and women can use their sexual organs to reproduce is no more morally relevant than *the fact* that gay and lesbian couples, like sterile or elderly heterosexual couples, cannot. New natural law proponents would seem at first to avoid naturalistic fallacies when they contend that the *actual* capability to reproduce is not what is morally relevant. They must do this in order to include within their conception of moral sex the penile-vaginal intercourse of sterile or elderly couples. They do not, however, stray too far from the finding of moral value in what is "natural" because they argue that although actual reproduction is not morally relevant, *how* sexual organs are used is. As long as reproductive sexual organs are used *as if* they were, in fact, reproductive, then the sexual conduct can be moral. In other words, what ends up mattering morally to NNL proponents, and what ends up distinguishing, in part, between marital and nonmarital relationships, is whether the sexual acts in question are "acts of the reproductive kind" since those are the only ones that can (regardless of whether they do in any particular instance) lead to reproduction.[96] It is only reproductive-like sexual acts that can lead to the creation of "a real organic union," a union that can only be formed between individuals with different and complementary sexual organs.[97] According to NNL, only through penile-vaginal intercourse is there a "unitary action in which the male and the female become literally one organism."[98] The sexual acts of lesbians and gay men, it is argued, "cannot make them a biological (and therefore personal) unit."[99]

This is all terribly mysterious. What is a biological unit? What is the connection between a biological unit and a personal unit? What matters morally to NNL is not actual reproduction, but the formation of a biological union that is apparently *only* possible through what are considered to be the *natural functionings* of certain bodily organs. We are not, however, given a definition of a "real organic union" that is normative. The only definition that we are given is a biological or physiological one, namely, it exists when one of several male sexual organs (the penis) is brought together with one of several female sexual organs (the vagina). If actual reproduction is not what matters normatively, then it is not at all clear why *nonreproductive* penile-vaginal intercourse by a sterile couple forms a biological union (and therefore a personal union) whereas *nonreproductive* same-gender sexual intercourse does not. In the end, the NNL argument seems to be based on what its proponents think is a self-evident intuition that penile-vaginal intercourse is natural whereas oral and anal sex are not; but there is no discernable *moral* argument left standing once NNL concedes that the capability to actually reproduce does not by itself allow us to distinguish between morally acceptable and unacceptable sexual acts.

That the capability to actually reproduce does not provide us with the required normative bite should not surprise us. What is at issue in assessments of the value of sexually intimate relationships goes deeper than the ability of the sexual partners to reproduce, or, for that matter, the ability or willingness to use sexual organs in certain prescribed ways. Although reproduction is, of course, necessary for the survival of the species, it is not a need or capability that determines whether particular forms of sexual expression, to quote Finnis again, are "a humanly appropriate use of sexual capacities."[100] What answers that question are the distinctly human attributes associated with emotions, vulnerabilities, and affiliations that accompany the use of our sexual capacities. It is for this reason that a moral conception of human sexuality that focuses so intently on what are considered to be the natural functions of bodily organs that uniquely lead to the formation of a "biological union" is highly reductionist. It reduces the full panoply of human aspirations and potentialities in matters of sexual intimacy to the use of two sexual organs in one particular way. (I will return to this issue in chapter 5, where I distinguish Finnis's conception of sexual morality that is based, in part, on the creation of a hierarchy of sexual acts with a gay and lesbian sexual ethic that rejects such a hierarchy.)

The conservative philosopher Roger Scruton, though not a proponent of NNL, has tried to articulate a moral argument critical of same-gender sexual intimacy based not on the physical complementarity between men and women that allows them to form a "biological union," but instead on the differences associated with gender attributes and characteristics. Thus Scruton argues that "in a world structured by gender, the other sex is forever a mystery to us."[101] Heterosexual intimacy, therefore, is a way of exposing ourselves to and challenging ourselves with the "strangeness" of the other. On the other hand, same-gender sexual intimacy is morally suspect because it is narcissistic: "In the heterosexual act, it might be said, I move out *from* my body towards the other, whose flesh is unknown to me; while in the homosexual act I remain locked within my body, narcissistically contemplating in the other an excitement that mirrors my own."[102]

Scruton's argument relating to the "narcissism" of same-gender intimacy, though not dependent on reproductive (or reproductive-like) sexual acts, is also highly reductive because it divides the entire human race into two neat and self-contained categories. The argument is based on the idea that if our sexual partner is of the same gender as we are, then his or her personal attributes, characteristics, and interests will be so similar to ours that there would be no real value in pursuing the kind of deep and meaningful mutuality that can accompany physical intimacy. According to this view, loving someone of the same gender is like loving our reflection in a mirror; it is more about loving ourselves than about loving another. Unfortunately for Scruton's view, human beings are (thankfully) much more complex creatures than it allows for. To suggest that there is no mystery or otherness in a sexual partner of the same gender is to reduce the full extent of human complexity and diversity to a handful of socially constructed gender traits. Differences based on sexual organs and gender attributes pale in comparison to the differences in interests, sensibilities, motivations, and aspirations among human beings. The reductionist moral perspective offered by NNL and Scruton serves the conservative purpose of trying, however desperately, to link sexual morality to sexual or gender distinctiveness. It presents us, however, with an unconvincing and highly simplified conception of what it means to be human.

New natural law proponents will undoubtedly defend themselves from the reductionist charge by arguing that what matters morally is not the use of sexual organs in a particular way but is instead the kind of unique "communion, companionship, *societas* and *amicitia*" that heterosexual spouses enjoy.[103] But the crucial point that they make is this: *Only when individuals engage in penile-vaginal intercourse are they able to actualize and realize* their relationships in such a way that makes their companionship and friendship valuable and distinct enough to be deemed marital in nature. Thus, NNL proponents Patrick Lee and Robert George argue that only heterosexuals through the act of coitus are able to connect their "bodily unity" with their "emotional and spiritual unity."[104] Lesbians and gay men, on the other hand, cannot, as Finnis puts it, "do what they may hope and imagine. Because their activation of one or even each of their reproductive organs cannot be an actualizing and experiencing of the marital good . . . [their sexual acts] can do no more than provide each partner with an individual gratification."[105] For Finnis, then, the mutuality that lesbians and gay men feel for each other is false and illusory; same-gender sexual acts, regardless of however much affection lesbians and gay men may think they feel for each other, are as morally worthless as, in Finnis's examples, masturbating or visiting a prostitute: it is all about using the body instrumentally in order to obtain individual gratification and physical pleasure rather than using it to attain true mutuality.[106]

New natural law theorists assure us that sexual pleasure itself is not the problem; the problem is when individuals seek to pursue sexual pleasure only for its own sake.[107] But the argument that lesbians and gay men always use their bodies instrumentally is unpersuasive. In chapter 5, I will explain how lesbians and gay men use sexual pleasure to transform themselves into ethical subjects in the face of societal oppression and animosity. But even more fundamentally, it is simply untrue that lesbians and gay men are incapable of attaining a real and meaningful mutuality through physical intimacy. The lives and experiences of lesbians and gay men tell us a very different story than the one told by the so-called self-evident truths of NNL. Those lives and experiences, as almost anyone who has a lesbian or gay man as a friend or family member knows, include meaningful and loving sexually intimate relationships. The social science studies of gay and lesbian relationships confirm that view.[108]

Lesbians and gay men use their sexual capacities in the same ways as do heterosexuals, namely, in order to create, express, and experience mutuality. Sometimes that mutuality is limited in duration to the sexual encounter itself, as when same-gender sexual partners who are not in an ongoing emotional relationship treat each other with respect and concern during sex. At other times, the mutuality extends to an emotional connection that goes beyond the sexual acts themselves. For countless gay and lesbian couples, sexual intimacy is valued not just for the sexual pleasure it provides, but for the bonds of affection and commitment that they simultaneously represent and engender. Only those who are so removed from and have no exposure to the daily lives of lesbians and gay men could possibly think otherwise. The moral conclusions of NNL in matters of same-gender sexuality are a good example of the dangers of making moral evaluations that are delinked from the lives of actual human beings and of the stories that they tell. The commitment, loyalty, trust, and affection—or to put it more succinctly, the love—that can be part of sexually intimate gay and lesbian relationships show how the sexuality of lesbians and gay men, like the sexuality of heterosexuals, is part of their humanity.

There is admittedly something intellectually unsatisfying about a debate in which one side contends that those who engage in same-gender sexual acts are incapable of actualizing and realizing true mutuality while the other side argues that they can. I suppose a skeptic like Richard Rorty could point to this fundamental disagreement to support the position that debates about what it means to be human are all hopeless anyway. Moral liberalism has no illusion that the deep moral chasm between, for example, NNL and lesbians and gay men can ever be bridged or reconciled. But the hope is not that John Finnis will be persuaded; the hope is that those who have heretofore quickly dismissed same-gender sexuality as immoral might be encouraged to consider the possibility that lesbians and gay men share with them human needs and capabilities associated with physical and emotional intimacy, a recognition that might serve as a means for finding moral and political common ground. The hope and expectation are that despite the efforts by some to claim "self-evident" moral differences, many if not most heterosexuals will eventually permit themselves to recognize, appreciate, and value the full humanity of lesbians and gay men, part of which they express and attain through their sexuality.

The Consequences for Society of Same-Sex Marriage. A discussion of the value of same-sex relationships and marriage would be incomplete without addressing the societal consequences of their recognition by the state. I believe that such a recognition will be good for society in at least two ways: (1) it will contribute to making marriage into a less patriarchal (and therefore more egalitarian) institution with positive ramifications for all of society and especially for women; and (2) it will provide greater stability to same-gender relationships, an especially important consideration given the large number of lesbians and gay men who are either having or adopting children. I discuss both of these points briefly below. I also address two of the principal consequentialist objections to same-sex marriage raised by opponents: (1) the idea that marriage as currently defined serves as a foundation for civil society and thus is crucial to the social order; and (2) the fear that the recognition of same-sex marriage will encourage promiscuity and sexual licentiousness. A third set of consequentialist (and moral) arguments raised by opponents of same-sex marriage involves the well-being of children. I begin to address those arguments in the next section of this chapter, and return to them in the last section of chapter 4.

In an era when the deontological liberalism of thinkers such as Rawls and Dworkin still reigns supreme, it is perhaps tempting to argue in favor of same-sex marriage only from the perspective of what is right without incorporating notions of what is good for society. But contemporary liberalism, in my view, has not been sufficiently cognizant of, and has failed to trumpet fully, the way in which enforcement of individual rights can benefit society at large. One does not have to abide by a consequentialist theory of individual rights to appreciate the limitations inherent in ignoring or minimizing the positive effects that the enforcement of individual rights can have on the broader society.

We can use the issue of interracial marriage to illustrate this point. By the end of the Civil War, almost every state in the nation had a law in its books that prohibited interracial marriage. (Before the emancipation of the slaves, Southern states refused to recognize the marriage of slaves as legally binding in society. Such a refusal was the quintessential denial of the humanity of a distinct group of persons—the love, commitment, and affection that one slave felt for another had no value and was of no interest to a deeply racist society.) The purpose of antimiscegenation laws was to keep the races separated while at the same time keeping the white race "pure." In this way, the institution of marriage played a role in the construction of racial difference that was akin to its role in the construction of gender difference.[109] It was not until 1967 that the Supreme Court in *Loving v. Virginia* struck down antimiscegenation statutes, holding them to be unconstitutional violations of equal protection and substantive due process. It is possible to justify the Court's ruling solely on grounds of individual rights to equality and liberty—that is—on the grounds that all individuals, regardless of race, should have the right to choose whom to marry. The Court in *Loving*, however, placed the issue in a broader societal and historical context by noting that the prohibitions against interracial marriage were "measures designed to maintain White Supremacy."[110] Although the ban against interracial marriage was still legally enforceable, it remained an important part of racial segregation and apartheid in America. It reinforced in the minds of many white Americans the view that members of racial minorities were both lesser and dangerous persons from whom the white race needed protection. When the antimiscegenation laws were struck down, apartheid in America suffered an important (though by no means deadly) blow. As Robin West notes, "the freedom of the individual to marry interracially has had profound social effects. To whatever degree . . . the moral point of the institution of marriage in a racist society with a slave past was once, at least in part, about preserving racial purity, it is no longer."[111] The striking down of antimiscegenation statutes has, of course, been important to those who fall in love and want to share a life with someone of a different race; but the Court's ruling also contributed to the formation of a better society, one that was, at the very least, less overtly racist.

Similarly, the elimination of the opposite-gender requirement for marriage will help diminish the patriarchal and gender-subordinating components of that institution. Marriage in the United States has played a crucial role in the promotion and maintenance of male power and privilege. The wife has historically been in a subordinate position to the husband, catering to his needs and priorities in the home while he pursues work, wealth, and recognition outside of it. As Nancy Cott, in her recent book on the history of marriage in the United States, notes, "the whole system of attribution and meaning that we call *gender* relies on and to a great extent derives from the structuring provided by marriage. Turning men and women into husbands and wives, marriage has designated the ways both sexes act in the world and the reciprocal relation between them."[112] Patriarchal internal family arrangements and practices have contributed immensely to women's second class status, not only inside the family, but outside of it as well. Inequality for women in the home has translated into economic, social, and political inequality outside of it.[113] Given this history of patriarchy and subordination, the argument that marriage *must* be between one man and one woman is an argument about maintaining certain power relationships and hierarchies that are based on gender roles and privileges.

Part of what drives the opposition to same-sex marriage is the concern that it will further destabilize what are taken to be the proper or necessary or natural gender divisions and roles within marriage.[114] This translates, whether consciously or unconsciously, into a concern that male privileges within marriage (and thus male privileges outside of it) will be further undermined. To be the male in a companionate marriage for most of American history has meant to be the recipient of advantages and benefits that emanate directly from the division of labor and responsibilities within the family according to gender roles. Committed and sexually intimate gay and lesbian relationships, on the other hand, are not defined or constituted by predetermined gender roles that have traditionally been incorporated into heterosexual marriage. When two men or two women seek societal recognition of their relationship as marital, they "subvert the belief that women and men take on separate but complementary roles within marriage and overtly resist the notion that marriage functions to support specifically defined gender roles."[115] Every time the sexual intimacy between two women or two men is accompanied by an emotional bond strong enough that they decide to make their lives into one, they must work out anew the internal arrangements and dynamics of their relationship rather than rely on arrangements and dynamics called for by predetermined gender roles. The assumption has been all along that being of opposite genders is a prerequisite for the formation of sexually intimate relationships that are enduring and enriching. Countless gay and lesbian couples are proving that gender is, in fact, *irrelevant* for purposes of forming such relationships and that the purported essentiality of gender reflects little more than the perceived essentiality of traditional gender roles and their accompanying male privileges. Same-sex marriage delinks marriage from gender; in the same way that the dismantling of a codified legal regime that prohibited interracial marriages has contributed to a lessening of institutional racism in America, degendering marriage will contribute to a reduction of sexism in America.[116]

It is possible to make too much of the effects that a recognition of same-sex marriage will have on degendering marriage as an institution and thus on reducing male privilege and female subordination in our society. It is not as if the day after same-sex marriage is recognized, heterosexual couples who abide by traditional gender roles in their relationships will cease to do so. The effect will be more attenuated than that, with the benefits becoming perceptible only over time. However, recognition of same-sex marriage—and, in fact, just the debate over the issue—encourages individuals to question centuries-old assumptions about the essentiality of gender in marital relationships. The mere fact that it will someday be possible for a couple to be married in the United States and yet for there to be no *husband* or no *wife* will contribute to the degendering of marital norms and social roles in American culture.

It was unfathomable to most white Americans a century ago that blacks should be free to marry whites and vice versa. It still seems true to most Americans today that men should only be allowed to marry women and vice versa. *Loving v. Virginia* changed marriage in America for the better; it contributed to the dismantling of racial apartheid. The recognition of same-sex marriage will also change marriage in America for the better; it will make it a more humane and egalitarian institution with fewer of the vestiges of gender-based hierarchies and domination. When lesbians and gay men someday receive the right to marry, it will not only be about their rights to autonomy and equality; it will also be about building a fairer and more just society.

Another instrumental reason why the recognition of same-sex marriages will be good for society has to do with encouraging stability in relationships. Once a society has decided that it will tolerate same-gender sexual conduct (by, for example, sparingly enforcing sodomy statutes even if it is constitutional to do so), there is little that society can do to prevent the formation of committed gay and lesbian relationships. The emotional intimacy that so often accompanies physical intimacy is not so easily deterred. It is in society's interest, once these relationships of love and commitment are going to be formed anyway, to promote their stability and continuity. (This argument is different from the one made earlier in the chapter that focused on stability and continuity in sexually intimate relationships from the perspective of the needs and capabilities of the individuals involved rather than from that of society at large.) The marital relationship brings with it certain rights and obligations, both legal and moral, that do not apply to committed relationships outside of marriage. Dissolution of the marital relationship is more complicated precisely because those rights and obligations do not go away upon termination. All of this contributes to a greater likelihood that the parties will try to work out differences and remain together (if that is indeed possible and advisable depending on particular circumstances) rather than easily and without meaningful consequences replacing one relationship with another.

The societal interest in promoting stability and continuity in committed same-gender relationships is particularly strong now that lesbians and gay men by the thousands are having and adopting children. It is in society's interest that these children be provided with security and continuity in their lives. The states of Hawaii and Vermont, in defending themselves against lawsuits that questioned the constitutionality of their bans against same-sex marriage, relied primarily on the "government's interest in furthering the link between procreation and child rearing."[117] With the large number of lesbians and gay men who are becoming parents, however, this argument is becoming increasingly nonsensical. As the Vermont Supreme Court pointed out in rejecting the argument in *Baker v. State*, "[i]f anything, the exclusion of same-sex couples from the legal protections incident to marriage exposes *their* children to the precise risks that the state argues the marriage laws are designed to secure against."[118] If the goal is to provide stability, continuity, and support for children, then the state has an interest in promoting stability, continuity, and support for the relationship of the parents (whether legal or de facto) even if they are of the same gender.

I will in the next section, and in the last section of chapter 4, have more to say on the issue of parenting by lesbians and gay men. In doing so, I will respond to the objections to same-sex marriage that are based on what is taken to be the essential link between marriage and children, as well as what are considered to be the potential harms to children who are raised by lesbians or gay men. I want to end this section by addressing some of the other consequentialist arguments put forward by opponents of same-sex marriage. One of those arguments, heard over and over again, is that a stable and well-functioning society depends on marriage being restricted to one man and one woman. This was the principal argument made by supporters of the Defense of Marriage Act. That statute defines marriage for purposes of federal law as limited to one man and one woman and seeks to exempt states from having to recognize same-sex marriages approved in other states.[119] The legislators who voted for the law argued that the institution of marriage, limited to one man and one woman, "is a fundamental pillar of our society and its values";[120] "a foundation of all that is stable and noble in our civilization";[121] "an institution basic not only to this country's foundation and to its survival but to every Western civilization";[122] and "a keystone to the stability, strength, and health of human society."[123]

As I noted earlier, it is indeed important to explore the connection between private ordering and the public good. That exploration, however, requires more than conclusory statements and overblown rhetoric. How is it, exactly, that allowing two men or two women to marry undermines the social order and the very fabric of the nation? It certainly undermines notions of patriarchy and the idea that gender is an essential element of marriage, but there is no reason to believe—as supporters of DOMA argued—that the very future of our society is at stake. The recognition of same-sex marriage in no way diminishes or tarnishes the value and meaning of the marriages of heterosexuals *except to the extent that that value and meaning are built on principles of gender difference.*

Almost a century ago, the Supreme Court held that a husband had a property interest in his wife and that, as a result, when she engaged in an adulterous relationship, he suffered an assault that injured both his person and his property. In supporting its holding, the Court argued that a husband's right to exclusive sexual intercourse with his wife is "a right of the highest kind, upon . . . which the whole social order rests."[124] We can now look back at this ruling with dismay at the way in which the Court casually and unconvincingly linked the sexual prerogatives of husbands to the stability of society itself. The arguments used by the pro-DOMA legislators are the intellectual descendants of this kind of conclusory and hyperbolic reasoning.

In order to support their position about the fundamental link between an institution of marriage that is exclusively heterosexual and the social order, opponents of same-sex marriage like to emphasize tradition: We have in this country only recognized marriages between men and women; surely, it is argued, that should counsel against changing the definition of marriage in the "radical" way that gay rights proponents suggest. The problem with relying on tradition is that much of the institutional inequality and discrimination suffered by minority groups in this country have at one point or another been part of the nation's traditions. As we know from our history, tradition by itself is a rather thin and unsteady reed upon which to defend institutions as currently defined from complaints of systematic discrimination and exclusion. Traditions are not irrelevant because there may be good reasons behind them; but simply relying on tradition, without more, is not enough.

Attempts by opponents of same-sex marriage to move beyond generalities in their consequentialist arguments prove to be no more successful. One favorite is to point to the alleged promiscuity of gay men. The argument runs like this: Men are more promiscuous than women. It is women who pressure or convince men to be monogamous. Gay men are not interested in sexual relationships with women so their natural promiscuity (as men) is not subject to any meaningful restraint. Recognition of gay marriages will mean that the institution of marriage will no longer be associated with monogamy. As a result, marriages will become less stable, which will be bad for society.[125]

The first interesting aspect of the promiscuity argument is that it is an argument *for* recognition of lesbian marriages. If what we want is monogamy in relationships and if women are more monogamous than men, then lesbian relationships should be recognized and encouraged. And yet, to my knowledge, no conservative opponent of gay rights argues that lesbian marriages should be recognized but that gay male ones should not. This suggests that opponents are not only being internally inconsistent with their arguments, but that what matters to them ultimately is not monogamy and stability in all sexually intimate relationships but monogamy and stability in relationships between men and women, which of course, takes us right back to the question of why marriage should be limited to relationships between a man and a woman. The promiscuity argument does not help us answer *that* question because it supports offering marital rights and benefits to lesbian couples.

Furthermore, the empirical assumptions of the promiscuity argument are open to challenge. Many who raise the alleged promiscuity of gay men as grounds for opposing the recognition of same-sex marriage rely on the same two studies, both of which were conducted over twenty years ago—most important *before* the AIDS epidemic—and one of which was limited to gay men in one city.[126] A more recent national survey of the sexual practices of both gays and straights concluded that the differences in the number of partners of gay men as opposed to straight men "do not appear very large" and are, under most variables (such as the number of sexual partners in the last year and the number of partners since turning eighteen), "not statistically significant."[127] Arguments about rampant promiscuity among gay men, then, appear to be based more on old stereotypes than on current facts. It does appear, however, that many lesbians and gay men do not believe that commitment and monogamy are necessarily synonymous. For example, in a recent study of 90 gay and lesbian couples, it was found that only 32 percent of the lesbians and 10 percent of the gay men discussed "the importance of monogamy as part of their commitment to their partners."[128] (Interestingly enough, even though most couples interviewed for the study did not view monogamy as an essential part of commitment, the vast majority of the couples—92 percent of the lesbians and 81 percent of the gay men—"either agreed to be monogamous or assumed the relationship was monogamous.")[129] The reasons why many lesbians and gay men do not view emotional commitment and sexual exclusivity as synonymous are complicated; they are based largely on the fears of assimilation by a historically marginalized and oppressed sexual minority as well as on an appreciation by members of that minority for the liberationist potential of sexual intimacy. The important point, however, is this: Lesbians and gay men have shown time and time again that they are capable of constructing long-term relationships where commitment, trust, respect, and mutuality exist. The fact that some lesbians and gay men do not equate those values with sexual exclusivity is not a sufficient ground for denying them the right to marry, especially in a society where lack of sexual exclusivity among married heterosexual couples is not exactly unheard-of.

Another consequentialist argument related to the issue of promiscuity that is raised against state recognition of gay and lesbian relationships is based on the idea, as Roger Scruton puts it, of a "functional justification" for the revulsion that many people feel toward homosexuality.[130] That revulsion, it is argued, plays an important social function in restraining the sexual impulses of all individuals in general and in teaching young people about the dangers of an unfettered sexuality in particular. Thus, opponents of same-sex marriage argue that state recognition of gay and lesbian relationships would, in effect, send the wrong message about the use of individuals' sexual capabilities and would lead to the weakening of other social taboos (such as incest and bestiality) that urge sexual restraint. Law professor Lynn Wardle, for example, argues that a recognition of same-sex marriage would send "the message of 'anything goes' in the way of sexual behavior, procreation, and parenthood [which] would wreck its greatest havoc among groups of vulnerable individuals who most need the encouragement of bright line laws and clear social mores concerning procreative responsibility."[131]

The attempt to use lesbians and gay men in this way is as morally bankrupt as it is pernicious. The argument amounts to using the lives of lesbians and gay men as instruments of social control. It tells lesbians and gay men that their needs and capabilities as human beings should be ignored and sacrificed in order to teach others (i.e., heterosexuals) that not all sexual desires or pleasures should be pursued. Lesbians and gay men, as human beings, have the right to be treated as ends rather than as means.

However society goes about teaching sexual moderation, it should not do so at the expense of the basic humanity of a large segment of its citizens who express and realize their needs and capabilities associated with physical and emotional intimacy with others of the same gender.

As one works through the different consequentialist arguments for opposing recognition of same-sex marriage, then, one finds little merit in them. The arguments are unconvincing and raise troubling moral issues of their own. I believe that the recognition of committed same-gender relationships will have a positive impact on society principally for the two reasons noted above: It will contribute to the reduction of gender-based oppression in our society while providing for greater stability in same-gender relationships, an especially important consideration as growing numbers of lesbians and gay men are choosing to become parents. I now turn to a discussion of parenting by lesbians and gay men in the final section of the chapter.

THE VALUE OF PARENTING BY LESBIANS AND GAY MEN

The interplay between human needs and capabilities is perhaps more evident in the parent-child relationship than in any other. Children at first have only needs, needs that must be satisfied if they are to have the opportunity to flourish as adults. What makes the satisfaction of children's needs possible is the capability of adults to provide for those needs. Parenting (like marriage), therefore, raises fundamental questions about our needs and capabilities as human beings to participate in relationships of care. There is arguably no more important need than that of a child to be cared for by an adult nor a more important capability than that of an adult to care for a child. The capability to provide for others, including children, is an integral part of our humanity. I am not suggesting, of course, that one has to have children in order to be fully human. What I am suggesting is that the capability to care for others is a constitutive human capability that we all share, one that is especially evident in the way in which adults nurture, protect, guide, and love children. These are the premises with which I believe a moral discussion relating to who should be entitled and encouraged to parent should begin.

Opponents of gay rights question whether the values and goodness usually associated with parenting are consistent with permitting or encouraging lesbians and gay men to become parents. In a long law review article, for example, Lynn Wardle attempts to make a comprehensive case against parenting by lesbians and gay men.[132] Wardle suggests that many lesbians and gay men seek to become parents for the wrong reasons, namely, to advance a political agenda and to earn recognition of parental rights that are meant more to benefit the adults than the children.[133] Like many opponents of gay rights who write in this area, Wardle glosses over the human attributes, in terms of needs and capabilities, that are implicated whenever individuals make the life-changing and life-affirming decision to become parents. When Wardle suggests that lesbians and gay men are thinking more of themselves than of their children when they decide to become parents, he suggests that they are selfishly putting their needs and desires ahead of their children. Such an accusation, however, is unfair because it simplifies and trivializes the human needs and capabilities that are implicated when adults rear children. It is only when the human needs and capabilities associated with caring for others are invoked by lesbians and gay men that conservative commentators such as Wardle treat them with skepticism, as if the love and commitment on the part of lesbians and gay men (for their partners and for their children) were really some sort of a ruse to hide political or self-serving motivations.

It may be that in the end, commentators who oppose parenting by lesbians and gay men and who perhaps know from personal experience how having and raising children can be an expression of one's needs and capabilities to love and care for others, and can reaffirm the depth, strength, and goodness of adult relationships, cannot accept that same-gender couples may experience the same. Gay and lesbian couples (or individuals) who decide to have and raise children do not act selfishly or with political motivations. In the end, that personal decision transcends political goals; it is an issue that goes to the core of what it means to be a human being because it entails the decision to love and care for a young, vulnerable, and highly dependent other. It is indeed ironic that lesbians and gay men have to defend their desire to love and nurture children when for the rest of the population such a desire is not only expected but is considered abnormal when it is lacking. (I will return to this issue in the next chapter when I discuss the pronatalist norms of the American society.)

A gay or lesbian individual, then, who wants to have and raise a child, is doing nothing more and nothing less than expressing and pursuing his or her humanity. At the heart of the disagreement over whether lesbians and gay men should be supported and encouraged in becoming parents is an assessment of whether they share sufficiently with others those human qualities that make for good parents. The burden must be on conservative opponents of gay rights to explain why sexual intimacy with someone of the same gender makes basic needs and capabilities associated with loving and caring for others, including children, less worthy of moral respect.

Conservatives have so far attempted to meet their burden by arguing that parenting by gay and lesbian individuals is harmful to children. Unlike in the case of same-sex marriage, where they allege that its recognition would harm the *institution* of marriage as a whole rather than the marriages of particular heterosexual couples, when it comes to parenting by lesbians and gay men, opponents of gay rights can point to identifiable (and vulnerable) children who are purportedly at risk of being harmed. For Wardle, for example, the purported harm arises from the greater likelihood that the children of gay and lesbian parents will themselves be gay or lesbian and from the purported fact that the gender roles, gender identities, and self-esteem of children raised by lesbians and gay men will be negatively affected by their parents' same-gender sexual orientation.[134]

The problem for Wardle and others who make similar arguments is that the empirical evidence suggests the opposite of what they claim. The available evidence from social science studies indicates that children of lesbians and gay men are not negatively affected in their emotional and social development.[135] Furthermore, putting aside the disputable assumption that it would in fact be harmful for children to become gay or lesbian adults, the studies indicate that the children of lesbians and gay men are not more likely to be lesbian or gay themselves.[136] The studies also show that neither the gender roles nor the gender identities of children raised by gay or lesbian parents are significantly different from those raised by heterosexual parents.[137] Although it is not unreasonable to think that children of lesbians and gay men may be more open to questioning the appeal of traditional gender roles (which would, in my opinion, be a positive development), current social learning theory and cognitive development theory tell us that parents actually play a relatively minor role in the encouragement of traditional gender role behavior; children learn most of that behavior from the many adults with whom they interact and from the culture at large.[138]

But the unease about parenting by lesbians and gay men goes deeper than concerns about the gender roles and identities of their children; the distress is also caused by what are perceived to be the intrinsic limitations of being raised by parents of only one gender. Many Americans believe that the complementary characteristics traditionally associated with "fathering" and "mothering" are correlated with one's gender. This is an area where feminism has been largely unsuccessful in dislodging deeply held views about the seemingly immutable relationship between gender, on the one hand, and particular parental abilities and qualities, on the other. But there is no reason to believe that the positive characteristics that we associate with fathering (such as providing and protecting) and mothering (such as nurturing and caring) are explained or determined by one's sex. That correlation is one more manifestation (admittedly one of the strongest) of our social construction of gender differences. Gay and lesbian parents—like single parents who have to be both "fathers" and "mothers" to their children—are beginning to chip away at that social construction of gendered parenting. As with marriage, a focus on parenting through "degendered" lenses allows us to concentrate on the real values and qualities that underlie the forms of human associations that we as a society have decided to privilege. As with marriage, the dispute over gay and lesbian parents implicates basic human needs and capabilities; those needs and capabilities have a complexity and a richness that are glossed over when we insist on grounding the value and meaning of parenting on gender differences and roles. To be a good parent—that is, to protect, nurture, provide, and care for a child—is not an expression of gender attributes; it is, instead, an expression (and realization) of one's humanity.

The bottom line, then, is that denying lesbians and gay men the opportunity to parent—or making it more difficult for them to parent—is a denial of their basic human needs and capabilities to love and care for others. Such a denial, in the absence of evidence that the children of lesbians and gay men are harmed by the same-gender sexual orientation of their parents, raises troubling moral questions because it places state institutions and policies in the business of denying individuals the ability to exercise, if they so wish, important aspects of their humanity through parenting. The social science literature shows that lesbians and gay men are as capable of loving and caring for their children and of rearing happy, healthy, and fulfilled children as are heterosexual parents. The moral respect that we owe the needs and capabilities of human beings to care for others requires us as a society to promote and provide for the needs and capabilities of lesbians and gay men to parent.

There is obviously more to be said about the issues raised by gay and lesbian parents. I will at the end of the next chapter, as I explore Michael Walzer's theory of internal moral and social criticism, address some of those issues by placing them in the context of the culture-specific meaning of parenthood in the United States.

I have argued in this chapter that human needs and capabilities associated with sexual intimacy and the loving and caring for others, which lesbians and gay men share with all human beings, merit the moral respect of society. As such, society has obligations to provide for and promote those needs and capabilities. I have explained in particular why gay and lesbian relationships and families are good and valuable forms of human associations that deserve the support and recognition of society. A sympathetic supporter of gay rights who is otherwise skeptical of the need or advisability of broaching the kind of moral arguments that I have raised in this chapter, however, may argue that the trend in the United States in the last few decades has been to emphasize notions of choice and autonomy in relationship and family matters rather than morality as such.[139] The better approach, it might be contended, is to support a further "de-moralization" of issues relating to committed relationships and families rather than to raise moral arguments about them, arguments that will only antagonize opponents and upon which there can be, in the end, no agreement. Lesbians and gay men, the skeptic might argue, should therefore simply ride the wave of "de-moralization" toward ever greater tolerance and acceptance.

I can offer three responses to the skeptic. First, I question whether arguments based on choice and autonomy are as morally neutral as proponents of "de-moralization" contend. As I noted in chapter 2, many liberals who purport to avoid moral questions in discussing intimate and familial relationships and their regulation by the state nonetheless place a high moral value on personal liberty and choice. It is a belief in the intrinsic goodness and value of autonomy and freedom that for many liberals serves as the foundation for their views on family law and policy (among many other issues). A vision of family law and policy that emphasizes autonomy and choice, therefore, is not necessarily one that is morally neutral. Second, although the trend in American family law and policy has been to emphasize issues of autonomy, the *range* of available choices remains nonetheless firmly constrained by a set of parameters— What is a "marital" relationship? Who is a "parent?" How do we best care for children?—that are determined largely through normative assessments based on the value of different kinds of relationships. In fact, some family law scholars have suggested, in my view correctly, that the focus on morality in the debates over family law and policy have not diminished as issues of choice and autonomy have become more prevalent. Instead, the nature of the moral debate has shifted to include issues of gender equity, parental responsibility and commitment, and caregiving and nurturing outside of traditional relationships.[140] Third, intimate human relationships of both the sexual and familial kind inevitably raise moral questions regarding whether those relationships are "consensual, exploitative, reciprocal, empowering, or debilitating,"[141] questions that cannot be fully addressed if we focus only on issues of negative liberty, the right to be left alone, and the right to choose. The characteristics of intimate relationships by their very nature raise a host of moral issues about human needs, capabilities, and above all, the transformative effects of human relationships. A moral and political philosophy of gay rights, therefore, must grapple with rather than avoid these admittedly bigger and more complicated moral questions. I believe that, unlike neutral or pragmatic liberalism, moral liberalism, with its focus on human needs, capabilities, and relationships, gives us the necessary tools to formulate forceful and convincing justifications for societal recognition and support of gay and lesbian relationships and families.

FOUR

Communitarianism

No debate in Anglo-American political philosophy has received greater attention in the last two decades than that between liberalism and communitarianism. The liberalism in that debate, however, has not been either pragmatic or moral liberalism. Instead, the main target of the communitarian critique of liberalism has been the neutral liberalism of John Rawls. Communitarians have criticized Rawlsian liberalism for its atomistic conception of the self, for separating the right from the good, and for paying insufficient attention to communal values and obligations.[1]

There are significant areas of agreement between pragmatism and communitarianism. Pragmatists and communitarians emphasize the embeddedness of individuals in relationships, groups, and communities as well as the importance of local norms and traditions in addressing questions of morality and justice. The pragmatist Richard Rorty, for example, agrees with the communitarian political philosopher Michael Walzer that questions of justice must be addressed not through principles of ostensibly universal applicability but rather internally through the norms and understandings of local communities.[2] Rorty parts company with communitarians, however, when he suggests that sacrificing communal ties and a strong sense of civic virtue may be the price that we have to pay in order to enjoy political freedom in a liberal democracy (ORT, 190). For Rorty, solidarity emerges not so much from communal ties and influences as from the hope and progress that, as we saw in chapter 2, he argues accompanies the promotion of liberal freedoms.

Moral liberalism also shares some common ground with communitarianism, though there are important areas of disagreement as well. Moral liberalism joins the communitarian Michael Sandel in his critique of Rawlsian liberalism for separating the right from the good. In the particular context of sexual orientation, as we have discussed, it is difficult to justify gay rights positions in the areas of marriage and parenting without a thicker conception of the good than that allowed by Rawlsian liberalism. The question of whether lesbians and gay men should have rights to marry and to parent is inextricably linked to questions of what is valuable and good in human relationships. Similarly moral liberalism, like communitarianism, understands that the well-being and autonomy of individuals are often dependent on their relationships with others. In addition, moral liberalism is cognizant of the importance of local specifications in addressing questions of justice. As we will see in this chapter, however, there are two important areas of disagreement between moral liberalism and communitarianism. First, moral liberalism, unlike communitarianism, recognizes the value of communities *of choice* in protecting the autonomy and dignity of individuals, especially those who belong to marginalized groups. (Communities of choice are those that individuals choose to participate in; they can be contrasted to given communities—such as the biological family and, for most people, religious communities—where membership is determined by birth.) Second, although moral liberalism recognizes that local interpretations and understandings are important whenever we discuss questions of justice, it also holds that it is sometimes necessary to rely on universal norms—specifically, those associated with basic human needs and capabilities that exist across time and place—to evaluate and critique local traditions and practices.

In this chapter, I explore the similarities and differences between moral liberalism and communitarianism and their relevance for a philosophy of gay rights. I focus on the writings of two leading American communitarian thinkers: Michael Sandel and Michael Walzer. Sandel's work is important because he has been the leading critic of the Rawlsian separation of the right from the good and because he has been an influential proponent of the role of community in protecting and promoting the well-being and freedom of individuals.[3] Many lesbians and gay men can attest to Sandel's view that communities can be sources of character, self-worth, dignity, and empowerment for individuals. Sandel's conception of community, however, raises difficulties for lesbians and gay men because he underestimates both the value of communities of choice in protecting and promoting freedom and the threats to autonomy and equality that sometimes emanate from given communities.

The strength of Walzer's communitarianism lies in its understanding of the important role that internal norms and shared traditions play in questions of justice. Thus, when deciding whether lesbians and gay men in the United States should be permitted to marry and become parents, it is important to determine what "marriage" and "parenthood" mean in the United States. We need, in other words, to grapple with the ways in which the American society defines those social goods and the criteria through which it distributes them. The limitations in Walzer's communitarianism inhere in its unwillingness to recognize that we sometimes need to go beyond strictly local understandings of the meanings of social goods in order to (1) address conflicting internal interpretations and (2) critique local practices that are both shared *and* oppressive of particular individuals and groups.

1. SANDELLIAN VALUES AND COMMUNITIES

Michael Sandel has been one of the most influential communitarian critics of Rawlsian liberalism. Sandel's critique can be winnowed down to two principal points. First, he rejects the notion that the right is prior to the good. Second, he rejects the idea that the self is prior to community. For Sandel, the right and the good, on the one hand, and the self and the many communities to which it belongs, on the other, are inevitably linked.

On the separation of the right from the good, Sandel has presented the most elaborate and convincing critique of Rawlsian moral bracketing. In an influential review of *Political Liberalism* that appeared in the *Harvard Law Review*, Sandel takes Rawls to task for promoting a political philosophy that seeks to avoid rather than to tackle the important moral controversies that inevitably spill over into the political debates of a democratic society.[4] As I argued in chapter 1, the Sandellian critique of moral bracketing is consistent with the realities of contemporary gay rights debates over same-sex marriage and parenting by lesbians and gay men. Sandel deserves credit for being the first political philosopher to encourage gay rights proponents to address issues of morality and the good directly rather than sidestepping them. It is important to note, however, that the argument for the removal of moral brackets is a procedural argument. It rejects the separation of the right from the good, but does not by itself tell us what the good is. I therefore proceed in this section to describe the conception of the good as promoted by Sandel's brand of communitarianism known as civic republicanism. In the next section, I address the implications of Sandel's substantive vision for lesbians and gay men.

Perhaps to a greater extent than any other contemporary American communitarian, Sandel has formulated a trenchant critique of the atomistic individual—one uncoupled from attachments and communities—in liberal political philosophy. In his highly regarded first book, *Liberalism and the Limits of Justice,* Sandel criticizes Rawlsian liberalism for its Kantian view of the self as unencumbered and disconnected from its ends and communities. Sandel argues that the "Rawlsian self is . . . an antecedently individuated subject, standing always at a certain distance from the interests it has" (LLJ, 62). For Sandel, such a view of the self fails to recognize that our attachments are constitutive of our identity and that our well-being and interests are inescapably linked to those of others. The Rawlsian self, Sandel concludes, "rules out the possibility that common purposes and ends could inspire more or less expansive self-understandings and so define a community in the constitutive sense, a community describing the subject and not just the objects of shared aspirations" (LLJ, 62).

According to Sandel, the realization of a just and democratic society is more likely to take place when individuals are active participants in the many communities to which they belong. This sense of communal participation and belonging promotes individual freedom and a true connection with and responsibility toward others. As a civic republican, Sandel wants the state to cultivate certain values, such as civic virtue, self-respect, and social responsibility, which encourage individuals to participate actively in their communities and self-government. Citizens should learn the virtue and value of a public orientation, that is, of subordinating when necessary private interests in favor of public concerns.

Sandel argues in his second book, *Democracy's Discontent: America in Search of a Public Philosophy,* that the myriad of communities to which individuals belong (e.g., families, schools, churches, and neighborhoods) play a crucial role in the elaboration of that which individuals believe is good, valuable, and just. Unlike Rawls, who for purposes of political justice seeks to separate citizens from the values they hold as members of nonpolitical communities, Sandel argues that citizens are (and should remain) fully embedded in the shared traditions and norms of their nonpolitical communities. Sandel, like other communitarians, argues that individuals in the real world do not exist prior to their ends or make moral or political decisions that involve questions of justice disconnected from their ties to other human beings. Instead, individuals have many ties of friendship, obligation, and loyalty that provide them with their sense of identity and bind them to the lives and well-being of others. These ties hold communities together and create the necessary conditions for freedom and justice. According to Sandel, a theory of political morality is seriously flawed if it does not consider the role that the links among human beings play in establishing and promoting traditional democratic values; a vision of individuals inextricably linked to their communities is consistent with the descriptive reality of most people's lives and appropriate as an ideal to which a theory of political morality and democracy should aspire.

As Sandel sees it, America has in the last few decades embraced in practice much of the theory of neutral liberalism. The American nation, Sandel argues, has come to define itself as a liberal procedural republic, constructed on a voluntarist vision of personhood that does not concern itself with particular ends but with the capacity of individuals to choose their own ends. The procedural republic aims to enforce and promote individual rights of autonomy while not requiring its citizens to abide by obligations that they do not choose voluntarily.

Sandel reminds us in *Democracy's Discontent,* however, that our nation has not always been a liberal procedural one. He notes, for example, that the contemporary liberal conception of rights was a creation of the twentieth century. He points out that "the Bill of Rights [did not] play an important role in protecting individual liberties against federal infringement" during its first one hundred years; "[l]iberty in the early republic," he adds, "had less to do with individual guarantees against government action than with the dispersion of power among branches and levels of government" (DD, 38). During the early part of the twentieth century, the Supreme Court, intent on promoting individual rights over ideals of self-government and the common good, superceded the traditional republican way of protecting freedom, namely, through the promotion of civic virtue and dispersed government. The Supreme Court's infamous decision in *Lochner v. New York*—where it struck down as unconstitutional a regulation protecting the welfare of workers—is important in this regard because it "established the priority of right[s]" by deeming the interests of individuals to contract to be more important than the societal good as determined by legislatures (DD, 43).[5] The Court, according to Sandel, has since *Lochner* been mostly in the business of promoting the values of the procedural republic. He uses the Court's privacy jurisprudence, among several other lines of cases, to support his claim. In that jurisprudence, the Court has chosen to emphasize issues of procedural voluntariness and choice rather than substantive judgments about the good.[6] The liberal theory behind the procedural republic, which according to Sandel pervades the Court's constitutional jurisprudence, insists on a form of state neutrality that asks citizens who challenge governmental action or who seek protection through governmental policies to bracket their identities and values "for the sake of political agreement" (DD, 116).[7] This bracketing brings with it a significant cost because it attains a superficial tolerance that alienates citizens from their government and society: "Respecting persons as unencumbered selves may afford a kind of social peace, but it is unlikely to realize the higher pluralism of persons and communities who appreciate and affirm the distinctive goods their different lives express" (DD, 116).

According to Sandel, the vision of the unencumbered self, free from all duties and responsibilities not freely chosen, is one that cuts across legal, political, and economic spheres. He argues that the procedural republic creates a sense of disillusionment among Americans as their communal identities become disconnected from their identities as citizens participating in the life of a democracy. Ultimately, the procedural republic has produced a displacement of community and left Americans isolated from each other, confused, and anxious about social institutions that are unresponsive to their needs. The result is a public discourse and a democracy that are rich in procedural guarantees and individual rights, but poor in substantive moral content, common purpose, and sense of civic unity.

Sandel wants to replace the liberal conception of the procedural republic with a civic republican vision that promotes the particular end of greater self-government by citizens. Sandel notes that "[t]he republican conception of freedom, unlike the liberal conception, requires a formative politics, a politics that cultivates in citizens the qualities of character self-government requires" (DD, 6). It is communities—civic, social, and religious—that are best able to cultivate the qualities of civic virtue and participation that Sandel believes are essential to a well-functioning democracy. He uses the example of Southern black churches during the civil rights era to illustrate how particular communities cultivate and foster a sense of civic virtue and participation that lead individuals, in this case African Americans, to strive *together* for political empowerment. "[T]he civic education and social solidarity cultivated in the black Baptist churches of the South," Sandel notes, "were a crucial prerequisite for the civil rights movement that ultimately unfolded on a national scale" (DD, 314).

According to Sandel, it is the given communities that we find ourselves in, such as family, school, church, neighborhood, and nation, as opposed to the communities that we choose, that are best able to instill character and transmit values. Sandel therefore emphasizes those "loyalties and convictions whose moral force consists partly in the fact that living by them is inseparable from understanding ourselves as the particular persons we are—as members of this family or community or nation or people, as bearers of this history, as sons and daughters of that revolution, as citizens of this republic" (LLJ, 179). He argues that a theory of political morality that does not recognize the importance of the connections between individuals and the given communities to which they belong fails to capture the complexity and depth of the character and identity of citizens. "[T]o have character," Sandel notes, "is to know that I move in a history I *neither summon nor command*, which carries consequences none the less for my choices and conduct" (LLJ, 179, emphasis added). Sandel argues that liberalism "cannot make sense of our moral experience, because it cannot account for certain moral and political obligations that we commonly recognize, even prize. These include obligations of solidarity, religious duties, and other moral ties that may claim us for reasons *unrelated to a choice*" (DD, 13, emphasis added). Ultimately, liberalism's prioritization of individualism and voluntariness is "eroding those forms of community—families and neighborhoods, cities and towns, civic and ethnic and religious communities—that situate people in the world and provide a source of identity and belonging" (DD, 294).

Although Sandel greatly values given communities, he does not have much interest in communities of choice. Voluntary associations are more about attaining the instrumental goals of their members than they are about the instillation and transmission of character and values. For Sandel, the important constitutive function of community arises precisely from its nonvoluntary components. As he explains, for members of a society, "community describes not just what they *have* as fellow citizens but also what they *are*, not a relationship they choose (as in voluntary association) but an attachment they discover, not merely an attribute but a constituent of their identity" (LLJ, 150).[8]

In short, for Sandel, the liberal understanding of the relationship between individuals and their communities fails to account for the ways in which the very identity, character, and values of individuals are the result of their embeddedness in distinct communities. To the extent, then, that Americans value liberty, equality, and other democratic principles, it is the result of their participation in a variety of communal entities that have promoted those values and transmitted them from one generation to the next to the point where they have become inseparable from the identity and character of American citizens. If we are concerned with the promotion of liberty and equality as values, therefore, we need to recognize and foster the bonds between citizens and their communities.

2. THE ROLE OF COMMUNITY IN THE LIVES OF LESBIANS AND GAY MEN

Given the hostility that emanates from the broader society, it is difficult for lesbians and gay men to lead free and dignified lives if they remain isolated from other gay and lesbian individuals. Isolation usually means a life in the closet—a life without much satisfaction or fulfillment—in which lies, deception, and a perceived need to go it alone undermine an individual's sense of self-worth and self-respect. As Kath Weston notes, "[t]he closet symbolizes isolation, the individual without society, a stranger even to self. Its imagery is consistent with the atomistic conceptions of a society in which individuated actors must struggle to communicate and gain legitimacy for private truths."[9] Only when the gay person comes out of the closet, when she declares openly that she is a member of a community that comes together to celebrate a sexuality and an identity that society devalues, can she begin to construct for herself a life that is both fulfilled and dignified. For lesbians and gay men, coming out of the closet means constructing a link between internal self-worth and public persona. Again, Kath Weston puts it well when she notes that "[i]n coming out, a person acts to create a sense of wholeness by establishing congruence between interior experience and external presentation, moving the inner into the outer, bringing the hidden to light, and transforming a private into a social reality."[10] The coming *out* of the closet for lesbians and gay men entails their coming *into* a set of communities that serve as sources of mutual support and care.[11] Those communities are of many different kinds and can include ones of friends, families, patrons of bars and coffeehouses as well as communities centered around religious faith, political activism, athletic pursuits, and so on.[12]

The historical and sociological literature is replete with accounts of the importance of community in the lives of lesbians and gay men, accounts that corroborate Sandel's views on the role of community in forming character and identity as well as fostering a sense of belonging and empowerment. The historian George Chauncey, for example, has described how the gay urban community in New York City in the first part of the twentieth century offered gay men "practical support in negotiating the demands of urban life [as they used their] gay social circles to find jobs, apartments, romance, and their closest friendships. Their regular association and ties of mutual dependence fostered their allegiance to one another, but gay culture was even more important to them for the emotional support it provided as they developed values and identities significantly different from those prescribed by the dominant culture."[13] Similarly, Elizabeth Lapovsky Kennedy and Madeline Davis, in their study of lesbians living in Buffalo in the 1930s and 1940s, conclude that community life centered around bars allowed lesbians to build relationships of camaraderie and solidarity that led to a sense of independence and freedom from the men and families in their lives as well as to the group-oriented consciousness that eventually produced an active participation in political movements.[14] Kath Weston, in her study of more contemporary lesbians and gay men living in San Francisco, writes about the freeing and empowering realization that by "joining together on the basis of a sexual identity, [they] could create enduring social ties. In the process, sexuality was reconstituted as a ground of *common experience* rather than a quintessentially *personal domain*."[15] The sociologist Peter Nardi also writes about how the strong and sustaining friendships of gay men serve as "a source of freedom from the limitations imposed by the culture on" gay lives.[16] There are many other similar accounts of the positive role that community plays in the lives of lesbians and gay men.[17]

For some, the idea that gay and lesbian communities reinforce a gay and lesbian identity is fraught with danger because of the threat of promoting the reification of a marginalized identity which in effect essentializes it.[18] For these critics, a gay and lesbian identity is nothing more than a socially constructed and marginalized identity whose main function is to serve as a juxtaposition to the privileged sexual identity as represented by heterosexuality. It is possible, however, to acknowledge the empowerment and sense of connectedness and belonging that emanate from the identity-conferring characteristics of communities without having to argue that there is an innate (or innately valuable) gay and lesbian identity that needs to be protected and advanced through community.[19] The value of community for lesbians and gay men, then, is not that it protects a pre-existing lesbian and gay identity. The value of gay and lesbian communities is that they provide protection and support to their members while serving as a source of social and political empowerment and solidarity in the face of societal stigmatization and oppression. As Peter Nardi notes, "to participate in spaces also occupied by others who have grown up with a stigmatized identity and who may have experienced—despite other significant differences—at least some similar forms of personal and social marginalization is a sociopolitical connection, perhaps one of brotherhood and sisterhood."[20]

Many lesbians and gay men, then, can attest to Sandel's view that communities can provide individuals with dignity and self-worth (internally) and empower them (externally). But there is an important element present in gay and lesbian communities that is missing from Sandel's given communities, namely, choice. Sandel is suspicious of communities of choice; for him, as noted earlier, the positive constitutive value of communities emanates from attachments that are *not* freely chosen. Sandel believes that communities of choice are primarily concerned with the attainment of instrumental ends and the pursuit of certain life goals that are determined by individuals *before* they join those communities. For Sandel, "community must be constitutive of the shared self-understandings of the participants and embodied in their institutional arrangements, not simply an attribute of certain of the participants' plans of life" (LLJ, 173). Ultimately, Sandel is not interested in communities of choice because choice suggests voluntariness, voluntariness suggests autonomy, and autonomy takes us right back to liberalism.

For lesbians and gay men, however, it is largely communities of choice that contribute to the self-respect, dignity, and social and political empowerment noted above. Not only do lesbians and gay men *choose* to join gay and lesbian communities, but most of those communities consider choice to be a highly valued norm. For example, as Kath Weston explains, lesbians and gay men use choice as a way of forming new family and kinship ties that can include close friends, current and former lovers, adopted children, and children from previous heterosexual relationships, among others.[21] The composition of gay families, in other words, is not predetermined and is thus not constitutive of a certain form of decreed identity. Instead, gay families are "[o]rganized through ideologies of love, choice, and creation."[22] Thus, by their very nature gay families are more fluid and accommodating than biological families: "In families we choose, the agency conveyed by 'we' emphasizes each person's part in constructing gay families, just as the absence of agency in the term 'biological family' reinforces the sense of blood as an immutable fact over which individuals exert little control."[23] This gay and lesbian conception of family recognizes the important value of family as a community, but places the responsibility on individuals to choose their own family's rules, obligations, dynamics, and composition. As Weston notes, "[b]y opening the door to the creation of families different in kind and composition, choice assign[s] kinship to the realm of free will and inclination. In the tradition of Thoreau's *Walden*, each gay man and lesbian bec[o]me[s] responsible for the exemplary act of creating an ideal environment."[24] Peter Nardi, in discussing gay male friendships, makes a similar point: "Networks of friendships, often reconceptualized as kinships of choice, become the source for developing communities of identity and equality. Unlike being born into a community of kin, an individual can choose a community of identity that provides norms and relationships that 'stimulate and develop her identity and self-understanding more adequately than her unchosen community of origin, her original community of place.' "[25]

Lesbians and gay men, therefore, do not wait passively to be constituted in the way that Sandel envisions individuals being constituted by their given communities; instead, lesbians and gay men actively form and create new attachments and associations built around principles of love, friendship, and choice. These communities also play an important role in character and identity formation, but the process is more fluid and variable than the one found in the given communities emphasized by Sandel. Sandel seems to believe that only those attachments that are chosen *for* us—as opposed to *by* us—impose character and identity through meaningful and lasting obligations. The reality, however, is that freely chosen obligations cannot be disregarded without, as Jeffrey Blustein puts it, a "sense of personal loss or self-betrayal. . . . Contrary to what some communitarians seem to think, an autonomous chooser of ends is capable of deep and meaningful commitments."[26] Ultimately, a discussion of the value of community for the lives and aspirations of individuals is incomplete if it does not address the role of choice in the formation of at least some communities that are important to them. Lesbians and gay men, at least, have shown how their communities of choice can provide them with a sense of belonging, a degree of personal freedom, and a measure of dignity.

In addition, as the feminist critics of communitarianism have noted, the unquestioned exaltation of given communities that are constitutive of predetermined identities is problematic given the inegalitarian and oppressive values and norms that are sometimes part of those very same communities.[27] Sandel speaks uniformly positively of the virtues and values fostered by given communities such as schools, families, churches, and neighborhoods; he does not address the fact that some of those communities have contributed to the promotion and transmission of racist, sexist, and homophobic views. Sandel's analysis of the positive values that can inhere in the communities he emphasizes is incomplete without a corresponding discussion of the negative values, which, at least in the United States, have also been part of those communities. A political discussion of the family without reference to its traditional patriarchal structure, for example, or of neighborhoods without acknowledging the long history of de jure and de facto housing discrimination on the basis of race, provides an incomplete view of the effects of given communities in the instillation and transmission of less than attractive views among some Americans.[28]

In fact, the same communities that Sandel believes can (1) help individuals in the constitutive process of identity and character formation and (2) revitalize American democracy have contributed to the oppression and stigmatization of lesbians and gay men. The list of examples that could be provided here is long. I will limit myself to briefly mentioning two examples. First, lesbians and gay men face a level of rejection and ostracization by their own biological families that is greater than that faced by just about any other group in America (including probably even criminals).[29] Whereas for other minorities, biological families can serve as sources of comfort and protection against the larger and often hostile society, many lesbians and gay men are either rejected outright by their families or are placed in the excruciatingly difficult position of having to choose between a relationship with their biological families and the leading of an honest and open life. A second example of the ostracization and pain inflicted on lesbians and gay men by given communities is provided by the African American churches—the same communities that Sandel praises in *Democracy's Discontent* as bastions of participatory democracy and civic virtue—that have turned their backs on their gay parishioners who are HIV positive.[30] In order to attain a degree of self-respect and self-worth, then, many lesbians and gay men have to at least partially *extricate* themselves from the very given communities that Sandel's civic republicanism values so highly.

The problem is that communities that are constitutive of a predetermined character and identity are not necessarily affirming of individual self-worth and dignity, or particularly interested in promoting personal autonomy. In fact, there is considerable tension between the inculcation of values by given communities and an individual's choices and preferences. Voluntarily created communities whose membership rules and obligations are subject to negotiation and bargaining are more likely to recognize "the possibility of disagreement and the contingent character of compromise."[31] The same cannot be said for Sandel's given communities, where the appropriate character and identity that are to be inculcated and transmitted through them have been determined long before the individual joins or, more often, is born into them. As a result, given communities often fail to promote tolerance and respect for individuals whom they view as having ideas, preferences, and values that undermine their norms and practices.

It is, of course, as dangerous to idealize communities of choice as it is to idealize given communities. Communities of choice—including gay and lesbian communities—sometimes trample on the choices and priorities of individual members in order to promote stability and cooperation. As Susan Krieger notes, in the context of discussing lesbian communities (and the same applies to gay male communities), "[t]he problems posed by lesbian communities are similar to those found in many other social groups and especially in minority groups, where efforts to achieve group solidarity and cohesiveness often conflict with efforts to foster individuality and to tolerate internal deviance."[32] Despite the tendency of communities of all kinds to prioritize cohesiveness over individuality, however, those communities created through the voluntary acts of their members usually allow greater room for flexibility, disagreement, and dialogue.[33]

In the end, however, it is not a matter of prioritizing communities of choice over given communities or vice versa. It is true that for some lesbians and gay men, communities of choice have completely replaced the more traditional given communities from which they came. But for most, the situation is more complex because they retain links and attachments to their given communities while simultaneously becoming deeply embedded into the communities they create around sexuality, choice, love, and friendship.[34] This complex struggle of multiple commitments and multiple sources of character, identity, and empowerment means that Sandel's effort to prioritize traditional, nonvoluntary communities is too simple. As Marilyn Friedman notes, "[t]he problem is not simply to appreciate community per se but rather to reconcile the conflicting claims, demands, and identity-defining influences of the variety of communities of which one is a part."[35]

Moral liberalism, I believe, strikes the appropriate balance between, on the one hand, a traditional liberalism that is insufficiently cognizant, as the communitarian critique tells us, of the role that ties and connections with others play in the leading of free and empowered lives and, on the other, a Sandellian communitarianism that values communities only when they are not chosen. As noted in the last chapter, moral liberalism understands that individuals attain their well-being and autonomy largely through relationships and attachments with others. Although the emphasis there was on intimate relationships (both sexual and familial), this section has explored how the ties and connections that are important to lesbians and gay men are broader in scope: They include the many communities of choice to which they belong and through which they seek support, solace, and protection from a hostile and disapproving society. Moral liberalism, then, agrees with the communitarian critique of traditional liberalism that views the self as being prior to and separated from its communities and attachments. Moral liberalism, however, rejects the idea that individuals are empty vessels that wait passively to be given an identity and character by their given communities. A limitation of communitarianism—and, as we will see in the next chapter, of postmodernism—is that it does not sufficiently account for the ability of individuals to participate actively in constructing the conditions that make it possible for them to lead free and dignified lives. Lesbians and gay men, through their formation of strong, thriving, and sustaining communities, have shown how even marginalized and oppressed individuals can significantly contribute to the creation of the necessary conditions that promote both their well-being and their freedom.

As I noted in chapter 3, moral liberalism, like all forms of liberalism, places the highest normative priority on the individual. It is the well-being and autonomy of *each* individual that matters. Sandel's political morality, on the other hand, places the highest normative value on communities and speaks of them as having value that is independent of their constitutive members. For Sandel, therefore, what seems to matter is that communities, mostly as currently constituted and understood, be promoted and strengthened. It is possible, however, to recognize, as moral liberalism does, the importance and value of communal ties and relationships while at the same time viewing them as secondary to or derivative of the individuals who constitute them. Even if Sandel is correct that traditional liberalism has either ignored or minimized the importance of community in the promotion of democratic processes and norms, we need to be careful not to go too far in the other direction by placing community values and priorities before those of individuals. The better choice is that offered by moral liberalism, one that recognizes that relationships and ties, both personal and communal, are an integral part of the ways in which individuals attain their well-being and exercise their autonomy while always keeping in mind that individuals are the ends and relationships and communities are the means.

3. WALZER AND JUSTICE

Michael Walzer is another leading communitarian critic of liberalism. Whereas Sandel's principal target of criticism has been liberalism's failure to recognize and value the embeddedness of individuals in the communities to which they belong, Walzer's main criticism of liberalism has been its proclivity for universalizing principles of justice. For Walzer, justice inheres in a society's shared traditions; by definition, therefore, different societies will have different interpretations of what is just. We are best able to capture the meaning of justice, Walzer argues, by paying attention to local norms and practices through moral and social criticism that is internal to shared understandings. As we will see, Walzer's political theory is thoughtful and complex. He has developed the most comprehensive theory of justice of any contemporary communitarian political thinker. In this section, I summarize that theory and in the next I apply it to the two issues that have been our primary concern from the beginning: same-sex marriage and parenting by lesbians and gay men.

The starting place for Walzer's theory of justice, as set forth in his book *Spheres of Justice,* is the shared traditions through which particular societies give meaning and value to social goods. "Goods in the world," he explains, "have shared meanings because [their] conception and creation are social processes. For the same reason, goods have different meanings in different societies" (SJ, 7). The distributive criteria that a particular society employs to allocate goods, like the meaning of the goods themselves, are dependent on social understandings and traditions. As a result, the justness of those distributions is "relative to the social meanings of the goods at stake" (SJ, 9). Given that justice inheres in shared understandings, therefore, a certain fluidity characterizes what social norms consider to be just or unjust: "Social meanings are historical in character; and so distributions, and just and unjust distributions, change over time" (SJ, 9). The analysis that Walzer proposes "is imminent and phenomenological in character. It will yield not an ideal map or a master plan but, rather, a map and a plan appropriate to the people for whom it is drawn, whose common life it reflects" (SJ, 26). As a result, Walzer disapproves of the view of the political philosopher as one isolated from the rest of society in an ivory tower thinking about the *a priori* conditions that are necessary for the creation of a just society. Instead, Walzer views the political philosopher as historian, anthropologist, and sociologist, immersing herself in the interpretation and evaluation of the shared traditions and understandings of a particular society.

Walzer argues that there are three different important paths for "doing moral philosophy": discovery, invention, and interpretation (ISC, 3). He is critical of the path of discovery—by which he means the attempt to discover principles of moral truth through internal reflection or reasoning— because it encourages the philosopher to "do" philosophy by separating herself from her social contexts. The result of such turning inward is often rather prosaic as the philosopher ends up "discovering" principles that "are already in our possession, incorporated, as it were, long ago, familiar and well-thumbed by now" (ISC, 6). The path of invention, which is the path that Walzer notes is preferred by thinkers such as John Rawls and Jürgen Habermas, emphasizes methodology and a design procedure to achieve ends that are right and just. Under this approach, philosophers seek to create or invent a morality "against which we can measure any person's life, any society's practices" (ISC, 13). Walzer is skeptical of such universalistic aspirations; we do not, he argues, need to invent and create new moral methodologies and principles when people in particular societies already share a moral culture and language. It is a mistake to ask them to replace that culture and language with the inventions by philosophers of universal methodologies and principles.

Walzer's preferred path for doing moral philosophy, then, is that of interpretation. This approach "lends itself less to abstract modeling than to thick description. Moral argument . . . is interpretative in character, closely resembling the work of a lawyer or judge who struggles to find meaning in a morass of conflicting laws and precedents" (ISC, 20). To critics who dismiss the interpretative approach as too positivistic and overly descriptive (i.e., as too concerned with what is as opposed to what ought to be), Walzer responds by noting that "the most interesting parts of the moral world are only in principle factual matters; in practice [moral facts] have to be 'read,' rendered, construed, glossed, elucidated, and not merely described" (ISC, 29). The interpretation of a shared tradition requires more than simply studying behavioral patterns because that tradition is "frequently expressed in general concepts—in its historical ideals, its public rhetoric, its foundational texts, its ceremonies and rituals" (ISC, 30). Moral interpretation, Walzer adds, "will sometimes confirm and sometimes challenge received opinion. And if we disagree with either the confirmation or the challenge, there is nothing to do but go back to the 'text'—the values, principles, codes, and conventions that constitute the moral world—and to the 'readers' of the text" (ISC, 30).

Given that different social goods within different societies are distributed according to different criteria, Walzer believes that the key to justice is to ensure that the distributive criteria (1) are consistent with the shared traditions of their society and (2) are applied only in their appropriate spheres. As Walzer explains, "[e]very social good or set of goods constitutes, as it were, a distributive sphere within which only certain criteria and arrangements are appropriate. Money is inappropriate in the sphere of ecclesiastical office; it is an intrusion from another sphere. And piety should make for no advantage in the marketplace, as the marketplace has commonly been understood" (SJ, 10). The key to justice, then, is to make sure that the distributive criterion that is appropriate in one sphere, according to a society's shared traditions, does not spill over and dominate other spheres. Walzer notes that most egalitarians concern themselves with ensuring that no distributive criterion monopolizes any particular sphere. He argues, however, that the focus should not be on whether a particular distributive criterion *monopolizes* a particular sphere, but on whether it *dominates* outside of its appropriate sphere. For example, the fact that money monopolizes the distribution of commodities in a capitalist society such as the American one is just because it is consistent with the society's shared meanings and traditions. Injustice results when the role and influence of money dominates the distribution of goods from other spheres such as religious, educational, and political spheres.

Walzer favors "complex equality," by which he means an acceptance of distributive monopolies—and thus inequalities—within specific spheres and a rejection of the domination by a distributive criterion outside of its proper sphere. As Walzer explains, complex equality

> establishes a set of relationships such that domination is impossible. In formal terms, complex equality means that no citizen's standing in one sphere or with regard to one social good can be undercut by his standing in some other sphere, with regard to some other good. Thus, citizen X may be chosen over citizen Y for political office, and then the two of them will be unequal in the sphere of politics. But they will not be unequal generally so long as X's office gives him no advantages over Y in any other sphere—superior medical care, access to better schools for his children, entrepreneurial opportunities, and so on (SJ, 19).

Complex equality is different from "simple equality"; under a regime of simple equality, the same distributive criterion applies across the spectrum of social goods. The idea of simple equality fails to capture the way in which different spheres operate under different distributive principles. For example, Walzer notes that the maxim " '[t]o each according to his needs,' may be acceptable—from an American perspective, given our shared traditions—for government services such as welfare, but it is an inappropriate criterion for the allocation of political power, religion, or marriage" (SJ, 25–26).[36] According to Walzer, neither that distributive maxim nor any other should apply *across* spheres.

Walzer also argues that the list of goods that a community decides to provide directly to individuals through its government rather than, for example, through market exchanges, will depend on the values and priorities of that community. He notes, however, that "[o]nce the community undertakes to provide some needed good, it must provide it to all the members who need it in proportion to their needs. The actual distribution will be limited by the available resources; but all other criteria, beyond need itself, are experienced as distortions and not as limitations of the distributive process" (SJ, 75). Walzer uses medical care as an example of a community-provided good. In the United States, the state provides health care through subsidies for some individuals (mainly the poor and elderly). Walzer argues that once the state, at the request of its citizens, participates in the provision of health care to some who are in need, it must allocate that good to everyone according to need and not wealth. In the United States, however, "no political decision has yet been made to challenge directly the system of free enterprise in medical care. And so long as that system exists, wealth will be dominant in (this part of) the sphere of security and welfare; individuals will be cared for in proportion to their ability to pay and not to their need for care" (SJ, 89). According to Walzer, this pattern of distribution of health care is unjust because it does not use the distributive principle (needs) called for by the shared tradition in the United States for the distribution of community-provided goods.[37]

It is important to emphasize that Walzer's theory does not prioritize any specific sphere or any specific distributive criterion. No spheres or distributive criteria are *ex ante* more valuable than others in the same way that no principle of justice, such as Rawls's difference principle or Dworkin's equality of resources, cuts across spheres. For Walzer, we avoid tyranny and injustice not by relying on principles of justice that are ostensibly applicable universally; instead, we do so by keeping distributive spheres separated from each other. Whereas Sandel's call for the removal of moral brackets is an effort to overlap purposefully the spheres of politics and morality, Walzer's strict separation of spheres is a form of bracketing writ large—bracketing that protects spheres from each other across society. Political, social, economic, and religious spheres must remain separated so that their respective distributive criteria do not influence the distribution of goods in other spheres.

4. INTERNAL SOCIAL CRITICISM: SAME-SEX MARRIAGE AND PARENTING BY LESBIANS AND GAY MEN

A discussion of gay rights issues from the perspective of Walzer's political philosophy does not begin with the traditional and familiar liberal ideals of autonomy, privacy, and tolerance. Instead, the starting place is an assessment of how society defines and distributes goods such as marriage and parenthood that are subject to gay rights disputes. From a gay rights perspective, Walzer's theory of internal social criticism has both benefits and limitations. By forcing us to grapple with the meaning of social goods and their respective distributive criteria as understood by shared traditions, Walzer helpfully reminds us of the importance of local understandings in moral and social criticism and wisely counsels against the use of abstract arguments that have little correlation to the ways in which particular societies give meaning to (and distribute) particular social goods.

There are two principal limitations, however, with Walzer's theory of internal social criticism. The first is that Walzer not only requires us to abide by norms that are internal to a given society, he also requires us to abide by norms internal to *specific* spheres within societies. In doing so, his approach disregards shared values that are important and relevant precisely because they cut across spheres. The second limitation is that a form of criticism that restricts itself to local traditions and practices does not give us the necessary means to criticize traditions and practices that are both shared by a society *and* are oppressive of and harmful to particular individuals and groups. In the following, I explore both the benefits and limitations of Walzer's theory of internal social criticism by discussing them in the contexts of same-sex marriage and parenting by lesbians and gay men.

THE CASE OF SAME-SEX MARRIAGE

Liberal theory, as I noted in chapter 3, generally relies on a distinction between a private sphere, which it considers to be outside of the concerns of political morality, and a public sphere that is the legitimate subject of societal regulation. Although the separation of spheres is a cornerstone of Walzer's theory of justice, he disagrees with the idea that there are some spheres that are "private" and thus somehow immune from considerations of justice. Thus, for example, he argues that it is "a mistake to think of kinship and love as a sphere different from all the others, as a sacred precinct . . . safe from philosophical criticism" (SJ, 227). As he explains it, "[t]he rules of kinship are an anthropological feast, wonderfully various and highly seasoned. There are a hundred ways in which the basic distributive question—Who . . . whom?—is asked and answered. Who can sleep with whom? Who can marry whom? Who lives with whom? Who eats with whom? Who celebrates with whom? Who must show respect to whom? Who is responsible for whom?" (SJ, 228). As a result, a social good such as that of marriage, through which so many people arrange their personal and intimate lives, is no different from any other social good that is subject to distribution; both its meaning and distributive criteria are determined through shared understandings. Those understandings vary considerably among societies and even change within societies with the passage of time. Walzer points out, for example, that in the West "before the Industrial Revolution . . . marriages were complex matters of exchange and alliance, carefully planned and elaborately negotiated" (SJ, 234). In Western societies until relatively recently, marriage was understood as playing an important part in the advancement of the economic fortunes and social positions of the prospective spouses' families. Parents participated in selecting whom their children married partly due to an abiding interest in promoting the family's political, social, and economic positions. In more contemporary times, however, these considerations have receded in importance, and the notion of choice as a more appropriate distributive criterion for the social good of marriage has emerged. As a result, a clearer separation currently exists between the sphere of marriage and the spheres of politics and economics so that decisions as to who should join whom in the former sphere are made largely independently of considerations emanating from the latter spheres.

Nancy Cott notes in her book on the history of marriage in the United States that the consent of individuals to be married has been a crucial component of marriage from the earliest days of the republic.[38] Of course, the fact that American women have traditionally chosen whom to marry does not mean that they have consented to the marked inequality that for most of our history, as Cott also shows, women have suffered once *in* the institution of marriage. It is difficult to dispute, however, that choice is a crucial criterion through which our society distributes marriage, quite apart from the conditions of gender inequality that might exist once the marriage is formed. Our social norms allow and encourage individuals to marry those whom they love. As the sociologist Steven Nock notes, "[t]he most widely shared normative aspect of contemporary marriage is the strong association between it and love. Mate selection in this country has become a matter of personal choice."[39]

It is possible then to argue, in applying Walzer's theory of internal social criticism, that denying lesbians and gay men the opportunity to marry is unjust because the prohibition is inconsistent with "the most widely shared normative aspect of contemporary marriage," namely, choice. Lesbians and gay men, to use Walzerian terminology, are simply asking for the benefit of the same distributive criterion that heterosexuals use to distribute among themselves the social good of marriage. A court in Alaska recently followed this line of reasoning in a case involving the constitutionality of that state's prohibition against same-sex marriage. In discussing the protections that constitutional principles of substantive due process affords individuals, the court stated that

> [t]he question presented by this case is whether the personal decision by those who choose a mate of the same gender will be recognized as [a] fundamental right. *Clearly, the right to choose one's life partner is quintessentially the kind of decision which our culture recognizes as personal and important. Though the choice of a partner is not left to the individual in some cultures, in ours it is no one else's to make.* . . . The relevant question is not whether same-sex marriage is so rooted in our traditions that it is a fundamental right, but whether the freedom to choose one's own life partner is so rooted in our traditions.[40]

If free choice guided by love is *the* most important criterion in the way in which our society currently distributes the social good of marriage, then that would argue in favor of recognizing same-sex marriages. The problem, of course, is that opponents of such recognition will quickly argue that *gender* constitutes another crucial distributive criterion in our culture's shared understanding of marriage. Our society, they will contend, has always considered gender to be an essential or constitutive part of marriage that limits—and is therefore prior to—free choice. Walzer's theory of internal social criticism has a difficult time helping us choose which one of these two different interpretations of the meaning of marriage is most appropriate given our (conflicting) shared traditions.

For gay rights proponents, one possible way of prioritizing choice over gender in determining the more appropriate meaning of marriage in our society is to point to the ways in which gender is becoming less relevant in many of our social, political, and economic institutions. If we as a society are moving toward greater gender equality and are therefore assigning less moral and political relevance to gender as such, then it would be consistent with that trend to de-emphasize gender as an essential element of marriage. Walzer would not allow us to argue in this way, however, because in order to be consistent with his theory of internal social criticism, we have to limit ourselves to the degendering that has taken place *within* the sphere of marriage. That presents a problem for gay rights proponents because though there are more marital heterosexual relationships today that are less driven by gender roles than a generation or two ago, gender roles within marriage nonetheless remain quite strong. Although husbands, for example, are generally doing more of their share of housework, wives continue to do significantly more even as growing numbers of them are also working outside of the home.[41] Women are also still the ones who are primarily responsible for caring for children who are part of a marriage.[42] It is not clear, therefore, if we simply limit ourselves to the sphere of marriage (or of the family), that degendering within that sphere has become prevalent enough for us to conclude that belonging to different genders (with their accompanying predetermined roles) is no longer a crucial part of the meaning of marriage according to our shared traditions. We could certainly make the normative argument that gender *ought* not to be a dispositive criterion in our understanding of marriage given the kind of deep inequality (both inside and outside of the family) that an emphasis on gender distinctions creates for women. It is that kind of argument that I made in chapter 3 when I noted the contribution that the recognition of same-sex marriages would make to the degendering of the institution of marriage, which would, in turn, contribute to the formation of a better, less sexist society. But it is difficult to make that argument solely from the perspective of practices and understandings within the sphere of marriage and the family as they currently exist, given that gender continues to play such an important role in the way in which many Americans define and practice their marital relationships.

Where we could find more powerful evidence of degendering is *outside* of the family, where women have made important strides in the political and economic spheres. But if we abide by Walzer's prescribed strict separation between spheres as a way of promoting just distributions, then we cannot use the (partial) degendering in the economic and political spheres to influence our evaluations of internal family practices. This seems unduly restrictive and creates an artificial separation between the family and other spheres akin to the liberal separation between private and public spheres. The allocation of power and roles within the family affect social, political, and economic arrangements outside of it, and vice versa.[43] One would think that a deemphasis on gender distinctions in social, political, and economic spheres should be relevant in assessing the appropriateness of gender distinctions within the family, including whether belonging to opposite genders should continue to be a defining characteristic of our understanding of marriage.

The degendering that is taking place in the American society is not the only norm that runs across spheres that might help us resolve the internal logjam created by the conflicting traditions represented by "choice" and "gender" in the meaning of marriage in our society. Another value that *cuts across* social, political, and economic spheres in the American society is a respect for individual autonomy and the idea that individuals should be able to make important decisions about their lives and their future. Issues of choice and personal autonomy are valued in American culture not only in terms of whom to marry, but also in terms of choosing political and social affiliations, as well as in deciding where and how one lives and works. Clearly some individuals, because of social and economic advantages, have a greater range of choices than others, yet it is difficult to deny that freedom of choice in broad areas of political, economic, and social life is a shared tradition among Americans. One would also think, therefore, that such a shared understanding that cuts across many different spheres should be relevant in helping us resolve the conflicting social meanings of marriage. Walzer's theory of internal social criticism, which constrains our use of shared traditions to those that are internal to specific spheres, then, turns out to be too limited.[44] It is not at all clear that we can, or should, limit ourselves to making arguments in favor of lifting the prohibition against same-sex marriage solely from within the sphere of marriage itself.

But even if Walzer's theory is too limited in its belief that the normative tools required to grapple with difficult issues of justice can be found in the shared traditions of particular spheres as they are currently understood, that does not necessarily undermine his broader point that moral and social criticism must remain internal to a society, and that the search for universal criteria that are meaningful and helpful in solving what are by their very nature local disputes and disagreements is hopeless. What undermines that broader point are the difficulties presented by those traditions that are widely shared but are nonetheless oppressive of and harmful to particular individuals and groups. Walzer has in this regard been criticized for suggesting that the hierarchical and inegalitarian caste system of India cannot be deemed unjust if it is consistent with the shared understandings of its participating members (SJ, 313). As one critic notes, "it is surely unreasonable to assign . . . overwhelming weight in deciding questions of justice and injustice to internal states of (real or apparent) consensus when these may depend so largely on force or ignorance."[45] Ronald Dworkin, for his part, criticizes Walzer for his relativism and for thinking of justice as our mirror (i.e., as simply reflecting what we do) rather than as our critic (MP, 219).

Our nation's shared traditions regarding homosexuality, as reflected in morality, religion, medicine, and law, have for most of the country's history either ignored lesbians and gay men altogether or sought to exclude them from countless social goods—including, of course, marriage and parenthood—because of an assessment that their sexuality is depraved, abnormal, and dangerous. Lesbians and gay men for most of our history have had no choice but to accept and even participate in those shared traditions, often by denying to others their true identity and sexuality, because to do otherwise presented grave and unacceptable personal risks. To limit ourselves to making arguments for change from within those traditions makes it less likely that we will ever be able to *transform* our society into one that values lesbians and gay men as truly equal human beings and that allows them to lead lives that are both free and dignified. This is why, as moral liberalism holds, we need to incorporate into our moral and social criticism those human commonalities that permit us to evaluate, both ethically and politically, local practices in terms of whether they promote or undermine the conditions necessary for the leading of full human lives. This search for commonalities does not mean that we have to transcend or step outside the interpretation of actual human practices. As Martha Nussbaum argues, and as we discussed in chapter 3, assessments as to what constitutes a full human life must be made from within interpretations of human history and practices. Thus, Nussbaum, like Walzer, prefers doing moral and political philosophy through interpretation, rather than through discovery or invention. Moral liberalism encourages us to search for human commonalities, as reflected in basic needs and capabilities, that are internal to experiences and practices, and that, while manifested in many different ways, are nonetheless shared by individuals living in different cultures and times.

Walzer acknowledges that there may be "certain internal principles, certain conceptions of social goods, [that] are reiterated in many, perhaps in all, human societies" (SJ, 314n). But whether such commonalities exist is for Walzer a matter of empirical as opposed to philosophical investigation. There are two problems with Walzer's position. First, by emphasizing only empirical investigations we are left with the limitations inherent in constraining ourselves to describing and understanding shared practices as they currently exist as opposed to assessing them ethically. For moral and social criticism to be meaningful, we need both empirical investigations *and* ethical evaluations. The former without the latter leaves us relying on descriptions of the status quo, or of what is "natural" as reflected in common human practices, without the necessary means for critiquing adequately those practices that are, as currently understood by large segments of the population, oppressive of and harmful to particular individuals and groups. The latter without the former leaves us relying on *a priori* principles and truths that are disconnected to the aspirations and vulnerabilities of real human beings. As the discussion of new natural law philosophy in chapter 3 sought to illustrate, such a disconnect between theory and the actual lives of real individuals can lead to misguided, and often harmful, assessments of moral value.

The second problem is that Walzer limits his (admittedly grudging) recognition that there may be relevant commonalities that apply to all human societies to those that are expressed through the meanings of social goods. The value of social goods, however, is derivative rather than fundamental. In other words, to the extent that social goods are valuable it is because of the benefits and opportunities they provide to the individuals whom they serve. A social good does not have a value that is independent of the individuals who benefit from its distribution. This is why moral liberalism searches for commonalities not at the level of social goods (marriage, jobs, wealth, and so on), but at the level of individuals. Moral liberalism does not ask which understandings of social goods are valuable because they are shared by *societies* across time and place; moral liberalism asks instead which attributes of *individuals*, as reflected in their needs and capabilities, are valuable because they are shared across time and place. A focus on individuals and their well-being, rather than on the value of social goods, allows us to raise justice-based objections when particular individuals and groups are treated in oppressive and harmful ways. A social good cannot be harmed, oppressed, or wronged if it is distributed in an improper way; it is human beings who suffer the consequences of unjust distributions (however defined), and as such, it is with them that our moral focus should remain. What should matter ultimately is not the protection and promotion of social goods as understood by the shared traditions of one or more societies, but the support and furtherance of the social conditions necessary to provide all individuals with the opportunity to lead lives that are fully human.

The shared traditions of most societies—including most Western ones—continue to demean gay and lesbian sexuality and relationships. To rely exclusively on the meaning of social goods as reflected in shared traditions gives us little comfort at the end of the day that individuals who are physically and emotionally attracted to others of the same gender will be permitted to lead free and dignified lives. The ability to criticize local practices from the perspective of shared human commonalities is crucial for individuals, such as lesbians and gay men, who have been simultaneously ignored and marginalized by local practices. On the other hand, it is undoubtedly true that there are dangers associated with any attempt to universalize, including the real possibility, as experience has shown time and time again, that what are defended as universal norms are reflections of the priorities of the powerful and privileged. As noted in chapter 3, there are two ways in which those dangers can be minimized. First, universal norms must be arrived at through interpretation of human experiences and practices rather than through the application of *a priori* reasoning or abstract principles that have no correspondence to the ways in which people lead their lives. Second, we must constantly remind ourselves that there are many different ways in which that which is universal can be manifested and expressed so that our search for commonalities does not lead us to threaten or undermine pluralism and diversity.

To return to the specific issue of same-sex marriage: in order to resolve the conflict over whether choice or gender should be the most important criterion in the distribution of marriage, we need to rely on moral evaluations that are consistent with but are grounded on considerations that go beyond the meaning of marriage as currently understood in the United States. Thus, for example, the conservative new natural law theorists prioritize what they consider to be the natural complementarity of men and women that they argue, as discussed in chapter 3, creates a biological and personal unity that has moral value and that exists only in heterosexual intimacy. For the new natural law theorist, therefore, the internal logjam between choice and gender in our shared understandings of marriage should be resolved in favor of the latter. For the follower of moral liberalism, on the other hand, what matters normatively is that individuals have the opportunity to meet basic human needs and exercise basic human capabilities. The moral liberal, therefore, will resolve the internal logjam as to the appropriate meaning of marriage in our society in favor of choice because she will view the needs and capabilities that lesbians and gay men have to love and care for others of the same gender in a sexually intimate relationship as constitutive elements of their humanity that society should promote and protect. The moral liberal will also point out how an emphasis on gender as a constitutive element of marriage has actually interfered with rather than promoted the basic needs and capabilities of many women.

To say that we need to go beyond Walzer's internal social criticism to moral considerations that are more universal in nature does not mean, of course, that that criticism is useless or besides the point. Walzer's internal criticism contributes in important ways to the framing of the issues and helps us to reject moral arguments that are not reflected in some way in our shared traditions as to the meaning of the social good in question (such as the way in which the new natural law arguments are reflected in the internal shared understanding of marriage that prioritizes gender and the way in which the arguments of moral liberalism are reflected in the internal prioritization of choice in marriage). Walzer's insistence that we grapple with the internal meanings of social goods and their respective distributive criteria is important because it reminds us that abstract arguments disconnected from the local meanings of goods that are subject to distribution by a particular society are unlikely to hold much moral weight. Walzer forces us to discuss and struggle with the different possible meanings of the social goods that are at issue in debates over justice, and therein lies the importance of his work.

Given that I have dedicated most of this section on same-sex marriage to a discussion of the limitations of Walzer's theory of internal social criticism, I want to use the next section on parenting by lesbians and gay men to show just how much can be accomplished through that kind of criticism. As in the area of marriage, I do not believe that arguments limited to shared traditions are sufficient to present a full justification as to why lesbians and gay men should be allowed and encouraged to become parents. That is why at the end of chapter 3, I presented arguments on behalf of gay and lesbian parents based on their needs and capabilities as human beings. But those arguments can certainly be supplemented with ones that are more particular to the ways in which our society, through its laws and norms, defines the meaning of parenthood.

THE CASE OF PARENTING BY LESBIANS AND GAY MEN

The meaning of parenthood in any society is a complicated issue that deserves detailed and extensive study. It is possible, however, to identify briefly, as I do below, some major themes that are crucial components of that meaning. My goal here is not to explore those themes exhaustively, but is instead to present them in a summarized fashion in order to illustrate how Walzer's internal social criticism can be applied to a specific subject of dispute involving gay rights in a way that helps us frame the issues and reach some normative conclusions based entirely on shared traditions and understandings.

Parenthood, like marriage, is a social good that is defined through laws and social norms, and as such is subject to distribution according to certain values. In the United States, those values are, in my opinion, the following: autonomy, universality, and responsibility. I explain below why I believe these are the three most important values that are constitutive of the meaning of parenthood in our society and then explain why all three are supportive of parenting by lesbians and gay men.

Autonomy.   Our shared traditions on parenthood highly value the freedom of adults to decide whether and when to become parents. Our norms do not support or encourage the interference by the state or the community with the life-changing decision of whether (and when) individuals should have children. Furthermore, for those who decide to become parents, our culture accords them significant respect and discretion in making important decisions regarding their children's well-being, education, and moral upbringing. All of these autonomy-based considerations are reflected in our constitutional doctrine. The Supreme Court has made it clear that individuals have a fundamental right to decide whether to have children.[46] That right has been understood as granting individuals the autonomy to make important decisions about their lives and bodies. The constitutionally protected right to use contraceptives (within and without marriage) reinforces the cultural norm that it is up to the individual (or couple) to decide whether and when to become parents.[47] As the Court has noted, "[t]his is understandable, for in a field that by definition concerns the most intimate of human activities and relationships, decisions whether to accomplish or to prevent conception are among the most private and sensitive."[48] Similarly, the Supreme Court has for almost a century now made it clear that parents have the right to make decisions regarding their children's education and well-being without interference by the state.[49] Adding further protection to the parent-child relationship, our laws also require that the state meet a high burden of showing abuse and neglect or abandonment of a child before involuntarily terminating parental rights.[50]

Universality.   There is considerably more to the meaning of parenthood in our society than the autonomy norms that have become deeply embedded in constitutional doctrine. The United States, despite long-term declines in birth rates and family size, remains a strong pronatalist society where individuals are expected to have children, in the same way that they are expected to marry.[51] This strong pronatalist sentiment runs throughout society, transcending categories of race, gender, age, religion, and class.[52] Thus, in 1998, only 19 percent of American women between the ages of 40 and 44 were childless.[53]

Although every society obviously has an interest in procreation, different cultures have different ways of expressing it. In the United States, beginning with the baby boom that followed World War II, parenthood has become "a major marker of adulthood" and a significant source of personal identity and actualization.[54] Our culture considers having children to be one of the most meaningful ways of pursuing happiness and fulfillment. Those who are voluntarily childless are deemed by the culture to be irresponsible, odd, and nonconformist. The motives of voluntarily childless women in particular are scrutinized with suspicion because they are viewed as having failed in their "duty" to have children.[55] The stigma is not significantly different for involuntarily childless couples, though those couples also have to deal with the added disgrace of a perceived physical deficiency or inadequacy. In involuntary childless couples, infertility is likely to be attributed to the woman even though men are as likely to be infertile.[56] Given that our society still defines and assesses women largely through their status and functioning as mothers, our norms equate childless women, whether they are so voluntarily or involuntarily, with failure, inadequacy, and disgrace.

It may appear at first that there is a conflict between, on the one hand, the value of autonomy, which as we have seen leaves it to individuals to decide whether to have children, and on the other, the universalistic or pronatalist norms that expect adults to have children and that stigmatize those who do not. That conflict can be mitigated, however, if we conceive of the value of autonomy as representing *rights* to parent whereas that of universality as representing *obligations* to parent. Parenthood in America, in other words, is both a right and a duty, though the duty these days is understood more as a duty owed to ourselves (in terms of pursuing happiness and fulfillment through our private lives) than to society at large.[57] The fact that the duty is more owed to ourselves than to others does not, however, minimize the stigma in the eyes of those others who view the lives of childless individuals as being, in crucial ways, incomplete and unfulfilled.

Responsibility.   The social meaning of parenthood is determined not only by questions of whether, when, and why individuals should become parents, but also by shared understandings of what being a *good* parent entails. In our culture, parents are expected to fulfill certain responsibilities toward their children that must be met for them to be deemed good parents. As law professor Elizabeth Scott notes in summing up the nature of those expectations, parents in our culture "are obligated to feed, clothe, shelter, discipline, socialize, educate, support, and love their children and to protect them from harm."[58] These expectations, as reflected in our social norms, "function to deter selfish behavior, encouraging parents to identify their own interests with those of their children."[59]

The norm of responsibility acts as a counterweight to that of autonomy. The meaning of parenthood in the United States, in other words, is not just about the rights of individuals to decide whether and how to parent; it is also about the needs of children and the corresponding *obligations* of care on the part of adults. In the United States, parents, and not extended families or the community or the state, are responsible for making sure that children are well taken care of and that their multiple needs are met. As with pronatalist norms, it is women who in our culture experience the brunt of the child responsibility norms because our society continues to hold them primarily responsible for the care of children. In fact, of the three norms associated with the meaning of parenthood in the United States identified above, two of them (universality and responsibility) are associated with obligations and one of them (autonomy) with rights. Not surprisingly, given our patriarchal culture, the norms associated with obligations and duties apply disproportionally to women.

The norms and values that in my estimation define the meaning of parenthood in the United States, then, are autonomy, universality, and responsibility. Walzer's theory of internal social criticism asks us to approach questions of justice raised by issues such as gay and lesbian parenting from within those norms and values. Before I discuss whether parenting by lesbians and gay men is consistent with the way in which we define parenthood in the United States, I want to discuss two other criteria that have also in the past been considered essential to the meaning of parenthood but which are less relevant in our society today: biology and marital status.

Although it is true that most American parents are biologically related to their children, biology no longer is a necessary element in our understanding of the meaning of parenthood in the United States. The main reason for this is the recognition, both legal and cultural, that adults who adopt children are as much the parents of those children as biological parents are of theirs.[60] Although the law has recognized this parity for many decades now, there was until more recently a strong social stigma associated with adoptive parenting. This stigma was so strong, in fact, that until relatively recently many adoptive parents did not inform their children, even when they became adults, that they had been adopted. Even though the stigma has not disappeared completely, it has significantly lessened in the last twenty years or so. Even if most Americans still prefer to have biological children rather than to adopt, those who adopt are as legitimate recipients of the label "parent" in our society as are those who are biologically related to their children.

The essentiality of biology to our shared understanding of parent-hood has also been undermined by the many heterosexuals who have di-vorced and remarried, and who have, as a result, helped to raise children to whom they are not biologically related. The delinking of biology from parenting is also reflected in doctrinal changes in the law that are beginning to recognize functional and intent-based parenting as the equivalent of biological parenting.[61] Although this area of the law is less well-established than adoption law, a growing number of courts are rec-ognizing that caretakers of children who are not biologically related to them but who have been *functioning* as parents should have the same rights and obligations as biological parents. Similarly, an intent to parent (as reflected, for example, in a surrogate contract) can under certain cir-cumstances be a sufficient ground for a finding of parenthood that trumps biological or genetic ties.[62] The connection between biology and parenthood, in other words, is no longer an essential or necessary one for the ways in which both our laws and culture define the meaning of who is a "parent."

It is interesting to note, in fact, that conservative opponents of par-enting by lesbians and gay men do not raise the link between biology and parenthood in discussing the issues associated with gay and lesbian parents as often as they raise the purported essentiality of reproductive (or, as we saw in chapter 3, of reproductive-like) sexual acts in the con-text of marriage. The difficulty for opponents of gay rights with relying on biology-based arguments is that changes in reproductive technology have made it possible for lesbians and gay men to have biological chil-dren. Lesbians are able to use donated sperm while gay men in some states have the option of contracting with surrogate mothers. In addi-tion, many openly gay and lesbian parents are raising biological children who were conceived in heterosexual marriages in the old-fashioned way (that is, without the assistance of technology). Biology, therefore, does not give opponents what they seek: a way of categorically distinguishing gay and lesbian parents from heterosexual parents.

Not so, of course, with marriage. As long as lesbians and gay men cannot marry, conservatives can continue to argue that marriage and parenthood are inextricably linked.[63] The problem with this argument is that the percentage of American families that fall under the tradi-tional model of children raised by a married man and woman living in the same home is shrinking rapidly (from 87 percent in 1970 to 69 percent in 2000).[64]

Conservatives respond to the changing demographics of the American family by arguing that even if the traditional model of the family is declin-ing as a descriptive matter, we should still aim for it as a policy goal because it remains the ideal and best way of raising children. There are at least two responses to this argument. First, millions of Americans know from their personal experiences of having been raised by single parents, or unmarried parents, or grandparents, that what conservatives dismiss as "less than ideal" family arrangements often provide forms of nurture, care, and support for children that are profound and enduring. By arguing that a married man and woman are essential to the formation of a family that is good for children, the defenders of the traditional family model are too quick to dismiss the value, contributions, and accomplishments of nontraditional families. Second, although it is not unreasonable to believe that everything else being equal, it is better to be raised by two parents rather than one and that marriage of the caretaking adults can offer stability and continuity in the lives of children, *neither* of those propositions is inconsistent with gay rights positions. In fact, it is ironic that it is more often than not the same conservatives who oppose parenting by lesbians and gay men who also oppose their marrying.[65] If one of the reasons for promoting the "ideal family," for example, is to prevent the harms that are claimed to accompany single parenthood and children born out of wedlock, then allowing lesbians and gay men—a growing number of whom are having or adopting children—to marry would reduce the number of both.

When we combine, therefore, conservatives' opposition to gay and lesbian parenting with their opposition to same-sex marriage, we are left with the realization that what really matters to them is not so much the *stability* in adult relationships that marriage offers (and which lesbians and gay men could take advantage of if permitted to marry, which would, in turn, benefit their children) but is instead, once again, the *gender* of the parents. (I addressed the issue of gender and parenting in chapter 3.) If what truly mattered in the conservatives' "ideal" conception of the family were in fact the stability and resources (both material and emotional) provided by families headed by two married individuals, that would argue in favor of recognizing same-sex marriages. Like biology, then, marriage by itself does not allow conservative opponents of gay rights to distinguish categorically between gay parents and straight parents, other than in the narrowly descriptive sense that under current law lesbians and gay men cannot marry and thus cannot, as married couples, raise children together.

If neither biology nor marriage, therefore, is an essential or necessary element of what it means to be either a parent or a good parent in the United States today, that leaves us with the three criteria identified above: autonomy, universality, and responsibility. All three of these are consistent with protecting the rights of current gay and lesbian parents and with encouraging and supporting future ones.

Autonomy. As noted above, our laws and social norms respect the choice of individuals to decide whether and when to have children. Our laws and culture have little tolerance for state-imposed restrictions on the decision of individuals to have children. The interests of autonomy, bodily integrity, and control over one's life almost always trump whatever concerns the state might try to promote by prohibiting or restricting individuals from having children, and those interests are not any different for lesbians and gay men from how they are for heterosexuals. In fact, given the fundamental nature of the right to have children, if the state tomorrow tried to prohibit or restrict the ability of lesbians and gay men to have biological children, such a ban would in all likelihood be struck down as unconstitutional.[66]

Universality.   Our shared pronatalist traditions and norms also argue in favor of parenting by lesbians and gay men. Lesbians and gay men who want to raise children are simply acting in the way that adults in the United States are expected to act. We cannot expect a gay or lesbian individual who lives in a society with such strong pronatalist norms to be immune from them. Lesbians and gay men are the only people in the United States who are the subject of concerted efforts to deny them the right to parent. The laws of some states, for example, prohibit lesbians and gay men *but no others* (including convicted criminals) from adopting.[67] As a result, lesbians and gay men find themselves in a perpetually stigmatized situation. If they choose to have children, they are accused of acting selfishly by trying to bring respectability to their otherwise morally suspect personal lives through the use of innocent and vulnerable children. If they choose *not* to have children, then they are subject to the same stigma that our society imposes on all childless individuals, viewing them as leading incomplete and unfulfilled lives. Lesbians and gay men in the United States who decide to raise children are not only, as I argued in chapter 3, expressing and exercising their basic human needs and capabilities to nurture and care for others, but they are also acting consistently with the pronatalist norms of their society.

Responsibility.   The social science literature indicates that lesbians and gay men as a group meet their responsibilities toward their children as well and as completely as do heterosexual parents.[68] The studies show that lesbians and gay men are parenting in ways *that are consistent with our society's definition of what it means to be a good parent*. Gay and lesbian parents are as loving, nurturing, and committed as are heterosexual parents.

The degree of consensus among experts on this issue was shown by the particulars offered by the state of Hawaii in 1996 in its defense of a lawsuit that alleged that its ban against same-sex marriage was unconstitutional. The state argued that it should be allowed to keep the ban because it had a compelling interest in encouraging the raising of children by heterosexual married couples and, by implication, an interest in discouraging the raising of children by lesbians and gay men. In order to establish this compelling interest at trial, the state called four expert witnesses to testify; three of those witnesses ended up, in parts of their testimony, considerably undermining the state's position. The first witness testified "that, in general, gay and lesbian parents are as fit and loving parents as non-gay persons and couples" and that "[s]ame-sex couples have the same capability as different-sex couples to manifest the qualities conducive to good parenting."[69] A second expert testified "that gay and lesbian couples can, and do, make excellent parents and that they are capable of raising a healthy child."[70] A third state witness testified "that the sexual orientation of a parent is not an indication of parental fitness."[71] (The court disregarded the testimony of a fourth witness called by the state because he testified that the social sciences are all suspect and that there is no scientific support for the theory of evolution.)[72]

The state's own witnesses, in other words, could not dispute the fact that lesbians and gay men, as a group, are raising their children well. This consensus among experts has led some courts to deem sexual orientation as irrelevant for purposes of determining what is in the best interests of children in the absence of specific evidence of harm, and others to conclude that children often benefit from having parents in committed relationships even if they are of the same gender.[73] It has also led the American Academy of Pediatrics, after reviewing the "growing body of scientific literature[,]" to conclude "that children who grow up with 1 or 2 gay and/or lesbian parents fare as well in emotional, cognitive, social, and sexual functioning as do children whose parents are heterosexual."[74]

In the face of convincing evidence that lesbians and gay men are good and responsible parents, opponents of gay rights rarely argue these days that lesbians and gay men are as a group irresponsible or unloving parents. Instead, the arguments are grounded on the idea that when it comes to parenting, love and nurture are not good enough. Lynn Wardle, for example, in his comprehensive critique of gay and lesbian parenting, suggests that whatever love, nurture, and care are provided by gay and lesbian parents, those goods are undermined and threatened by the parents' same-gender sexuality. Thus, Wardle asks rhetorically: "Is 'experiencing love and security' really the highest, ultimate value for child welfare? . . . Many variables affect child development, and to categorically state that nurturing/caring is always more important than parental sexuality is to state more than the evidence supports."[75] Wardle then proceeds to discuss the dangers of promiscuity, child molestation, domestic violence, and having sex in front of one's children as if any of that behavior has anything to do with the question of whether lesbians and gay men are capable of being good parents. Of course, a parent who molests her child or who has sex in front of her child is a bad parent, regardless of how much love and nurture that parent otherwise provides to her child.

In making this obvious point, however, Wardle misses the broader and more important one, namely, that lesbians and gay men (as a group), as the social science literature indicates, are caring, loving, nurturing, and being responsible for their children in ways that make them morally indistinguishable from straight parents (as a group). The fact that a highly respected family law scholar such as Professor Wardle feels compelled to resort to raising issues associated with child molestation and the consequences for children of their parents engaging in sexual conduct in front of them, in order to make the point that love and nurture does not always trump "sexuality," and that therefore lesbians and gay men should be discouraged from parenting, is a sign of the thinness of his empirical and normative arguments.

There is a lot more that can be said about both the values associated with parenthood in the United States and the ways in which parenting by lesbians and gay men is consistent with those values. The purpose of this brief discussion has been to explore some general themes on both of those issues. These are the kinds of arguments and considerations that can be raised from within Walzer's theory of internal social criticism that permit us to show, at least in part, why the exclusion of lesbians and gay men from the good of parenting is unjust. Walzer's theoretical model encourages us to grapple with what it means to be a parent, and, just as important, with what it means to be a *good* parent, in our society. Those meanings are on the side of present and prospective gay and lesbian parents.

FIVE

Postmodernism

It is possible to think of the reluctance that many liberal and progressive theorists feel toward the incorporation of notions of morality into discussions of political philosophy as forming a "continuum of skepticism." Neutral liberalism is at one end of that continuum. It is the least skeptical of the theories because it does not question either objective morality or truth—it simply doubts whether we can reach "reasonable and workable political agreement . . . on the truth of comprehensive doctrines" (PL, 63). Pragmatism (along with the communitarianism of Michael Walzer) is next on the continuum of skepticism. It also does not question our ability to make morally defensible judgments, but believes that those judgments are necessarily local as defined by internal customs, traditions, and understandings. We can reach moral conclusions, pragmatists hold, but only "by our lights" (PLM, 8). Next and last on the continuum is postmodernism, which does present us with an epistemological challenge to the ability of individuals to reach moral conclusions (whether universal or local) that are anything more than a reflection of power relations and systems of knowledge.

It is helpful to think of these theoretical perspectives as constituting a *continuum* because there are nuances and overlaps along the way. Although the ends of the continuum are quite distinct—there are, for example, stark differences between the neo-Kantianism of Rawls and Dworkin and the anti-Enlightenment positions of postmodernist philosophers—there are also gradations within the three categories (neutral liberalism, pragmatism, and postmodernism) identified above. Thus, the later Rawls is much closer to Rorty in his prioritization of politics over philosophy than Dworkin is. For his part, Rorty straddles the line between pragmatism and postmodernism whereas Posner does not.

In this chapter, I turn my attention to postmodernism. Given that postmodern moral and political philosophy is an immense subject matter, it is impossible to do it justice in one book, much less in one chapter.

In order to focus the discussion to a manageable degree, therefore, I concentrate on one narrow but important sliver of postmodernist philosophy, namely, Michel Foucault's writings on sexual ethics. Those writings shed further light on two of the principal issues explored in this book. First, they contribute to the discussion of whether it makes sense to think of certain human capabilities, and in particular of a capacity for autonomy, as universal. Second, they help us argue against the prevailing notion held by many opponents of gay rights that they have a monopoly on issues of sexual morality and ethics.

Liberals generally believe that human beings have a capacity for autonomy or self-determination.[1] Postmodernists, however, prefer to speak of agency rather than of autonomy; for them, the concept of autonomy is illusory because it suggests a subject or a self that can exist or function independently of the social forces that constitute it. But we need not view autonomy in such a way. In fact, some contemporary liberal theorists argue that a capacity for autonomy is recognizable and understandable only from within public meanings and social forces that in important ways determine that capacity. In this chapter, I rely on Foucault's later work to explain how the conception of agency held by some postmodernists is not terribly different from some liberal understandings of autonomy. At the same time, by emphasizing that Foucault, at least in his later years, believed that we can contribute to our own conditions of freedom and that we are, as a result, not always the helpless pawns of social forces beyond our control, I hope to show liberals that there is real value in Foucault's ideas.

The debates and disagreements between liberals and postmodernists are reflected in disputes within gay rights philosophy. The liberal philosopher Richard Mohr, for example, warns of the "perils of postmodernity for gay rights."[2] Mohr is particularly concerned about the relativism of postmodernism because he views it as undercutting arguments for both equality and freedom. On the other hand, postmodernists are highly skeptical of liberal ideas and priorities. The postmodernist queer theorist David Halperin, for example, contends that "lesbians and gay men . . . far from having been the beneficiaries of liberal, humanist notions of freedom, truth, and rationality, have tended rather to be the targets of a new kind of terror carried out in their name."[3]

Instead of adding to this legitimate though ultimately divisive debate, I try in this chapter to find some common ground on which both postmodernist queer theorists and liberal supporters of lesbians and gay men can stand. I seek to find this common ground in Foucault's later work and interviews, and in particular in his last two books: Volumes II and III of *The History of Sexuality*. Although no philosopher has had a greater impact on gay and lesbian studies than Foucault, that influence emanates largely from Volume I of *The History of Sexuality*; those interested in gay issues have paid scant attention to the other two volumes.

Volume I has been particularly influential in supporting the view that sexual orientation is socially constructed, a view that these days is shared by almost everyone in the social sciences and humanities who writes on issues of sexuality.[4] Postmodernist queer theorists go one step further by combining this antiessentialist understanding of sexuality with an antifoundationalist moral and political philosophy that rejects universal norms and values.[5]

In this chapter, I question whether an antifoundationalist conception of political morality must necessarily follow an antiessentialist understanding of sexual orientation. In particular, I argue that the universalist idea that we all as human beings share a capacity for autonomy, which has important implications for issues of sexuality, is not inconsistent with the view that sexual orientation categories and the meaning of sexual acts are socially constructed. Even if our identities (sexual and otherwise) are nothing more than the effects of social discourses and power relations, we still retain, as Foucault recognized at the end of his life, a capacity for autonomy, or as he would put it, an ability to participate actively in the constitution of our selves through practices of freedom. I believe that the need to protect and promote a capacity for autonomy is a universal concern that can contribute to the development of an alternative sexual ethic for marginalized sexual minorities, even if the sexual identities of those minorities form themselves entirely through processes of social construction.

The first reason, then, for delving into Foucault's writings on sexual ethics is to explore their (surprising) contributions to the question of whether human beings share a universal capacity for autonomy. The second reason is that those writings help us examine the meaning of a contemporary gay and lesbian sexual ethic. It is my contention that the legal, medical, and moral decodification of homosexuality that has taken place in the United States over the last forty years has allowed for the emergence of a gay and lesbian sexual ethic. The process through which such an ethic has emerged is similar to the care of the self and the practices of freedom that Foucault argues in Volumes II and III of *The History of Sexuality* were constitutive of sexual ethics in ancient Greece and Rome. Furthermore, a contemporary gay and lesbian sexual ethic emphasizes particular substantive values—such as openness, mutuality, and pleasure—making it a powerful and appealing alternative to the conception of sexual ethics held by the Christian tradition and its secular variation found in new natural law philosophy that makes moral judgments based, in part, on the nature of particular sexual acts. Foucault's writings contribute significantly to an understanding of the substantive values of a gay and lesbian sexual ethic. The existence of such an ethic challenges the conventional notion held by opponents of gay rights that sexual morality and ethics are only on one (their) side of the gay rights controversies that are part of our nation's moral, political, and legal debates.

1. FOUCAULT AND SEXUAL ETHICS

As noted, while academic commentators interested in issues of sexual orientation have been greatly influenced by *The History of Sexuality*, Volume I, they have barely paid attention to Foucault's writings on sex and sexuality that followed the publication of that book. In the first section below, I summarize Volume I and explain its implications for an anti-essentialist conception of sexual orientation. In the second section, I describe Foucault's post-Volume I shift on issues of sexuality from a focus on pervasive and hegemonic power relations and systems of knowledge to an emphasis on the ability of the subject to transform itself through practices of freedom. For Foucault, those practices of freedom are the constitutive elements of an ethical life. In the third section, I explore what Foucault takes to be the practices of freedom that constituted sexual ethics in ancient Greece and Rome.

THE HISTORY OF SEXUALITY, VOLUME 1

In *The History of Sexuality*, Volume I, Foucault explains how the discourse on sexuality in Western countries went through a transformation in the seventeenth century. At the beginning of that century, "sexual practices had little need of secrecy" (HS1, 3). People discussed sexual matters openly and "[c]odes regulating the coarse, the obscene, and the indecent were quite lax" (HS1, 3). By the end of the century, however, what we can characterize as the modern era of sexuality began. Two principal phenomena defined this era. First, areas of enforced silence were established where matters of sexuality were not to be discussed; these areas included the relationship "between parents and children, for instance, or teachers and pupils, or masters and domestic servants" (HS1, 18). At the same time, a second phenomenon took place, namely, an explosion of discourses concerning sex. Through discourses of science, medicine, and psychiatry, so-called experts began to study and analyze sex at a great level of detail. Different disciplines sought to schematize human sexuality through an endless discussion and cataloging of sexual desires, tendencies, and acts. That schematization centered around four different axes: (1) the hysterization of women's bodies; (2) the pedagogization of children's sex; (3) the socialization of procreative behavior; and (4) the psychiatrization of pleasure that was deemed perverse. As Foucault notes, "[u]nder the authority of a language that had been carefully expurgated so that it was no longer directly named, sex was taken charge of, tracked down as it were, by a discourse that aimed to allow it no obscurity, no respite" (HS1, 20).

It is possible to view the two phenomena mentioned above, namely, the establishment of areas of silence and of intense discourse, as dichotomous and contradictory. In fact, however, the two were very much connected. The relationship is perhaps clearest in nineteenth century Victorian sexual norms that simultaneously silenced and incited sexuality. In the Victorian bourgeoisie home, "silence [was] the rule. The legitimate and procreative couple laid down the law. The couple imposed itself as model, enforced the norm, safeguarded the truth, and reserved the right to speak while retaining the principle of secrecy" (HS1, 3). At the same time, however, well-established institutional discourses regarding sexuality represented "a political, economic, and technical incitement to talk about sex. And not so much in the form of a general theory of sexuality as in the form of analysis, stocktaking, classification, and specification, and of quantitative or causal studies" (HS1, 23–24). Studies of populations, of birthrates and the appropriate age to marry, of fertility and infertility, of childhood sexuality, of sexual normality and abnormality, of sexual crimes and other infractions against nature, and of debilitating and frustrating sexual desires, all created a discourse on sexuality that was extensive and multifaceted. "What is peculiar to modern societies," Foucault writes, "is not that they consigned sex to a shadow existence, but that they dedicated themselves to speaking of it *ad infinitum*, while exploiting it as *the* secret" (HS1, 35).

In his early writings, which discuss topics from mental illness to penal discipline to sexuality, Foucault seeks to show the hegemony of power and the relationship between power and experiences (e.g., madness, illness, sex) and systems of knowledge (e.g., medicine, psychology, criminology).[6] According to Foucault, observation, surveillance, and classification by scientists and social scientists alike create disciplinary regimes from which emanate diffuse and noncentralized sources of power. Medical hospitals, mental hospitals, prisons, schools, and other institutions develop their own disciplinary techniques that are reflected in the power relations used to train, regulate, and control people. The liberal fixation with the abuse of power by the state and the Marxist fixation with the abuse of power by the ruling class are unsatisfying for Foucault because they largely ignore the dispersed regimes of power found everywhere in society. "Power is not something that is acquired, seized, or shared, something that one holds on to or allows to slip away; power is exercised from innumerable points, in the interplay of nonegalitarian and mobile relations" (HS1, 94). From this perspective, individuals are constituted by power relations and systems of knowledge; there is nothing to individuals—including their sexuality—that is either natural or true. What we consider to be natural or true about ourselves is nothing more than the effects of societal forces as reflected in power/knowledge.

As a result, according to Foucault, the promise of liberation from repression, proposed by psychiatry in general and Freud in particular, offers a dangerous hope. The possibility of overcoming repression suggests the possibility of liberation, of being outside of relations of power. But, Foucault argues, such a liberation is impossible. In fact, there is in *The*

History of Sexuality, Volume I, little sense that the subject is its own agent; there is little hope that the self can be anything but one that is defined and constrained by the discourses that are themselves effects of power relations. Neither truth in a universal sense nor individual agency provide any solace or hope for liberation from power relations.

Foucault's view of power and his rejection of philosophical metaprinciples of truth and justice in *The History of Sexuality*, Volume I (as well as in his earlier work), places him firmly in the postmodernist camp and subjects him to criticism by those who find his vision overly pessimistic and relativistic. Although Foucault remains a controversial figure among non-postmodernist philosophers, queer theorists openly embrace his conception of sexuality as presented in Volume I. It is no coincidence, they argue, that the term "homosexual" first appeared at the end of the nineteenth century, when the modernist discourses of sexuality were at their apogee.[7] In an effort to categorize, analyze, and schematize human sexuality, political, religious, scientific, and medical systems of power/knowledge imposed an identity (and a discourse) on those individuals who engaged in same-gender sexual conduct. What before had been viewed simply as sexual acts (such as sodomy) now became the basis for a socially constructed identity. As Foucault quips, "[t]he sodomite had been a temporary aberration; the homosexual was now a species" (HS1, 43).[8]

Queer theorists argue that because sexual identities such as the "homosexual" arise from particular societal contexts and discourses, sexual orientation cannot be an essential or constitutive part of human beings that is in any way natural or universal. Society both creates the category of "the homosexual" and then seeks to marginalize it by contrasting its supposed perversity to the normality of the other socially constructed category, namely, "the heterosexual." Queer theorists, therefore, follow Foucault in contending that there is no objective essence and no universal truth to human sexuality. The perceived abnormality of homosexuality is the result of contemporary power struggles for domination of the discourse on sexuality. The focus, queer theorists argue, needs to be on recasting the discourse with the understanding that stepping outside of the power relations that determine the nature of the discourse is impossible.

A minority of scholars take issue with the antiessentialism of postmodernist queer theory.[9] These thinkers believe "that there are objective, intrinsic, culture-independent facts about what a person's sexual orientation is."[10] For these writers, there have always been homosexuals, even if different societies have perceived them in different ways at different times. Studies suggesting the possibility of a biological or physiological basis for sexual orientation have added some support to the essentialist position, though, as noted in chapter 3, the meaning of those studies remains highly controversial.[11]

I do not here take a position on the constructionism versus essentialism debate on matters of sexual orientation. That debate has received sufficient attention elsewhere. I assume here that queer theorists are correct that sexual orientation categories are socially constructed and that there is nothing of essence or universal about them. I make this assumption because I do not think that it undermines my broader point, namely, that even if systems of power/knowledge define a subject's sexuality, it is still possible to promote a sexual ethic that leaves a significant role for him or her as an autonomous agent who can engage in self-defining and self-transformative practices. In order to begin supporting this view, I turn now to Foucault's later writings and interviews on sexual ethics.

FOUCAULT'S SHIFT

After Foucault published *The History of Sexuality*, Volume I, it took him an additional eight years to publish Volume II (*The Use of Pleasure*) and Volume III (*The Care of the Self*). During those intervening years, Foucault redirected his philosophical interests. He spoke about the change five months before his death in 1984 in an interview titled "The Ethics of the Concern for Self as a Practice of Freedom." Foucault's inquiries shifted away from a study of the hegemonic and coercive practices of disciplines and professions and toward an interest in asceticism, "not in the sense of a morality of renunciation but as an exercise of the self on the self by which one attempts to develop and transform oneself, and to attain . . . a certain mode of being" (ECS, 282). Individuals in ancient Greek and Roman civilizations practiced this care of the self to a much greater extent than those in the modern era; for this reason, Foucault turned his attention to antiquity, writing Volumes II and III of *The History of Sexuality* about a period that came centuries before the one he discussed in Volume I.

In the interview, Foucault makes clear that power is omnipresent (a point he had made many times before), but such omnipresence is not inconsistent with freedom (a point he had not emphasized previously). For Foucault, power exists in all human relationships, including those not directly connected to political or social institutions. Power relations exist whenever "one person tries to control the conduct of the other," which encompasses just about any form of human interaction, including "amorous, institutional, [and] economic" (ECS, 291). But we should not despair about the omnipresence of power relations because those relations are "mobile, reversible, and unstable" (ECS, 292). Power relations have these characteristics precisely because the individuals who are their subjects retain some freedom. Foucault explains this as follows:

> [I]n power relations there is necessarily the possibility of resistance because if there were no possibility of resistance (of violent resistance, flight, deception, strategies capable of reversing the situation), there would be no power rela-

tions at all. This being the general form, I refuse to reply to the question I am sometimes asked: "But if power is everywhere, there is no freedom." I answer that if there are relations of power in every social field, this is because there is freedom everywhere (ECS, 292).

Domination—as opposed to power relations—exists when there is no possibility of resistance—that is—when resistance proves to be "only stratagems that never succeed[ ] in reversing the situation" (ECS, 292). The main difference between power and domination is that the former allows for freedom whereas the latter does not. Domination exists when the relations of power are "perpetually asymmetrical and allow an extremely limited margin of freedom" (ECS, 292). As an example, Foucault points to the domination of women by men "in the conventional marital structure of the eighteenth and nineteenth centuries" (ECS, 292). Foucault, however, emphasizes that "[t]he idea that power is a system of domination that controls everything and leaves no room for freedom cannot be attributed to me" (ECS, 293).

Although Foucault in *The History of Sexuality*, Volume I, had noted that resistance is a constitutive element of power, he was by 1984 much more explicit in his acknowledgment that the possibility of resistance means the possibility of *freedom*. This new focus on the possibility and practices of freedom calls for a different (or perhaps more complete) view of the self. The self in Foucault's prior writings—including in *The History of Sexuality*, Volume I—was passive, as he emphasized how power relations and systems of knowledge constitute it. Although Foucault had recognized the possibility of resistance, he was in his earlier work not particularly explicit (or optimistic) about the nature of such resistance. The later Foucault, however, became explicitly interested in the concept of freedom and in how "the subject constitutes itself in an *active* fashion through practices of the self" (ECS, 291, emphasis added). Foucault's later work focuses on ethics, which he defines as "the kind of relationship you ought to have with yourself . . . and which determines how the individual is supposed to constitute himself as a moral subject of his own actions."[12] What *does* remain constant in Foucault's writings is the view that the practices of freedom do not arise from within the self. Instead, the practices "are models that [the self] finds in his culture and are proposed, suggested, imposed upon him by his culture, his society, and his social group" (ECS, 291).[13]

Foucault, in another interview, argues that "human beings . . . understand themselves" through "truth games" or "technologies" of which there are four major types:

(1) technologies of production, which permit us to produce, transform, or manipulate things; (2) technologies of sign systems, which permit us to use signs, meanings, symbols, or signification; (3) technologies of power, which

determine the conduct of individuals and submit them to certain ends or domination, an objectivizing of the subject; (4) technologies of the self, which permit individuals to effect by their own means, or with the help of others, a certain number of operations on their own bodies and souls, thoughts, conduct, and way of being, so as to transform themselves in order to attain a certain state of happiness, purity, wisdom, perfection, or immortality.[14]

Whereas the earlier Foucault wrote primarily about the third technology, the later Foucault wrote almost exclusively about the fourth. All four technologies go to the definition of the self, but the first three are entirely external to it. The fourth set of technologies differs; it understands the self as playing an active role in its own constitution and transformation.

By focusing on the technologies of the self, the later Foucault explores the relationship between freedom and ethics and how an individual can lead a life that is both free and ethical if he or she engages in a process of reflection with the ultimate goal of self-transformation. As he puts it, "[f]reedom is the ontological condition of ethics. But ethics is the considered form that freedom takes when it is informed by reflection" (ECS, 284). Foucault here can be understood as making "two important claims: first, ethics is what gives a coherent form to the exercise of freedom; and second, coerced practice can never be strictly speaking, ethical practice (which, importantly enough, Foucault refers to as the practice *of freedom*)."[15] It was practices of freedom that intrigued Foucault during the last years of his life, in particular those engaged in by individuals in ancient Greece and Rome who sought to care for themselves through an aesthetics of existence.[16]

An aesthetics of existence is made of "those intentional and voluntary actions by which men not only set themselves rules of conduct, but also seek to transform themselves, to change themselves in their singular being, and to make their life into an *oeuvre*, that carries certain aesthetic values and meets certain stylistic criteria" (HS2, 10–11). While today we tend to equate art with objects, the concept of art or aesthetics for the Greeks was much broader than that, and included living one's life as a work of art.[17] As David Halperin puts it, "[w]hat Foucault understood by an 'art of existence' . . . was an ethical practice that consisted in freely imposing on the form of one's life a distinctive shape and individual style, and thereby transforming oneself in accordance with one's own conception of beauty or value."[18] Foucault views an aesthetics of existence as a process of self-transformation whereby the subject seeks (some) freedom from its socially constituted self. Thus, in matters of sexuality, we "practice freedom . . . by liberating our desire [so] that we will learn to conduct ourselves ethically in pleasure relationships with others" (ECS, 284). This conception of ethical practices is consistent with Foucault's more general view of philosophy, which he sees as the attempt "to learn to what extent the effort to think one's own history can free thought from what [one] silently thinks, and so enable [one] to think differently" (HS2, 9).[19]

Sexual ethics in ancient Greece and Rome were problematized in such a way that the focus was on the practices of the self and not on codes of conduct (whether legal, scientific, or religious). In fact, as Foucault sees it, the problematization of sex in antiquity raised issues of ethics and not of morality. Morality for Foucault "means a set of values and rules of action that are recommended to individuals through the intermediary of various prescriptive agencies such as the family (in one of its roles), educational institutions, churches, and so forth" (HS2, 25). Although the sources of moral values can be quite varied, those values are usually represented in codes of conduct. When we speak of morality, according to Foucault, we compare "the real behavior of individuals in relation to the rules and values that are recommended to them" by the codes of conduct (HS2, 25). But when we speak of ethics, we speak of "the manner in which one ought to 'conduct oneself'—that is, the manner in which one ought to form oneself as an ethical subject acting in reference to the prescriptive elements that make up the [moral] code[s]" (HS2, 26).

Morality, then, is a codification of normative principles understood as universal rules of general applicability that are meant "to embrace every area of behavior" (HS2, 29). Ethical precepts, on the other hand, are not universal rules of behavior; instead, they are determined by "what is required of the individual in the relationship he has with himself, in his different actions, thoughts, and feelings as he endeavors to form himself as an ethical subject" (HS2, 30). Different periods in the history of sexuality have seen the presence of both morality and ethics, though there have been marked differences in the emphasis of one over the other. To be schematic about it, we can divide the history of sexuality in the West into four parts. Chronologically we begin with Greek and Roman antiquity where the problematization of sexuality was based on the practices of the self (ethics) rather than on a codification of rules of universal applicability (morality). Thus, Foucault argues that in antiquity there were few references to codes that sought to prescribe morally permissible—and proscribe morally impermissible—sexual conduct. Instead, the focus was on the practices of freedom through which the self defined itself as an ethical (and thus a free) subject. I explain all of this in more detail in the next section.

The second period was the Christian period when the emphasis in matters of sexual morality shifted from ethics and the practices of the self to "a very strong 'juridification'—more precisely, a very strong 'codification'—of the moral experience" (HS2, 30). In the transition "[f]rom [a]ntiquity to Christianity, we pass from a morality that was essentially the search for personal ethics to a morality as obedience to a system of rules."[20] Those rules, as they relate to sexuality, were perhaps best exemplified by the penitentials of early Christianity, which were codes of conduct—relied upon by priests during confessions—that set forth in great detail the sexual sins (as defined by the Church) and their corresponding penances.[21]

Although Foucault does not elaborate on Christian sexual morality in great detail, his work is sprinkled with references to the differences in the problematization of sexuality between antiquity and Christianity.[22] In addition to the already mentioned codification, Christian sexual morality called not for the self-transformation of the ethical subject but instead for the self-renunciation of impure desires. Christian sexual morality was dominated by the dangers of lustful desires and the need to atone for those desires, mainly through confession.

The modern period, described by Foucault in *The History of Sexuality*, Volume I, emphasized the codification of sexual rules—much like the Christian era that preceded it. Religious codes, however, became less hegemonic (though they retained considerable influence) while scientific, medical, and psychiatric codes became more important. Modern discourses on sexuality focused on the debilitating effects (physical, psychological, and moral) of sexual desire. There was continuity from the earlier Christian period in the sense that the focus remained on the need to control improper desires and to avoid sexual acts that were considered immoral or abnormal. This focus differed from the one in antiquity, which emphasized learning how to use sexual pleasures in order to transform oneself.

Although Foucault was never explicit on this issue, I think it is possible to speak of our contemporary era as a fourth period in the history of sexuality in the West. There is continuity between the modern period and the contemporary period (as there was between the Christian period and the modern era) given that legal, medical, and moral codes retain some importance in determining the discourses of sexuality. But the contemporary era is characterized by a *partial* decodification that has allowed a return of sorts to a focus on the practices of the self, albeit to very different practices from the ones found in Greek and Roman antiquity. I will discuss later in this chapter the contemporary decodification of sexual morality and its implications for the emergence of a gay and lesbian sexual ethic. Before I do so, however, it is necessary to have a better idea of how Foucault interprets the practices of the self that were common in antiquity in order to understand fully what I mean by "a return of sorts to a focus on the practices of the self."

SEXUAL ETHICS IN CLASSICAL ANTIQUITY

In classical antiquity, according to Foucault, sexuality for privileged individuals—that is—for free male citizens, was problematized around the subject's ethical work on itself.[23] This self-formative process is one through "which the individual delimits that part of himself that will

form the object of his moral practice, defines his position relative to the
precept he will follow, and decides on a certain mode of being that will
serve as his moral goal" (HS2, 28). I explore below how Foucault conceives of this self-formative process. I pay particular attention to it in the
context of the problematization in antiquity of male homosexual conduct. The point of doing so is not to argue that there should be a return
to the way in which ancient societies dealt with homosexual behavior.
Instead, the point is to see the similarities between antiquity and the
contemporary period in their emphases on the ethical practices of the
self and their deemphases on codes of conduct that seek to construct a
sexual morality based on universal distinctions between acceptable and
unacceptable sexual acts.

In *The Use of Pleasure*, Foucault identifies "four great axes of experience" that for the Greeks represented the most important areas where
there was a need to establish an ethical relationship with the self. The
axes were "the relation to one's body, the relation to one's wife, the relation to boys, and the relation to truth" (HS2, 32). In these different
contexts, Foucault discusses at some length the "notion of *aphrodesia*,
through which one can grasp what was recognized as the 'ethical substance' in sexual behavior" (HS2, 37). "The *aphrodesia* are the acts, gestures, and contacts that produce a certain form of pleasure" (HS2, 40).
For the Greeks, as I explain below, the "ethical substance" of that pleasure was not linked to particular sexual acts or to the objects of sexual
desire (male or female); what mattered instead were the following: (1)
moderation and (2) an active and reflective approach to sex.

The Greeks associated excess in matters of sexuality with a failure to
care for the self. They viewed sex as just another form of appetite that
needed to be controlled. They also thought that being a master of oneself and living one's life as a work of art required moderation and restraint. The purpose of sexual ethics was not, as it would become in
Christianity, to resist desire. The Greeks were not subjects of sexual desire (i.e., their sexuality was not defined or constrained by the need to
understand or control sexual desire). Instead, the key to their sexual
ethic was to *use* sex in certain acceptable ways.

The discouragement of particular sexual practices in ancient Greece
was not justified in terms of their abnormal nature or the improper desires that led individuals to want to engage in them; rather, the sexual
practices that were condemned were those that resulted from immoderation and a lack of self-restraint. The importance of moderation as a
norm of sexual ethics, in fact, runs throughout *The Use of Pleasure*.[24]
What constituted means of self-restraint for the Greeks were not codes
of conduct, but were instead voluntary and self-imposed limitations on
the uses of sexual pleasure. Sexual ethics were not, as they would become under Christianity, about rules of conduct based on the distinction
between natural (or good) and unnatural (or bad) sexual acts; instead,

they were about "prudence, reflection, and calculation in the way one distributed and controlled [one's sexual] acts" (HS2, 54). The crucial point to understand is that individuals were not expected to comply with norms of sexual moderation and austerity as universal prescriptions and proscriptions; rather, the norms were understood as "principle[s] of stylization of conduct for those who wished to give their existence the most graceful and accomplished form possible" (HS2, 250–51). Whether an individual led an ethical sexual life, then, was not determined by his faithful adherence to a code of conduct but by the way in which he fashioned and used his sexuality to exercise control over his sexual appetites while leading a graceful and stylized existence.[25]

The absence of codes of conduct that distinguished between acceptable and unacceptable sexual acts explains why same gender sexual intimacy was not problematized in antiquity at the level of gender. In other words, nothing about the *gender* of two males who were sexually intimate with each other made that intimacy ethically or morally suspect.[26] It would be too easy, however, to conclude that ancient Greek culture was simply tolerant of homosexual conduct. The Greeks did problematize homosexual acts; they just did it differently from how contemporary Western societies do.

In ancient Greece there was little interest in sexual relations between men of similar ages or between boys.[27] The problematization was instead of relationships between adult men and boys: "A male relationship gave rise to a theoretical and moral interest [only] when it was based on a rather pronounced difference on either side of the threshold separating adolescence from manhood" (HS2, 195). The older man was expected to play the active role, not just sexually but also socially and morally. The older man was required to provide guidance, education, and support for the younger man. There needed to be, however, moderation and self-control on *both* sides: The older man "was expected to show his ardor, and to restrain it"; the younger man "had to be careful not too yield too easily; he also had to keep from accepting too many tokens of love, and from granting his favors heedlessly and out of self-interest, without testing the worth of his partner" (HS2, 196). Through this ethic of moderation, each partner sought to make himself into "a subject of ethical behavior" (HS2, 203). The idea was to engage in an active form of reflection with the goal of incorporating prudence and moderation into one's sex life.

The ancient Greeks disapproved of sexual immoderation and passivity; the latter entailed allowing sexual acts to take place without engaging in an active process of reflection, an omission that was associated with femininity. To be active vis-à-vis sexual pleasures meant to use them for the creation of a better self; to be active meant to be strong, to control, and to moderate one's use of sexual pleasures. The problematization, then, did not apply when the object of the sexual interest was of the same gender as the subject. It applied, instead, when there was a lack of attention to the care of the self. As Foucault notes, "[i]n the eyes of the Greeks, what constituted ethical negativity par excellence was clearly not the loving of both sexes, nor was it the preferring of one's sex over the other; it consisted in being passive with regard to the pleasures" (HS2, 85–86).

Foucault discusses other forms of sexual problematization in ancient Greece (such as "the relation to the body and to health, [and] the relation to wives and to the institution of marriage"), but it was through sexual intimacy between men and boys "that the question of the relations between the use of pleasures and access to truth was developed, in the form of an inquiry into the nature of true love" (HS2, 229). The initial dissymmetry in the power and age of the partners could, through reflection and self-control, lead to true reciprocity and the "convergence of love" (HS2, 239). The reciprocity existed because the older man became as much the object of attention as the boy; the older man's wisdom and experience became the boy's object of love. The older man, "through the complete mastery that he exercises over himself, will turn the game upside down, reverse the roles, establish the principle of the renunciation of the *aphrodesia*, and become, for all young men who are eager for truth, an object of love" (HS2, 241). Thus, Foucault notes that in the last pages of Plato's *Symposium* there is a complete role reversal, with the handsome young boys enamored of the old and wise Socrates and anxious for him to return their attention (HS2, 241).

According to Foucault, the importance of the care of the self continued in the Greco-Roman era of the first two centuries A.D. (Foucault discusses sexuality in this era in *The Care of the Self.*) In fact, in the early part of the Roman Empire there was, if anything, a perceived need for an "intensification of the relation to oneself by which one constituted onself as the subject of one's acts" (HS3, 41). The Romans, like the ancient Greeks, paid little attention to universal codes of behavior. They also did not problematize sexual intimacy on the basis of the gender of the parties.[28]

There were, however, changes in the forms of problematizations that distinguished Rome in the first two centuries after the death of Christ from Greek antiquity and which, to some extent, presage some of the types of sexual problematizations found in later Christianity and even in the modern era. The first of these changes was the greater involvement of medicine in matters of sexuality as sex became viewed as potentially debilitating and as exposing individuals to illnesses (HS3, 112–18, 141–43).[29] A second important change was a reduced interest in the relationship between male adults and boys and a corresponding greater problematization of the relationship between husband and wife.[30] This change of focus did not mean that individuals ceased to engage in same-gender sexual conduct or even that they were discouraged from doing so. Instead, there was "a decline in the interest one took in [such conduct]; a fading of the importance it was granted in philosophical and moral debate" (HS3, 189). Foucault identifies several reasons for this decline, including: greater control by parents in the elite classes over their children; the availability of young slaves—who did not raise the same concerns about status and passivity as did the children of the elites—as objects of sexual pleasures; the greater institutionalization of education, which reduced the mentoring role of adult males; and the greater "valorization of marriage" (HS3, 190).

The increased focus on marriage meant a privileging of sexual relations within marriage coupled with a concern for the dangers of non-marital sexuality. As the Roman Empire era progressed, there was an increasing codification of natural law and a greater acceptance of universal rules of conduct as applied to sexuality. With the move toward a universalization of rules, there was a corresponding emphasis on "forms of prohibitions" such as the discouragement of adultery.[31] These changes presaged the Christian era, with its comprehensive religious codification of sexual morality, which, in turn, gave way to the modern era with its secular codes of conduct and its systems of knowledge for the production and schematization of human sexuality that Foucault captured so eloquently in *The History of Sexuality*, Volume I.

2. AGENCY VERSUS AUTONOMY IN FOUCAULT'S LATE WRITINGS

As already noted, most scholars who write about homosexuality abide by an antiessentialist understanding of sexual orientation. Foucault's highly influential *The History of Sexuality*, Volume I, provides strong support for the idea that sexual orientation categories are not natural or universal but are instead the effect of power relations and disciplinary discourses (such as medical and psychiatric). Prior to writing Volumes II and III, it was also quite clear that Foucault was not only an antiessentialist on issues of sexuality, but was also a committed philosophical antifoundationalist who rejected the idea of universal principles or norms. Although *The Use of Pleasure* and *The Care of the Self* by no means turned Foucault into a Kantian liberal, it is nonetheless intriguing that he in those two books for the first time wrote extensively about practices of *freedom*. In my estimation, Volumes II and III allow us to consider whether it is possible to delink antiessentialism on issues of sexuality from antifoundationalism on issues of moral and political philosophy. I argue in this section that Foucault in his later work had a conception of the self that allows for an understanding of its capacity for autonomy as constituting a universal good that is necessary for the development of an alternative sexual ethic. Foucault's later work, in fact, leads one to the conclusion that the difference between (at least some understandings of) liberal autonomy and postmodernist agency is not as marked as some queer theorists have argued.

As with many of Foucault's philosophical ideas, his conception of the self was complicated and not always consistent throughout his career. As we have seen, the earlier Foucault viewed the self as a largely passive creature who is constituted by power relations and systems of knowledge that are beyond its control. In the earlier part of Foucault's career, then, it was common for him to write sentences such as the following: "it is one . . . of the prime effects of power that certain bodies, certain gestures, certain discourses, certain desires, come to be identified and constituted as individuals."[32]

As we have also seen, however, the later Foucault came to have a different conception of the self. The later Foucault by no means denied the importance of power/knowledge in the formation of individual identities and he *never* argued that it was possible for individuals to step outside of it. But the self for the later Foucault was no longer hopelessly passive; instead, the self in the later works played an active role in its own constitution through self-defining and self-transformative practices, including sexual ones. The issue that I want to explore in this section is whether the later Foucault, in allowing that the subject can play an active role in constituting and defining itself, was speaking of a capacity for autonomy that is in any way similar to the way in which autonomy is viewed by some liberals. If the answer to that question is yes, then I believe that Foucault's later writings can help us find some common ground between liberal and postmodernist supporters of gay rights.

Postmodernists are as a rule extremely skeptical of the concept of autonomy. The philosopher Ladelle McWhorter, for example, criticizes "liberal theorists [for] their delusions of autonomy."[33] Similarly, the highly influential queer theorist Judith Butler sees autonomy as an illusion held by dominant groups such as men.[34] Individual autonomy for these thinkers is a liberal ruse that views the individual as being separate from and existing prior to society. For postmodernists there is no such Archimedean point from which we can apply (or celebrate) neutral and universal values such as autonomy.

Postmodernists, however, cannot completely give up on the idea that the self has *some* control over its life because to do so would be to give up all hope of a progressive political agenda. If the self is indeed nothing more than a reflection of systems of power/knowledge, there is little room for optimism that it can, in any meaningful way, resist or undermine existing social relationships and practices. A conception of the self that requires us to view it as being nothing more than the effect of power/knowledge would lead to despondency and hopelessness about the human condition. Thus, while postmodernists reject the idea of autonomy, they frequently invoke that of agency. The self as an agent is not prior to society. Instead, it is defined and constructed by society; within those parameters, however, there is enough room to oppose and subvert existing modes of power/knowledge. As Butler puts it, "[e]ven within the theories that maintain a highly qualified or situated subject, the subject still encounters its discursively constituted environment in an oppositional epistemological frame. The culturally enmired subject negotiates its constructions, even when those constructions are the very predicates of its own identity."[35] The political theorist Mark Bevir also makes it clear that in his view there is an important distinction between autonomy and agency. "Autonomous subjects," he argues, "would be able, at least in principle, to have experiences, to reason, to adopt beliefs, and to act, outside of all social contexts."[36] He contrasts such ultimately illusory liberal subjects to

> [a]gents [who] exist only in specific social contexts, but these contexts never determine how they try to construct themselves. Although agents necessarily exist within regimes of power/knowledge, these regimes do not determine the experiences they can have, the ways they can exercise their reason, the beliefs they can adopt, or the actions they can attempt to perform. Agents are creative beings; it is just that their creativity occurs in a given social context that influences it.[37]

Clearly, the concept of an aesthetic of existence as a form of ethical practice as envisioned by Foucault in *The History of Sexuality*, Volumes II and III, requires at the very least the kind of agency that Butler and Bevir describe. Foucault's aesthetic of existence envisions the self as participating in its own constitution and transformation as it negotiates the construction of its identity. The issue is whether such a view of agency is significantly different from the conception of autonomy held by some liberals.

Postmodernist theorists usually rely on an understanding of autonomy that is consistent with a Kantian/Rawlsian conception of the self that views it as standing apart from its social contexts. As noted in chapter 1, the early Rawls, at least, understood the capacity of individuals to make important choices about their lives as being prior to the ends that they actually choose, ends which, when aggregated with those of others, form distinctive social contexts. Similarly, for Kant, as J.B. Schneewind notes, "self-governance [is] a necessary feature of human beings, one not dependent on or created by society."[38] It is not necessary, however, to abide by a Kantian/Rawlsian view that the self can be separated from (or is prior to) its social contexts in order to believe that the self has a capacity for autonomy. A believer in autonomy "need not deny that the self is a cultural product, rather than a divine or natural one."[39] There are liberal political philosophers, in fact, who *do* incorporate the social situatedness of subjects into their conceptions of autonomy. One of them is Martha Nussbaum whose capabilities approach, as we saw in chapter 3, is grounded on an interpretation and evaluation of the real lives of individuals as they take place in particular affiliative and social contexts. Another liberal philosopher who departs from a Kantian/Rawlsian conception of the self is Stephen Macedo. In his book *Liberal Virtues*, Macedo notes that a liberal conception of autonomy starts with the proposition that "[a] crucial feature in the move from autarchy to autonomy is the development of the capacity critically to assess and even actively shape not simply one's actions, but one's character itself, the source of our actions."[40] The exercise of that capacity, however, takes place *within* particular social contexts and public meanings. As Macedo notes (in a passage with which I believe the later Foucault would have been in complete agreement):

> We can control our own actions but not the public meanings of our actions, for we act in a context largely given. We are not autonomous in the sense of being "radically free" or able to create the values that define the moral problems we face, or to make words mean whatever we choose. Our freedom and the autonomy we strive for are not the consequence of an ability to extricate ourselves from this network of public meanings. We are objects and not only agents of critical interpretation.[41]

Macedo also recognizes that the identity of the self is not fixed, but is instead contingent on dynamic forces that are both internal (reflection and self-evaluation) and external (commitments, attachments, social contexts, and language). "The desires, convictions, and even the identity of the autonomous liberal subject are never fixed or closed: they are to some degree malleable and open to revision in response to the broad vista of human experience."[42] "Liberal autonomy," Macedo adds, "engages our understanding and responsibility at a deep level by engaging the capacity critically to reflect upon morality and personal identity, itself already constituted by projects, plans, commitments, and strong evaluations."[43]

Macedo in *Liberal Virtues* is responding to the communitarian critique of liberalism and not explicitly to postmodernism. But the communitarian critique of the atomistic individual, separated from communities and social attachments, is similar to the postmodernist critique of the liberal conception of the self. Macedo is one of several liberal political philosophers who have taken the communitarian critique of liberalism seriously and who have, in response, presented restructured understandings of liberalism.

As discussed in chapter 3, feminists have also criticized a conception of the self that gives a descriptive emphasis and a normative priority to the separateness of individuals. Feminists, therefore, have generally been skeptical of a conception of autonomy that equates it with individualism and the right to be left alone. Many feminists instead emphasize the role that ties, relationships, and an ethic of care play in the construction of identities and the attainment of well-being of all individuals, and in particular of women. A conception of the self that views it as largely defined through social attachments, relationships, and commitments, however, has not prevented, as we also saw in chapter 3, liberal feminists from recognizing and valuing a capacity for autonomy. As Catriona Mackenzie and Natalie Stoljar put it, "we can accept that social relations influence and perhaps constitute agents' senses of themselves and their capacities, without concluding that capacities such as autonomy are nonexistent."[44] That capacity for autonomy plays an important role in the ability of women to give shape to their lives and to define who they are rather than accepting definitions provided by a male-dominated society.

The conception of autonomy held by restructured forms of liberalism closes the gap between liberalism and the later Foucault. Although Foucault never spoke of an autonomous subject that can define itself independently of systems of power/knowledge, and though liberal philosophers such as Macedo are more optimistic than Foucault ever was about the moral guidance that reason and principles of justice can provide to individuals, the later Foucault's belief in a capacity for agency is not significantly different from Macedo's belief in a capacity for autonomy. In fact, Bevir, in discussing Foucault's distinction between morality and ethics, notes that,

> [m]orality, in any sphere, represents a set of imposed rules to follow, which is not truly to exercise one's agency, not to be free, but only to regulate oneself. Agency and freedom really appear only when we question moral rules by interpreting them creatively in an ethics, although equally we can develop an ethics only because we possess a capacity for agency and freedom. We are agents, but we exercise our agency properly only when we resist the pressures of normalization by challenging a morality through our personal, ethical conduct.[45]

If we substitute the word "agency" with "autonomy" in this passage, there is nothing with which a liberal such as Macedo would disagree. While trying to distinguish Foucauldian postmodernist agency from liberal autonomy, Bevir acknowledges that for the *former* to exist, social forces must allow for a "space . . . where individuals [can] decide what beliefs to hold and what actions to perform."[46] Bevir's understanding of Foucauldian agency comes awfully close to liberal autonomy—there is no more traditional bedrock principle of liberalism, after all, than the need to create the necessary space for individuals to be able to choose their own beliefs and actions.

David Halperin is a good example of a postmodernist queer theorist who believes that everything about individuals (including their sexual orientation) is socially constructed. Yet, at the same time, those individuals, Halperin implicitly acknowledges, have a capacity for autonomy. Halperin sides with the earlier Foucault's conception of the subject when he (Halperin) notes that it "is not an identity or a substance" (i.e., there is nothing to the subject that exists apart from the effects of social constructions).[47] And yet, practically in the same breath, Halperin adds a crucial qualifier: "Nonetheless, insofar as the subject is an *ethical* subject, a subject of ethical practices, it is to that extent a free subject, for that is what it means, definitionally, to *be* an ethical subject."[48] Halperin adds that "[t]he kind of power that Foucault is interested in . . . , far from en-slaving its objects, constructs them as subjective agents and preserves them in their *autonomy*, so as to invest them all the more completely."[49] It seems to me, however, that one cannot have it both ways: Either there is nothing to the self that is independent of the effects of social forces *or* the self, even from within regimes of power/knowledge, has the capacity to exercise some autonomy in actively constructing itself. If the latter proposition is correct, then the sharp contrast that postmodernist queer theorists seek to draw between their understanding of human agency and (some) liberal understandings of human autonomy is not as great as may at first appear.

The postmodernist philosopher Ladelle McWhorter, in writing about issues of sexuality, also rejects a conception of the self that is independent of power/knowledge. For McWhorter, there is no constitutive part of the self that is not an effect of power/knowledge.[50] When we scratch at the surface and try to strip away our sexual identity, for example, there is nothing below that particular layer that is not itself constituted by social forces. For McWhorter, the sexual self as well as the knowing self are so-cially constructed. Social construction, in other words, goes all the way down; there is for her "no epistemic stopping point."[51] And yet, McWhorter grounds her philosophy and politics on the ability of individ-uals to engage in *transformative* practices by which she means practices, chosen by individuals, that lead to self-expansion and self-definition as a way of attaining if not freedom, then at least some measure of meaningful agency.[52] She argues that there is no inconsistency between her concep-tion of the self and her faith in transformative practices because, as she puts it, "I can exercise agency despite (and even because of) the fact that my very existence as a subject is a form of subjection."[53] It seems to me, however, that McWhorter, like Halperin, is trying to have it both ways. On the one hand, she follows postmodern theory in arguing that no parts of human beings are constituted independently of social forces. And yet, at the same time, she recognizes that we are capable of *choosing* among different kinds of practices in order to *transform* ourselves. Whether we call that capacity agency or autonomy is less important than the fact that it is a constitutive part of ourselves that is in some measure able to stand apart from power/knowledge in order to work on a self that ultimately becomes a *different* one than the one that would exist if it did not work to resist social forces through transformative practices. Again, I believe such a view of the self is consistent with a liberal concep-tion of a human capacity for autonomy.

In thinking about the role of self-transformative practices, or what Foucault calls practices of freedom, it is important to keep in mind the distinction between self-definition and self-discovery. Foucault very much rejects the latter because it suggests that there exists a true self that is somehow prior to power/knowledge and that is therefore amenable to discovery. If we believe that self-discovery is possible, in other words, power relations and systems of knowledge can obstruct that discovery. For Foucault, however, practices of freedom are not relevant to self-discovery but to self-definition, that is, to the working of the self by the self. This self-definition is not a Kantian/Rawlsian one whereby the individual defines itself largely independently of its social ties and contexts; rather, the process of self-definition for Foucault is a highly contextualized one that takes place within, not outside of, social forces. The process of self-definition as understood by Foucault is one of self-transformation. That transformation is "not a distant flight away from the conditions of our being but, instead, a metamorphosis, or morphing, of the virtuality of our lives, building concretely upon the experience of the present so as to realize our freedom as a practice."[54] It is clear then, that when Foucault alludes to a capacity for autonomy in his later writings, he does not have in mind autonomous subjects that are somehow separate from or independent of social forces. As Jeremy Moss puts it, "Foucault [sees] the freedom that subjects have to work on themselves not as an abstract freedom, but as dependent on the resources they ha[ve] at their disposal, both in terms of their own capacities and the structures of society."[55] The capacity for autonomy, in other words, must be cultivated internally (through a care of the self) and promoted externally (through modes of power that encourage the capacity and discourage submission and domination).

When we apply this theoretical framework to a gay and lesbian sexuality, we see how lesbians and gay men develop a sexual ethic not independently of societal norms, but very much from within them. The ethic has to be developed from within those norms because it is those norms that define the homosexual identity to begin with. Even as that identity is being determined by power relations and systems of knowledge, however, the opportunity for resistance presents itself. The socially defined gay and lesbian subject seeks to transform itself through practices of freedom. This transformative process requires a self that has the capacity to participate in its own definition, that is, a capacity for at least partial autonomy or self-determination. It is true, as law professor Richard Fallon puts it, that the self "is not a bare, vanishing, purely rational entity that stands outside the world and judges it."[56] In this sense, the postmodernists are correct. Nonetheless, even if "the self is a creature in and of the world, [it is also] one capable of at least partially transforming herself through thought, criticism, and self-interpretation."[57] And it is this possibility of partial transformation that for Foucault entails the possibility of freedom, which, in turn, exists wherever there is power because power (as opposed to domination) requires freedom as a consti-

tutive element. If power is everywhere, then, so is the possibility of freedom. Although postmodernists emphasize the former when they discuss
Foucault, they rarely mention the latter. If you take away the capability
of the subject to exercise its autonomy, then you take away the possibility of freedom and the possibility of engaging in ethical practices. Such
scenarios do, of course, exist when there is domination (i.e., the impossibility of resistance). But Foucault's discussion of sexuality is rarely about
domination; it is instead about power. And it is the omnipresence of
power that accounts for the omnipresence of the possibility of freedom.

The capacity for autonomy, in my view, plays a foundational or universal role in the development of an alternative sexual ethic. The marginalized sexual subject, who works on the crafting of an alternative sexual
ethic through reflection and self-transformation, must be given the opportunity to exercise its capacity for autonomy. Without that opportunity, the development of a sexual ethic that is different from and resistant
to the societal norms relating to sexuality would be impossible. (I will in
the next section explore the particular meaning of one such alternative
sexual ethic, namely, a gay and lesbian one.) The role that autonomy
plays in that development is not culture-specific. Instead, it is appropriate to speak of the *capacity* of the sexual subject to exercise its autonomy
as a form of universal good. The need to protect and promote a capacity
for autonomy is a universal concern that can contribute to the development of an alternative sexual ethic for marginalized sexual minorities,
even if the sexual identities of those minorities form themselves entirely
through a process of social construction.

It is important to emphasize what is and what is not universal about
this process. The need of individuals to exercise their capacity for autonomy is universal. However, the ways in which sexuality is problematized,
which then leads some individuals (if they have the opportunity) to approach their sexuality ethically in response to that problematization, will
vary across time and place. As we have seen, the way in which the Greeks
problematized same-gender sexual conduct was very different from the
contemporary problematization of homosexuality. Similarly, the substantive content of the sexual ethic that develops in response to the differing
forms of problematization will be different across history and cultures.
There is no such thing, in other words, as a universal sexual ethic.

The later Foucault, then, allows us to build a bridge across the seemingly irreconcilable differences between liberals and postmodernists.
Foucault's writings emphasize the postmodernist idea that social forces
largely determine the identity of the self (including its sexual orientation). At the same time, however, Foucault's conception of ethics recognizes a capacity for autonomy as the self seeks to care for itself through
self-constitutive and self-transformative practices of freedom. The conception of ethics held by the later Foucault, in other words, requires a
self that is to some degree capable of self-authorship. If even someone

like Foucault, who was of course no liberal, can acknowledge the importance of the capacity for autonomy as individuals participate in the constitution of their identity through practices of freedom, perhaps there is more to the capacity for autonomy than postmodernists have been willing to admit. On the other hand, Foucault's acknowledgment in his later works that the omnipresence of power is not inconsistent with freedom can perhaps allay the fears of those liberals who believe that to pursue the implications of Foucault's writings is to somehow give up on the idea of human freedom. Again, as Foucault noted several months before he died, "[t]he idea that power is a system of domination that controls everything and leaves no room for freedom cannot be attributed to me" (ECS, 293).

If liberals can lower their philosophical guards when approaching Foucault's ideas, they may be more willing to explore the implications of his trenchant observations about the role of power in society. Liberals tend to view power only in its negative form, focusing largely on the need to contain power in order to protect the individual; Foucault emphasizes power in its positive form, as a constitutive element of all interactions and relationships among individuals, not as a force that can be isolated. There is no need to fear the omnipresence of power, then, as long as we understand that the ability of power to constrain freedom is always accompanied by its ability to provide *for* freedom. A conception of power that views it only as a force from which we need protection is too limited because power helps to constitute individuals. Power, in other words, plays a crucial role in constructing the very individuals whose autonomy liberals want to protect.

I do not want to suggest that Foucault completely reconciles the hegemonic influences of power relations and systems of knowledge as emphasized in his earlier work with the recognition that individuals have a capacity for autonomy implied in his later work.[58] My point instead is that, at least in the context of sexuality, it is possible to do some of the reconciling *for* Foucault if we separate the social construction of sexual orientation categories from the capability of individuals (once society places them in those categories) to work on and transform themselves. That transformation will never be so complete so as to lead to a radically new and free self that emerges from the socially constructed one. Instead, what can take place is a process whereby the individual tries (sometimes successfully and sometimes not) to engage in self-transformative practices that affect the impact of social forces in the constitution of the self. It is in these self-transformative practices that freedom for marginalized sexual minorities resides. If what I am suggesting is in fact possible, then the connection between antiessentialism on matters of sexual orientation and antifoundationalism or antiuniversalism on matters of moral and political philosophy is not as immutable as postmodernist queer theory holds.

3. CODES OF CONDUCT AND A GAY AND LESBIAN SEXUAL ETHIC

For the remainder of this chapter, I apply the issues discussed so far to an exploration of the meaning of a contemporary gay and lesbian sexual ethic. The development of such an ethic, with its own processes and values, has allowed lesbians and gay men to work on their ethical self-definition and self-transformation. As in Greek and Roman antiquity, the development of a sexual ethic such as the contemporary gay and lesbian one, which allows for an active participation by the individual in the leading of a sexually ethical life, is accompanied by a deemphasis on a regime of sexual morality that seeks to find the value, truth, and meaning of sexuality through codes of conduct.

In thinking about what we can learn from the sexual ethics of classical antiquity, it is important to emphasize that it would be too simplistic to interpret ancient Greek culture as encouraging freedom and tolerance in matters of (homo)sexuality. Foucault repeatedly counsels against such an idealized interpretation of Greek sexual norms (HS2, 187; 192–93; 197). Those norms were not about freedom and tolerance per se; they were instead about using male homosexual acts (in particular those between adults and adolescents) as the best way of constituting oneself through reflection, moderation, and self-transformation. Foucault also makes it clear that he is not calling for a return to Greek sexual ethics. Opportunities for the ethical use of pleasures and a care of the self were available only to men from the ruling classes. It was not deemed possible (or beneficial) for women, foreigners, or slaves to engage in the process of caring for the self in an ethical way. Clearly, the ancient Greek society, with its oppressive class and gender hierarchies, is not one that we should aim to replicate.

But it is possible to emphasize a different point altogether, namely, that a sexual ethic that allows for a meaningful care of the self places little importance on a code of conduct that makes normative distinctions based on the nature of different sexual acts. It is not a matter, then, of emulating the Greeks—it is a matter of recognizing that a sexual ethic does not have to be grounded in codes of conduct that tell us which sexual acts (and thus which sexual desires) are "good" and which are "bad." To the extent that we think that the value, truth, and meaning of sex is to be found in codes of conduct that seek to make normative distinctions among sexual acts, there is considerably less room for the kind of self-defining and self-transformative ethical practices that existed in ancient Greece and Rome. It is my view that the partial legal, medical, and moral *de*codification of homosexuality that has taken place over the last forty years in the United States has allowed for the emergence of a gay and lesbian sexual ethic, one that offers a powerful and appealing alternative to traditional Christian sexual ethics.

In the first section, I briefly summarize a rather extensive subject, namely, the legal codification of homosexuality that began in the United States in the late nineteenth century. In doing so, I rely heavily on Bill Eskridge's excellent book on the history of the legal regulation of same-gender sexual conduct in the United States.[59] As we will see, the legal codification of homosexuality paralleled the intensification of medical and psychiatric discourses of sexuality identified by Foucault in *The History of Sexuality,* Volume I. I also in the first section trace the partial *de*codification of homosexuality that has taken place in American law in the last forty years. In the second section, I discuss the role that moral codes of conduct (as opposed to *legal* codes of conduct) currently play in assessments of the morality of same-gender sexual acts. In the United States today, there is no longer a consensus that moral codes of sexual conduct that privilege particular sexual acts and prohibit others can serve as normative foundations for assessments of the goodness and value (or lack thereof) of sex and sexuality. This process of moral decodification, when coupled with a partial legal decodification of homosexuality, has allowed for the emergence of a gay and lesbian sexual ethic. I explore the processes, values, and some of the implications of that ethic in the third and last section.

As I have noted throughout this book, many opponents of gay rights dismiss the sexual practices of lesbians and gay men as lacking moral value. Many of these critics abide by a conception of sexual morality and ethics that limits the range of acceptable sexual conduct to that engaged in by individuals of different genders, preferably within the institution of marriage. From this perspective, although society may have prudential reasons for not criminalizing same-gender sexual acts, it should never view such sex as moral. In fact, as I have also noted, opponents of state recognition of same-sex marriage often base their opposition on the perceived immorality of same-gender sexual conduct, which they argue constitutes a threat to the values system inherent in the traditional view of marriage.

Conservatives, then, have largely monopolized the discussion of sexual morality and ethics in the context of gay rights. In the last few decades, however, lesbians and gay men have constructed a distinct sexual ethic with its own processes and values. The later Foucault, by writing so provocatively about nontraditional sexuality within a framework of sexual ethics, helps us understand how lesbians and gay men, despite the accusations of many opponents of gay rights, approach their sexuality ethically. It is indeed ironic that Foucault—who for most of his career as a philosopher tried to stay away from staking out positive normative positions—gives us such helpful tools in elaborating on the meaning and values of a gay and lesbian sexual ethic.

THE LEGAL CODIFICATION AND PARTIAL DECODIFICATION OF SAME-GENDER SEXUAL CONDUCT

The law has historically served as an important source for rules of conduct that relate not only to coerced sexual acts but also to consensual ones. Thus sodomy, for example, which is often in criminal statutes referred to as a crime against nature or as a form of deviate sexual intercourse, has been subject to criminal penalties in the United States regardless of whether consent is involved.[60] The law, through sodomy statutes and in many other ways (as we will see), has assisted in the simultaneous creation and marginalization of a homosexual identity in the United States.

Foucault, however, has very little interest in or use for the law. He sees the law as the kind of traditional source of power that has been overemphasized by historians and philosophers alike. For Foucault, an emphasis on the law is misplaced because it offers a view of power relations that places the sovereign (however defined) at the center of power. According to Foucault, political theory should cease to "privilege . . . law and sovereignty," and instead analyze power through its diffusion (HS1, 90). Foucault does not believe that real power expresses itself through institutions such as legislatures and courts. Instead, he sees power as being highly diffuse, spread throughout society in a myriad of different kinds of disciplines and systems of knowledge. For Foucault, these "mechanisms of power . . . are probably irreducible to the representation of law" (HS1, 89). "[T]he juridical system," Foucault notes, "is utterly incongruous with the new methods of power whose operation is not ensured by right but by technique, not by law but by normalization, not by punishment but by control, methods that are employed on all levels and in forms that go beyond the state and its apparatus" (HS1, 89).

Some commentators have noted that Foucault underestimates the role that the law plays in affecting the societal structures and relations that frame the more diffuse kinds of power relations that he explores in his writings.[61] Given that Foucault has little faith in the ability of the law to affect meaningfully the power relations and disciplines that are the main foci of his historical and philosophical analyses, it is perhaps not surprising that he also underestimates the role that the law plays in the formation of sexual identities and moralities. There is very little in *The History of Sexuality*, Volume I, about legal discourse or rules; instead, as we have seen, Foucault's focus in that book is primarily on the disciplines of medicine and psychiatry. As I will argue, however, the law, at least in the United States beginning at the end of the nineteenth century, played an important role—alongside the discourses identified by Foucault—in the creation of a homosexual identity and in reifying a conception of homosexuality as dangerous and depraved.

The story of the codification of consensual same-gender sexuality in American law began with the application of English sodomy (or buggery) statutes in the colonies. After independence, all of the new American states enacted sodomy statutes.[62] Prior to the late nineteenth century, however, the criminal act of sodomy was not connected to a particular sexual identity. Society, in other words, did not assign a distinctive sexual identity to those who engaged in sodomy. This changed at the end of the nineteenth century as science and medicine helped to create sexual identities known as inverts, perverts, transsexuals, and homosexuals. Although these identities had different meanings and characteristics, they had one common denominator: a seeming refusal by some individuals to abide by what medical and psychiatric experts (in reflecting broader cultural norms) considered to be appropriate gender roles and behaviors.[63] The gender nonconformists flouted the strict societal norms regarding appropriate male and female personalities, male and female dress, and male and female subjects of sexual desire.

Sodomy statutes, as a means of regulating same-gender sexual conduct, were inadequate in an era when American doctors began to view the turning to one's own gender for sexual intimacy as "a dangerous sickness."[64] They proved inadequate because prior to the 1880s they only prohibited anal sex; they did not prohibit oral sex or mutual masturbation between men, or sex of any kind between women.[65] In addition, convicting a defendant of consensual sodomy proved difficult since the testimony of an adult accomplice was required.[66] Beginning in the 1880s, therefore, state legislatures enacted a slew of new laws to deal with the problem—identified by science and medicine—of sexual inversion and gender noncompliance. The scope of sodomy statutes was expanded to include oral sex. And just as important, new laws were enacted that criminalized public indecency, sexual solicitation, cross-dressing, seduction of minors, and obscenity.[67] These laws, violations of which were easier to prove than violations of sodomy statutes, became a powerful weapon in the regulation and oppression of homosexuals and other gender nonconformists.

Starting in the 1880s, then, the state significantly increased its legal regulation of same-gender sexual behavior. It would be a mistake, however, to view the law as the primary source of meaning in the construction of a homosexual identity; to believe so would be to ignore Foucault's insights about the multiplicity of sexuality discourses, most of which do not emanate directly from state regulation. But as Eskridge notes, the law played a "supporting role" in the creation and marginalization of a homosexual identity given that the "law reinforced social pressure by *normalizing* sex around marital procreation."[68] Sex outside of such procreation became subject to increasing legal regulation. At the same time that medical and psychiatric discourses led to "a unique construction of identity crystallized around same-sex desire,"[69] the law became much more active and aggressive in its regulation of that desire.

World War I brought further changes in the legal regulation of same-gender sexuality. The war itself was a period of relative tolerance of sexual and gender nonconformity as the nation focused its attention elsewhere and as male friendships and camaraderie were encouraged. After the war, however, there was a regulatory shift from prewar practices. The culture began to view homosexuals not only as medical and psychiatric aberrations, but also as immoral and predatory. There was a growing sense, for example, that children needed to be protected from homosexuals. As Eskridge puts it, "[t]he state's goals [became] to control and punish the psychopathic homosexual, to harass and drive underground homosexual communities and their expression, and to exclude homosexuals from citizenship—all in the name of protecting children from a dangerous force threatening their development into heterosexuals."[70] Eskridge documents how sodomy and other criminal prosecutions specifically targeted at homosexuals (for disorderly conduct, lewd conduct, and solicitation) increased substantially during the postwar period. Furthermore, the state harassed homosexuals in public places (such as bars, parks, streets, and cafes) where they sought to meet and associate.[71] The state also, in the period between the wars, intensified its censorship of gay books, magazines, and theater. "The homosexual was not only a sexual outlaw but one who by World War II had clearly caught the eye of the government."[72]

World War II, like World War I, saw a period of relative tolerance toward gender and sexual nonconformity.[73] As the nation refocused on domestic issues after the war, however, the repression of homosexuals increased, even beyond the levels that were seen in the period after World War I. In the late 1940s and during the 1950s, government agencies hunted down lesbians and gay men through the use of the criminal law with a ferocity not seen before or since. As Eskridge explains, "[t]he state between 1946 and 1961 imposed criminal punishments on as many as a million lesbians and gay men engaged in consensual adult intercourse, dancing, kissing, or holding hands."[74] Police departments created special vice or morals squads that specialized in the targeting of homosexuals. Police stakeouts, raids, and undercover operations became "much more aggressive and invasive than they had been before the war."[75]

In addition to the aggressive enforcement of the criminal law, the 1940s and 1950s saw the implementation of policies that identified and expelled homosexuals from government jobs while excluding gay applicants from those jobs altogether. Lesbians and gay men were subject to governmental harassment, surveillance, and witch-hunts with an intensity that matched the treatment of communists and other leftists during the McCarthy era.[76] In the end, however, though the persecution of homosexuals led to the destruction of thousands of lives, it did not accomplish the government's "stated goal of discouraging and erasing homo-sexual subcultures."[77] In fact, the persecution of lesbians and gay men created a shared sense of identity as they began to organize and fight back in the 1960s and 1970s.[78] As Eskridge puts it, "[i]ronically, the American antihomosexual terror [campaign] helped create a homosex-ual rights movement."[79]

The law played a complicated role in this new development; although it remained (as it remains today) a source of oppression and discrimina-tion, the law in the 1960s began to retreat somewhat from the oppres-sive regulation of same-gender sexual conduct. The first sign of this partial retreat was the American Law Institute's vote in 1955 to decrim-inalize consensual sodomy in its Model Penal Code. In 1961, Illinois became the first state actually to decriminalize sodomy. Since 1961, thirty-one additional states and the District of Columbia have decrimi-nalized sodomy, either legislatively or through judicial rulings based on state constitutional grounds.[80] Six of those states (and the District of Columbia) have done so after the Supreme Court upheld the federal constitutionality of Georgia's sodomy statute in *Bowers v. Hardwick*.[81]

Beginning in the 1960s, prosecutions for sodomy began to de-crease, as did prosecutions for other activities such as cross-dressing and solicitation. Vague and overly broad solicitation, lewdness, disor-derly conduct, and vagrancy laws that states used for decades to harass and oppress lesbians and gay men, began to receive greater attention from legislatures and scrutiny by courts. Beginning in the 1960s, legis-latures started "repealing broadly phrased vagrancy and disorderly conduct laws and replacing them with statutes criminalizing specified acts of public disorder."[82] Furthermore, as the Supreme Court strengthened individual rights of speech and association during the civil rights era, there were unintended positive consequences for les-bians and gay men. Judicial rulings gave lesbians and gay men greater legal protection allowing them to speak, associate, socialize, and orga-nize.[83] Gay publications, organizations, bars, and cafes began to prolif-erate as lesbians and gay men for the first time were afforded partial protection by the law.

Ironically, then, after decades of legal persecution and oppression, les-bians and gay men began to turn to the law for protection. Vermont's enactment of legislation that provides to gay and lesbian couples who enter into civil unions the same rights and benefits enjoyed by married heterosexual couples is only the most recent and dramatic example of this phenomenon. There have been many others along the way, includ-ing the enactment of state and local laws that protect lesbians and gay men from employment and housing discrimination, the issuing of exec-utive orders banning discrimination in federal civilian agencies, as well as the recognition by many (though by no means all) judges that the sexual orientation of gay and lesbian parents is not inconsistent with the best interests of children.[84] The result of all of this is that the law today is as often the protector of lesbians and gay men as it is their oppressor.

Of course, many law-based oppressions remain and we should not minimize their impact. Examples are many and include the following: (1) nineteen states still criminalize sodomy; (2) harassment of gay men through solicitation and public lewdness laws, though less prevalent than in the period after World War II, has by no means disappeared;[85] (3) the military continues to discriminate openly against lesbians and gay men and such discrimination has been found by courts to pass constitutional muster;[86] (4) three states (Florida, Mississippi, and Utah)[87] currently prohibit lesbians and gay men from adopting children, and the view that gay and lesbian parents do not deserve the same legal protections as heterosexual parents still persists.[88]

Despite these remaining law-based oppressions, the law as a codifier of sexual morality today plays a much less important role in the subordination of lesbians and gay men than it did forty short years ago. The law by and large no longer provides a hierarchy of consensual sexual conduct that seeks to distinguish between permissible and impermissible sexual acts. Even states that still have sodomy statutes on the books rarely enforce them.[89] In the same way that adultery and fornication statutes have become largely irrelevant (both legally and morally), laws that still oppress lesbians and gay men have lost their ability to impact significantly the debate regarding the morality or appropriateness of same-gender sexual acts. Even though there remains a considerable societal hostility and animosity toward lesbians and gay men, those who share those feelings can no longer rely, as they once did, on having their views consistently reflected in the law. In fact, the Supreme Court has held that to the extent that a law is nothing more than the codification of animosity toward lesbians and gay men, it violates the Constitution's equal protection clause.[90] Our contemporary legal institutions and rules, which simultaneously protect and oppress lesbians and gay men, send mixed signals about the status of homosexuality in our society— signals that largely cancel themselves out.

This retrenchment in the ability of the law to serve as a code of conduct that distinguishes between permissible and impermissible consensual sexual acts allows for the development of an alternative sexual ethic, as individuals have a greater opportunity to affect the meaning of their sexual acts and sexuality. Foucault in his later work recognized that the absence of codes of conduct allows for the development of a sexual ethic that is not based on universal rules. As we have seen, the absence of codes of conduct permitted the flourishing of an ethic as a care of the self in Greek and Roman antiquity. Similarly, in the United States over the last forty years, the law's contribution to the elaboration of universal standards that affect the perceived morality of consensual sexual activity has waned. This partial decodification has allowed for the emergence of a gay and lesbian sexual ethic, that though different in substance from a Greek sexual ethic, is procedurally similar in that it encourages the individual to engage in an ethical process of reflection and self-transformation.

I want to make it clear that what I mean by a partial legal decodification of (homo)sexuality entails the lessening of the law's ability to make distinctions between permissible and impermissible consensual sexual acts. In this sense, decodification means not the absence of law, but the absence of law as a form of normative hierarchy that seeks to distinguish among different kinds of sexual acts. Thus, by using the term "decodification," I do not want to suggest that our society has as a descriptive matter embraced, or that it should as a normative matter aspire to construct, a libertarian framework that considers the absence of codes or regulations sufficient to guarantee freedom and personal autonomy in matters of sexuality. As I have argued throughout this book, the libertarian view that requires only that the state not interfere with consensual relationships proves to be insufficient for lesbians and gay men who depend on the state (and the law) to protect them from discrimination and oppression, and to provide them with membership in certain institutions such as parenthood and (potentially) marriage.

It is also important to note that what I refer to as a partial decodification of consensual sexual acts has not been limited to the law. The same applies to other disciplines such as psychiatry. In 1973, the American Psychiatric Association removed homosexuality from the list of mental illnesses contained in its *Diagnostic and Statistical Manual of Mental Disorders* (DSM).[91] The DSM, like the laws that regulate consensual sexuality, is a code of conduct that distinguishes between acceptable (or normal) and unacceptable (or abnormal) sex.[92] As long as homosexuality was officially listed as a mental illness, the medical and psychiatric professions could continue to subject lesbians and gay men to their commands and standards. Over the last thirty years, however, the importance of codes in the medical regulation of homosexuality has receded considerably as substantial numbers of American medical doctors, psychiatrists, and psychologists no longer view homosexuality as a disease.[93]

Although I do not attempt to explore in greater detail the medical decodification of homosexuality, that phenomenon, like the legal decodification of homosexuality, has allowed for the emergence of a gay and lesbian sexual ethic. As these codes play less of a role in defining the meaning of homosexuality in our society, lesbians and gay men have been able, through a process of self-definition and self-transformation, to give ethical meaning to their sexuality and their sexual acts. Before I turn to a detailed discussion of the content of a gay and lesbian sexual ethic, I want to discuss another kind of decodification of sexuality that has taken place in the United States in the last few decades—namely, a *moral* one.

MORAL (DE)CODIFICATION OF SEXUALITY

The idea of a sexual morality based on a code of conduct that is tied to particular sexual acts has its roots in a Christian sexual ethic. That ethic has two principal components, both of which are traceable to the biblical writings of St. Paul and to the fourth- and fifth-century writings of St. Augustine. The first component is that sex must take place within marriage in order to be moral. The second component is that even within marriage, sexual acts must be limited to those that are reproductive in nature. According to the Christian tradition, only procreative, marital intercourse can turn sexual pleasure into a moral good because only such sex is about more than physical pleasure; it is also about the creation of new life and, what Aquinas called, the *fides* of the marital union. By *fides*, Aquinas meant the union of the mind and body of the two spouses into a unique form of community characteristic of the marital relationship.[94]

Rather than track the historical development of a Christian sexual ethic,[95] I want to return briefly to the new natural law philosophy of John Finnis, which seeks to present an ostensibly secular variation of the Christian sexual ethic. Finnis's moral code of sexual conduct, which I discussed in chapter 3, is the philosophical equivalent of a legal codification of prohibited sexual acts. In the same way, however, that the relevance of legal codes on issues of sexual morality has waned, so has the relevance of a moral code of conduct that relies in a significant way on the nature of particular sexual acts to distinguish between morally acceptable and unacceptable sex.

Finnis states that one of the questions that interest him is "whether certain types of [sexual] *acts* are morally right or wrong."[96] Feelings of love, mutuality, and friendship in sexual intimacy matter but only if they are expressed from within the institution of marriage *and* if they accompany sexual acts that have "procreative significance."[97] As Finnis notes, "wrongful sex acts are more seriously immoral the 'more distant' they are from *marital* sexual intercourse."[98] It is possible, therefore, to construct a hierarchy of sexual acts based on Finnis's conception of sexual morality:

1. Uncontracepted penile-vaginal sex by a married couple
2. Contracepted penile-vaginal sex by a married couple
3. Oral or anal sex by a married couple
4. Any kind of sex by an unmarried heterosexual couple
5. Masturbation
6. Any kind of sex with someone of the same gender

For Finnis, only the first kind of sexual intimacy on this list is moral. All others, including contracepted penile-vaginal sex by a married couple, are not. There is a hierarchy for Finnis because the further one moves away from marital reproductive sex, the more immoral the sex becomes. Although Finnis undoubtedly believes that same-gender intimacy (item six in the hierarchy) is worse than contracepted penile-vaginal sex by a married couple (item two), the common denominator of acts two through six is that they are motivated largely by a desire to experience physical pleasure. Masturbation and same-gender intimacy are at the bottom of the hierarchy for Finnis because he cannot conceive of any reason for engaging in those acts other than the seeking of pleasure. For Finnis, as noted in chapter 3, no meaningful human connection, and no actual mutuality, can arise from sexual conduct that has no resemblance to marital reproductive sex.

It is the nature of sexual acts that for Finnis often plays a determinative role in the moral assessment of sexuality. Thus, for example, the same married heterosexual couple can have the same level of love and respect for each other, and yet if one day they engage in uncontracepted penile-vaginal sex, they use their sexuality morally, but if on the next day they use a condom or engage in oral sex, they use it immorally. Although Finnis is not dismissive or unmindful of the importance of mutuality, the determinative role in his conception of sexual morality is often played not by mutuality but by the nature of the sexual act itself. No degree of love, respect, or concern for the other will make sexual acts two through six in the foregoing hierarchy free of moral suspicion.

There are many Americans today whose conception of sexual morality remains wedded to a hierarchical list of particular kinds of sexual acts (even if some would draw the line between moral and immoral sexual acts at different places than does Finnis), or who, at the very least, view all sexual acts outside of marriage as immoral.[99] On the other hand, there are many Americans (gay and straight) who have delinked their conception of sexual morality from a Finnisian hierarchy of sexual acts. This delinking began at the start of the twentieth century and reached its apogee in the decades after World War II. As the twentieth century progressed, more Americans began to view sex as having functions that went beyond reproduction and included the deepening of emotional bonds and the enjoyment of physical pleasure.[100]

The tension between a traditional conception of sexual morality founded on a code of conduct that seeks to distinguish between permissible and impermissible consensual sexual acts and one that deemphasizes the importance of privileged sexual acts (such as penile-vaginal sex within marriage) remains quite strong in our society. Many of our most divisive political issues, from abortion to homosexuality to teenage sexuality, reflect this tension. It is, in a sense, easier for those who subscribe to a traditional conception of sexual morality to articulate a concise sexual ethic because they can point to a hierarchy of sexual acts that uses marriage and reproduction to distinguish between moral and immoral sexual conduct. Conversely, the articulation is more challenging for those of us who reject the linkage between sexual ethics and a hierarchical code of particular sexual acts, but it is certainly not impossible. In fact, the Sexuality Information and Education Council of the United States (SIECUS) recently took out a full-page ad in the *New York Times* to explain how its understanding of sexual ethics differs from what I have here described as the traditional Christian sexual ethic. The ad was titled a "Religious Declaration on Sexual Morality, Justice, and Healing" and listed several principles including "Sexuality is God's life-giving and life-fulfilling gift" and "Our faith traditions celebrate the goodness of creation, including our bodies and our sexuality."[101] One of the principles set forth in the ad is particularly relevant to our discussion and is worth quoting in its entirety:

> **Our culture needs a sexual ethic focused on personal relationships and social justice** *rather than particular sexual acts.*
>
> All persons have the right and the responsibility to lead sexual lives that express love, justice, mutuality, commitment, consent, and pleasure. Grounded in respect for the body and for the vulnerability that intimacy brings, this ethic fosters physical, emotional, and spiritual health. It accepts no double standards and applies to all persons, without regard to sex, gender, color, age, bodily condition, marital status, or sexual orientation.[102]

Alternatives to a conception of sexual ethics that is founded on a hierarchical code of conduct look to normative values that are delinked from particular sexual acts. In the next and last section of the book, I discuss what I take to be the values of one such alternative, namely, that offered by a contemporary gay and lesbian sexual ethic.

A GAY AND LESBIAN SEXUAL ETHIC

The shift away from the legal, medical, and moral codification of same-gender sexuality has had important implications for the emergence of a gay and lesbian sexual ethic. The deemphasis of codes as sources of sexual morality has allowed lesbians and gay men to construct and abide by a new form of sexual ethic, an ethic that has both procedural and substantive components. I discuss both of those components below. Before I do so, however, I want to acknowledge a possible criticism of my treating lesbians and gay men in a unitary fashion without emphasizing the differences between them. I believe that there is sufficient common ground between lesbians and gay men in terms of how they construct ethical lives through their sexuality that permits us to speak in broad terms of a gay *and* lesbian sexual ethic. I do not believe, for example, that lesbians and gay men experience or celebrate the values of openness, mutuality, and pleasure, which I identify below as constitutive of a gay and lesbian sexual ethic, in significantly different ways. When one emphasizes commonalities, however, there is always the danger of minimizing important differences. Lesbians, for example, have to deal with their own distinct oppression as women in a society that retains strong patriarchal norms and practices. It also appears that some lesbians have a more fluid sense of their sexual identity than do most gay men.[103] Explorations of these differences and others are important and merit their own separate projects. I believe, however, that there are enough commonalities that make it fruitful to speak of a gay and lesbian sexual ethic that is broad enough to encompass the intimate lives and aspirations of both groups.

The Process of a Gay and Lesbian Sexual Ethic.   The procedural component of a gay and lesbian sexual ethic consists of a process of self-definition that is similar to what Foucault describes as a care of the self. A gay and lesbian sexual ethic emerges as lesbians and gay men give ethical meaning to their sexual practices through reflection and self-transformation. The ethical meaning of gay and lesbian sexuality will not be found in societal sexual norms, most of which aim to stigmatize and marginalize lesbians and gay men based on their sexual conduct. Instead, the gay or lesbian individual must turn inward to reflect and elaborate on the ethical meaning of his or her sexual practices. The legal, medical, and moral decodification of sexuality as represented by the waning of rigid normative hierarchies of sexual acts has given lesbians and gay men greater opportunities to craft their own ethical sexual lives. Although the sexual orientation of lesbians and gay men may very well be socially constructed, they are nonetheless able to exercise their capacity for autonomy in such a way that allows them to give ethical meaning to their lives. Through self-defining and self-transformative practices, lesbians and gay men are able to attain a modicum of freedom in a society that otherwise is oppressive of their sexuality.

Opponents of gay rights often refer derisively to a gay and lesbian "lifestyle." Lesbians and gay men often respond that just because one engages in sex with someone of the same gender does not mean that one leads a different lifestyle. But opponents of gay rights may be on to something when they speak of a gay lifestyle, even if the implications of their observations (or, perhaps more accurately, of their accusations) are the opposite of what they contend. For Foucault, a gay style of life is a positive, not a negative, because a gay life can be styled and crafted through the relationship that the gay person has toward his or her sexuality. The style emanates from the creative and transformative possibilities of same-gender sex. Thus Foucault asks: "Is it possible to create a homosexual mode of life? . . . It seems to me that a way of life can yield a culture and an ethics. To be 'gay,' I think, is not to identify with the psychological traits and the visible marks of the homosexual but to try to define and develop a way of life."[104] As David Halperin puts it, "Foucault in effect seizes on that most abjected and devalued feature of gay male self-fashioning, namely, *style* . . . and finds in it a rigorous, austere, and transformative technology of the self which produces concrete pos-

sibilities for the development of personal autonomy."[105] The practices of
the self engaged in by lesbians and gay men lead to "new forms of relationship, new modes of knowledge, new means of creativity, and new
possibilities of love."[106]

In a gay and lesbian sexual ethic, then, what distinguishes ethical sexual conduct from unethical sexual conduct is not the nature of the sexual
act itself but is instead how the individual uses sex to craft an ethical life.
Thus, Edmund White has it exactly wrong when he argues that sex is
about aesthetics and not about ethics.[107] It is precisely the fact that sex
can be an integral part of an aesthetics of existence that imbues it with
ethical meaning. A gay and lesbian sexual ethic is about crafting a certain
relationship with the self. I use the word "crafting" purposefully because
it suggests active participation by the individual in the molding and creating of an ethical life, akin to the work that a craftsman or an artist does
in creating an object of beauty. "Sex is not a fatality," Foucault notes,
"it's a possibility for creative life."[108]

It is true, of course, that not every lesbian and gay man views her or
his sexual life through the rather rarefied prism of aesthetics. But all sexually active lesbians and gay men must at some point and at some level
cope with the dissonance between their sense of self-worth and self-
regard as sexual beings and the societal norms that deem their sexuality
to be abnormal, perverse, and immoral. Coping with this dissonance requires the constructing and crafting of ethical sexual lives that are built
around an alternative sexual ethic. This process does not require endless
self-redefinition and self-transformation; lesbians and gay men do not
constantly reevaluate their ethical assessments of their sexual lives. It is
reasonable to assume that they, like everyone else, find routine and stability in ethical judgments appealing. Before they can settle into a routine, however, there is ethical work to be done as they reflect on what
their sexuality means to them quite apart from what society tells them it
should mean. They must construct ethical lives where love, relationships, families, and communities are built around a form of sexuality that
most of the rest of society considers at best odd and at worst perverse
and immoral. Lesbians and gay men have to *themselves* give ethical
meaning to their sexual lives; society will not do it for them. Lesbians
and gay men must transform themselves from the perverse, abnormal,
and immoral persons that society deems them to be into individuals who
use their sexuality as a way of crafting ethical lives. They must, as Sarah
Hoagland puts it, "create meaning through [their] living."[109]

The Substance of a Gay and Lesbian Sexual Ethic.   I should acknowledge at the start of this discussion of the substantive component
of a gay and lesbian sexual ethic that Foucault never explicitly gave his
conception of ethics a substantive content; he never intended, in other
words, to tell people what to do or how to go about doing it. Given the

constant barrage of accusations made by opponents of gay rights about the supposed immorality of gay and lesbian sexuality, however, it is normatively acceptable and politically necessary to explore the substantive elements of a gay and lesbian sexual ethic.

The process of ethical self-transformation in which many lesbians and gay men engage today has led to the emergence of substantive values that are constitutive of a gay and lesbian sexual ethic. In my estimation, that ethic includes the values of openness, mutuality, and pleasure. I discuss each of those values below. Before I do, however, I want to make it clear that I am not suggesting that these are the only values that are part of a gay and lesbian sexual ethic or that the way in which I interpret them is the only way of doing so. Others may want to offer additional values or describe the values that I identify in different ways. My goal is less to offer a definitive and final interpretation of a contemporary gay and lesbian sexual ethic than it is to argue for the existence of such an ethic that, regardless of its precise contours, constitutes a powerful and appealing alternative to the traditional Christian sexual ethic.

Openness. An important value in a gay and lesbian sexual ethic is openness, a straightforward value that need not detain us long. Foucault in *The History of Sexuality*, Volume I, notes that society's power relations and systems of knowledge simultaneously create, marginalize, and silence sexual identities that are considered abnormal or perverse. The principle of openness addresses the silencing element in the triad noted by Foucault. By remaining silent, we as lesbians and gay men contribute to our own marginalization. For lesbians and gay men, to be silent about issues of sexuality is to implicitly contribute to society's disapproval of homosexuality.

It is common for lesbians and gay men to be told, "you do whatever you want to do, just don't assume that others want to hear about it." That is an ethically untenable principle for a gay or lesbian person to abide by because the silencing only deepens the stigmatization and marginalization of the conduct that then, in turn, reinforces the silence. Through openness, lesbians and gay men can attempt to break this never-ending loop. The starting point of a gay and lesbian sexual ethic, then, entails a refusal to contribute to our own silencing.

In many ways, the AIDS crisis has made it impossible for homosexuals—and gay men in particular—to keep our sexuality hidden. Remaining in the closet in the face of such death and suffering threatens one's integrity and self-respect. Whereas sex can be kept private and hidden, death and dying cannot. A gay and lesbian sexual ethic encourages lesbians and gay men to find strength and dignity through the very same sexual acts that societal norms rely on to marginalize and oppress them. With AIDS, gay men have the additional need to seek strength and dignity in the face of a deadly epidemic and under the onslaught of vituperative attacks by some conservatives (mostly Christian evangelicals) who equate AIDS with a just punishment for immoral behavior. Under such conditions, the first step toward using one's sexuality ethically is an open acknowledgment of it.

Mutuality. Mutuality is a second substantive value in a gay and lesbian sexual ethic, one that serves as common ground for bringing together different ways of thinking about the role of sex in the lives of lesbians and gay men. The sociologist Steven Seidman has identified two primary strains in gay sexual culture. The first is libertarian and holds that the only normative restraint on sexual activity should be lack of consent. The second is romanticist and views sex instrumentally as creating and strengthening emotional bonds between individuals.[110] The tension between these two viewpoints manifests itself periodically in criticisms by gay commentators about promiscuity and an excessive focus on sex among some in the gay male community.[111] Following such complaints, there is often a response by other gay commentators who view any criticism of a free and unrestrained sexuality as a threat to gay liberation and as a dangerous incorporation of traditional and conservative heterosexual values (such as monogamy and marriage) into the gay sexual culture.[112] An inclusive gay sexual ethic, therefore, must somehow reconcile the different perspectives of the libertarian and romanticist camps. In my estimation, the value of mutuality in matters of sexuality (by which I mean a reciprocal respect and concern for the needs and vulnerabilities of sexual partners) provides the framework for an inclusive sexual ethic that brings together both libertarians and romanticists within the gay and lesbian community.

Mutuality entails more than mere consent because mutuality presupposes a respect and concern for the other person, neither of which is required by consent. In fact, some libertarians within the gay community have argued that since the only relevant issue in matters of sex is consent, consensual sex is outside "of the realm of morality."[113] If we demand mutuality, however, we make it clear that the sexual actor must accept a minimum level of moral responsibility for the well-being of the other person; if the actor does not meet the needs and concerns of the other person, the sexual act will lack the requisite degree of mutuality. A concern for mutuality also requires a recognition of the sexual other as a vulnerable human being. Sexual intimacy by its very nature requires a letting go, a trusting of the other, and a lowering of self-protective mechanisms, all of which can make the parties feel vulnerable and insecure. By being respectful and considerate of the other, however, sex that takes place in a context of mutuality helps the other turn initial feelings of vulnerability and insecurity into ones of self-assurance and self-respect.

Mutuality is, of course, often present in sexual intimacy that is part of loving and committed relationships (though as I will argue, mutuality can also be present in sexual encounters where there is no affectional connection between the parties). It is a shame that Foucault, in his extensive discussions of sexuality, does not speak more of the affectional implications of sexual acts. As Mark Poster notes, "the great lacuna of Foucault's history of sexuality [is] a relative and remarkable absence of discussion about the affective nuances of sexual relations."[114] In at least one interview given toward the end of his life, however, Foucault addresses the ethical implications of the affection and love that can accompany same-gender sexual acts. What Foucault says is fascinating (which makes one wish he had said more!). He starts by noting that society is less troubled by gay sex than it is by gay love. A same-gender sexual act does not by itself raise "troubling [questions about] affection, tenderness, friendship, fidelity, camaraderie, and companionship, things that our rather sanitized society can't allow a place for without fearing the formation of new alliances and the tying together of unforeseen lines of force."[115] It is precisely because same-gender intimacy can lead to new emotional possibilities and new loves that society fears it. "To imagine a sexual act that doesn't conform to law or nature is not what disturbs people. But that individuals are beginning to love one another—there's the problem."[116] Foucault's astute observations are reflected in our current debates over same-sex marriage. Our society today, as David Halperin puts it, has an "easier [time] legaliz[ing] gay sex than gay marriage."[117] Although in most states gay sex is no longer a criminal act, no jurisdiction recognizes same-sex marriage.

With the exception of the recent enactment of the Vermont civil union statute, lesbians and gay men in the United States have failed in their attempts to gain meaningful state recognition of and protection for their relationships. Despite the absence of predetermined relational frameworks (legal and otherwise) upon which to rely, it is nonetheless remarkable how lesbians and gay men have, over the last few decades, created new types of relationships and loves with their own distinctive characteristics and forms. For example, as noted in chapter 4, friendship, love, and choice are the constitutive elements of gay families which makes them less dependent on predetermined biological or legal structures. Thus, by their very nature, gay families are more fluid, variable, and accommodating than traditional heterosexual families, which are primarily defined through biological and legal ties. Similarly, as discussed in chapter 3, committed and sexually intimate gay and lesbian relationships cannot rely on predetermined gender roles that have traditionally been incorporated into heterosexual intimate relationships. When gay or lesbian partners decide that their sexual intimacy leads to emotional bonds that are strong enough to make their lives into one, therefore, they must work out the arrangements and dynamics of their relationship with little societal or legal guidance. The structure and form of gay and lesbian relationships and families do not depend on predetermined concepts of law and biology or on presumptions about gender roles. Instead, the structure and form are provided almost exclusively by the mutuality (as reflected in reciprocity and support) that exists between the partners.

The later Foucault has been criticized for emphasizing an ethics of individualism that ignores relationships, communal ties, and collective action.[118] In Foucault's defense, he makes it clear that the care of the self as practiced in antiquity "constituted, not an exercise in solitude, but a true *social* practice" (HS3, 51, emphasis added). He adds that though "[t]he care of the self is ethical in itself[,] . . . it [also] implies complex relationships with others in so far as this *ethos* of freedom is also a way of caring for others" (ECS, 287). These statements notwithstanding, it is true that Foucault was not as explicit as he perhaps should have been about the relational and associational components of his conception of ethics.

In any event, what is important for our purposes is to note that a gay and lesbian sexual ethic is not an individualistic ethic in the libertarian sense where the primary norm is freedom constrained only by issues of consent—rather, it is a group-oriented ethic (or ethos) developed by individuals whom society has marginalized and stigmatized because of their sexuality and whose ethical values and practices of freedom are direct responses to that oppression. The creation of gay and lesbian relationships, families, and communities results from lesbians and gay men reflecting on, and working through, the meaning and purpose of their sexuality. The bonds that build and cement gay and lesbian relationships, families, and communities most often originate from a sexual attraction that is different from the societal norm. That different and stigmatized attraction leads lesbians and gay men to a myriad of connections and associations that provide the support and affirmation that is denied by the broader society. Gay and lesbian relationships, families, and communities are the collective manifestations of a process of self-definition and self-transformation in which lesbians and gay men engage as they seek to build ethical lives based, in part, on sexual intimacy. For lesbians and gay men, caring for others, defining and transforming the self, and sexuality are all bound together. As Mark Blasius notes, "[l]esbians and gay men use their sexuality throughout the course of life to create diverse relationships and to integrate sexual freedom within relationships as a source of revitalization, innovation, and self-invention."[119]

While gay sex has led to the formation of new kinds of relationships and connections based on love and commitment, the principle of mutuality in sexual relations can also be satisfied outside of an affectional context. It is possible, for example, for mutuality to be present in an anonymous S/M sexual encounter. One of the aspects of S/M that fascinated Foucault was the fluidity of its internal power relations. The uninformed outsider may view an S/M encounter simply as the sexual domination of one party over another. But the power dynamics within an S/M sexual encounter can shift at any time. As Foucault noted, "the S&M game is very interesting because it's a strategic relation, but it is always fluid. Of course, there are roles, but everybody knows very well that those roles can be reversed. Sometimes the scene begins with the master and slave, and at the end the slave has become the master."[120] The fluidity of power in an S/M encounter imbues it with mutuality, which is the polar opposite of a rigid domination of one sexual partner over the other. In fact, Blasius discusses the fluidity of power in gay and lesbian S/M sex as well as in so-called butch/femme lesbian relationships. He notes that in both situations, as well as in a more general gay and lesbian sexuality, "[t]here may be a top and a bottom, but 'who' is 'what' is ambiguous and reversible in terms of power. It is not only that people may switch roles. . . . Rather, to the extent that people invent an erotic power game, it is understood as an invention, and neither position is reinforced by social power relations as it is in heterosexuality."[121]

Sex that lacks mutuality is inconsistent with a gay and lesbian sexual ethic because such sex cannot play a role in either the creation of gay and lesbian relationships, families, and communities, or in maintaining equality and a balance of power between sexual partners. Mutuality is a crucial component of a gay and lesbian sexual ethic; it explains the role of sex in both committed relationships and in sexual encounters where there is no affectional commitment but there is nonetheless a minimum of respect and concern for the other individual as a distinct human being with his or her own needs, expectations, and vulnerabilities. A gay and lesbian sexual ethic gives more weight to mutuality than does the sexual morality of a conservative thinker such as John Finnis who, as we have seen, seeks to defend a secular version of traditional Christian sexual morality. For Finnis, no amount of mutuality can mitigate the intrinsic immorality of some sexual acts. So, for example, the respect and concern that two gay men may have for each other as they engage in sexual acts (whether or not in a committed relationship) is never enough to overcome the fact that they are engaging in the *wrong* kinds of sexual acts. This view places Finnis in the indefensible position of having to argue that which bodily orifice is penetrated and by whom has a greater moral significance than the mutuality that may exist between the parties. A gay and lesbian sexual ethic, on the other hand, values mutuality while simultaneously refusing to find value or disvalue in the nature of particular sexual acts.

A gay and lesbian sexual ethic values mutuality because it assists lesbians and gay men in constructing affectional relationships, loving families, and enriching communities around a form of sexuality that a large segment of the society deems to be immoral and perverse. Without mutuality in sexual intimacy, lesbians and gay men could not create and maintain those collective entities; it is mutuality, through the trust and confidence in others that it provides, which partly makes up for the lack of predetermined and supportive structures (afforded by law, biology, and gender roles) that are characteristic of heterosexual relationships and families. In addition, mutuality plays a crucial role for those lesbians and gay men who choose to engage in sex in the absence of affectional commitment. The principle of mutuality allows for the delinking of sex from commitment (for those who so choose) without compromising the necessary respect for the other person and without incorporating into the sexual encounter society's predetermined power relations and hierarchies such as those represented by traditional gender roles.

Pleasure.   The third important value that I take to be constitutive of a gay and lesbian sexual ethic is pleasure. For Foucault, an emphasis on sexual pleasure requires a corresponding deemphasis on sexual desire. As he explains it, the Christian conception of sex is centered around controlling lustful desires. The modern conception is centered around understanding and categorizing sexual desire. The ancient Greeks approached sex differently because they delinked sex from desire; neither the subject nor the object of desire was of ethical interest to them. Instead, what mattered was sexual pleasure, and how the individual came to it and incorporated it into his ethical life.

The idea that sex should be governed by desire is so ingrained in our consciousness that it is, at first glance, difficult to imagine sex without desire. But that is precisely what Foucault asks us to entertain: to take sex out of the sphere of desire and place it in the sphere of pleasure. Foucault explains this idea as follows:

> I am advancing this term [pleasure], because it seems to me that it escapes the medical and naturalistic connotations inherent in the notion of desire. That notion has been used as a tool, as a grid of intelligibility, a calibration in terms of normality: "Tell me what your desire is and I will tell you who you are, whether you are normal or not, and then I can validate or invalidate your desire." . . . The term "pleasure" on the other hand is virgin territory, unused, almost devoid of meaning. There is no "pathology" of pleasure, no "abnormal" pleasure. It is an event "outside the subject," or at the limit of the subject, taking place in that something which is neither of the body nor of the soul, which is neither inside nor outside—in short, a notion neither assigned nor assignable.[122]

Although scientific, medical, and religious discourses have defined and manipulated sexual desire, in other words, sexual pleasure remains a "virgin territory" that has largely escaped analysis and categorization.[123] Even though various disciplines and moral perspectives have sought to distinguish between normal and abnormal sexual desires, little moral attention has been paid to sexual pleasure, other than to warn of its dangers. Foucault believes that there is a positive and normative side to sexual pleasure because it can be used to construct new kinds of lives. As

Ladelle McWhorter notes, "Foucault advocates the use of pleasure and the expansion of our capacities for pleasure as a means of resisting sexual normalization and creating different lives for ourselves."[124]

Pleasure is an appropriate focus for a gay and lesbian sexual ethic that seeks to challenge traditional sexual moralities and discourses grounded on the distinction between normal and abnormal sexual *desires*. A gay and lesbian sexual ethic embraces and celebrates sexual pleasure. In doing so, it must constantly work to counteract the idea that it is pleasure that makes sex morally suspect. For a gay and lesbian sexual ethic, pleasure is a normative good; it is the pleasure of sex that leads individuals to use sex and sexuality in the construction of new kinds of lives. As Michael Warner notes, "[p]leasures once imaginable only with disgust, if at all, become the material out of which individuals and groups *elaborate themselves*."[125] When we evaluate sex from the perspective of pleasure rather than desire, we shift the focus away from codes of conduct that seek to distinguish between moral and immoral sexual desires and toward the ways in which individuals *use* sexual pleasures to transform themselves.

For Foucault pleasure is both creative and transformative. Sadomasochistic sex, for example, was intriguing for Foucault because he saw it as expanding the possibilities of pleasure. Even though an outsider might view S/M as painful and violent, such a view, according to Foucault, "is stupid."[126] Instead, S/M is about "inventing new possibilities of pleasure with strange [or different] parts of the body—through the erotization of [nongenital] parts of the body."[127] Sadomasochism, Foucault concludes, is "the real creation of new possibilities of pleasure, which people had no idea about previously."[128] Gay and lesbian sex, like S/M sex, explores the boundaries of pleasure as a means of self-definition. In response to society's stigmatization of same-gender intimacy, the gay or lesbian individual asks himself or herself the following: *How do I use sexual pleasure to simultaneously constitute and transform myself? It is the seeking of this sexual pleasure that makes me a "homosexual" and yet it is through this pleasure that I can work on myself as an ethical person. It is through a reflective posture vis à vis the pleasure of sex that I can escape the normalizing and stigmatizing efforts by society to link my sexual conduct to supposed abnormal sexual desires.*

An emphasis on pleasure, of course, makes lesbians and gay men vulnerable to accusations of hedonism and moral relativism. Such accusations are best addressed by emphasizing that pleasure is only one of the values of a gay and lesbian sexual ethic and that the value of mutuality, another constitutive element of such an ethic, places limits on the uses of pleasure. Particular sexual pleasures in particular contexts violate what I take to be a gay and lesbian sexual ethic if in the seeking of pleasure, the individual fails to respect the needs, expectations, and vulnerabilities of the sexual partner. Furthermore, no one denies that a life that is only concerned with pleasure is an empty and unsatisfying one.[129] However, sexual pleasures that are part of the cultivation of the self, that are aimed to better the self and create links of mutuality and respect with others, ought to be seen as ethical regardless of which bodily orifice is penetrated or the gender of the penetrator. A gay and lesbian sexual ethic is not meant to justify any and all sexual pleasures; rather, such an ethic acknowledges "that the imaginative and intelligent pursuit of pleasure *requires* a certain amount of work (in the sense of exertion) and that it *does* a certain amount of work (in the sense of transformation)."[130]

The key ethical precept, then, is not to be passive vis-à-vis sexual pleasure. Like the ancient Greeks, the key is to work with pleasure in order to transform oneself. The result of this transformation for contemporary lesbians and gay men will, of course, be different from the transformation of the privileged males in ancient Greece. These differences, however, are consistent with Foucault's views since, as already mentioned, he did not want us simply to embrace the sexual ethics of antiquity. Instead, he wanted sexual ethics to focus on the need to transform the self rather than on universal codes of conduct that seek to distinguish moral sexual acts from immoral ones. For the contemporary lesbian or gay man, the transformation that can be achieved through the values of openness, mutuality, and pleasure is a transformation from an individual who is marginalized and stigmatized to one who, through reflection and self-definition, leads an ethical life characterized by dignity and self-respect.

Some Concluding Thoughts on a Gay and Lesbian Sexual Ethic. Many heterosexuals also emphasize openness, mutuality, and pleasure in their sexual relations; lesbians and gay men obviously do not have a monopoly on these values. It is therefore possible to articulate and defend a progressive sexual ethic that applies to everyone regardless of sexual orientation. Gayle Rubin, in her influential essay on human sexuality, explains such an ethic in this way: "A [sexual ethic] should judge sexual acts by the way partners treat one another, the level of mutual consideration, the presence or absence of coercion, and the quantity and quality of pleasures they provide."[131] What is different for lesbians and gay men is that, unlike heterosexuals, society defines them morally as human beings, not just as *sexual* human beings, through their sexuality. As Ladelle McWhorter notes of her unsuccessful efforts to overcome society's definition of her based on her sexual identity:

> Very quickly . . . I was made to understand that society would not allow me *not* to be a sexual subject and that if I persisted in engaging in homosexual acts I would have to be a homosexual subject and be outcast and ridiculed as such. What kind of moral subject I would be was exhaustively defined by my homosexuality; nothing I might do would mitigate society's moral condemnation of me. My sexuality, not my morality, determined who I truly was.[132]

The gay or lesbian individual uses his or her sexuality to construct and fashion an ethical life through a process that does not replicate itself for heterosexuals because their sexuality is already ethically privileged. Although heterosexuals can, of course, lead sexually ethical lives, they do not construct for themselves an ethical sexual life in the face of societal norms that equate their very sexuality with abnormality, perversity, and immorality.

The relationship that heterosexuals have with their sexuality is not unlike the relationship that white Americans have with the color of their skin. Many, if not most, white Americans cannot comprehend the reactions and sensitivities that African Americans have toward issues of race because black skin is problematized in the United States in a very different way from white skin. Black skin is marginalized and oppressed, whereas white skin stands in a relationship of supremacy vis-à-vis black skin. W.E.B. Du Bois wrote famously about the double-consciousness that African Americans experience as a "sense of always looking at one's self through the eyes of others, of measuring one's soul by the tape of a world that looks on in amused contempt and pity."[133] Similarly, heterosexuality is defined and receives its many privileges when juxtaposed to the supposed immorality and perversity of homosexuality. Lesbians and gay men, on the other hand, are defined and measured "through the eyes of others" as society sits in moral judgment of them almost entirely through their sexuality.

There are in this regard interesting parallels between a gay and lesbian sexual ethic and a feminist sexual ethic. Although female heterosexual sexuality has not been as despised as gay and lesbian sexuality, it has had to cope with its own distinctive set of taboos requiring circumspection and subservience to the desires of men. There is a long-standing myth that men enjoy sex more than women, and this belief has led to all kinds of misperceptions and stereotypes about women's sexuality. Believing that women have less interest in or use for sex helps reinforce cultural norms that sex is primarily about satisfying the physical needs of men, and that the role of women, here as in so many different areas of American life, is to serve men. In fact, one of the goals of the early women's liberation movement was to address the double standard that applied to women's sexuality.

It is not surprising, therefore, that there are commonalities between what I take to be a contemporary gay and lesbian sexual ethic and the sexual ethic of the early women's liberation movement. That movement pursued goals that included the need: (1) to discuss *openly* female sexuality (including lesbianism); (2) to demand a minimum degree of *mutuality* and respect between men and women in intimate relationships; and (3) to promote awareness that women can also get *pleasure* from sex.[134] Given the problematization by society of women's sexuality, the attempts by women to cope with their marginalization and oppression, to lead lives of dignity and self-respect, are imbued with an ethical content, a content that is simply nonexistent and largely incomprehensible for heterosexual men. The same is true for lesbians and gay men who must create ethical lives, from within a society that views their sexuality as intrinsically immoral, through reflection and self-transformation, and through the promotion of values such as openness, mutuality, and pleasure.

As society moves toward greater tolerance and acceptance of gay and lesbian relationships, however, an interesting question emerges: what happens to the process of ethical self-definition and self-transformation once gay sex is no longer viewed as morally problematic? If society someday ceases to morally problematize same-gender sexual intimacy, then the opportunity to engage in self-transformative practices through that intimacy will be reduced. That does not mean, however, that gay sex will become ethically or morally valueless, in the same way that contemporary society's failure to problematize morally consensual opposite-gender sexuality does not render it valueless. If and when gay sex is no longer morally problematic in the minds of a clear majority of Americans, that will mean that norms such as openness, mutuality, and the value of sexual pleasure will be more morally relevant to the sexual ethic of most Americans than the nature of particular sexual acts or the gender of the parties involved. A gay and lesbian sexual ethic, in other words, will be part of, or at least be consistent with, largely accepted sexual norms.

There are some in the gay community who are afraid of the day when gay sex might lose its transgressive meaning and outsider status. For these individuals, lesbians and gay men must never become part of the sexual mainstream of society because to do so will be to give in to conservative, heterosexist values. I do not see it that way; I do not see much value in transgression for the sake of transgression. The ultimate goal should not be transgression—a morally limited concept that does not by itself tell us what we should transgress *against*—but the reduction, and eventual elimination, of oppression.[135]

If society someday ceases to problematize morally gay and lesbian sexuality, then I think lesbians and gay men should happily trade in their stigmatization and marginalization for the opportunity to live open and dignified lives in a society that values them as full and equal human beings. If society someday no longer problematizes morally gay and lesbian sexuality, that will not mean that society will have simply co-opted lesbians and gay men into accepting its values. If the moral problematization of same-gender intimacy ends someday, those values will have been *modified* in order to account for the sexuality and relationships of lesbians and gay men. If, for example, same-sex marriage is one day recognized in the United States, that will mean that the gender of spouses will become irrelevant for purposes of marriage. This development will mean that centuries-old ideas about gender roles and privileges within marriage will be undermined and weakened. As noted in chapter 3, the transformative impact of such a change should not be underestimated. True acceptance of gay and lesbian sexuality and relationships will require a meaningful transformation of society's sexual norms that should help allay the concerns of some about the co-optation of lesbians and gay men into existing values.

Although some on the left will be skeptical of the notion that a gay and lesbian sexual ethic should (ever) be part of a mainstream sexual ethic, some on the right will argue that the values of a gay and lesbian sexual ethic as I have explained them here do not speak of the need for *restraint* on matters of sex. A traditionalist will argue that a gay and lesbian sexual ethic will allow individuals to do whatever they want as long as they reflect on the meanings of their sexual acts and use those acts to define and transform themselves. The traditionalist will point out that a code of conduct, such as the one that is part of traditional Christian sexual morality, places certain sexual acts out of bounds. Not so a gay and lesbian sexual ethic.

There are at least two responses to this argument. First, as already noted, the value of mutuality in sexual relationships—a constitutive element of a gay and lesbian sexual ethic—acts as a restraint on sexual conduct. A gay and lesbian sexual ethic demands that the needs, expectations, and vulnerabilities of sexual partners be respected because it is through that mutuality that gay relationships, families, and communities are formed and maintained. In addition, it is that mutuality that protects and promotes equality and a balance of power in gay and lesbian sexual encounters that take place outside of an affectional context.

Second, there are other moral and ethical norms (that are not explicitly about sex) that are always applicable to sexual relationships and encounters. The duty not to cause pain or suffering, the duty not to deceive or mislead, the duty to treat others as ends rather than merely as means for the attainment of our own ends, to name just three, are moral obligations that apply whenever humans interact, including interactions that have a sexual component. The traditionalists, however, want to go beyond those kinds of generalized moral restraints by automatically placing certain sexual acts outside of acceptable moral bounds. It is precisely the efforts by traditionalists to mandate sexual restraint through a code of conduct that is based on the gender of the parties involved and on the particular bodily orifices that are used that have caused unacceptable suffering and oppression. What a gay and lesbian sexual ethic questions most fundamentally is the traditionalist idea that there is intrinsic moral (un)worthiness associated with particular sexual acts.

NOTES

INTRODUCTION—WHY MORALITY?

1. See William N. Eskridge Jr., *Gaylaw: Challenging the Apartheid of the Closet* (Cambridge: Harvard University Press, 1999), p. 60.
2. See *The Wolfenden Report: Report of the Committee on Homosexual Offenses and Prostitution* (American edition, New York: Stein & Day, 1963).
3. Ibid., ¶61.
4. Ibid.
5. John D'Emilio, *Sexual Politics, Sexual Communities: The Making of a Homosexual Minority in the United States, 1940–1970* (Chicago: University of Chicago Press, 1983), p. 112.
6. See Richard D. Mohr, *Gays/Justice: A Study of Ethics, Society, and Law* (New York: Columbia University Press, 1988), chs. 5–7.
7. 478 U.S. 186, 196 (1986).
8. Brief for Respondent, pp. 26–27, *Bowers v. Hardwick*, 478 U.S. 186 (1986), quoting *Poe v. Ullman*, 367 U.S. 497, 545 (1961) (Harlan, J., dissenting). Twelve years later, the Georgia Supreme Court, in a case involving a *heterosexual* defendant, struck down on state constitutional grounds the same statute that was at issue in *Bowers*. See *Powell v. State*, 510 S.E.2d 18 (Ga. 1998).
9. Chai Feldblum suggests that there may be benefits to raising issues of morality even when advocating for legislation that would protect lesbians and gay men from employment discrimination. See Chai R. Feldblum, "Sexual Orientation, Morality, and the Law: Devlin Revisited," 57 *University of Pittsburgh Law Review* 237, 300–12 (1996).
10. Michael J. Sandel, "Political Liberalism," 107 *Harvard Law Review* 1765, 1788 n.52 (1994).
11. See William J. Bennett, *The Book of Virtues: A Treasury of Great Moral Stories* (New York: Simon & Schuster, 1993).
12. *Face the Nation* (CBS television broadcast, Dec. 8, 1996).
13. Sen. Burns, 142 Cong. Rec. S10117 (Sept. 10, 1996).
14. See John Finnis, "Law, Morality, and 'Sexual Orientation,'" 69 *Notre Dame Law Review* 1049, 1049–1053 (1994). There are also a growing number of Americans who believe that lesbians and gay men should be provided with the kind of protection against discrimination in employment and housing that is afforded to other minorities. When President William Clinton issued an order banning discrimination against lesbians and gay men by federal civilian agencies, for example, surveys showed that 70 percent of Americans supported his decision. See Richard L. Berke, "Chasing the Polls on Gay

Rights," *New York Times*, Aug. 2, 1998, §4, p. 3. In 1996, a bill that would
have prohibited discrimination on the basis of sexual orientation failed in the
United States Senate by only one vote. See John E. Yang, "Senate Passes Bill
Against Same-Sex Marriage; In First Test on Hill, Measure to Prohibit Employment Discrimination is Defeated 50–49," *Washington Post*, Sept. 11,
1996, p. A1. Surveys continue to show, however, that a substantial majority
of Americans (around two thirds) are opposed to the recognition of same-sex
marriage. See Hanna Rosin and Richard Morin, "In One Area, Americans
Still Draw a Line on Acceptability," *Washington Post*, January 11, 1999, p. 8
(national edition); "More Folks Say Gay is OK, But Most Oppose Marriages," *USA Today*, March 19, 1996, p. 3A.

15. Finnis, "Law, Morality, and 'Sexual Orientation,' " p. 1076. The conservative
philosopher Robert George also believes that society has a legitimate interest
in enforcing public morality in many instances, including through the prohibition of same-sex marriage. See Robert P. George and Gerard V. Bradley,
"Marriage and the Liberal Imagination," 84 *Georgetown Law Journal* 301
(1995). George nonetheless recognizes the importance of an enforceable and
meaningful right to privacy. See Robert P. George, *Making Men Moral: Civil
Liberties and Public Morality* (New York: Oxford University Press, 1995), pp.
210–17. See also Harry M. Clor, *Public Morality and Liberal Society: Essays
on Decency, Law, and Pornography* (Notre Dame: Notre Dame Press, 1996),
p. 83 (recognizing "limiting criteria" in the otherwise valid regulation of
public morality that would counsel against the enforcement of "criminal
statutes against homosexual conduct among consenting adults in private").

16. I will not in this book discuss the normative foundations of a right to privacy.
For thoughtful elaborations on such foundations with particular attention to
constitutional issues, see Mohr, *Gays/Justice*, chs. 2–4; David A. J. Richards,
Sex, Drugs, and the Law: An Essay on Human Rights and Overcriminalization
(Totowa, NJ: Rowman & Littlefield, 1982); Vincent J. Samar, *The Right to
Privacy: Gays, Lesbians, and the Constitution* (Philadelphia: Temple University
Press, 1991).

17. Most of the issues, priorities, and concerns that I will raise in this book in relation to lesbians and gay men are also applicable to bisexual and transgendered individuals. Adding "bisexuals and trangendered" to the dozens of
times that I will refer to "lesbians and gay men" in this book, however, would
be cumbersome. I also prefer not to use acronyms—such as LGBT—to refer
to people. The least dissatisfactory option, then, is to use "lesbians and gay
men" accompanied by this early caveat that I wish to include bisexual and
transgendered individuals within the ambit of my arguments.

18. See e.g., Posner, SR.

19. See e.g., David M. Halperin, *One Hundred Years of Homosexuality* (New
York: Routledge, 1990).

20. See e.g., Judith P. Butler, *Bodies that Matter: On the Discursive Limits of "Sex"*
(New York: Routledge, 1993).

21. For ways of dividing social constructionists in matters of sexuality into categories that are somewhat different from the ones that I have used here, see
Edward Stein, "Conclusion: The Essentials of Constructionism and the Construction of Essentialism," in *Forms of Desire: Sexual Orientation and the Social Constructionist Controversy*, ed. Edward Stein (New York: Routledge,

1992), pp. 325, 338–44; Carole S. Vance, "Social Construction Theory: Problems in the History of Sexuality," in *Homosexuality, Which Homosexuality?*, eds. Anja van Kooten Niekerk and Theo van der Meer (London: GMP Publishers, 1989), pp. 13, 18–23.

22. Peter M. Cicchino, "Building on Foundational Myths: Feminism and the Recovery of 'Human Nature': A Response to Martha Fineman," 8 *American University Journal of Gender, Social Policy and the Law* 73, 84 (1999).

23. For an eloquent defense of this view, see Michael Warner, *The Trouble with Normal: Sex, Politics, and the Ethics of Queer Life* (New York: Free Press, 1999).

24. The connection between Mill and Warner's ideas is noted by Martha Nussbaum in "Experiments in Living," *The New Republic*, Jan. 3, 2000, pp. 31, 32.

25. The sections on Dworkin are organized slightly differently. I divide the discussion of Dworkin into his earlier and later works. Both sections have a descriptive and an evaluative component to them, unlike the discussions of Rawls, Rorty, Posner, Sandel, Walzer, and Foucault that try, as much as possible, to separate description from evaluation.

CHAPTER ONE—NEUTRAL LIBERALISM

1. Another important proponent of neutral liberalism is Bruce Ackerman. See Bruce A. Ackerman, *Social Justice in the Liberal State* (New Haven: Yale University Press, 1980).

2. See Ladelle McWhorter, *Bodies and Pleasures: Foucault and the Politics of Sexual Normalization* (Bloomington: Indiana University Press, 1999).

3. See ibid., pp. 215–25. See also Francisco Valdes, "Queer Margins, Queer Ethics: A Call to Account for Race and Ethnicity in the Law, Theory, and Practice of 'Sexual Orientation,' " 48 *Hastings Law Journal* 1293, 1311 (1997) (noting that "nothing to date suggests that present-day Queer activism and theorizing . . . is inclined to abandon [a] broad anti-discrimination quest").

4. See Mark Blasius, *Gay and Lesbian Politics: Sexuality and the Emergence of a New Ethic* (Philadelphia: Temple University Press, 1994).

5. See Urvashi Vaid, *Virtual Equality: The Mainstreaming of Gay and Lesbian Liberation* (New York: Anchor Books, 1995), pp. 178–80.

6. Shane Phelan, "Queer Liberalism?," 94 *American Political Science Review* 431, 441 (2000).

7. Not all queer theorists abide by a political model of individual rights. Judith Butler, for example, has eschewed a traditional civil rights model in favor of transgressive practices aimed at undermining socially constructed identities. See Judith P. Butler, *Gender Trouble: Feminism and the Subversion of Identity* (New York: Routledge, 1990). Although Butler's work has been highly influential inside the academy, it is not clear that her emphasis on resistance to power through performative transgressions (such as drag) translates into a coherent or viable political vision. See Max H. Kirsch, *Queer Theory and Social Change* (New York: Routledge, 2000), p. 8; Martha C. Nussbaum, "The Professor of Parody," *The New Republic*, Feb. 22, 1999, p. 37; Momin Rah-

man, *Sexuality and Democracy: Identities and Strategies in Lesbian and Gay Politics* (Edinburgh: Edinburgh University Press, 2000), pp. 131–42.

8. See Michael Warner, *The Trouble with Normal: Sex, Politics, and the Ethics of Queer Life* (New York: Free Press, 1999).

9. See Michael J. Sandel, "Political Liberalism," 107 *Harvard Law Review* 1765, 1772 (1994).

10. Sandel, LLJ, p. xi (introduction to 2nd edition, 1998).

11. See Sandel, "Political Liberalism," pp. 1782–89.

12. See Chai R. Feldblum "Sexual Orientation, Morality, and the Law: Devlin Revisited," 57 *University of Pittsburgh Law Review* 237 (1996).

13. Rawls adds that "a central feature of political liberalism is that it views all . . . arguments [based on comprehensive secular doctrines in] the same way it views religious ones, and therefore these secular philosophical doctrines do not provide public reasons. Secular concepts and reasoning of this kind belong to first philosophy and moral doctrine, and fall outside of the domain of the political" (IPR, 780).

14. Sandel, "Political Liberalism," p. 1778.

15. Rawls, PL, p. iv n.31 (introduction to paperback edition, 1996).

16. Ibid.

17. Sandel, "Political Liberalism," p. 1778.

18. For a more positive assessment of the value of Rawls's constraints on public reasoning as they apply to the issue of same-sex marriage, see Linda C. Mc-Clain, "Deliberative Democracy, Overlapping Consensus, and Same-Sex Marriage," 66 *Fordham Law Review* 1241, 1248–52 (1998). Morris Kaplan has also expressed optimism that Rawls's understanding of the social bases of self-respect as a primary good and the interests of individuals in associational freedom are enough to require "social recognition of the associations, intimate and otherwise, through which [individuals] express their moral personality." Morris B. Kaplan, *Sexual Justice: Democratic Citizenship and the Politics of Desire* (New York: Routledge, 1997), p. 31. Kaplan's discussion of Rawls, in this otherwise excellent book, is relatively brief and does not address the concerns that I raise here, namely, the thinness of Rawls's account of moral personality and the problems associated with the constraints that he places on public reasoning.

19. See Robert P. George, "Public Reason and Political Conflict: Abortion and Homosexuality," 106 *Yale Law Journal* 2475 (1997).

20. Although both Michael Sandel and Robert George criticize Rawls for his separation of the right from the good, Sandel is generally supportive of gay rights positions, see Sandel, "Political Liberalism," pp. 1786–88, whereas George clearly is not. See Robert P. George and Gerard V. Bradley, "Marriage and the Liberal Imagination," 84 *Georgetown Law Journal* 301 (1995).

21. See *In re M.M.D.*, 662 A.2d 837 (D.C. Cir. 1995); *In re Adoption of Tammy*, 619 N.E.2d 315 (Mass. 1993); *In re Jacob*, 660 N.E.2d 397 (N.Y. 1995). Some courts have contended that in ruling in favor of gay or lesbian parties in cases involving children, they need not make normative evaluations regarding the same-gender relationships of the adults. Thus, for example, the Vermont Supreme Court, in ruling on a petition brought by the partner of a lesbian parent to adopt the latter's children, stated that "[w]e are not called upon to approve or disapprove of the relationship between" the partners. *In re*

B.L.V.B., 628 A.2d 1271, 1276 (Vt. 1993). Even if the court was technically correct that it was not called upon to "approve or disapprove of the relation-ship" between the adults, it had to conclude, before it could approve the adoption petition, that the relationship was good and valuable for the chil-dren. Not all relationships between adults who head a family (regardless of their sexual orientation) will be in the best interests of children, and courts in family law cases, though not called upon to rule directly upon the morality of the relationship between the adults, must nonetheless evaluate the goodness and value, from the children's perspective, that is characteristic of that rela tionship.

22. It is an implicit tenet of political liberalism that engaging in moral bracketing is a sign of respect for the deeply held views of others. We respect others' philosophical, moral, and religious views, it is thought, by not bringing into discussions about justice and rights our own comprehensive views. Although I will not address this issue here, it can be argued that real respect actually re-quires the opposite. As Cheryl Misak notes, "[w]e respect others not by ig-noring their comprehensive views, but by engaging those views—by attend-ing their beliefs, challenging them, learning from them, and arguing with them." Cheryl Misak, *Truth, Politics, Morality* (New York: Routledge, 2000), p. 28. It is this kind of respect for the views of others, it can be argued, that engenders a true and meaningful form of reciprocity.

23. See Patrick Devlin, *The Enforcement of Morals* (New York: Oxford University Press, 1965).

24. As Chai Feldblum points out, Lord Devlin did not actually oppose the Wolfenden Committee's recommendation to decriminalize male homosexual sodomy. Devlin "did not believe [that] the collective societal judgment re-garding homosexuality rose to the level of public indignation and disgust he believed was necessary for societal morality to be given the force of law." Feldblum, "Sexual Orientation, Morality, and the Law," p. 315, citing De-vlin, *The Enforcement of Morals*, p. ix.

    For more recent defenses of the use of morality in the setting of public pol-icy, see Harry M. Clor, *Public Morality and Liberal Society: Essays on Decency, Law and Pornography* (Notre Dame: Notre Dame Press, 1996); Robert P. George, *Making Men Moral: Civil Liberties and Public Morality* (New York: Ox-ford University Press, 1995). Both Clor and George, though agreeing with Lord Devlin that the state often has a legitimate role to play in the promotion of morality, argue that such promotion is only appropriate when there are substan-tive and defensible—as opposed to merely majoritarian—moral values at stake.

25. John Stuart Mill, *On Liberty* (ed , David Spitz, New York: W.W. Norton & Co., 1975 (1859)), pp. 10–11.

26. Ibid., p. 11.

27. For similar criticism, see Patrick Neal, *Liberalism and its Discontents* (New York: New York University Press, 1997), ch. 2; Michael J. Perry, *Morality, Politics, and Law* (New York: Oxford University Press, 1988), pp. 67–69.

28. See Nicholas Bamforth, *Sexuality, Morals and Justice: A Theory of Lesbian and Gay Rights Law* (Washington, D.C.: Cassell, 1997), pp. 128–29.

29. See e.g., William Bennett, "Leave Marriage Alone," *Newsweek*, June 3, 1996, p. 27; Charles Krauthammer, "When John and Jim Say 'I Do': If Gay Mar-riages are O.K., Then What About Polygamy? or Incest?," *Time*, July 22,

1996, p. 120. In a speech on the floor of the House of Representatives in support of the Defense of Marriage Act, Henry Hyde, the Republican Congressman from Illinois and the then-Chairman of the House Judiciary Committee, argued that "most people do not approve of homosexual conduct. They do not approve of incest. They do not approve of polygamy, and they express their disapprobation through the law." Rep. Hyde, 142 Cong. Rec. H7501 (July 12, 1996).

30. See *Romer v. Evans,* 517 U.S. 620, 648 (1996) (Scalia, J., dissenting).
31. Dworkin raises similar issues in "Liberal Community," 77 *California Law Review* 479 (1989). Dworkin began to refer to neutrality as a derivative as opposed to a fundamental value in an essay titled "Why Liberals Should Care about Equality" (MP, 205–13).
32. See Ronald Dworkin, *Freedom's Law: The Moral Reading of the American Constitution* (Cambridge: Harvard University Press, 1990), pp. 1–38; Ronald Dworkin, *Law's Empire* (Cambridge: Harvard University Press, 1986); Ronald Dworkin, "In Praise of Theory," 29 *Arizona State Law Journal* 353 (1997).
33. Although Dworkin refers to this critique as communitarian, I think it is most helpfully thought of as perfectionist.
34. For a similar argument, see Jean Hampton, "The Moral Commitments of Liberalism," in *The Idea of Democracy,* eds. David Copp et al. (New York: Cambridge University Press, 1993), p. 292.
35. Dworkin discusses his conception of equality of resources in detail in, "What is Equality? Part 2: Equality of Resources," 10 *Philosophy & Public Affairs* 283 (1981). Dworkin's most important essays on equality have been collected in a single volume. See Ronald Dworkin, *Sovereign Virtue: The Theory and Practice of Equality* (Cambridge: Harvard University Press, 2000).
36. Dworkin, "Liberal Community," p. 483.
37. Dworkin distinguishes between two different models for determining "the source and nature of the value a life can have for the person whose life it is" (FLE, 240). The first model is consequentialist whereas the second is Aristotelian in that it holds "that the value of a good life lies in the inherent value of a skillful performance of living" (FLE, 241). Dworkin prefers the second model because it allows individuals to pursue goals and relationships that are enriching and meaningful even if they do not have measurable consequences.
38. Dworkin, for example, notes that his conception of equality "is suspicious of critical paternalism because it rejects its root assumption: that a person's life can be improved just by forcing him into some act or abstinence he thinks valueless" (FLE, 265).

CHAPTER TWO—PRAGMATIC LIBERALISM

1. Rawls explains his position as follows: "Political liberalism does not question that many political and moral judgments of certain specified kinds are correct and it views them as reasonable. . . . [I]t [also] does not argue that we should be hesitant and uncertain, much less skeptical, about our own beliefs. Rather, we are to recognize the practical impossibility of reaching reasonable and workable political agreement in judgment on the truth of comprehensive

doctrines" (PL, 63). Rawls adds that "[i]t is vital to the idea of political liberalism that we may with perfect consistency hold that it would be unreasonable to use political power to enforce our own comprehensive view, which we must, of course, affirm as either reasonable or true" (PL, 138).

2. Cheryl Misak, *Truth, Politics, Morality* (New York: Routledge, 2000), p. 21. Richard Rorty, in an essay originally published in 1988, tried to enlist Rawls as an ally in his antifoundationalist quest. See "The Priority of Democracy to Philosophy" (ORT, 175–96). There are crucial differences, however, between the two since Rorty, unlike Rawls, is convinced that there is no such thing as objective truth. If truth were God, Rorty would be an atheist whereas Rawls (for purposes of political morality only) would be an agnostic. Several years after the publication of "The Priority of Democracy to Philosophy," Rorty acknowledged that he and Rawls part ways when the latter rejects historicism, that is, when he rejects the idea that, when we speak about justice, we should limit ourselves to arguing from within the particular practices and norms of particular societies. See Rorty, "Justice as a Larger Loyalty," in *Justice and Democracy: Cross-Cultural Perspectives*, eds. Ron Bontekoe and Marietta Stepaniants (Honolulu: University of Hawaii Press, 1997), pp. 9, 14.

3. See Ronald Dworkin, "Objectivity and Truth: You'd Better Believe It," 25 *Philosophy & Public Affairs* 87 (1996). For a similar argument see Thomas Nagel, *The Last Word* (New York: Oxford University Press, 1997), ch. 6.

4. Dworkin, "Objectivity and Truth," p. 89.

5. Ibid. Dworkin has been skeptical of skepticism for a long time. In an essay originally published in 1978 titled simply "Liberalism," he argued that "[l]iberalism cannot be based on skepticism. Its constitutive morality provides that human beings must be treated as equals by their government, not because there is no right and wrong in political morality, but because that is what is right" (MP, 203). Dworkin also believes that there are right and wrong answers to hotly disputed legal controversies. See *Law's Empire* (Cambridge: Harvard University Press, 1986), ch. 7; "Is There Really No Right Answer in Hard Cases?" (MP, 119–45); "Hard Cases" (TRS, 81–130).

6. Rorty is characterized as a postmodernist as often as he is labeled a pragmatist. Although many of Rorty's epistemological ideas fit quite comfortably within postmodernism, it is more helpful to think of him as a pragmatist, especially in a discussion of political philosophy.

7. Cornel West, *The American Evasion of Philosophy: A Genealogy of Pragmatism* (Madison: University of Wisconsin Press, 1989), p. 86. In this passage West refers to the work of John Dewey, but the same view of philosophy is held by other pragmatists. According to William James, for example, the pragmatist philosopher "turns away from abstraction and insufficiency from verbal solutions, from bad *a priori* reasons, from fixed principles, closed systems, and pretended absolutes and origins. He turns towards concreteness and adequacy, towards facts, towards action, and towards power." William James, *Pragmatism* (Cambridge: Harvard University Press, 1975 (1907)), p. 31. John Stuhr notes that for pragmatists, philosophy is not "to be understood as a purely theoretical quest for eternal truths or knowledge of an ultimate and unchanging reality. Its job no longer [is] to [divide] experience into the real and unreal, the substantial and the insubstantial. Instead, it must be practical, critical, and reconstructive; it must aim at the successful transformation or

amelioration of the experienced problems which call forth and intrinsically situate it, and its success must be measured in terms of this goal." John J. Stuhr, "Introduction," in *Pragmatism and Classical American Philosophy: Essential Readings and Interpretative Essays*, ed. John J. Stuhr (New York: Oxford University Press, 2000), p. 3. For an engaging discussion of the lives and ideas of early American pragmatist philosophers, see Louis Menand, *The Metaphysical Club: A Story of Ideas in America* (New York: Farrar, Straus and Giroux, 2001).

8. For book-length treatments of Rorty's work, see e.g., Norman Geras, *Solidarity in the Conversation of Humankind: The Ungroundable Liberalism of Richard Rorty* (New York: Verso, 1995); David L. Hall, *Richard Rorty: Prophet and Poet of the New Pragmatism* (Albany: State University of New York Press, 1994); Ronald A. Kuipers, *Solidarity and the Stranger: Themes in the Social Philosophy of Richard Rorty* (Lanham, Md.: University Press of America, 1997).

9. For two exceptions, see Nicholas Bamforth, *Sexuality, Morals and Justice: A Theory of Lesbian and Gay Rights Law* (Washington, D.C.: Cassell, 1997), pp. 118–20; Bart Schultz, "The Private and Its Problems—Pragmatism, Pragmatist Feminism, and Homophobia," 29 *Philosophy of the Social Sciences* 281 (1999).

10. James makes this point as follows: "There can *be* no difference anywhere that doesn't *make* a difference elsewhere—no difference in abstract truth that doesn't express itself in a difference in concrete fact and in conduct consequent upon that fact, imposed on somebody, somehow, somewhere and somewhen." James, *Pragmatism*, p. 30. Dewey writes that "[j]ust as to say an idea was true all the time is a way of saying *in retrospect* that it has come out in a certain fashion, so to say that an idea is 'eternally true' is to indicate *prospective* modes of application which are indefinitely anticipated. Its meaning, therefore, is strictly pragmatic. It does not indicate a property inherent in the idea as intellectualized existence, but denotes a property of use and employment." John Dewey, *The Middle Works, 1899–1924*, vol. 4 (Carbondale and Edwardsville: Southern Illinois University Press, 1976–1983), p. 71.

11. Richard Rorty, "Truth and Freedom: A Reply to Thomas McCarthy," 16 *Critical Inquiry* 633, 635 (1990). "[T]he aim of a just and free society," Rorty argues, should be to let "its citizens be as privatistic, 'irrationalist,' and aestheticist as they please so long as they do it on their own time—causing no harm to others and using no resources needed by those less advantaged" (CIS, xiv).

12. Rorty also praises the "private" Foucault and criticizes the "public" one in "Moral Identity and Private Autonomy: The Case of Foucault," in *Essays on Heidegger and Others* (New York: Cambridge University Press, 1991), p. 193. Rorty's efforts to relegate Foucault to the private sphere are highly debatable. As I will argue in chapter 5, and as many who write on issues of sexual orientation have noted, Foucault's work has played an invaluable role in better understanding the processes and oppressions that are involved in society's definition and regulation of sexuality. I believe that David Hall is therefore correct when he notes that "Foucault, the ironist, wrote of pain and humiliation in a manner that could sensitize us as much as any novelist so called. Thus, it seems Rorty must allow Foucault his due as an ironist whose words have *public* relevance." Hall, *Richard Rorty*, p. 156.

13. See Richard J. Ellis, "Achievement Gap," *The National Review*, June 22, 1998 (noting that Rorty "is assailed from the Right as an irresponsible liberal relativist").

14. See Ronald Dworkin, "Pragmatism, Right Answers, and True Banality," in *Pragmatism in Law and Society*, eds. Michael Brint and William Weaver (Boulder: Westview Press, 1991), p. 359.

15. See e.g., Richard J. Bernstein, "Rorty's Liberal Utopia," 57 *Social Research* 31 (1990); Nancy Fraser, "Solidarity or Singularity? Richard Rorty Between Romanticism and Technology," in *Reading Rorty*, ed. Alan R. Malachowski (Cambridge, Mass.: Blackwell, 1990), p. 303; John Tamborino, "Philosophy as the Mirror of Liberalism: The Politics of Richard Rorty," 30 *Polity* 57 (1997). Indeed, it is ironic (in a non-Rortian sense) that for a thinker who believes that there is no final word on anything since everything is vulnerable to redescription, Rorty nonetheless argues that "J.S. Mill's suggestion that governments devote themselves to optimizing the balance between leaving people's private lives alone and preventing suffering seems to me pretty much *the last word*" (CIS, 63) (emphasis added).

16. See Rorty, "Truth and Freedom," pp. 636–37.

17. See e.g., La. Rev. Stat. §14:89 (1986); Mich. Stat. §750.158 (1991).

18. The full quotation is as follows: "Copulation of humans with animals is repudiated because it treats human sexual activity and satisfaction as something appropriately sought in a manner as divorced from the actualizing of an intelligible common good as is the instinctive coupling of beasts—and so treats human bodily life, in one of its most intense activities, as appropriately lived as merely animal. The deliberate genital coupling of persons of the same sex is repudiated for a very similar reason." John M. Finnis, "Law, Morality, and 'Sexual Orientation,' " 69 *Notre Dame Law Review* 1049, 1069 (1994).

19. See Moisés Kaufman and the Members of the Tectonic Theater Project, *The Laramie Project* (New York: Vintage Books, 2001), p. 58. In his recent study of the attitudes of middle-class Americans, the sociologist Alan Wolfe found that many of those he surveyed "had no trouble finding these words, all of which cropped up in [his] interviews when the subject of homosexuality was raised: 'abnormal,' 'immoral,' 'sinful,' 'unacceptable,' 'sick,' 'unhealthy,' 'untrustworthy,' 'mentally ill,' 'wrong,' 'perverted,' and 'mentally deficient.' " Alan Wolfe, "The Homosexual Exception," *New York Times*, Feb. 8, 1998, §6 (Magazine), pp. 46, 47. For a further discussion of Wolfe's findings, see Alan Wolfe, *One Nation, After All* (New York: Penguin Books, 1998), pp. 72–81.

20. See Ladelle McWhorter, *Bodies and Pleasures: Foucault and the Politics of Sexual Normalization* (Bloomington: Indiana University Press, 1999), pp. 101–06.

21. David A. J. Richards, *Identity and the Case for Gay Rights: Race, Gender, Religion as Analogies* (Chicago: Chicago University Press, 1999), pp. 183–84. Cheshire Calhoun explores how lesbians and gay men are viewed by society exclusively in sexual terms in *Feminism, the Family, and the Politics of the Closet: Lesbian and Gay Displacement* (New York: Oxford University Press, 2000).

22. See Rep. Coburn, 142 Cong. Rec. H7444 (July 11, 1996).

23. Rorty's utopian vision includes within it a picture of "a planetwide democracy, a society in which torture, or the closing down of a university, on the

other side of the world is as much a cause for outrage as when it happens at home." Richard Rorty, "Philosophy and the Future," in *Rorty and Pragmatism: The Philosopher Responds to his Critics*, ed. Herman J. Saatkamp Jr. (Nashville: Vanderbilt University Press, 1995), pp. 197, 203.

24. See Amartya Sen, "East and West: The Reach of Reason," *N.Y. Review of Books*, July 20, 2000, p. 33; Amartya Sen, "Human Rights and Asian Values," *The New Republic*, July 14/21, 1997, p. 33.

25. 517 U.S. 620, 631 (1996).

26. Ibid., p. 635.

27. Andrew Sullivan, "Gay Marriage Supported by Hannah Arendt," *The New Republic*, May 6, 1996, p. 6.

28. See *Baker v. State*, 744 A.2d 864 (Vt. 1999).

29. Ibid., p. 889.

30. Ibid., citing *Dred Scott v. Sandford*, 60 U.S. (How.) 393 (1856).

31. *Baker*, p. 889 (emphasis added).

32. Mario Vargas Llosa, "Why Literature?," *The New Republic*, May 14, 2001, pp. 31, 32.

33. As Robin West notes, if we are shown a picture of a suffering person without "cultural indicators of that person's identity, our sympathetic response is much less likely to be filtered through nationalist identification." Robin West, "Is the Rule of Law Cosmopolitan?," 19 *Quinnipiac Law Review* 259, 289 (2000). "That we currently tailor our moral sympathies to the dictates of nationalism," West adds, "hardly shows that such a cribbed response is central to our nature." Ibid.

34. For the importance of narrative in the advancement of gay rights, see William N. Eskridge Jr., "Gaylegal Narratives," 46 *Stanford Law Review* 607 (1994); Marc A. Fajer, "Can Two Real Men Eat Quiche Together? Stortytelling, Gender-Role Stereotypes, and Legal Protection for Lesbians and Gay Men," 46 *University of Miami Law Review* 511 (1992).

35. Leonard Kriegel, "Uncle Tom and Tiny Tim: Some Reflections on the Cripple as Negro," 38 *American Scholar* 412, 418 (1969). Raimond Gaita makes a similar point when he notes that "[o]nly when one's humanity is fully visible will one be treated as someone who can intelligibly press claims to equal access to goods and opportunities." Raimond Gaita, *A Common Humanity: Thinking About Love and Truth and Justice* (New York: Routledge, 2000), p. xvi.

36. Martha C. Nussbaum, *Upheavals of Thought: The Intelligence of Emotions* (New York: Cambridge University Press, 2001), p. 319.

37. Rorty adds that "[m]oral development in the individual, and moral progress in the human species as a whole, is a matter of re-marking human selves so as to enlarge the variety of the relationships which constitute those selves" (PSH, 79). Norman Goras discusses how Rorty sometimes relies on a particular conception of human nature in *Solidarity in the Conversation of Humankind*, ch. 2.

38. Nussbaum distinguishes between a realism that is based on metaphysical principles and one that is internal to human experience (HFS, 205–08). For an elaboration on this point, see Martha C. Nussbaum and Amartya Sen, "Internal Criticism and Indian Rationalist Traditions," in *Relativism: Interpretation and Confrontation*, ed. Michael Krausz (Notre Dame: University of Notre Dame Press, 1989), p. 299.

39. See Martha C. Nussbaum, *Cultivating Humanity: A Classical Defense of Reform in Liberal Education* (Cambridge: Harvard University Press, 1997), pp. 85–112; Martha C. Nussbaum, *Poetic Justice: The Literary Imagination and Public Life* (Boston: Beacon Press, 1995); Martha C. Nussbaum, *Love's Knowledge: Essays on Philosophy and Literature* (New York: Oxford University Press, 1990).

40. Nussbaum has criticized Rorty for emphasizing national pride and identity over "a more international basis for political emotion and concern." See Martha C. Nussbaum, "Patriotism and Cosmopolitanism," in *For Love of Country: Debating the Limits of Patriotism*, ed. Joshua Cohen (Boston: Beacon Press, 1996), pp. 2, 4.

41. Rorty at one point notes that "everything we say and do and believe," including our philosophy and politics, "is a matter of fulfilling human needs and interests" (PSH, xxvii). It is those needs and interests, rather than the traditional dichotomies between morality and prudence or objectivity and subjectivity, that should drive philosophical discussions. (Those discussions, as we have seen, are for Rorty worth our while only if they help us plan a practical course of action). At first glance it may seem that he uses the adjective "human" in a universal sense since the phrase "human needs and interests" is not on its face limited to particular societies or cultures. Rorty, however, would undoubtedly argue that a discussion of "human needs and interests" would be useless unless we discuss them in the context of particular local practices and understandings. The problem is that there is very little in Rorty's work that tells us what the important human needs and interests (whether socially contingent or not) might be. One would think that if the task of philosophy is, in fact, to help us determine a plan of action for "fulfilling human needs and interests," we would need to have some discussion of what exactly those needs and interests might be.

42. Robert Lipkin makes a similar point in "Pragmatism—The Unfinished Revolution: Doctrinaire and Reflective Pragmatism in Rorty's Social Thought," 67 *Tulane Law Review* 1561, 1595–1619 (1993).

43. As Thomas McCarthy notes, "the forms of justification prevalent in our culture means, in many pursuits at least, attempting to construct arguments that claim to be valid transculturally." Thomas McCarthy, "Private Irony and Public Decency: Richard Rorty's New Pragmatism," 16 *Critical Inquiry* 355, 361 (1990).

44. See Richard A. Posner, *Economic Analysis of Law* (Boston: Little, Brown, 1972); Richard A. Posner, *The Economics of Justice* (Cambridge: Harvard University Press, 1981); Richard A. Posner, *The Federal Courts: Crisis and Reform* (Cambridge: Harvard University Press, 1985); Richard A. Posner, *Law & Literature: A Misunderstood Relation* (Cambridge: Harvard University Press, 1988); Richard A. Posner, *The Problems of Jurisprudence* (Cambridge: Harvard University Press, 1990).

45. Posner discusses his pragmatic approach to jurisprudence in many recent writings, including in PLM, ch. 4; Richard A. Posner, *Overcoming Law* (Cambridge: Harvard University Press, 1995), ch. 19; Richard A. Posner, "Pragmatic Adjudication," 18 *Cardozo Law Review* 1 (1996).

46. In addition to his extended discussions of homosexuality in *Sex and Reason*, there are shorter discussions in PLM, 173–82, 249–52; Posner, *Overcoming*

Law, ch. 26; Richard A. Posner, "Should There Be Homosexual Marriage? And If So, Who Should Decide?," 95 *Michigan Law Review* 1578 (1997).

47. Posner distinguishes between academic moralists and moral entrepreneurs. The former fruitlessly limit themselves to abstract and intellectual arguments; the latter get things done by appealing to emotions and loyalties (PLM, 42–44).

48. See Alfred C. Kinsey et al., *Sexual Behavior in the Human Male* (Philadelphia: W.B. Saunders & Co., 1948), pp. 638–41.

49. Martha Ertman has criticized Posner for largely ignoring lesbians in *Sex and Reason*. See Martha Ertman, "Denying the Secret of Joy: A Critique of Posner's Theory of Sexuality," 45 *Stanford Law Review* 1485 (1993).

50. Posner makes clear that what he categorizes as "deviant" sexual practices "are not 'unnatural,' at least in a biological sense; rather, they are peripheral to procreative sexuality" (SR, 99).

51. For an argument that we have sufficient data available to conclude that allowing lesbians and gay men to serve openly in the military would not undermine military effectiveness, see Elizabeth Kier, "Homosexuals in the U.S. Military: Open Integration and Combat Effectiveness," 23 *International Security* 5 (1998).

52. See F. Carolyn Graglia, *Domestic Tranquility: A Brief Against Feminism* (Dallas: Spence Publishing, 1998), p. 182; Roger Scruton, "Gay Reservations," in *The Liberation Debate: Rights at Issue*, ed. Michael Leahy and Dan Cohn-Sherbok (Routledge: New York, 1996), pp. 108, 110–13.

53. See e.g., Ertman, "Denying the Secret of Joy"; William N. Eskridge Jr., "A Social Constructionist Critique of Posner's *Sex and Reason*: Steps Toward a Gaylegal Agenda," 102 *Yale Law Journal* 333 (1992); Pamela S. Karlan, "Richard Posner's Just So Stories: The Phalacies of *Sex and Reason*," 1 *Virginia Journal of Social Policy and the Law* 229 (1993); Gillian K. Hadfield, "Flirting with Science: Richard Posner on the Bioeconomics of Sexual Man," 106 *Harvard Law Review* 479 (1992); Robin West, "Sex, Reason, and a Taste for the Absurd," 81 *Georgetown Law Journal* 2413 (1993). Posner responds to his feminist critics in *Overcoming Law*, ch. 16.

54. See Martha C. Nussbaum, " 'Only Grey Matter'? Richard Posner's Cost-Benefit Analysis of Sex," 59 *University of Chicago Law Review* 1689, 1699 (1992).

55. Jean Cohen, "Is There a Duty of Privacy? Law, Sexual Orientation, and the Construction of Identity," 6 *Texas Journal of Women and the Law* 47, 112 (1996). Katharine Bartlett makes a similar argument when she notes that Posner dismisses the preferences of those who view all premarital sex as sinful and harmful. By "[i]gnoring the preferences of such individuals, which economic theory purports to take at face value, Posner's [appeal to] 'reason' is nothing other than a trumping of their morally based assessment of harm with his own." Katharine T. Bartlett, "Rumpelstiltskin," 25 *Connecticut Law Review* 473, 481 (1993).

56. Ronald Dworkin, "Darwin's New Bulldog," 111 *Harvard Law Review* 1718, 1735–36 (1998).

57. Ibid.

58. As Alison Jaggar notes, "[e]ven the standard of physical survival cannot be used as a value-free criterion for determining human needs, for it raises normative questions about how long and in what conditions humans can and

should survive." Alison M. Jaggar, *Feminist Politics and Human Nature* (Totowa, NJ: Rowman and Allanheld, 1983), p. 20. Dworkin concurs: "We cannot evaluate a morality by asking whether it helps society to 'survive,' because the morality a society adopts will almost always determine not whether it survives, but the form in which it does so." Dworkin, "Darwin's New Bulldog," pp. 1734–35.

59. See Charles Taylor, *Sources of the Self: The Making of the Modern Identity* (Cambridge: Harvard University Press, 1989), p. 9.

60. Although Kinsey's studies on sexuality continue to be cited with some frequency, his methodology has been the subject of much criticism. See e.g., Robert T. Michael et al., *Sex in America: A Definitive Survey* (Boston: Little, Brown, 1994), pp. 17–21.

61. 10 U.S.C. §654(a)(15) (2001).

62. Ibid. at §654(b)(1)(A).

63. Opinion of the Justices, 530 A.2d 21, 24 (N.H. 1987). The statutory provision was repealed in July, 1999.

64. Eskridge, "A Social Constructionist Critique," p. 360.

65. Posner cites only two studies on the durability and quality of same-gender relationships: Philip Blumstein and Pepper Schwartz, *American Couples: Money, Work, Sex* (New York: Morrow, 1983) and Lawrence A. Kurdek and J. Patrick Schmitt, "Relationship Quality of Partners in Heterosexual Married, Heterosexual Cohabiting, and Gay and Lesbian Relationships," 51 *Journal of Personality and Social Psychology* 711 (1986). See SR, 306–07 nn. 41–42. Other studies available before the publication of *Sex and Reason* include Alan P. Bell and Martin S. Weinberg, *Homosexualities: A Study of Diversity Among Men and Women* (New York: Simon & Schuster, 1978); Susan E. Johnson, *Staying Power: Long-Term Lesbian Couples* (Tallahassee: Naiad Press, 1990); J. Harry, "Gay Male and Lesbian Family Relationships," in *Contemporary Families and Alternative Lifestyles: Handbook on Research and Theory*, eds. Eleanor Macklin and Roger H. Rubin (Beverly Hills: Sage, 1983), p. 216; Letitia Anne Peplau and Steven L. Gordon, "The Intimate Relationships of Lesbians and Gay Men," in *Changing Boundaries: Gender Roles and Sexual Behavior*, eds. Elizabeth Rice Allgeier and Naomi B. McCormick (Palo Alto: Mayfield, 1983), p. 226; S.M. Duffy and C.E. Rosbult, "Satisfaction and Commitment in Homosexual and Heterosexual Relationships," 12 *Journal of Homosexuality* 1 (1985); Natalie S. Eldridge and Lucia A. Gilbert, "Correlates of Relationship Satisfaction in Lesbian Couples," 14 *Psychology of Women Quarterly* 43 (1990); Lawrence A. Kurdek, "Relationship Quality of Gay and Lesbian Cohabiting Couples," 15 *Journal of Homosexuality* 93 (1988); Lawrence A. Kurdek, "Correlates of Relationship Satisfaction in Cohabiting Gay and Lesbian Couples: Integration of Contextual, Investment, and Problem-Solving Models," 61 *Journal of Personality and Social Psychology* 910 (1991); Lawrence A. Kurdek and J. Patrick Schmitt, "Partner Homogamy in Married, Heterosexual Cohabiting, Gay, and Lesbian Couples," 23 *Journal of Sex Research* 212 (1987).

More recent studies include Christopher Carrington, *No Place Like Home: Relationships and Family Life Among Lesbians and Gay Men* (Chicago: University of Chicago Press, 1999), Suzanne Later, *The Lesbian Family Life Cycle* (New York: The Free Press, 1995); Gretchen A. Stiers, *From This Day*

Forward: Commitment, Marriage, and Family in Lesbian and Gay Relationships (New York: St. Martin's Press, 1999); Leslie Koepka et al., "Relationship Quality in a Sample of Lesbian Couples with Children and Child-Free Lesbian Couples," 41 *Family Relations* 224 (1992); Lawrence A. Kurdek, "Relationship Outcomes and Their Predictors: Longitudinal Evidence from Heterosexual Married, Gay Cohabiting, and Lesbian Cohabiting Couples," 60 *Journal of Marriage & Family* 553 (1998); Lawrence A. Kurdek, "Assessing Multiple Determinants of Relationship Commitment in Cohabiting Gay, Cohabiting Lesbian, Dating Heterosexual, and Married Heterosexual Couples," 44 *Family Relations* 261 (1995); Lawrence A. Kurdek, "Developmental Changes in Relationship Quality in Gay and Lesbian Cohabiting Couples," 31 *Developmental Psychology* 86 (1995); Richard A. Mackey et al., "Psychological Intimacy in the Lasting Relationships of Heterosexual and Same-Gender Couples," 43 *Sex Roles* 201 (2000); Karlein M.G. Schreurs and Bram P. Buunk, "Closeness, Autonomy, Equity and Relationship Satisfaction in Lesbian Couples," 20 *Psychology of Women Quarterly* 577 (1996).

66. Cohen, "Is There a Duty of Privacy?," p. 111.
67. See Edward O. Laumann et al., *The Social Organization of Sexuality: Sexual Practices in the United States* (Chicago: Chicago University Press, 1994), ch. 8. As Laumann's study makes clear, answering the empirical question of how many lesbians and gay men there are in the United States depends on the more normative question of how we should define who is a lesbian or a gay man. The numbers very much depend on how we answer that second question. If our determinative criterion is those who have experienced same-gender sexual desire, then the numbers are higher (7.7% of men and 7.5% of women) than if we use same-gender sexual conduct (4.9% of men and 4.1% of women) or self-identification (2.8% of men and 1.4% of women) as the most appropriate criterion. See ibid., pp. 292–97.
68. Cohen, "Is there a Duty of Privacy?," p. 112.
69. E.M. Forster, *Maurice* (New York: New American Library, 1973).
70. Nussbaum, "Only Gray Matter?," p. 1721.
71. It is interesting to note the way in which Nussbaum's discussion of integrity in the context of Posner's understanding of human sexuality mirrors Bernard Williams's criticism of utilitarianism for failing to account for the value of integrity. Utilitarianism, Williams argues, fails to acknowledge that individuals often prioritize those commitments with which they are "deeply and extensively involved and identified" over utility. See Bernard Williams, "A Critique of Utilitarianism," in J.J.C. Smart and Bernard Williams, *Utilitarianism: For and Against* (New York: Cambridge University Press, 1973), pp. 77, 116. To ask an individual to put those commitments aside in the pursuit of utility "is to alienate him in a real sense from his actions and the source of his action in his own convictions. . . . It is thus, in the most literal sense, an attack on his integrity." Ibid., pp. 116–17. Jeffrey Blustein defends utilitarianism from what he takes to be Williams's broader point that individuals will lose their sense of integrity if they act as utilitarianism requires. Blustein, however, does not take issue with Williams's narrower point, which is the one more relevant to our discussion of Posner, namely, that utilitarianism does not account for integrity as a separate value that is often at odds with utility. See Jeffrey Blustein, *Care and Commitment: Taking the Personal Point of View* (New York:

Oxford University Press, 1994), pp. 76–77. For other elaborations on the meaning and implications of integrity, see Stephen L. Carter, *Integrity* (New York: Basic Books, 1996); Mark S. Halfon, *Integrity: A Philosophical Inquiry* (Philadelphia: Temple University Press, 1989); Lynne McFall, "Integrity," 98 *Ethics* 5 (1987).
72. Bartlett, "Rumpelstiltskin," p. 483.
73. Blustein, *Care and Commitment*, p. 231.

CHAPTER THREE—MORAL LIBERALISM

1. John Locke, *Second Treatise of Government*, ed. Peter Laslett (New York: Cambridge University Press, 1988 (1694)), ¶63.
2. John Stuart Mill, *On Liberty* (ed., David Spitz, New York: W.W. Norton & Co., 1975 (1859)), p. 21.
3. See e.g., Virginia Held, *Feminist Morality: Transforming Culture, Society, and Politics* (Chicago: Chicago University Press, 1993); Alison M. Jaggar, "Love and Knowledge: Emotion in Feminist Epistemology," in *Gender/Body/Knowledge: Feminist Reconstructions of Being and Knowing*, eds. Alison M. Jaggar and Susan R. Bordo (New Brunswick: Rutgers University Press, 1989), p. 145.
4. See e.g., Ladelle McWhorter, *Bodies and Pleasures: Foucault and the Politics of Sexual Normalization* (Bloomington: Indiana University Press, 1999).
5. Jeffrey Reiman has written about a moral liberalism that seeks to "establish a universal moral ideal on a universal foundation, namely the rationality of human beings." Jeffrey H. Reiman, *Critical Moral Liberalism: Theory & Practice* (Lanham, Md.: Rowman and Littlefield, 1997), p. 2. In emphasizing rationality to the exclusion of the many other needs and capabilities that define us as human, Reiman's conception of moral liberalism is in my estimation framed too narrowly. As I will argue later in this chapter, there are needs and capabilities that are not associated with reason that are nonetheless important sources of human dignity and that have crucial ramifications for issues of political morality.
6. For critical assessments of this skepticism, see Louise M. Antony, " 'Human Nature' and Its Role in Feminist Theory," in *Philosophy in a Feminist Voice: Critiques and Reconstructions*, ed. Janet A. Kourany (Princeton: Princeton University Press, 1998), p. 63; Charlotte Witt, "Feminist Metaphysics," in *A Mind of One's Own: Feminist Essays on Reason and Objectivity*, eds. Louise M. Antony and Charlotte Witt (Boulder: Westview Press, 1993), p. 273.
7. The feminist and postmodernist literature on the body, both highly influenced by the writings of Michel Foucault, is extensive. For a representative sample, see Judith Butler, *Bodies that Matter: On the Discursive Limits of "Sex"* (New York: Routledge, 1993); Susan Bordo, *Unbearable Weight: Feminism, Western Culture, and the Body* (Berkeley: University of California Press, 1993); Jaggar and Bordo, *Gender/Body/Knowledge*; McWhorter, *Bodies and Pleasures*.
8. For discussions of needs and their implications for moral and political philosophy, see e.g., David Braybrooke, *Meeting Needs* (Princeton: Princeton University Press, 1987); *Necessary Goods: Our Responsibilities to Meet Others'*

Needs, ed. Gillian Brock (Lanham, Md.: Rowman and Littlefield, 1998); Len Doyal and Ian Gough, *A Theory of Human Need* (New York: Guilford Press, 1991); David Wiggins, *Needs, Values, Truth: Essays in the Philosophy of Values* (New York: Blackwell, 1987).

9. See Amartya Sen, *Resources, Values and Development* (Cambridge: Harvard University Press, 1984), p. 514.

10. Nussbaum argues that her capabilities approach is a somewhat modified though generally faithful descendent of Aristotle's ethical and political writings. See e.g., Martha C. Nussbaum, "Nature, Function, and Capability: Aristotle on Political Distribution," *Oxford Studies in Ancient Philosophy*, Supp. Vol. I (1988), p. 145; Martha C. Nussbaum, "Aristotle on Human Nature and the Foundations of Ethics," in *World, Mind and Ethics*, eds. J.E.J. Altham and Ross Harrison (New York: Cambridge University Press, 1995), p. 86. Some, however, have questioned whether Aristotle's writings can support the weight of Nussbaum's arguments. See e.g., Richard Mulgan, "Was Aristotle an 'Aristotelian Social Democrat'?," 111 *Ethics* 79 (2000). Nussbaum responds to Mulgan in "Aristotle, Politics, and Human Capabilities," 111 *Ethics* 102, 108–116 (2000).

11. Nussbaum's most important writings on the capabilities approach, in order of publication, are: "Nature, Function, and Capability"; ASD; "Non-Relative Virtues: An Aristotelian Approach," in *The Quality of Life*, ed. Martha C. Nussbaum and Amartya Sen (New York: Oxford University Press, 1993), p. 242; "Aristotle on Human Nature and the Foundations of Ethics"; "Human Capabilities, Female Human Beings," in *Women, Culture and Development*, eds. Martha C. Nussbaum and John Glover (New York: Oxford University Press, 1995), p. 61; "The Good as Discipline, the Good as Freedom," in *Ethics of Consumption: The Good Life, Justice, and Global Stewardship*, eds. David A. Crocker and Toby Linden (Lanham, Md.: Rowman and Littlefield, 1998), p. 312; "Women and Cultural Universals," in Martha C. Nussbaum, *Sex and Social Justice* (New York: Oxford University Press, 1999), ch. 1; "Capabilities, Human Rights, and the Universal Declaration," in *The Future of International Human Rights*, eds. Burns H. Weston and Stephen P. Marks (Ardsley, NY: Transnational Publishers, 1999), p. 25; WHD.

12. Nussbaum notes that her capabilities approach does not entail a complete theory of justice. Some issues that the capabilities approach does not address with much precision include the appropriate balance between private incentives and public regulation, intergenerational justice, and the possible need for international redistributative mechanisms (WHD, 75, 75 n.75).

13. See Nussbaum, "Capabilities, Human Rights, and the Universal Declaration."

14. Nussbaum also worked for several years as a research advisor to the World Institute for Development Economics Research (WIDER) based in Helsinki and associated with the United Nations University. She discuses the work of WIDER, her participation in that work, and how philosophy can contribute to international development in "Public Philosophy and International Feminism," 108 *Ethics* 762 (1998). Those themes are also discussed in Nussbaum and Sen, *The Quality of Life*; Nussbaum and Glover, *Women, Culture, Development*. The economist and philosopher Amartya Sen has also promoted a capabilities approach to international development. He has urged that assess-

ments of development focus on capabilities rather than on traditional measurements such as per capita GNP. See e.g., Amartya Sen, *Development as Freedom* (New York: Knopf, 1999); Sen, *Resources, Values and Development*. Nussbaum discusses the relationship between her work and Sen's (including their differences) in WHD, 11–15.

15. See Martha C. Nussbaum, *Upheavals of Thought: The Intelligence of Emotions* (New York: Cambridge University Press, 2001); Martha C. Nussbaum, *Poetic Justice: The Literary Imagination and Public Life* (Boston: Beacon Press, 1995), ch. 3; Nussbaum, "The Feminist Critique of Liberalism," in *Sex and Social Justice*, p. 55.

16. Nussbaum makes this point as follows: "Human nature cannot, and need not, be validated from the outside, because human nature just *is* an inside perspective, not a *thing* at all, but rather the most fundamental and broadly shared experiences of human beings living and reasoning together." Nussbaum, "Aristotle on Human Nature," p. 121.

17. Antony, " 'Human Nature' and its Role in Feminist Theory," p. 85.

18. Nussbaum discusses the celibacy example in "The Good as Discipline, the Good as Freedom," p. 321.

19. Nussbaum acknowledges that it is sometimes necessary to promote actual functionings. Examples include making education for children mandatory, as well as promoting health and safety through building codes, food and medicine safety rules, environmental regulations, and so on (WHD, 89–95)

20. For an elaboration of Nussbaum's critique of Rawls on this point, see ASD 207–17, 226–27; "Nature, Function, and Capability," pp. 150–54. For other references to the capabilities approach as constituting an overlapping consensus, see WHD, 5, 14, 76.

21. Nussbaum did so explicitly for the first time in a paper first read in 1994 and published in 1998. See Nussbaum, "The Good as Discipline, the Good as Freedom."

22. See ibid., p. 314, citing PL, 181.

23. Martha C. Nussbaum, "Political Animals: Luck, Love, and Dignity," 29 *Metaphilosophy* 273, 284 (1998).

24. See Joseph Raz, *The Morality of Freedom* (New York: Oxford University Press, 1986), p. 369.

25. Ibid., p. 204.

26. Ibid. Raz views the harm principle as imposing both positive and negative obligations on the state. "It is a mistake," he argues, "to think that the harm principle recognizes only the duty of governments to prevent loss of autonomy. Sometimes failing to improve the situation of another is harming him." Ibid., pp. 415–16. I discuss Raz's conception of the harm principle in more detail in "Moral Foundations for a Discourse on Same-Sex Marriage: Looking Beyond Political Liberalism," 85 *Georgetown Law Journal* 1871, 1919–30, 1936–42 (1997). Raz is a self-described liberal perfectionist. Nussbaum, on the other hand, rejects the label of perfectionist. See Nussbaum, "Aristotle, Politics, and Human Capabilities," p. 128. I will not here explore whether it is proper to think of Nussbaum as a perfectionist, though it should be noted that both Raz and she consider autonomy to be an intrinsic good essential to human flourishing that, as such, should be promoted through state policies that go beyond noninterference. In "Moral Foundations for a

Discourse on Same-Sex Marriage" I elaborate on the positive implications of Raz's liberal perfectionism for the recognition of same-sex marriage.

27. Nussbaum argues that for the full exercise of human capabilities to be possible, capabilities that are internal to the individual must be *"combined with* suitable external conditions." (WHD, 85, emphasis in original).

28. Two influential perspectives that disagree with moral liberalism on this point are the new natural law philosophy of John Finnis and Robert George. See John Finnis, "Law, Morality, and 'Sexual Orientation,' " 69 *Notre Dame Law Review* 1049 (1994); Robert P. George, *Making Men Moral: Civil Liberties and Public Morality* (New York: Oxford University Press, 1995), and the communitarianism of Alasdair McIntyre and Michael Sandel. See Alasdair McIntyre, *After Virtue: A Study in Moral Theory* (Notre Dame: University of Notre Dame Press, 1981); Sandel, DD.

29. 517 U.S. 620 (1996).

30. Peter Cicchino distinguished between the state basing public policy on "bare public morality," by which he meant encouraging or discouraging behavior that has no empirical connection to any good other than the increase or decrease in the conduct itself, and the state acting on value judgments that are widely accepted and shared, such as "that physical health is an integral part of human flourishing." See Peter M. Cicchino, "Reason and the Rule of Law: Should Bare Assertions of 'Public Morality' Qualify as Legitimate Government Interests for the Purposes of Equal Protection Review?," 87 *Georgetown Law Journal* 139, 140–41 (1998).

31. Resources and wealth are obviously relevant to a society's ability to provide for and protect the opportunities of individuals to meet their basic human needs and exercise their basic human capabilities. The distribution of some goods in some societies, however, is not subject to limitations based on resources and wealth. This is true of the two goods that are the focus of this book (marriage and parenthood), at least in developed nations. I therefore do not here address the otherwise important question of how social resources and wealth affect questions of justice in the promotion and protection of basic human needs and capabilities.

32. Alison M. Jaggar, *Feminist Politics and Human Nature* (Totowa, NJ: Rowman and Allanheld, 1983), p. 48.

33. Robin West, "Rights, Capabilities, and the Good Society," 69 *Fordham Law Review* 1901, 1913 (2001).

34. See Rebecca M. Ryan, "The Sex Right: A Legal History of the Marital Rape Exemption," 20 *Law & Social Inquiry* 941 (1995); Elizabeth M. Schneider, "The Violence of Privacy," 23 *Connecticut Law Review* 973 (1991); Reva B. Siegel, " 'The Rule of Law': Wife Beating as Prerogative and Privacy," 105 *Yale Law Journal* 2117 (1996).

35. See Nussbaum, "The Feminist Critique of Liberalism," pp. 63–65.

36. Carol Gilligan, *In a Different Voice: Psychological Theory and Women's Development* (Cambridge: Harvard University Press, 1982), p. 100. Another book that has had a great influence in the articulation of a feminist ethic of care is Nel Noddings, *Caring: A Feminine Approach to Ethics and Moral Education* (Berkeley: University of California Press, 1984).

37. The literature in this area is vast. For some representative works, see Annette C. Baier, "The Need for More than Justice," in *Science, Morality and Femi-*

nist Theory, eds. Marsha Hanen and Kai Nielsen (Calgary: University of Calgary Press, 1987), p. 41; Owen Flanagan and Kathryn Jackson, "Justice, Care, and Gender: The Kohlberg-Gilligan Debate Revisited," 97 *Ethics* 622 (1987); Held, *Feminist Morality*; Sara Ruddick, *Maternal Thinking: Towards a Politics of Peace* (Boston: Beacon Press, 1989).

38. See e.g., Nancy Fraser and Linda J. Nicholson, "Social Criticism without Philosophy: An Encounter between Feminism and Postmodernism," in *Feminism/Postmodernism*, ed. Linda J. Nicholson (New York: Routledge, 1990), p. 19; Elizabeth V. Spellman, *Inessential Woman: Problems of Exclusion in Feminist Thought* (Boston: Beacon Press, 1988).

39. See e.g., Angela P. Harris, "Race and Essentialism in Feminist Legal Theory," 42 *Stanford Law Review* 581 (1990); Martha Minow, *Making All the Difference: Inclusion, Exclusion, and American Law* (Ithaca: Cornell University Press, 1990), pp. 229–39; Carol B. Stack, "The Culture of Gender: Women and Men of Color," in *An Ethic of Care: Feminist and Interdisciplinary Perspectives*, ed. Mary J. Larrabee (New York: Routledge, 1993), p. 108.

40. See e.g., Diemut Elisabet Bubeck, *Care, Gender, and Justice* (New York: Oxford University Press, 1995), ch. 5; Marilyn Friedman, *What Are Friends For?: Feminist Perspectives on Personal Relationships and Moral Theory* (Ithaca: Cornell University Press, 1993), ch. 5; Susan Moller Okin, "Reason and Feeling in Thinking about Justice," in *Feminism and Political Theory*, ed. Cass R. Sunstein (Chicago: Chicago University Press, 1990), p. 15.

41. See Eva Feder Kittay, *Love's Labor: Essays on Women, Equality, and Dependency* (New York: Routledge, 1999); Virginia Held, "Non-Contractual Society: A Feminist View," in *Science, Morality, and Feminist Theory*, p. 111.

42. As David Gauthier puts it, "the contractarian insists that a society could not command the willing allegiance of a rational person if, without appealing to her feelings for others, it afforded her no expectation of net benefit." See David Gauthier, *Morals by Agreement* (New York: Oxford University Press, 1986), p. 11. Although Rawls's difference principle is concerned with those at the bottom of society's socioeconomic hierarchies, individuals in the original position choose the difference principle as a norm of justice not out of a sense of responsibility or obligation toward those at the bottom of the heap but because they do not know, once the veil of ignorance is removed, whether *they* will be at the top or at the bottom. The risk averse individual in Rawls's original position, therefore, is usually understood as acting from what it perceives to be in its own best interest, without any sense of obligation or belonging to others. Susan Moller Okin has questioned this traditional interpretation of Rawls's contractarianism. She suggests that it is also possible to read Rawls as arguing that a capacity for empathy and caring is necessary if individuals are to develop a capacity for justice. See Okin, "Reason and Feeling in Thinking about Justice," pp. 21–24.

43. See Okin, "Reason and Feeling in Thinking about Justice," pp. 17–21; Bernard Williams, "Persons, Character, and Morality," in *Moral Luck: Philosophical Papers, 1973–1980* (New York: Cambridge University Press, 1981), ch. 1.

44. See Lawrence Kohlberg, *The Psychology of Moral Development* (San Francisco: Harper & Row, 1984), pp. 229–34.

45. Friedman, *What are Friends For?*, p. 98.

46. Ibid.

47. See Annette C. Baier, "Hume, the Women's Moral Theorist?," in *Women and Moral Theory*, eds. Eva Feder Kittay and Diana T. Meyers (Totowa, NJ: Rowman and Littlefield, 1987), p. 37.

48. For a helpful summary of different feminist critiques of autonomy, see Catriona Mackenzie and Natalie Stoljar, "Introduction: Autonomy Refigured," in *Relational Autonomy: Feminist Perspectives on Autonomy, Agency, and the Social Self*, eds. Catriona Mackenzie and Natalie Stoljar (New York: Oxford University Press, 2000), pp. 3, 5–12.

49. Marilyn Friedman, "Autonomy, Social Disruption, and Women," in *Relational Autonomy*, pp. 35, 40 (emphasis in original).

50. Jennifer Nedelsky, "Reconceiving Autonomy: Sources, Thoughts and Possibilities," 1 *Yale Journal of Law and Feminism* 7, 12 (1989).

51. Robin West, "Universalism, Liberal Theory, and the Problem of Gay Marriage," 25 *Florida State University Law Review* 705, 721 (1998).

52. *Griswold v. Connecticut*, 381 U.S. 479 (1965); *Eisenstadt v. Baird*, 405 U.S. 438 (1972).

53. 478 U.S. 186, 191 (1996).

54. Ibid., p. 205 (Blackmun, J., dissenting).

55. Ibid., quoting *Paris Adult Theatre I v. Slaton*, 413 U.S. 49, 63 (1973).

56. Gilligan, *In a Different Voice*, pp. 73–97. In an essay published a few years after *In a Different Voice*, Gilligan explained that under an ethic of care, "[t]he connection between the fetus and the pregnant woman becomes the focus of attention and the question becomes whether it is responsible or irresponsible, caring or careless, to extend or to end this connection. In this construction, the abortion dilemma arises because there is no way not to act, and no way of acting that does not alter the connection between self and others. To ask what actions constitute care or are more caring directs attention to the parameters of connection and the costs of detachment, which become subjects of moral concern." Carol Gilligan, "Moral Orientation and Moral Development," in *Women and Moral Theory*, pp. 19, 24.

57. Nancy Felipe Russo et al., "U.S. Abortion in Context: Selected Characteristics and Motivations of Women Seeking Abortions," 48 *Journal of Social Issues* 183, 200 (1992).

58. 394 U.S. 557 (1969). Although the Court decided *Stanley* on free speech rather than on substantive due process grounds, it stated that whatever interest the state might have in regulating obscene materials does not justify "reach[ing] into the privacy of one's home." Ibid., p. 565.

59. 381 U.S. 479 (1965); 405 U.S. 438 (1972).

60. 388 U.S. 1 (1967); 434 U.S. 374 (1978).

61. 431 U.S. 494 (1977).

62. 530 U.S. 57 (2000); 268 U.S. 510 (1925); 262 U.S. 390 (1923).

63. *Roberts v. United States Jaycees*, 468 U.S. 609, 619 (1983).

64. Milton C. Regan, Jr., *Alone Together: Law and the Meanings of Marriage* (New York: Oxford University Press, 1999), p. 24.

65. Brenda Almond, "Human Bonds," in *Applied Philosophy: Morals and Metaphysics in Contemporary Debate*, eds. Brenda Almond and Donald Hill (New York: Routledge, 1991), pp. 59, 71.

66. See Onora O'Neill, "Between Consenting Adults," 14 *Philosophy & Public Affairs* 252, 272 (1985).

67. See J. Michael Bailey and Richard C. Pillard, "A Genetic Study of Male Sexual Orientation," 48 *Archives of General Psychiatry* 1089 (1991); Dean H. Hamer et al., "A Linkage Between DNA Markers on the X Chromosome and Male Sexual Orientation," 261 *Science* 321 (1993); Simon LeVay, "A Difference in Hypothalamic Structure Between Heterosexual and Homosexual Men," 253 *Science* 1034 (1991). Many have questioned the validity and significance of these studies. See e.g., Edward Stein, *The Mismeasure of Desire: The Science, Theory, and Ethics of Sexual Orientation* (New York: Oxford University Press, 1999), ch. 7; McWhorter, *Bodies and Pleasures*, pp.13–34; Janet E. Halley, "Sexual Orientation and the Politics of Biology: A Critique of the Argument from Immutability," 46 *Stanford Law Review* 503, 529–46 (1994).

68. See *Frontiero v. Richardson*, 411 U.S. 677, 686 (1973). Janet Halley argues that what has really been at issue in the Supreme Court's equal protection jurisprudence has not been the immutability of characteristics used to distinguish among groups of individuals as such, but rather the "process implications often associated with apparently immutable traits." See Janet E. Halley, "The Politics of the Closet: Towards Equal Protection for Gay, Lesbian, and Bisexual Identity," 36 *UCLA Law Review* 915, 923 (1989).

69. See e.g., *High Tech Gays v. Defense Indus. Sec. Clearance Office*, 895 F.2d 563, 573–74 (9th Cir. 1990); *Woodward v. United States*, 871 F.2d 1068, 1076 (Fed. Cir. 1989).

70. This is the position taken by the Catholic Church when it seeks to distinguish between lesbians and gay men, who as persons are worthy of respect and compassion, and same-gender sexual acts, which are deemed to be "intrinsically disordered and in no case to be approved of." See "Some Considerations Concerning the Response to Legislative Proposals on the Non-discrimination of Homosexual Persons" (July 23, 1992). The complete text of this Vatican statement can be found in *Voices of Hope: A Collection of Positive Catholic Writings On Gay and Lesbian Issues*, eds. Jeannine Gramick and Robert Nugent (Mt. Rainier, Md.: New Ways Ministry, 1995), p. 229. For other important official Vatican statements that discuss homosexuality, see "The Congregation for the Doctrine of the Faith's Letter to the Bishops of the Catholic Church on the Pastoral Care of Homosexual Persons," 16 *Origins* 377 (1986); "Declaration on Certain Questions Concerning Sexual Ethics," 5 *Origins* 486, 489 (1976).

71. For a short essay that has helpful citations to sources on cross-cultural studies of family arrangements, see Arland Thornton, "Comparative and Historical Perspectives on Marriage, Divorce and Family Life," in *Promises to Keep: Decline and Renewal of Marriage in America*, eds. David Popenoe et al. (Lanham, Md.: Rowman and Littlefield, 1996), p. 69.

72. Joseph Raz, "Liberalism, Skepticism, and Democracy," 74 *Iowa Law Review* 761, 783 (1989).

73. See Arthur Aron and Elaine N. Aron, *Love and the Expansion of Self: Understanding Attraction and Satisfaction* (Washington, D.C.: Hemisphere, 1986). Robert Nozick noted how romantic love expands the self by blurring the lines between the individuals involved, creating a new identity for both. See Robert Nozick, *The Examined Life: Philosophical Meditations* (New York: Simon & Schuster, 1989), pp. 68–86.

74. Carl E. Schneider, "The Law and the Stability of Marriage: The Family as a Social Institution," in *Promises to Keep*, pp. 187, 190.
75. Regan, *Alone Together*, p. 12. Regan argues that "[g]enuine intimacy seems to require the ability to adopt [an] internal stance toward marriage, in which the relationship is taken as a given without reference to individual costs and benefits." Ibid., p. 11. "That stance," Regan adds, "focuses on the health of a larger relational unit whose viability is a shared concern." Ibid, pp. 11–12.
76. For representative and thoughtful articulations of the feminist and queer theory critiques of same-sex marriage, see Claudia Card, "Against Marriage and Motherhood," 11 *Hypatia* 1 (Summer, 1996); Paula L. Ettelbrick, "Since When is Marriage a Path to Liberation?," in *Lesbian and Gay Marriage: Private Commitments, Public Ceremonies*, ed. Suzanne Sherman (Philadelphia: Temple University Press, 1992), p. 20; Nancy D. Polikoff, "We Will Get What We Ask For: Why Legalizing Gay and Lesbian Marriage Will Not 'Dismantle the Legal Structure of Gender in Every Marriage,' " 79 *Virginia Law Review* 1535 (1993); Michael Warner, *The Trouble with Normal: Sex, Politics, and the Ethics of Queer Life* (New York: Free Press, 1999), ch. 3.
77. Cheshire Calhoun, *Feminism, the Family, and the Politics of the Closet: Lesbian and Gay Displacement* (New York: Oxford University Press, 2000), p. 133.
78. Most of the studies that have evaluated the dynamics and responsibility-sharing arrangements of gay and lesbian couples have concluded that same-gender relationships are more egalitarian and less role-driven than heterosexual relationships. See e.g., Philip Blumstein and Pepper Schwartz, *American Couples: Money, Work, Sex* (New York: Morrow, 1983); J. Lynch and M. Reilly, "Role Relationships: Lesbian Perspectives," 12 *Journal of Homosexuality* 53 (1985); Lawrence A. Kurdek, "The Allocation of Household Labor in Gay, Lesbian, and Heterosexual Married Couples," 49 *Journal of Social Issues* 127 (1993). This appears to be the case even after gay and lesbian couples assume childrearing responsibilities, which is when many previously egalitarian heterosexual relationships tend to shift toward more traditional allocations of family responsibilities and labor. See Raymond W. Chan et al., "Division of Labor Among Lesbian and Heterosexual Parents: Associations with Children's Adjustment," 12 *Journal of Family Psychology* 402 (1998).

     It should be noted that a recent study has questioned the almost unanimous consensus in the literature that lesbian and gay relationships are more egalitarian than heterosexual relationships. See Christopher Carrington, *Home: Relationships and Family Life Among Lesbians and Gay Men* (Chicago: Chicago University Press, 1999). Many of the same-gender couples in this study were found to abide by a traditional model characterized by one partner being primarily responsible for work outside of the home while the other being mostly responsible for work inside of it. Obviously, however, it is by definition impossible for members of same-gender relationships to assign themselves roles based on gender. Whatever allocation of labor and other responsibilities same-gender partners settle on, therefore, it is more likely to be the result of discussion, negotiation, and personal interests than it is in heterosexual relationships.
79. See Pepper Schwartz, "Peer Marriage: What Does It Take to Create a Truly Egalitarian Relationship?," in *Family in Transition*, eds. Arlene J. Skolnick and Jerome H. Skolnick (Boston: Allyn and Bacon, 11th ed., 2001), p. 182.

80. See Card, "Against Marriage and Motherhood," p. 11.
81. See e.g., Maura I. Strassberg, "Distinctions of Form or Substance: Monogamy, Polygamy and Same-Sex Marriage," 75 *North Carolina Law Review* 1501 (1997).
82. See William N. Eskridge Jr., *Equality Practice: Civil Unions and the Future of Gay Rights* (New York: Routledge, 2002), pp. 210–13. The Netherlands in 2001 became the first nation to recognize same-sex marriages.
83. See *Baker v. State*, 744 A.2d 864 (1999).
84 See Andrew Sullivan, "State of the Union," *The New Republic*, May 8, 2000, pp. 18, 22.
85. See Greg Johnson, "Vermont Civil Unions: The New Language of Marriage," 25 *Vermont Law Review* 15, 19 (2000). Bill Eskridge argues that though we should be troubled by the inequality that remains between marital and civil union relationships, the legal recognition of the latter is an important and useful incremental step in eventually attaining full equality for lesbians and gay men. See Eskridge, *Equality Practice*, ch. 4.
86. Finnis, "Law, Morality, and 'Sexual Orientation,' " p. 1070.
87. John Finnis, "Virtue and the Constitution of the United States," 69 *Fordham Law Review* 1595, 1598 (2001).
88. See John Finnis, *Natural Law and Natural Rights* (New York: Oxford University Press, 1980), ch. 3. Robert George, another leading proponent of new natural law, notes that to assert that some goods are self-evidently good does not imply that "that they are undeniable or, still less, that no one denies them. What it does imply is that the practical intellect may grasp them, and practical judgment can affirm them without the need for a derivation." Robert P. George, "Recent Criticism of Natural Law Theory," 55 *University of Chicago Law Review* 1371, 1389 (1988).
89. See Finnis, *Natural Law and Natural Rights*, ch. 4.
90. See Finnis, "Law, Morality, and 'Sexual Orientation,' " pp. 1064–65. The theologian Germaine Grisez, whose ideas have greatly influenced new natural law philosophy, also considers marriage to be a basic good that is not reducible to either friendship or the transmission of life. See Germain Grisez, *The Way of the Lord Jesus: Living a Christian Life*, Vol. 2 (Chicago: Franciscan Herald Press, 1993), p. 568 n.43.
91. See George, *Making Men Moral*.
92. Lynn Wardle puts this point as follows: "The ubiquity of heterosexual marriage, the fact that marriage has exclusively referred to a heterosexual union in all cultures and across all time, suggests that it is not a matter of social construct." Lynn D. Wardle, "Legal Claims for Same-Sex Marriage: Efforts to Legitimate a Retreat from Marriage by Redefining Marriage," 39 *South Texas Law Review* 735, 750 (1998). See also Gerard V. Bradley, "Same-Sex Marriage: Our Final Answer?," 14 *Notre Dame Journal of Law, Ethics, and Public Policy* 729, 747 (2000) (referring to marriage as a "pre-political (and thus natural) institution"). Cheshire Calhoun has noted how the understanding of marriage as a pre-political institution was shared by many of the legislators who supported the Defense of Marriage Act. See Calhoun, *Feminism, the Family, and the Politics of the Closet*, pp. 123–28. Nussbaum summarizes and criticizes the argument that families have "natural" characteristics that are prior to society and law in WHD, 252–61.

93. Finnis, "Law, Morality, and 'Sexual Orientation,' " p. 1064.
94. For similar arguments see Robert P. George and Gerard V. Bradley, "Marriage and the Liberal Imagination," 84 *Georgetown Law Journal* 301 (1995); Patrick Lee and Robert P. George, "What Sex Can Be: Self-Alienation, Illusion, or One-Flesh Union," 42 *American Journal of Jurisprudence* 135 (1997).
95. See David Hume, *A Treaty on Human Nature* (eds. David F. Norton and Mary J. Norton, New York: Oxford University Press, 2000 (1740)).
96. See Finnis, "Law, Morality, and 'Sexual Orientation,' " p. 1067.
97. See Lee and George, "What Sex Can Be," p. 143.
98. Ibid., p. 144.
99. Finnis, "Law, Morality, and 'Sexual Orientation,' " p. 1066.
100. Ibid., p. 1070.
101. See Roger Scruton, *Sexual Desire: A Moral Philosophy of the Erotic* (New York: Free Press, 1986), p. 283.
102. Ibid., p. 310.
103. See Finnis, "Law, Morality, and 'Sexual Orientation,' " p. 1064.
104. Lee and George, "What Sex Can Be," p. 144.
105. Finnis, "Law, Morality, and 'Sexual Orientation,' " p. 1066.
106. Ibid., p. 1067.
107. See John Finnis, "The Good of Marriage and the Morality of Sexual Relations: Some Philosophical and Historical Observations," 42 *American Journal of Jurisprudence* 97, 102–11 (1997).
108. See sources cited in note 65, chapter 2.
109. See Nancy F. Cott, *Public Vows: A History of Marriage and the Nation* (Cambridge: Harvard University Press, 2000), ch. 2.
110. 388 U.S. 1, 11 (1967).
111. West, "Universalism, Liberal Theory, and the Problem of Gay Marriage," p. 721.
112. Cott, *Public Vows*, p. 3.
113. See Susan Moller Okin, *Justice, Gender, and the Family* (New York: Basic Books, 1989).
114. I say in part because there is also what Cheshire Calhoun calls a "separate axis of oppression" at play in the refusal to recognize same-sex marriage, one that involves heterosexual—as opposed to male—privilege and which can be overlooked if we focus exclusively on issues of gender. See Calhoun, *Feminism, the Family, and the Politics of the Closet*, pp. 2–14.
115. Gretchen A. Stiers, *From This Day Forward: Commitment, Marriage, and Family in Lesbian and Gay Relationships* (New York: St. Martin's Press, 1999), p. 110.
116. See Nan D. Hunter, "Marriage, Law, and Gender: A Feminist Inquiry," 1 *Law and Sexuality* 9 (1991); West, "Universalism, Liberal Theory, and the Problem of Gay Marriage."
117. *Baker v. State,* 744 A.2d 864, 881 (Vt. 1999). In the Hawaii case, the State argued *inter alia* that it had "a compelling interest to promote the optimal development of children . . . [and] all things being equal, it is best for a child that it be raised in a single home by its parents, or at least by a married male and female." *Baehr v. Miike,* 23 *Family Law Reporter* 2001 (Haw. Cir. Ct., Dec. 3, 1996), ¶19.

118. *Baker*, p. 882.
119. Several commentators have questioned the constitutionality of the second aim of the Defense of Marriage Act. See Andrew Koppelman, "Dumb and DOMA: Why the Defense of Marriage Act is Unconstitutional," 83 *Iowa Law Review* 1 (1997); Mark Strasser, *The Challenge of Same-Sex Marriage: Federalist Principles and Constitutional Protections* (Westport, CT: Praeger, 1999), ch. 8.
120. Rep. Ensign, 142 Cong. Rec. H7493 (July 12, 1996).
121. House of Representatives Report (Judiciary Committee), 104–664 (July 9, 1996), p. 12.
122. Rep. Barr, 142 Cong. Rec. H7275 (July 11, 1996).
123. Sen. Byrd, 142 Cong. Rec. S10109 (Sept. 10, 1996).
124. *Tinker v. Colwell*, 193 U.S. 473, 484 (1904).
125. For different variations on this argument that do not limit themselves to the issue of same-sex marriage, see Norman Podhoretz "How the Gay Rights Movement Won," *Commentary*, Nov. 1996, p. 40; Roger Scruton, "Gay Reservations," in *The Liberation Debate*, eds. Michael Leahy and Dan Cohn-Sherbok (New York: Routledge, 1996), p. 108.
126. The often-cited studies are Blumstein and Schwartz, *American Couples*, pp. 271–72; David P. McWhirter and Andrew M. Mattison, *The Male Couple: How Relationships Develop* (Englewood Cliffs, NJ: Prentice Hall, 1984), pp. 252–59. The McWhirter and Mattison study was limited to gay men living in San Diego. For examples of the use of these studies by opponents of same-sex marriage, see George W. Dent Jr., "The Defense of Traditional Marriage," 15 *Journal of Law and Politics* 581, 625 n.229 (1999) (McWhirter and Mattison); Finnis, "The Good of Marriage and the Morality of Sexual Relations," p. 130, n.131 (Blumstein and Schwartz).
127. Edward O. Laumann et al., *The Social Organization of Sexuality: Sexual Practices in the United States* (Chicago: Chicago University Press, 1994), pp. 316, 314. This survey supports the more anecdotal findings of greater monogamy in the gay male population following the appearance of AIDS. See Michelangelo Signorile, *Life Outside* (New York: Harper Collins, 1997), ch. 6.
128. Stiers, *From This Day Forward*, p. 52.
129. Ibid., p. 53.
130. See Scruton, "Gay Reservations," p. 122.
131. Lynn D. Wardle, " 'Multiply and Replenish': Considering Same-Sex Marriage in Light of State Interests in Marital Procreation," 24 *Harvard Journal of Law and Public Policy* 771, 799 (2001). For a typical essay that discusses the parade of horribles, including bestiality and incest, that would purportedly follow the recognition of same-sex marriage, see Dent, "The Defense of Traditional Marriage," pp. 623–29.
132. See Lynn D. Wardle, "The Potential Impact of Homosexual Parenting on Children," 1997 *University of Illinois Law Review* 833.
133. In opposing parenting by lesbians and gay men and arguing that the law should make it difficult for them to parent, Wardle complains that, "[t]he manipulation of child-oriented rules of law for the political purposes and benefits of adults is troubling." Ibid., p. 840. He adds that when the partners of gay and lesbian parents seek to adopt the latter's children, "[t]he objective seems to be to provide a clear basis for claiming relational rights if the same-

sex relationship breaks up, rather than to provide for the best interests of the child." Ibid., p. 882. Wardle concludes that "[c]hildren are the innocent victims who suffer the most from choices their parents make to experiment for personal self-gratification." Ibid., p. 897.

134. See Wardle, "The Potential Impact of Homosexual Parenting on Children," pp. 852–57. For another attempt to explain the purported harms to children from having lesbian or gay parents, see Paul Cameron, "Homosexual Parents: Testing 'Common Sense'—A Literature Review Emphasizing the Golombok and Tasker Longitudinal Study of Lesbians' Children," 85 *Psychological Reports* 282 (1999).

135. See "Technical Report: Coparent or Second-Parent Adoption by Same-Sex Parents," 109 *Pediatrics* 341, 342–43 (2002). Janice Pea and I have written a point-by-point rebuttal to all of Wardle's harm-based arguments. See Carlos A. Ball and Janice Farrell Pea, "Warring with Wardle: Morality, Social Science, and Gay and Lesbian Parents," 1998 *University of Illinois Law Review* 253.

136. On the issue of the sexual orientation of the children of lesbians and gay men, see e.g., J. Michael Bailey et al., "Sexual Orientation of Adult Sons of Gay Fathers," 31 *Developmental Psychology* 124 (1995); Ghazala Alzal Javaid, "The Children of Homosexual and Heterosexual Single Mothers," 23 *Child Psychiatry & Human Development* 235 (1993); Richard Green, "Sexual Identity of 37 Children Raised by Homosexual or Transsexual Parents," 135 *American Journal of Psychiatry* 692 (1978).

137. See e.g., Charlotte J. Patterson, "Children of the Lesbian Baby Boom: Behavioral Adjustment, Self-Concepts, and Sex Role Identity," in *Lesbian and Gay Psychology: Theory, Research, and Clinical Applications*, eds. Beverly Greene and Gregory M. Herek, (Thousand Oaks, Ca.: Sage, 1994), p. 156; Richard Green et al., "Lesbian Mothers and their Children: A Comparison with Solo Parent Heterosexual Mothers and their Children," 15 *Archives of Sexual Behavior* 167 (1986); Julie Schwartz Gottman, "Children of Gay and Lesbian Parents," in *Homosexuality and Family Relations*, eds. Frederick W. Bozett and Marvin B. Sussman (New York: Harrington Park Press, 1990), p. 177. For a discussion of the implications of these studies, see Ball and Pea, "Warring with Wardle," pp. 291–99.

138. See Susan Golombok, "Lesbian Mother Families," in *What Is a Parent?: A Socio-Legal Analysis*, eds. Andrew Bainham et al. (Portland, Or.: Hart Publishing, 1999), p. 161.

139. To support this position, the skeptic can cite to Carl E. Schneider, "Moral Discourse and the Transformation of American Family Law," 83 *Michigan Law Review* 1803 (1985).

140. See Naomi R. Cahn, "The Moral Complexities of Family Law," 50 *Stanford Law Review* 225 (1997); Jane C. Murphy, "Rules, Responsibility and Commitment to Children: The New Language of Morality in Family Law," 60 *University of Pittsburgh Law Review* 1111 (1999). As David Meyer, looking into the future puts it, "[f]amily in the 21st century will be less defined by tradition . . . but neither will it be solely a matter of personal choice; instead, there is growing acceptance that family ultimately must be defined by modern consensus about what is essentially good and special about that relation." David D. Meyer, "What Family for the 21st Century?: The Bonds and Bounds of Childrearing," 50 *American Journal of Comparative Law* 101, 118 (2002).

141. Jean Cohen, "Is There a Duty of Privacy? Law, Sexual Orientation, and the Construction of Identity," 6 *Texas Journal of Women and the Law* 47, 111 (1996).

CHAPTER FOUR—COMMUNITARIANISM

1. The liberal-communitarian debate has spawned an immense literature. For a representative sample, see *Communitarianism: A New Public Ethics*, ed. Markate Daly (Belmont, Ca.: Wadsworth, 1994); *Democratic Community* (Nomos XXXV), eds. John W. Chapman and Ian Shapiro (New York: New York University Press, 1993); *Liberalism and Its Critics*, ed. Michael J. Sandel (New York: New York University Press, 1984); Elizabeth Frazer and Nicola Lacey, *The Politics of Community: A Feminist Critique of the Liberal-Communitarian Debate* (Toronto: Toronto University Press, 1993); Stephen Mulhall and Adam Swift, *Liberals & Communitarians* (Cambridge, Mass.: Blackwell Press, 1996); *New Communitarian Thinking: Persons, Virtues, Intentions, and Communities*, ed. Amitai Etzioni (Charlottesville: University of Virginia Press, 1995); *The Communitarian Challenge to Liberalism*, eds. Ellen Frankel Paul et al. (New York: Cambridge University Press, 1996); *The Liberalism-Communitarianism Debate: Liberty and Community Values*, ed. C.F. Delaney (Lanham, Md.: Rowman and Littlefield, 1994). The most important communitarian critics of liberalism are generally considered to be Alasdair MacIntyre, Michael Sandel, Charles Taylor, and Michael Walzer.
2. See Richard Rorty, "Justice as a Larger Loyalty," in *Justice and Democracy: Cross-Cultural Perspectives*, eds. Ron Bontekoe and Marietta Stephaniants (Honolulu: University of Hawaii Press, 1997), p. 9.
3. Sandel is also the only leading communitarian thinker who has at least attempted to address gay rights issues. See Michael J. Sandel, "Moral Argument and Liberal Toleration: Abortion and Homosexuality," 77 *California Law Review* 521, 533–38 (1989); Michael J. Sandel, "Political Liberalism," 107 *Harvard Law Review* 1765, 1786–89 (1994).
4. See Sandel, "Political Liberalism."
5. 198 U.S. 45 (1905).
6. As Sandel sees it, when the Court first announced a constitutional right to privacy in *Griswold v. Connecticut*, 381 U.S. 479 (1965), a case that involved the right of married couples to have access to contraceptives, it did so not on the basis of needing to protect voluntary choices but on the basis of a judgment of the good that *certain* choices could produce: "[T]he Court vindicated privacy not for the sake of letting people lead their sexual lives as they choose, but rather for the sake of affirming and protecting the social institution of marriage" (DD, 96). In *Griswold*, according to Sandel, the Court employed a substantive moral judgment about the social good of marriage rather than focusing on issues of voluntariness and choice. In later privacy cases, however, the Court limited its moral outlook to a voluntarist view of personhood and the need to protect individual autonomy. In *Eisenstadt v. Baird*, 405 U.S. 438 (1972), for example, the Court, in order to protect the personal autonomy of individuals to live however they choose, including those who choose to have sex outside of marriage, struck down another law pro-

hibiting the distribution of contraceptives. Sandel identifies the Court's theoretical shift in *Eisenstadt* as a redescription of privacy rights bearers from "persons *qua* participants in the social institution of marriage to persons *qua* individuals, independent of their roles or attachments" (DD, 97). The Court,
Sandel adds, "protected privacy in *Eisenstadt*, not for the social practices it
promotes but for the individual choice it secures" (DD, 97). Sandel is also
critical of the dissenting opinions in *Bowers v. Hardwick*, 478 U.S. 186
(1986), because they emphasized voluntariness and choice rather than "defending homosexual intimacies in terms of the human goods they share with
intimacies already protected by the Court" (DD, 104).

7. As examples of citizens who were successful in petitioning their governments
for protection, but who lost that protection when courts prioritized the rights
of individuals over the needs of the community, Sandel points to (1) Jews in
Skokie, Illinois, who wanted to keep Nazis from marching in their town, and
(2) feminist activists in Indianapolis who wanted to protect women from the
harmful effects of pornography (DD, 85–88).

8. Michael Walzer also criticizes the liberal view that "existing patterns of association" are the result of voluntary and contractual arrangements. Most people's associations and attachments, Walzer argues, develop within the communities into which they were born, communities that "express . . .
underlying identities . . . which . . . are not so much chosen as enacted."
Michael Walzer, "The Communitarian Critique of Liberalism," 18 *Political
Theory* 6, 15 (1990).

9. Kath Weston, *Families We Choose: Lesbians, Gays, Kinship* (New York: Columbia University Press, 1991), p. 50.

10. Ibid. For explorations of the coming out process, see Gershen Kaufman and
Lev Raphael, *Coming Out of Shame: Transforming Gay and Lesbian Lives*
(New York: Doubleday, 1996); Laura A. Markowe, *Redefining the Self: Com-
ing Out as Lesbian* (Cambridge, Mass.: Blackwell, 1996); Marc E. Vargo, *Acts
of Disclosure: The Coming-Out Process of Contemporary Gay Men* (New York:
Haworth Press, 1998).

11. Mark Blasius has written about a gay and lesbian ethos that emerges when the
gay self joins with gay others. That ethos, Blasius argues, entails "a shared
way of life through which lesbians and gay men invent themselves, recognize
each other, and establish a relationship to the culture in which they live."
Mark Blasius, "An Ethos of Lesbian and Gay Existence," 20 *Political Theory*
642, 645 (1992). As part of that ethos, the gay self works to define itself
through its connection to others. "[I]n the formation of an ethos, the earlier
posed 'How shall I live?' becomes inextricably connected to 'How shall *we*
live?' The stake that one has in the morale and destiny of the local lesbian and
gay community, that makes one's 'self' possible, becomes a stake in civic involvement in [a] wider sociohistorical existence." Ibid., p. 659.

12. See Simon LeVay and Elisabeth Nonas, *City of Friends: A Portrait of the Gay
and Lesbian Community in America* (Cambridge: MIT Press, 1995).

13. George Chauncey, *Gay New York: Gender, Urban Culture and the Making of
the Gay Male World, 1890–1940* (New York: Basic Books, 1994), pp. 2–3.

14. Elizabeth Lapovsky Kennedy and Madeline D. Davis, *Boots of Leather, Slippers
of Gold: The History of a Lesbian Community* (New York: Routledge, 1993),
p. 66.

15. Weston, *Families We Choose*, p. 123 (emphasis added).
16. Pater M. Nardi, *Gay Men's Friendships: Invincible Communities* (Chicago: Chicago University Press, 1999), p. 166.
17. See e.g., *Creating a Place for Ourselves: Lesbian, Gay, and Bisexual Community Histories*, ed. Brett Beemyn (New York: Routledge, 1997); John D'Emilio, *Sexual Politics, Sexual Communities: The Making of a Homosexual Minority in the United States, 1940–1970* (Chicago: University of Chicago Press, 1983); Kristin G. Esterberg, *Lesbian and Bisexual Identities: Constructing Communities, Constructing Selves* (Philadelphia: Temple University Press, 1997); Susan Krieger, *The Mirror Dance: Identity in a Women's Community* (Philadelphia: Temple University Press, 1983); Esther Newton, *Cherry Grove, Fire Island: Sixty Years in America's First Gay and Lesbian Town* (Boston: Beacon Press, 1993).
18. See e.g., Momin Rahman, *Sexuality and Democracy: Identities and Strategies in Lesbian and Gay Politics* (Edinburgh: Edinburgh University Press, 2000), ch. 1.
19. This is a distinction that I failed to explain adequately in my previous discussion of these issues in my article "Communitarianism and Gay Rights," 85 *Cornell Law Review* 443, 468–76 (2000).
20. Nardi, *Gay Men's Friendships*, p. 3.
21. See Weston, *Families We Choose*, p. 3.
22. Ibid., p. 27.
23. Ibid., p. 38.
24. Ibid., p. 110.
25. Nardi, *Gay Men's Friendships*, p. 192, quoting Marilyn Friedman, *What Are Friends For?: Feminist Perspectives on Personal Relationships and Moral Theory* (Ithaca: Cornell University Press, 1993), p. 252.
26. Jeffrey Blustein, *Care and Commitment: Taking the Personal Point of View* (New York: Oxford University Press, 1991), p. 5.
27. See Frazer and Lacey, *The Politics of Community*; Marilyn Friedman, "Feminism and Modern Friendship: Dislocating the Community," in *Feminism and Community*, eds. Penny A. Weiss and Marilyn Friedman (Philadelphia: Temple University Press, 1995), p. 187; Donna Greschner, "Feminist Concerns with the New Communitarians: We Don't Need Another Hero," in *Law and the Community: The End of Individualism?*, eds. Allan C. Hutchinson and Leslie J. M. Green (Toronto: Carswell, 1989), p. 119.
28. As Mary Lyndon Shanley notes, "[t]he story that Sandel tells is suffused with a nostalgia that distorts the historical record by ignoring instances in which appeals to community values would have deprived members of minority groups of a political voice; it is a story that glides over and obscures oppression." Shanley, "Liberalism and the Future of Democracy," 49 *Stanford Law Review* 1271, 1290 (1997).
29. Kath Weston reports that when some of the lesbians and gay men whom she interviewed came out to their biological families, they were "institutionalized, threatened with electroshock therapy, kicked out of the house, reduced to living on the street, denied an inheritance, written out of a will, battered, damned as a sinner, barred from contact with younger relatives, shunned by family members, or insulted in ways that encouraged [them] to leave." Weston, *Families We Choose*, p. 61.

30. See Reginald Glenn Blaxton, " 'Jesus Wept': Black Churches and HIV," *Harvard Gay & Lesbian Review*, Winter 1998, p.13; Sheryl Gay Stolberg, "Epidemic of Silence: Eyes Shut, Black America Is Being Ravaged by AIDS," *New York Times*, June 29, 1998, p. A1.

31. Christopher J. Berry, "Shared Understanding and the Democratic Way of Life," in *Democratic Community*, pp. 67, 78.

32. Susan Krieger, "Lesbian Identity and Community: Recent Social Science Literature," *Signs*, Autumn 1982, p. 91. See also Esterberg, *Lesbian and Bisexual Identities*, p. 114 (reporting that lesbian and bisexual women in a small, northeastern town found that "[w]omen described the [lesbian] community as close yet closed, cohesive yet claustrophobic").

33. Marilyn Friedman notes that friendships and communities of urban dwellers, which are communities of choice, are less likely to be oppressive than the given communities emphasized by communitarians. See Friedman, "Feminism and Modern Friendship," pp. 199–204.

34. Ellen Lewin in her studies of lesbian mothers and of gay and lesbian commitment ceremonies, describes how many lesbians and gay men maintain their ties to their biological families, often in the face of initial hostility or uncertainty on the part of the biological relatives, at the same time that they seek to construct new families and kinships. See Ellen Lewin, *Lesbian Mothers: Accounts of Gender in American Culture* (Ithaca: Cornell University Press, 1993), pp. 75–94; Ellen Lewin, *Recognizing Ourselves: Ceremonies of Lesbian and Gay Commitment* (New York: Columbia University Press, 1998), pp. 87–122.

35. Friedman, "Feminism and Modern Friendship," p. 194.

36. Another example of simple equality is the liberal maxim of "equality of opportunity." Such a maxim may be appropriate in the United States for the distribution of jobs, but it does not describe, for example, the way that our government allocates services or our polity chooses its leaders. David Miller defines simple equality as follows: "[A]n idea of equality [is] 'simple' when it holds that equality requires the equal possession or enjoyment of some advantage X. A society is egalitarian, on this view, when all its members are equal in respect of X; that is, they equally enjoy the stuff or the condition represented by X. There are as many notions of simple equality as there are plausible contenders for the X in this formula: candidates include property, income, opportunity, rights, resources, capacities, and welfare." David Miller, "Complex Equality," in *Pluralism, Justice, and Equality*, eds. David Miller and Michael Walzer (New York: Oxford University Press, 1995), p. 197.

37. Michael Rustin points out that Walzer's discussion of the justness of the distribution of health care in the United States overlooks the possibility that the combination of market and government provision might be consistent with the nation's shared traditions. See Michael Rustin, "Equality in Post-Modern Times," in *Pluralism, Justice, and Equality*, pp. 17, 34–35.

38. See Nancy F. Cott, *Public Vows: A History of Marriage and the Nation* (Cambridge: Harvard University Press, 2000), p. 3.

39. Steven L. Nock, *Marriage in Men's Lives* (New York: Oxford University Press, 1998), p. 24.

40. See *Brause v. Bureau of Vital Statistics*, 24 *Family Law Reporter* 2015 (Alaska Super. Ct., Feb. 27, 1998) (emphasis added). In response to the court's rul-

ing, which held that the state had the burden of showing a compelling interest in order to continue enforcing its ban against same-sex marriage, the voters in Alaska approved an amendment to the constitution that explicitly prohibits same-sex marriage. See Liz Ruskin, "Limit on Marriage Passes in Landslide," *Anchorage Daily News*, Nov. 4, 1998, p. A1.

41. For a review of the literature on this subject, see Beth Ann Shelton, "Understanding the Distribution of Housework Between Husbands and Wives," in *The Ties That Bind: Perspectives on Marriage and Cohabitation*, eds. Linda J. Waite et al. (Hawthorn, NY: Aldine de Gruyter, 2000), p. 343.

42. See Elizabeth S. Scott, "Social Norms and the Legal Regulation of Marriage," 86 *Virginia Law Review* 1901 (2000).

43. See Susan Moller Okin, *Justice, Gender, and the Family* (New York: Basic Books, 1989). Okin notes that although Walzer emphasizes the ways in which spheres outside of the family improperly reflect its internal inequalities, "he pays almost no attention to the continued operation of the gender structure within the family." Ibid., p. 114.

44. Amy Gutmann makes a similar point when she argues that "the social meanings of some goods are multiple and the multiple meanings sometimes conflict, leading us to look for moral considerations that can adjudicate among the conflicting meanings. These moral considerations lead us beyond a search for the real social meaning of the good in question to moral considerations that are not internal to the sphere." Gutmann, "Justice Across the Spheres," in *Pluralism, Justice, and Equality*, p. 99.

45. Rustin, "Equality in Post-Modern Times," p. 31. Martha Nussbaum, in discussing the lives of Indian women, notes the ways in which they adapt their preferences based on the limitations imposed by oppressive social conditions. She argues that it is sometimes necessary, therefore, in thinking about what should be our most important considerations of justice, to depart from or criticize those preferences (WHD, ch. 2).

46. See *Roe v. Wade*, 410 U.S. 113 (1973), *Skinner v. Oklahoma*, 316 U.S. 535 (1942).

47. See *Roe v. Wade; Eisenstadt v. Baird*, 405 U.S. 438 (1972); *Griswold v. Connecticut*, 381 U.S. 479 (1965).

48. *Carey v. Population Services International*, 431 U.S. 678, 685 (1977).

49. See *Troxel v. Granville*, 530 U.S. 57 (2000); *Pierce v. Society of Sisters*, 268 U.S. 510 (1925); *Meyer v. Nebraska*, 262 U.S. 390 (1923).

50. See e.g., Calif. Fam. Code §§7820–7829 (1994 & Supp. 2001).

51. See Elinor Burkett, *The Baby Boon: How Family-Friendly America Cheats the Childless* (New York: The Free Press, 2000); Marian Faux, *Childless By Choice: Choosing Childlessness in the Eighties* (New York: Anchor Press, 1984); *Pronatalism: The Myth of Mom & Apple Pie*, eds. Ellen Peck and Judith Senderowitz (New York: Thomas Y. Crowell, 1974); Elaine Tyler May, *Barren in the Promised Land: Childless Americans and the Pursuit of Happiness* (New York: Basic Books, 1995); Jean E. Veevers, *Childless by Choice* (Toronto: Butterworths, 1980).

52. See Veevers, *Childless by Choice*, p. 3.

53. See "Fertility of American Women," *Current Population Reports* (Census Bureau. Washington, D.C., 1998), Table A. That number was up since 1976 when the percentage was an even smaller 10 percent. See ibid. (Figure 1). In

1998, the percentage of childless women between the ages of 40 and 44 divided according to racial and ethnic groups was as follows: white women, 19.5 percent; black women, 17 percent; Asian and Pacific Islander women, 17 percent; Hispanic women, 14.5 percent. See ibid. (Table A).

54. See May, *Barren in the Promised Land*, p. 9.

55. See Faux, *Childless by Choice*, ch. 2; Myra J. Hird and Kimberly Abshoff, "Women without Children: A Contradiction in Terms?," 31 *Journal of Comparative Family Studies* 347 (2000); Carolyn M. Morel, *Unwomanly Conduct: The Challenges of Intentional Childlessness* (New York: Routledge, 1994), ch. 4; Veevers, *Childless by Choice*, pp. 7–8.

56. See Charlene E. Miall, "Community Constructs of Involuntary Childlessness: Sympathy, Stigma and Social Support," 31 *Canadian Review of Sociology and Anthropology* 392 (1994); Charlene E. Miall, "The Stigma of Involuntary Childlessness," 33 *Social Problems* 268 (1986). "The fact that reproduction remains primarily a woman's problem is due less to women's biological capacity for pregnancy and more to cultural norms that still place motherhood at the center of female identity." May, *Barren in the Promised Land*, p. 258.

57. See May, *Barren in the Promised Land*.

58. Scott, "Social Norms and the Legal Regulation of Marriage," p. 1912.

59. Ibid, p. 1913.

60. This was seen most clearly a few years ago in the strong and almost unanimous criticism of the Illinois Supreme Court in the now infamous "Baby Richard" case. The court in that case ordered that a four-year-old boy be removed from the home of his adoptive parents, who had raised him since he was born, and be handed over to his biological father. See *In re Petition of Doe*, 638 N.E.2d 181 (Ill. 1994).

61. See Katharine T. Bartlett, "Rethinking Parenthood as an Exclusive Status: The Need for Legal Alternatives when the Premise of the Nuclear Family Has Failed," 70 *Virginia Law Review* 879 (1984); Nancy D. Polikoff, "This Child Does Have Two Mothers: Redefining Parenthood to Meet the Needs of Children in Lesbian-Mother and Other Nontraditional Families," 78 *Georgetown Law Journal* 459 (1990).

62. See Richard F. Storrow, "Parenthood by Pure Intention: Assisted Reproduction and the Functional Approach to Parentage," 53 *Hastings Law Review* 597 (2002).

63. See Lynn D. Wardle, " 'Multiply and Replenish': Considering Same-Sex Marriage in Light of State Interests in Marital Procreation," 24 *Harvard Journal of Law and Public Policy* 771 (2001).

64. See "America's Families and Living Arrangements," *Current Population Reports* (Census Bureau: Washington, D.C., 2000), p. 7.

65. Lynn Wardle is a good example of this common phenomenon. Compare Wardle, "'Multiply and Replenish'" with Wardle, "The Potential Impact of Homosexual Parenting on Children," 1997 *University of Illinois Law Review* 833.

66. Adoption is different because it is considered a statutory privilege rather than a constitutional right. Adoption bans for lesbians and gay men may nonetheless be constitutionally vulnerable under an equal protection analysis, especially after *Romer v. Evans*, 517 U.S. 620 (1996). A federal district court, however, has recently denied a constitutional challenge to the Florida law that

prohibits lesbians and gay men from adopting. See *Lofton v. Kearney,* 157 F. Supp. 2d 1372 (S.D. Fla. 2001).

67. See Fla. St. §63.042(3) (1995); Miss. St. §93–17–3(2) (1999); Ut. St. §78–30–1(3)(b) (2000). The Florida statute bars all lesbians and gay men from adopting. The Mississippi statute bars gay and lesbian couples, though not individuals, from adopting. The Utah statute bars all unmarried cohabiting couples from adopting, but it was clearly aimed at lesbians and gay men. See Nora Stephens, "Don't Adopt These Bills," *Salt Lake City Tribune,* Feb. 20, 2000, p. A1.

68. For reviews of the literature see Carlos A. Ball and Janice Farrell Pea, "Warring with Wardle: Morality, Social Science, and Gay and Lesbian Parents," 1998 *University of Illinois Law Review* 253; Charlotte J. Patterson, "Children of Lesbian and Gay Parents," 63 *Child Development* 1025 (1992).

69. Testimony of Dr. Kyle Pruett, *Baehr v. Miike,* 23 *Family Law Reporter* 2001 (Haw. Cir. Ct., Dec. 3, 1996), ¶¶34–35.

70. Testimony of Dr. David Eggebeen, Ibid., ¶52.

71. Testimony of Dr. Thomas Merrill, Ibid.,¶71.

72. Testimony of Dr. Richard Williams, Ibid., ¶¶59–61.

73. See e.g., *Conkel v. Conkel,* 509 N.E.2d 983 (Ohio App. 1987); *Van Driel v. Van Driel,* 525 N.W.2d 37 (S.D. 1994); *In re M.M.D.,* 662 A.2d 837 (D.C. Cir. 1995); *In re Adoption of Tammy,* 619 N.E.2d 315 (Mass. 1993); *In re Jacob,* 660 N.E.2d 397 (N.Y. 1995).

74. "Technical Report: Coparent or Second-Parent Adoption by Same-Sex Parents," 109 *Pediatrics* 341 (2002).

75. Wardle, "The Potential Impact of Homosexual Parenting on Children," p. 865.

CHAPTER FIVE—POSTMODERNISM

1. Although most forms of liberalism see the capability of individuals to reason as that which defines them as human and gives them a capacity for autonomy, moral liberalism, as we saw in chapter 3, takes a more expansive view of what it means to be human by also accounting for basic needs and capabilities associated with the body, emotions, and relationships. In addition, moral liberalism believes, as we also saw in chapter 3, that the exercise of the human capacity for autonomy takes place within and is dependent on our relationships and attachments to others.

2. See Richard D. Mohr, "The Perils of Postmodernity for Gay Rights," 8 *Canadian Journal of Law & Jurisprudence* 5 (1995).

3. David M. Halperin, *Saint Foucault: Towards a Gay Hagiography* (New York: Oxford University Press, 1995), p. 123. As noted in chapter 1, even though queer theorists are skeptical of liberal theory, many remain, at the level of practice, committed to a liberal model of individual rights that promotes autonomy and equality.

4. The late historian John Boswell and Richard Mohr are two notable and important exceptions. See John Boswell, "Concepts, Experience, and Sexuality," in *Forms of Desire: Sexual Orientation and the Social Constructionist Controversy,* ed. Edward Stein (New York: Routledge, 1990), p. 133; Richard D.

Mohr, *Gay Ideas: Outing and Other Controversies* (Boston: Beacon Press, 1992), ch. 7.

5. See e.g., Judith Butler, *Gender Trouble: Feminism and the Subversion of Identity* (New York: Routledge, 1990); Halperin, *Saint Foucault*; Ladelle McWhorter, *Bodies and Pleasures: Foucault and the Politics of Sexual Normalization* (Bloomington: Indiana University Press, 1999).

6. See Michel Foucault, *Madness and Civilization: A History of Insanity in the Age of Reason* (New York: Vintage Books, 1988 (1965)); Michel Foucault, *The Birth of the Clinic: An Archaeology of Medical Perception* (New York: Pantheon Books, 1973); Michel Foucault, *Discipline and Punish: The Birth of the Prison* (New York: Pantheon Books, 1977). Foucault's earlier works were archaeological and genealogical. The former entails the study of truth as a form of representation and discourse. The latter entails the study of truth as a form of domination, subjugation, and power. See Arnold I. Davidson, "Archaeology, Genealogy, Ethics," in *Foucault: A Critical Reader*, ed. David Couzens Hoy (New York: Blackwell, 1986), pp. 221–25. As I will discuss later in this chapter, Foucault in his later work was interested mostly in ethics, which he conceived to be "a study of the self's relationship to itself." Ibid., p. 228.

7. See Jonathan Katz, *Gay/Lesbian Almanac: A New Documentary* (New York: Harper & Row, 1983), pp. 147–50; David M. Halperin, *One Hundred Years of Homosexuality* (New York: Routledge, 1990), p. 15.

8. Foucault adds that while under "ancient civil or canonical codes, sodomy was a category of forbidden acts . . . [in] [t]he nineteenth century [the] homosexual became a personage, a past, a case history, and a childhood, in addition to being a type of life, a life form, and a morphology. . . . Nothing that went into his total composition was unaffected by his sexuality" (HS1, 43).

9. See Boswell, "Concepts, Experience, and Sexuality"; Mohr, *Gay Ideas*, ch. 7.

10. Edward Stein, "Introduction," in *Forms of Desire*, pp. 3, 5.

11. See sources cited in note 67, chapter 3.

12. Foucault, "On the Genealogy of Ethics: An Overview of Work in Progress," in Michel Foucault, *Ethics: Subjectivity and Truth*, ed. Paul Rabinow (New York: The New Press, 1997), pp. 253, 263.

13. Foucault in another interview explained this point as follows: "I believe . . . that the subject is constituted through practices of subjection, or, in a more autonomous way, through practices of liberation, of liberty, as in Antiquity, on the basis, of course, of a number of rules, styles, inventions to be found in the cultural environment." Michel Foucault, "An Aesthetics of Existence," in Michel Foucault, *Politics, Philosophy, Culture: Interviews and Other Writings, 1977–1984*, ed. Lawrence D. Kritzman (New York: Routledge, 1988), pp. 47, 50–51.

14. Foucault, "Technologies of the Self," in *Ethics: Subjectivity and Truth*, pp. 223, 225.

15. Andrew W. Lamb, "Freedom, the Self and Ethical Practice According to Michel Foucault," 35 *International Philosophical Quarterly*. 449, 456 (1995).

16. Foucault notes that when discussing issues of morality and ethics we are today much more comfortable with the concept of "knowing oneself" than we are with "caring for oneself." But the latter "was, for the Greeks, one of the main

principles of cities, one of the main rules for social and personal conduct and for the art of life." Foucault, "Technologies of the Self," p. 226. In contrast, today "[w]e find it difficult to base rigorous morality and austere principles on the precept that we should give more care to ourselves than to anything else in the world." Ibid., p. 228. For the Greeks, as for the later Foucault, however, the "critical function of philosophy derives from the Socratic injunction 'Take care of yourself,' in other words, 'Make freedom your foundation, through the mastery of yourself' " (ECS, 301).

17. Foucault makes this point as follows: "What strikes me is the fact that, in our society, art has become something that is related only to objects and not to individuals or to life. That art is something which is specialized or done by experts who are artists. But couldn't everyone's life become a work of art? Why should the lamp or the house be an art object but not our life?" Foucault, *On the Genealogy of Ethics*, p. 261.

18. Halperin, *Saint Foucault*, pp. 69–70.

19. Foucault elsewhere notes that "[t]he main interest in life and work is to become someone else that you were not in the beginning." Michel Foucault, "Truth, Power, Self," in *Technologies of the Self: A Seminar with Michel Foucault*, eds. Luther H. Martin et al. (Amherst: University of Massachusetts Press, 1995), p. 9.

20. Foucault, "An Aesthetics of Existence," p. 49.

21. See Pierre J. Payer, *Sex and the Penitentials: The Development of a Sexual Code, 550–1150* (Toronto: University of Toronto Press, 1984). Between the sixth and the twelfth century, the penitentials were "the principal agent in the formation and transmission of a code of sexual morality." Ibid. The penitentials were quite explicit in their codification. In terms of homosexual acts, sodomy was the most serious sin and received the longest period of penance, but other acts such as fellatio and mutual masturbation between men, and fornication between women, were also proscribed. See ibid., pp. 40–44.

22. When Foucault died, he was working on a fourth volume of the *History of Sexuality*, which was to cover the Christian period that followed antiquity and preceded modernity. The manuscript of the fourth volume remains unpublished.

23. Foucault notes that sexual ethics in Greece were "ethics for men: an ethics thought, written, and taught by men and addressed to [free] men" (HS2, 22). Foucault has been criticized for paying insufficient attention to women in his discussion of sexual ethics in ancient Greece. See Amy Richlin, "Foucault's History of Sexuality: A Useful Theory for Women?," in *Rethinking Sexuality: Foucault and Classical Antiquity*, eds. David H.J. Larmour et al. (Princeton: Princeton University Press, 1997), pp. 138, 148; Kate Soper, "Productive Contradictions," in *Up Against Foucault: Explorations of Some Tensions Between Foucault and Feminism*, ed. Caroline Ramazanoğlu (New York: Routledge, 1993), pp. 29, 41.

24. There are nineteen entries under "moderation" in the index to *The Use of Pleasure* (HS2, 287–88).

25. I use the male pronoun because, as already noted, sexual ethics in ancient Greece were addressed primarily to men.

26. The view that neither Greek law nor customs prohibited or penalized homosexual conduct is supported by the leading book in the field. See K.J. Dover,

Greek Homosexuality (Cambridge: Harvard University Press, 1978). Although some scholars have argued that this is an incorrect assessment of the historical record, see David Cohen and Richard Saller, "Foucault on Sexuality in Greco-Roman Antiquity," in *Foucault and the Writing of History*, ed. Jan Goldstein (Cambridge, Mass.: Blackwell, 1994), pp. 35, 37–39; the Dover/Foucault position on this issue is accepted by most classicist scholars. See Halperin, *One Hundred Years of Homosexuality*, pp. 4–7; Martha C. Nussbaum, "Platonic Love and Colorado Law: The Relevance of Ancient Greek Norms to Modern Sexual Controversies," 80 *Virginia Law Review* 1515, 1544–47 (1994).

27. John Boswell noted that though the relationship between adult males and boys in ancient Greece may have been "an idealized cultural convention," this does not mean that those kinds of relationships—as opposed to relationships between male adults—were more prevalent. See John Boswell, *Christianity, Social Tolerance, and Homosexuality* (Chicago: Chicago University Press, 1980), p. 28.

28. See Craig A. Williams, *Roman Homosexuality: Ideologies of Masculinity in Classical Antiquity* (New York: Oxford University Press, 1999).

29. Even though medicine was now more involved in issues of sexuality, the nature of that involvement was different from what took place much later. In the modern era, the involvement of medicine "was to be organized as a domain that would have its normal forms and its morbid forms, its specific pathology, its nosography and etiology—to say nothing of its therapeutics" (HS3, 141). In Greco-Roman culture, medicine viewed sexual acts as problematic because they could lead to physical illnesses caused by the expenditure of energy (HS3, 142).

30. In the Greco-Roman era, "[m]arriage, as an individual tie capable of integrating relations of pleasure and of giving them a positive value . . . , constitute[d] the most active focus for defining a stylistics of moral life" (HS3, 192). See also Mark Poster, "Foucault and the Tyranny of Greece," in *Foucault: A Critical Reader*, pp. 205, 215 (noting that "[i]n place of the elaborate subculture surrounding the love of boys, the wife [in the early Roman period] became the centre of the man's sexuality and accordingly the locus in which he constituted his subjectivity").

31. See Poster, "Foucault and the Tyranny of Greece," p. 216.

32. Michel Foucault, "Two Lectures," in *Power/Knowledge: Selected Interviews and other Writings, 1972–1977*, ed. Colin Gordon (New York: Pantheon, 1980), pp. 78, 98.

33. McWhorter, *Bodies and Pleasures*, p. xvi.

34. See Butler, *Gender Trouble*, p. vii.

35. Ibid., p. 143. Butler adds that agency is found within repetitive processes of gender regulation when they allow for new possibilities "that contest the rigid codes of hierarchical binarisms." Ibid., p. 145. For Butler, there is no prediscursive subject; both the subject and its agency are fully constituted by culture and discourse. Carl Stychin provides the following explanation of a postmodernist conception of agency: agency emanates from "the necessarily incomplete delineation of the boundaries of any discourse." Carl Stychin, *Law's Desire: Sexuality and the Limits of Justice* (New York: Routledge, 1995), p. 21. This incompleteness "allows for intervention, resistance, and subver-

sion of the terms of the system. The active role of the agent, through her creative intervention and resistance, ultimately contributes to the social construction of identity." Ibid., p. 22.

36. Mark Bevir, "Foucault and Critique: Deploying Agency Against Autonomy," 27 *Political Theory* 65, 67 (1999).

37. Ibid. Sarah Hoagland, writing more as a lesbian feminist than as a postmodernist, calls autonomy a "thoroughly noxious concept" because it suggests separation, independence, and self-sufficiency. Sarah L. Hoagland, *Lesbian Ethics: Toward New Value* (Palo Alto: Institute of Lesbian Studies, 1988), p. 144. Rather than autonomy, Hoagland prefers to speak of "aotokoenomy," a concept that envisions individuals making choices in a community of others who also make choices. Hoagland adds that aotokoenomy "is not a matter of us controlling our environment but rather of our acting within it and being a part of it." Ibid., p. 145.

38. J. B. Schneewind, "The Use of Autonomy in Ethical Theory," in *Reconstructing Individualism: Autonomy, Individuality, and the Self in Western Thought*, eds. Thomas C. Heller et al. (Palo Alto: Stanford University Press, 1986), pp. 64, 69.

39. Ibid., p. 72.

40. See Stephen Macedo, *Liberal Virtues: Citizenship, Virtue, and Community in Liberal Constitutionalism* (New York: Oxford University Press, 1990), p. 216.

41. Ibid., p. 225.

42. Ibid., p. 223. Macedo adds that "[o]ur very identity may be open to revision, but we are not simply adrift . . . because autonomous persons are not passive but active centers of self-direction, always constituted by a range of commitments, attachments, and allegiances." Ibid., p. 226.

43. Ibid., p. 220.

44. Catriona Mackenzie and Natalie Stoljar, "Introduction: Autonomy Refigured," in *Relational Autonomy: Feminist Perspectives on Autonomy, Agency, and the Social Self*, eds. Catriona Mackenzie and Natalie Stoljar (New York: Oxford University Press, 2000), pp. 3, 8. See also Linda C. McClain, "Toleration, Autonomy, and Governmental Promotion of Good Lives: Beyond 'Empty Toleration' to Toleration as Respect," 59 *Ohio State Law Journal* 19, 128 (1998) (noting that "a liberal conception of autonomy does not require a model of the self as immune from the process of social construction").

45. Bevir, "Foucault and Critique," p. 76.

46. Ibid., p. 68.

47. See Halperin, *Saint Foucault*, p. 212 n.137.

48. Ibid.

49. Ibid., p. 18 (emphasis added).

50. See McWhorter, *Bodies and Pleasures*, ch. 2.

51. Ibid., p. 50.

52. McWhorter gives a personal account of how the practices of gardening and dancing, for example, have allowed her to expand her interests and experiences and have therefore permitted her to expand her sense of self. See ibid., pp. 162-75.

53. Ibid., p. 79. I discuss McWhorter's ideas in more detail in Carlos A. Ball, "Essentialism and Universalism in Gay Rights Philosophy: Liberalism Meets

Queer Theory," 26 *Law & Social Inquiry* 271, 274–85 (2001).

54. Thomas Dumm, *Michel Foucault and the Politics of Freedom* (Thousand Oaks, Ca.: Sage, 1996), p. 15.

55. Jeremy Moss, "Introduction: The Later Foucault," in *The Later Foucault: Politics and Philosophy*, ed. Jeremy Moss (Thousand Oaks, Ca.: Sage, 1998), pp. 1, 5.

56. Richard H. Fallon Jr., "Two Senses of Autonomy," 46 *Stanford Law Review* 875, 888 (1994).

57. Ibid. Seyla Benhabib similarly notes that even if we concede that subjectivity can only be structured within narratives and culture, "we must still argue that we are not merely extensions of our histories, that vis-à-vis our own stories we are in the position of author and character at once." Seyla Benhabib, *Situating the Self: Gender, Community and Postmodernism in Contemporary Ethics* (New York: Routledge, 1992), p. 214.

58. Christopher Norris, for one, argues that Foucault "left himself no room for manouevre when it came to explaining how subjects could exercise a degree of ethical autonomy or choice, a margin of freedom that would not be fore-closed by the pervasive workings of power/knowledge." Christopher Norris, *The Truth About Postmodernism* (Cambridge, MA: Blackwell, 1993), p. 47.

59. See William N. Eskridge Jr., *Gaylaw: Challenging the Apartheid of the Closet* (Cambridge: Harvard University Press, 1999).

60. See e.g., Mich. Comp. Laws. Ann. §750.158 (1991); Okla. St. Title 21 §886 (2001); Texas Penal Code Ann. §21.01, §21.06 (1994).

61. Alan Hunt and Gary Wickham note that Foucault's rather circumscribed view of the law is similar to that held by the nineteenth-century legal philosopher John Austin who conceived of the law only as commands issued by the sovereign and enforced through sanctions. See Alan Hunt and Gary Wickham, *Foucault and the Law: Towards a Sociology of Law as Governance* (Boulder: Pluto, 1994), p. 60. They argue that Foucault "unnecessarily marginalised" the role of the law and the state "with respect to the coordination and condensation of the forms of power." Ibid., p. 71. They add "that, contrary to Foucault, disciplinary power is not opposed to law, but rather . . . law has been a primary agent of the advance of new modalities of power, law constitutes distinctive features of their mode of operation." Ibid., p. 65. Similarly, Duncan Kennedy criticizes Foucault's conception of the law because it fails to recognize that power relations "between parties [are themselves] conditioned through and through by a preexisting legal context." Duncan Kennedy, *Sexy Dressing Etc.* (Cambridge: Harvard University Press, 1993), p. 120.

62. See Eskridge, *Gaylaw*, p. 157; Katz, *Gay American History*, pp. 16–23. The English sodomy statutes applied during the colonial period can be traced back to the Reformation Parliament of 1533. That body, in turn, secularized criminal offenses previously regulated by the Catholic Church.

63. See George Chauncey Jr., "From Sexual Inversion to Homosexuality: Medicine and the Changing Conceptualization of Female Deviance," 58–59 *Salgamundi* 114 (1982–83).

64. Eskridge, *Gaylaw*, p. 22. Jonathan Katz provides a fascinating cross section of excerpts from the medical literature on homosexuality from the end of the nineteenth century to the 1970s. See Katz, *Gay American History*, pp. 129–51.

65. Justice White got his history wrong, therefore, when he argued in *Bowers v. Hardwick* that the conduct for which Mr. Hardwick was arrested (oral sex) had been a criminal offense for centuries. See *Bowers v. Hardwick*, 478 U.S. 186, 192 (1986). Oral sex was not a crime in either England before 1885, or, more important, in the United States at the time of enactment of the Fourteenth Amendment.

66. See Eskridge, *Gaylaw*, p. 24.

67. Ibid., pp. 29–34.

68. Ibid., p. 52.

69. Steven Seidman, *Embattled Eros: Sexual Politics and Ethics in Contemporary America* (New York: Routledge, 1992), p. 146.

70. Eskridge, *Gaylaw*, p. 40.

71. Ibid., 44–45. George Chauncey describes how the regulation of homosexuality in New York City in the 1920s and 1930s became progressively more intense and pernicious as governmental agencies (such as the police and the alcohol regulation authorities) aggressively enforced laws against homosexuals. See George Chauncey, *Gay New York: Gender, Urban Culture and the Making of the Gay Male World, 1890–1940* (New York: Basic Books, 1994), pp. 331–54.

72. Eskridge, *Gaylaw*, p. 43.

73. See John D'Emilio, *Sexual Politics, Sexual Communities: The Making of a Homosexual Minority in the United States, 1940–1970* (Chicago: Chicago University Press, 1983), pp. 24–31

74. Eskridge, *Gaylaw*, p. 60.

75. Ibid., p. 64. See also Robert L. Jacobson, " 'Megan's Law': Reinforcing Old Patterns of Anti-Gay Police Harassment," 87 *Georgetown Law Journal* 2431, 2433–40 (1999).

76. See John D'Emilio, "The Homosexual Menace: The Politics of Sexuality in Cold War America," in *Passion and Power: Sexuality in History,* eds. Kathy Peiss et al. (Philadelphia: Temple University Press, 1989), p. 226.

77. Eskridge, *Gaylaw*, p. 82.

78. For an historical overview of this process, see D'Emilio, *Sexual Politics, Sexual Communities*; Eric Marcus, *Making History: The Struggle for Gay and Lesbian Rights, 1945–1990* (New York: HarperCollins, 1992).

79. Eskridge, *Gaylaw*, p. 83.

80. See ibid., pp. 328–37 (Appendix "A1") (state-by-state history of sodomy statutes).

81. 478 U.S. 186 (1986). The six states are Georgia, Kentucky, Montana, Nevada, Pennsylvania, and Tennessee.

82. Eskridge, *Gaylaw*, p. 110.

83. The most important early case that specifically recognized the rights of association of gay individuals was *One Eleven Wings & Liquors, Inc. v. Division of Alcoholic Beverage Control*, 235 A.2d 12 (N.J. 1967). In that case, the New Jersey Supreme Court set aside penalties imposed by the state against bar owners because they had allowed lesbians and gay men to congregate. In reaching its decision, the New Jersey court relied, in part, on United States Supreme Court cases such as *NAACP v. Alabama,* 357 U.S. 449 (1958) and *Griswold v. Connecticut,* 381 U.S. 479 (1965).

84. See Eskridge, *Gaylaw*, pp. 356–61 (Appendix "B2") (listing states and municipalities that have laws against sexual orientation discrimination); Exec.

Order No. 13,087, 63 Fed. Reg. 30,097 (1998) (further amendment to Exec. Order No. 11,478, Equal Employment Opportunity in the Federal Government); *In re M.M.D.*, 662 A.2d 837 (D.C. Cir. 1995); *In re Adoption of Tammy*, 619 N.E.2d 315 (Mass. 1993); *In re Adoption of B.L.V.B.*, 628 A.2d 1271 (Vt. 1993).

85. See Jacobson, "Megan's Law," pp. 2454–55.

86. See e.g., *Able v. United States*, 155 F.3d 628 (2nd Cir. 1998); *Holmes v. California Army National Guard*, 124 F.3d 1126 (9th Cir. 1997) *Thomasson v. Perry*, 80 F.3d 915 (4th Cir. 1996).

87. See Fla. St. §63.042(3) (1995); Miss. St. §93–17–3(2) (1999); Ut. St. §78–30–1(3)(b) (2000).

88. See Lynn D. Wardle, "The Potential Impact of Homosexual Parenting on Children," 1997 *University of Illinois Law Review* 833.

89. Even when not enforced, however, sodomy statutes still have negative implications for gay and lesbian individuals in areas of civil law affecting families, employment, and immigration. See Diana Hassel, "The Use of Criminal Sodomy Laws in Civil Litigation," 79 *Texas Law Review* 813 (2001).

90. See *Romer v. Evans*, 517 U.S. 620 (1996).

91. See Ronald Bayer, *Homosexuality and American Psychiatry: The Politics of Diagnosis* (New York: Basic Books, 1981), pp. 101–54. The American Psychological Association took a similar step in 1975. See *www.apa.org/pi/lgbpolicy/against.html* (as of May 17, 2002).

92. The most recent edition of the DSM lists exhibitionism, fetishism, pedophilia, sexual masochism, sexual sadism, transvestic fetishism, voyeurism, and gender identity disorder as psychiatric illnesses. See *Diagnostic and Statistical Manual of Mental Disorders (DSM IV)* (Washington, D.C.: American Psychiatric Association, 1994), pp. 522–38.

93. See Bayer, *Homosexuality and American Psychiatry*, pp. 155–78.

94. See John Finnis, "The Good of Marriage and the Morality of Sexual Relations: Some Philosophical and Historical Observations," 42 *American Journal of Jurisprudence* 97, 107–08 (1997).

95. For helpful sources on such a development, see e.g., Boswell, *Christianity, Social Tolerance and Homosexuality*; James Brundage, *Law, Sex and Christian Society in Medieval Europe* (Chicago: Chicago University Press, 1987); Philip L. Reynolds, *Marriage in the Western Church: The Christianization of Marriage During the Patristic and Early Medieval Periods* (New York: E.J. Brill, 1994).

96. See John M. Finnis, "Law, Morality, and 'Sexual Orientation,' " 9 *Notre Dame Journal of Law, Ethics, and Public Policy* 30 n.48 (1995). This is the same essay as the one cited in the following note with some additional comments by Finnis added to the footnotes.

97. See John M. Finnis, "Law, Morality, and 'Sexual Orientation,' " 69 *Notre Dame Law Review* 1049, 1067 (1994). As discussed in chapter 3, for Finnis sexual acts have "procreative significance" if they in general could lead to reproduction, regardless of whether they actually do so in any particular instance. In this way, Finnis prioritizes penile-vaginal intercourse even when engaged in by a sterile or elderly couple.

98. See Finnis, "The Good of Marriage and the Morality of Sexual Relations," p. 98.

99. A comprehensive survey of almost 2,500 Americans conducted in the early 1990s (known as the National Health and Social Life Survey) found that approximately one third of the respondents believed that all extramarital sex is wrong. See Robert T. Michael et al., *Sex in America: A Definitive Survey* (Boston: Little Brown, 1994), pp. 232–33. Nearly half believed that "sex should be part of a loving relationship, but that it need not always be reserved for marriage." Ibid., p. 233. A little more than one quarter of the respondents believed that "sex need not have anything to do with love." Ibid.

100. See e.g., Nancy F. Cott, *Public Vows: A History of Marriage and the Nation* (Cambridge: Harvard University Press, 2000), pp. 181–82 ; John D'Emilio and Estelle B. Freedman, *Intimate Matters: A History of Sexuality in America* (Chicago: Chicago University Press, 1988), pp. 239–274; Steven Seidman, *Romantic Longings: Love in America, 1830–1980* (New York: Routledge, 1991), pp. 65–156.

101. See "Religious Declaration on Sexual Morality, Justice, and Healing," *New York Times*, Jan. 25, 2000, p. A19.

102. Ibid. (emphasis added).

103. See Laura S. Brown, "Lesbian Identities: Concepts and Issues," in *Lesbian, Gay, and Bisexual Identities over the Lifespan*, eds. Antony R.D. Augelli and Charlotte J. Patterson (New York: Oxford University Press, 1995), p. 3.

104. Michel Foucault, "Friendship as a Way of Life," in *Ethics: Subjectivity and Truth*, pp.135, 137–38.

105. Halperin, *Saint Foucault*, pp. 73–74.

106. Ibid., p. 79.

107. "Sexual habit . . . to my mind is . . . an aesthetic rather than an ethical issue, a matter (so long as no one is hurt) of what gives pleasure rather than what is good or right." Edmund White, *States of Desire: Travels in Gay America* (New York: Dutton, 1980), p. 38.

108. Michel Foucault, "Sex, Power, and the Politics of Identity," in *Ethics: Subjectivity and Truth*, p. 163.

109. Hoagland, *Lesbian Ethics*, p. 13.

110. See Seidman, *Embattled Eros*, pp. 172–73.

111. See Gabriel Rotello, *Sexual Ecology: AIDS and the Destiny of Gay Men* (New York: Dutton, 1997); Michelangelo Signorile, *Life Outside* (New York: HarperCollins, 1997); Larry Kramer, "Gay Culture, Redefined," *New York Times*, Dec. 12, 1997, p. A35.

112. See Michael Bronski, "Behind the SexPanic! Debate," *Harvard Gay & Lesbian Review*, Spring 1998, p. 29; Caleb Crain, "Pleasure Principles: Queer Theorists and Gay Journalists Wrestle Over the Politics of Sex," *Lingua Franca*, Oct. 1997, p. 27; Sheryl Gay Stolberg, "Gay Culture Weighs Sense and Sexuality," *New York Times*, Nov. 23, 1997, §4, p. 1. The citations in this and in the previous note relate to the intracommunity debate that took place in the 1990s. Seidman recounts in great detail the debate that took place in the 1980s. See Seidman, *Embattled Eros*, pp. 154–70.

113. Seidman, *Embattled Eros*, p. 171.

114. Poster, "Foucault and the Tyranny of Greece," p. 214. Poster suggests that "[p]erhaps the reason for the omission lies in Foucault's aversion to Freudian discourse, laden as it is with the question of conscious and unconscious feelings." Ibid.

115. Foucault, "Friendship as a Way of Life," p. 136.
116. Ibid., pp. 136–37. Foucault notes the bind that some institutions find themselves in when they simultaneously foment and discourage same-gender camaraderie and companionship. An example is the military, "where love between men is ceaselessly provoked [*appelé*] and shamed. Institutional codes can't validate these relations with multiple intensities, variable colors, imperceptible movements and changing forms. These relations short-circuit [the codes] and introduce love where there's supposed to be only law, rule, or habit." Ibid., p. 137.
117. Halperin, *Saint Foucault*, p. 98.
118. See Terry Eagleton, *The Ideology of the Aesthetic* (Cambridge, MA: Blackwell, 1990), p. 393; Herbert Grabes, "Ethics, Aesthetics, and Alterity," in *Ethics & Aesthetics: The Moral Turn of Postmodernism*, eds. Gerhard Hoffmann & Alfred Hornung (Heidelberg: C. Winter, 1996), pp. 13, 20–21; Jean Grimshaw, "Practices of Freedom," in *Up Against Foucault*, pp. 51, 68; Lois McNay, *Foucault and Feminism: Power, Gender, and the Self* (Boston: Northeastern University Press, 1993), pp. 163–64.
119. Mark Blasius, *Gay and Lesbian Politics: Sexuality and the Emergence of a New Ethic* (Philadelphia: Temple University Press, 1994), p. 109.
120. Foucault, "Sex, Power, and the Politics of Identity," p. 169.
121. Blasius, *Gay and Lesbian Politics*, p. 91.
122. See Halperin, *Saint Foucault*, pp. 93–94. A slightly different translation of the same interview can be found in David Macey, *The Lives of Michel Foucault* (New York: Pantheon Books, 1993), p. 365.
123. As Foucault notes, "[p]leasure is something which passes from one individual to another; it is not secreted by identity. Pleasure has no passport, no identification papers," quoted in Halperin, *Saint Foucault*, p. 95. See also McWhorter, *Bodies and Pleasures*, p. 184 (noting that "attempts to quantify pleasure and measure it, to capture it in terms of statistically manipulable developmental norms, have not met with much success").
124. McWhorter, *Bodies and Pleasures*, p. 177.
125. Michael Warner, *The Trouble with Normal: Sex, Politics, and the Ethics of Queer Life* (New York: Free Press, 1999), p. 12 (emphasis added).
126. Foucault, "Sex, Power, and the Politics of Identity," p. 165.
127. Ibid.
128. Ibid.
129. This is a point that Robert Nozick made when he hypothesized about the lack of appeal in plugging into a machine that would "give you any experience that you desired." See Robert Nozick, *Anarchy, State, and Utopia* (New York: Basic Books, 1974), p. 42.
130. Halperin, *Saint Foucault*, p. 107.
131. Gayle Rubin, "Thinking Sex: Notes for a Radical Theory of the Politics of Sexuality," in *Pleasure and Danger: Exploring Female Sexuality*, ed. Carole S. Vance (Boston: Routledge and K. Paul, 1984), pp. 267, 283.
132. McWhorter, *Bodies and Pleasures*, p. 101.
133. W.E.B. Du Bois, *The Souls of Black Folk* (New York: Signet/Penguin Books, 1995), p. 3. For a thoughtful analogy between racism and homophobia that discusses, among other matters, Du Bois's concept of double consciousness, see David A.J. Richards, *Identity and the Case for Gay Rights: Race, Gender,*

Religion as Analogies (Chicago: University of Chicago Press, 1999), ch. 1.

134. See e.g., Kate Millet, *Sexual Politics* (New York: Doubleday, 1970); The Boston Women's Health Book Collective, *Our Bodies, Ourselves: A Book By and For Woman* (New York: Simon and Schuster, 1973).

135. Foucault recognizes that transgression is a concept that lacks a positive content. See Michel Foucault, "A Preface to Transgression," in Michel Foucault, *Aesthetics, Method, and Epistemology*, ed. James D. Faubion (New York: New Press, 1998), pp. 69, 74. As Mark Bevir notes, once we distinguish, as we must, between "good and bad transgressions, then transgression itself is unlikely to remain the cornerstone of our theory of freedom." Bevir, "Foucault and Critique," p. 79.

INDEX

Abortion
  and moral liberalism, 97
  and political values, 26
  and public reason, 25–26
Adaptationist conception of
  morality, 60, 66
Adoption
  and parenting by lesbians and gay
    men, 165
  and prohibition of lesbians and
    gay men, 200
Aesthetic of existence
  and Foucault, 179, 187
  and gay sexual ethics, 206
Agency versus autonomy
  and postmodernism, 185–193
AIDS
  and gay and lesbian sexual ethic,
    207–208
Alaska
  and gay rights, 157
  and same-sex marriage, 157
American Law Institute
  and decriminalization of sodomy,
    199
American Psychiatric Association
  and homosexuality, 201
Ancient Greece
  and codes of conduct, 182–183
  and excess, 182
  and passivity, 183–184
  and pleasure, 182–184, 212, 214
  and reciprocity, 184
  and relationships between men
    and boys, 183–184
  and self-restraint, 182–183

  and sexual ethics, 173, 180–184,
    194, 200–201
Antidiscrimination laws
  state and local, 3, 52–53, 199
Antiessentialism
  and sexuality, 173, 174, 176,
    185, 193
Antifoundationalism
  and postmodernism, 173, 185
Antimiscegenation laws, 126–127
Aristotle
  and pragmatic liberalism, 43
Autonomy
  and moral liberalism, 75–137
  and parenting by lesbians and gay
    men, 163, 167–168
  and postmodernism, 172–217
  and relationships and
    attachments, 91–100

Baker v. State, 129
Beliefs
  and pragmatic liberalism, 44
Bennett, William
  and same-sex marriage, 4
Bevir, Mark
  and agency versus autonomy,
    187, 189
Biological families
  rejection and ostracization of gay
    members, 149
Blackmun, Justice Harry
  and *Bowers v. Hardwick*, 97
Blasius, Mark
  and mutuality, 210
  and relational rights, 16

Blustein, Jeffrey
   and communitarianism, 148
Bowers v. Hardwick, 3, 96–97, 111,
   199

Calhoun, Cheshire
   and same-sex marriage, 112
Card, Claudia
   and same-sex marriage, 113
Chauncey, George
   and gay community, 146
Civic republicanism, 141–142, 149
Civil unions, 116–117, 199–200,
   209
   and Vermont, 116, 199–200,
   209
Codes of conduct
   and gay and lesbian sexual ethic,
   194–217
   and sexual ethics, 180–183
Codification of homosexuality, 195,
   196–199, 202–203
Cohen, Jean
   and majoritarian preferences, 65
   and sexuality, 70, 72
Coming out, 145
Communitarianism, 7, 139–170
   and communities of choice,
   144–151
   and complex equality, 153–154
   criticism of John Rawls, 139
   and critique of liberalism, 7
   and feminism, 148
   and gay families, 147
   and given communities, 144–151
   and human commonalities,
   160–161
   and moral bracketing, 141, 143,
   154
   and moral liberalism, 90, 107,
   139–140, 150–151, 160
   and neutral liberalism, 142
   and new natural law, 160–161
   and postmodernism, 150
   and pragmatic liberalism, 49
   and pragmatism, 139

   and relationships and
   attachments, 141–142
   and Sandel, 7, 141–151
   and social goods, 154, 159–163
   and Walzer, 7, 151–163, 170
Communities of choice
   and communitarianism, 144–151
Community
   role in the lives of lesbians and
   gay men, 145–151
Companionate marriage, 108–111,
   115, 127
Complex equality
   and communitarianism, 153–154
Continuity strategy
   of Dworkin, 38
Contractarianism
   discontinuity strategy, 38
   and feminist critique, 94
   and neutral liberalism, 18, 38, 78
Cott, Nancy
   and marriage, 127, 156
Criminalization of sex acts, 31, 33,
   65, 96, 197
Cruelty and humiliation
   and pragmatic liberalism, 46–48,
   50, 52

Davis, Madeline
   and lesbian community, 146
Decodification of homosexuality,
   199–204
Defense of Marriage Act, 4, 33, 50,
   130
Degendering trend
   and same-sex marriage, 157–158
Dehumanization of lesbians and
   gay men
   equating sodomy with bestiality,
   50
   viewed only in sexual terms,
   50–51
Denmark
   and same-sex marriage, 116
Derrida, Jacques
   and ironist theory, 46

and pragmatic liberalism,
    48
Descartes, René
    and pragmatic liberalism, 43
Descriptions and redescriptions
    and perceived human
        commonalities, 55
Devlin, Lord
    and enforcement of majoritarian
        morality, 31–33, 40
Dewey, John
    and liberal optimism, 47, 51
    and pragmatic liberalism, 42–43
Discontinuity strategy
    of Rawls, 38
Discrimination
    and employment, 3–4
DOMA. *See* Defense of Marriage
    Act.
Domestic partnership legislation,
    64
Domination
    versus power relations, 178, 192
Dred Scott v. Sandford, 53
Du Bois, W.E.B.
    and African Americans, 215
Dworkin, Ronald
    and communitarianism, 159
    continuity strategy, 38
    and human sexuality, 62
    individual ethics and the liberal
        society, 37–40
    later writings, 37–40
    and liberal equality, 30–37
    and moral bracketing, 30–37
    and neutral liberalism, 6, 30–40
    and pragmatic liberalism, 41–42,
        45, 48
    and societal regulation of
        homosexuality, 31

Eisenstadt v. Baird, 98
Emerson, Ralph Waldo
    and pragmatism, 42
Emotional intimacy
    and physical intimacy, 104–109

Equality
    and Dworkin's Tanner lectures,
        37, 39
    and employment, 36
    and neutral liberalism, 30, 32, 36
    and race, 36
    of resources, 38–39
    and same-sex marriage, 36
Eskridge, Bill
    and persecution of homosexuals,
        68
    and same-sex marriage, 116
    and state regulation of sexual
        conduct, 195, 197–199
Ethics
    individual, 37–40
    and morality, 180–181, 189
External preferences
    and criminalization of sex acts, 31
    role in setting public policy,
        31–32

Fairness
    and justice, 17–21
Fallon, Richard
    and self-transformation, 191
Feminism
    and autonomy, 188–189
    and communitarianism, 148
    and critique of marriage, 112–113
    and moral liberalism, 77, 92–96,
        99
Finnis, John, 4
    and basic goods, 118
    and sexual ethics, 202–203
    and homosexual intimacy,
        117–118, 123–125
    and mutuality, 211
Florida
    and adoption law, 200
Forster, E.M.
    and *Maurice*, 72
Foucault, Michel
    and aesthetic of existence, 179,
        187
    and ironist theory, 46–47

Foucault, Michel (continued)
  and postmodernism, 7–8, 16,
    172–196, 205, 209–213
  and pragmatic liberalism, 42–43,
    48
  and sexual ethics, 7–8, 172–185,
    205, 209–213
Foundationalism, 41–42
Friedman, Marilyn
  and community, 150
  and moral liberalism, 95

Gay and lesbian sexual ethic, 173,
    191–192, 194–217
  and codes of conduct, 194–217
  and mutuality, 208–212
  and openness, 207
  and pleasure, 212–214
  process of, 205–206
  substance of, 206–214
Gay families
  and communitarianism, 147
  and postmodernism, 209
Gay lifestyle, 205–206
Gay marriage. See Same-sex
    marriage.
Gay relationships
  longevity of, 69
  societal recognition of, 4, 10–12,
    25, 27
  validation of, 4
Gay rights
  in Great Britain, 2, 31
  history of, 2–4
  and communitarianism,
    155–162, 166–170
  and issues of sexual exclusivity,
    13
  and moral liberalism, 100–137
  and neutral liberalism, 24–29,
    32–37
  and pragmatic liberalism, 48–50,
    52–57, 63–64, 68–70
  and privacy, 4–5
  and state of Alaska, 157
  and state of Florida, 200

  and state of Georgia, 199
  and state of Hawaii, 116, 129,
    168
  and state of Illinois, 199
  and state of Mississippi, 200
  and state of New Hampshire, 68
  and state of Utah, 200
  and state of Vermont, 53, 116,
    129, 199–200, 209
Gay sex
  versus gay love, 209
George, Robert
  and homosexual intimacy, 124
Georgia
  and gay rights, 199
Griswold v. Connecticut, 98

Habermas, Jürgen
  and communitarianism, 152
Halperin, David
  and autonomy, 189–190
  and gay rights, 172
  and same-sex marriage, 209
Hardwick, Michael, 3
Harm principle
  of John Stuart Mill, 12, 32, 46,
    62–63, 65–66, 88
Hawaii
  and gay rights, 116, 129, 168
  and same-sex marriage, 116, 129,
    168
Heidegger, Martin
  and pragmatic liberalism, 43
Homosexual intimacy
  alleged narcissism of, 123
Homosexuality
  choice versus immutable trait,
    101–102
  proportion of the population, 71
  societal regulation of, 31,
    195–203
Hope
  and pragmatic liberalism, 47, 52
Human commonalities, 37, 51–58,
    84, 120, 160–161
  and communitarianism, 160–161

and intimacy, 57
and moral liberalism, 84, 120
and pragmatic liberalism, 51–58
Human flourishing
and moral liberalism, 85, 118
and new natural law, 118
Human sexuality
and biology, 61–62
and "deviant" behavior, 63
and discussions of morality, 71–72
moralistic biological discourse
on, 72
moralistic Christian discourse on,
72
and pragmatic liberalism, 58–73
and rational choice theory, 61–62
and same-sex marriage, 64
Hume, David
and naturalistic fallacies,
121–122

Illinois
and decriminalization of sodomy,
199
Individual ethics
and the liberal society, 37–40
Intergenerational sex, 13–14,
183–184
Internal social criticism
and parenting by lesbians and gay
men, 162–170
and same-sex marriage, 155–162
Ironist theory
and pragmatic liberalism, 45–46
and private sphere, 45–46
and public sphere, 46

Jaggar, Alison
and moral liberalism, 92
James, William
and pragmatism, 42–43
Justice
and fairness, 17–21
and local norms and practices,
151–155
political conception of, 20

and the self's ties and
connections, 23

Kant, Immanuel
and pragmatic liberalism, 43, 187
Kennedy, Elizabeth Lapovsky
and lesbian community, 146
Kinsey, Alfred
and studies on sexuality, 62
Kinsey scale, 62, 67–68
Kohlberg, Lawrence
and moral liberalism, 95
Kriegel, Leonard
and marginalized persons, 55
Krieger, Susan
and lesbian community, 149

Language
and moral liberalism, 83
and pragmatic liberalism, 43–45,
55–56
Lee, Patrick
and homosexual intimacy, 124
Liberalism
communitarian critique of, 7,
139, 141–145, 188
moral, 7, 39, 75–137
neutral, 6, 15–40
pragmatic, 6, 41–73
Libertarianism, 66
Lochner v. New York, 143
Locke, John
and moral liberalism, 77–78
and pragmatic liberalism, 43
Loving v. Virginia, 98, 126, 128

Macedo, Stephen
and autonomy, 188–189
Mackenzie, Catriona
and autonomy, 189
Majoritarian morality, 31–34
role in setting public policy,
31–33, 39–40
and same-sex marriage, 33
and sodomy laws, 32–33
Majoritarian preferences, 65–66

Marriage
and gender-based privileges, 128
interracial, 126–128
patriarchal and inegalitarian
characteristics, 112–113,
126–129, 157–158
and subordination of women, 113
Marxism
and pragmatic liberalism, 47–48
Maurice, 72–73
McWhorter, Ladelle, 16
and pleasure, 213
and sexual identity, 214
Meyer v. Nebraska, 98
Military service
effect of gay soldiers on morale of
heterosexual soldiers, 64
and lesbians and gay men, 64, 68
Mill, John Stuart
harm principle, 12, 32, 46,
62–63, 65–66, 88
and liberalism, 16
and moral liberalism, 77
Mississippi
and adoption law, 200
Mohr, Richard
and postmodernism, 172
Monogamy
and same-sex marriage, 131–132
Moral bracketing
and communitarianism, 141,
143, 154
and neutral liberalism, 1, 6, 24,
29–37
and parenting by lesbians and gay
men, 29
and same-sex marriage, 29
and Sandel, 141, 143
and Walzer, 154
Moral decodification of sexuality,
202–204
Moral evaluations
versus moral judgments, 10–11
Moral liberalism, 7, 39, 75–137,
150–151

addressing views of neutral
liberals, 89
and autonomy, 75–137
and choice, 136–137
and communitarianism, 90, 107,
139–140, 150–151, 160
and conception of self, 75
and feminism, 92–96, 99
and gay rights, 100–137
and human flourishing, 85,
118
and language, 83
and new natural law, 90,
118–125
and Nussbaum, 6–7, 78–91
and postmodernism, 77, 119
and pragmatism, 107
and same-sex marriage, 102–103,
107–133
and state coercion, 88
Moss, Jeremy
and freedom, 191
Mutuality
and gay and lesbian sexual ethic,
208–212
and slave/master sexual
encounters, 210–211, 213

Nardi, Peter
and gay community, 146–148
Nedelsky, Jennifer
and moral liberalism, 96
Needs and capabilities
and leading full human lives,
75–137
The Netherlands
and same-sex marriage, 116
Neutral liberalism, 6, 15–40, 142
and communitarianism, 142
and contractarianism, 38
and Dworkin, 6, 30–40
and equality of resources, 38–39
and fairness, 17–21
and fundamental principles of
justice, 17–21

and issues of equality, 30, 32, 36
and moral bracketing, 1, 6, 24, 29
versus moral liberalism, 15–16
and parenting by lesbians and gay
    men, 15–16, 24, 27–28
and political values, 20, 25
and public reason, 20–21, 25
and Rawls, 6, 16–30
and same-sex marriage, 25–27
New Hampshire
and gay rights, 68
New natural law
and basic goods, 118–119
and communitarianism, 160–161
and human flourishing, 118
and moral liberalism, 90,
    118–120
and same-gender sexuality,
    120–125
Nietzsche, Friedrich
and ironist theory, 46
and pragmatic liberalism, 43
NNL. See New natural law.
Nock, Steven
and marriage, 156
Nussbaum, Martha
and autonomy, 187
and basic human capabilities,
    80–87
and ethical judgments, 65
and human commonalities,
    55–56, 58
and Maurice, 72
and moral liberalism, 7, 78–88,
    91–92, 108

Openness
and AIDS, 207–208
and gay lesbian sexual ethic,
    207–208

Parenting by lesbians and gay men
and adoption, 165, 200
alleged selfishness of, 134
and autonomy, 163, 167–168

and conclusions of American
    Academy of Pediatrics, 169
effect on children of parents'
    sexual orientation, 70
and human commonalities,
    133–134
and internal social criticism,
    162–170
and issue of biological
    relatedness, 165–166
and issues of equality, 36
moral arguments regarding,
    28–29, 35
and moral bracketing, 29
and neutral liberalism, 15–16, 24,
    27–28
in New Hampshire, 68
and responsibility, 164–170
and same-sex marriage, 121, 129
and universality, 163–164, 168
value of, 133–137
Passivity
and ancient Greece, 183–184
and postmodernism, 186
Phelan, Shane
and rights, 17
Physical and emotional intimacy
and same-sex marriage, 104–109
Pierce v. Society of Sisters, 98
Plato
and pragmatic liberalism, 43
Pleasure
and ancient Greece, 182–184,
    212, 214
versus desire, 212–213
and gay and lesbian sexual ethic,
    212–214
Political liberalism
of Rawls, 17–30
and Rawls's veil of ignorance,
    18–19
Political values
and abortion, 26
and neutral liberalism, 20, 25
and same-sex marriage, 26–27

Polygamy
    and state regulation of sexual
        conduct, 34–35, 114
Posner, Richard
    and gay rights, 63–64, 69–70
    normative theory of sex
        regulation, 62–66
    and homosexuality, 62–63, 67–73
    and morally indifferent sex, 59,
        68
    and pragmatic liberalism, 6, 58–73
Poster, Mark
    and mutuality, 209
Postmodernism, 7–8, 42, 45, 48,
        150, 171–217
    agency versus autonomy,
        185–193
    and antifoundationalism, 185
    and autonomy, 172–217
    and communitarianism, 150
    and feminism, 188–189
    and freedom, 177–179, 185,
        188–194
    and moral liberalism, 77, 119
    and power and knowledge,
        176–178, 186, 190, 192–193,
        196
    and pragmatic liberalism, 42, 45,
        48
    and self-transformation, 179,
        190–194, 205–207, 210,
        213–214, 216
Power and knowledge
    and postmodernism, 176–178,
        186, 190, 192–193, 196
Pragmatic liberalism, 6, 41–73
    and beliefs, 44
    and building solidarity, 47, 51,
        53, 55–56
    and dealing with nonliberals, 47
    and Dewey, 42–43
    and Emerson, 42
    and feminism, 45, 55
    and functional normativism,
        64–65

    and hope, 47, 52
    and human commonalities,
        51–58
    and human sexuality, 58–73
    and invention of morality, 45
    and ironist theory, 45–46
    and James, 42–43
    and language, 43–45, 55–56
    and Marxism, 47–48
    and minimization of cruelty and
        humiliation, 46–48, 50, 52
    morality versus prudence, 45
    and Posner, 58–73
    and postmodernism, 42, 45, 48
    private sphere versus public
        sphere, 45–48
    and rights, 45
    and Rorty, 42–58
    and truth, 43
    and utility, 43, 45
    and vocabulary, 46–48, 58
Pragmatism
    Darwinian, 66
    empirical, 60
Private sphere
    and vocabulary of self-creation,
        46–47
Promiscuity
    of gay men, 126, 131–132
    gay men versus straight men,
        131–132
Public power
    and neutral liberalism, 21
Public reason
    and abortion, 25–26
    and neutral liberalism, 20–21, 25
    and same-sex marriage, 25
    and societal recognition of gay
        relationships, 27
Public sex, 13–14
Public sphere
    and vocabulary of justice, 46–47

Queer theorists
    critique of marriage, 112–113

and postmodernism, 172,
176–177, 185–186, 189–190,
193
and skepticism of liberalism, 16

Rawls, John
on abortion, 25–26
and conception of the self, 18,
187
constraints on public reasoning,
29
critique by communitarianism,
139–142
and the difference principle, 18
discontinuity strategy, 38
and gay rights, 24–30
and the liberty principle, 18
and moral liberalism, 77–78,
118
and moral personhood, 22
and neutral liberalism, 6, 16 30
and pragmatic liberalism, 41–42
Rawlsian liberalism, 17–30
communitarian critique of, 23
ontological critique of, 22–23
perfectionist critique of, 23–24
Raz, Joseph
and moral liberalism, 88, 108
"Real" homosexuals versus
opportunistic homosexuals,
62–63, 67–69, 71
Recognition of gay relationships
and state coercion, 33–34
Regan, Milton
and moral liberalism, 98
Relationships and attachments
and communitarianism,
141–142
and importance to autonomy,
91–100
Resistance
and power, 178
Responsibility
and parenting by lesbians and gay
men, 164–170

Richards, David
and resistance to gay rights
positions, 50
Rights of inclusion
burden of justification, 49–50
Romer v. Evans, 35, 52–53, 91
Rorty, Richard
and communitarianism, 139
and moral liberalism, 118
and pragmatic liberalism, 6,
42–58

Same-sex marriage
consequences for society,
125–133
critique from the left, 112–117
critique from the right, 117–133
and degendering trend, 157–158
and Denmark, 116
and destabilization of gender
roles, 127–128
and internal social criticism,
155–162
and issue of promiscuity, 126, 132
and majoritarian morality, 33
and monogamy, 131–132
and moral bracketing, 29
and moral liberalism, 102–103,
107–133
and the Netherlands, 116
and neutral liberalism, 15–16,
24–26
and parenting by lesbians and gay
men, 121, 129
and physical and emotional
intimacy, 104–109
and political values, 27
and pragmatic liberalism, 53
and public reason, 25
and state coercion, 33
and state of Alaska, 157
and state of Hawaii, 116, 129, 168
and state of Vermont, 53, 116,
129
value of, 103–133

Sandel, Michael
   and communitarianism, 7,
      139–151
   and moral bracketing, 141, 143
   perfectionist critique of neutral
      liberalism, 23–24, 26
   and values and communities,
      141–145
Sartre, Jean-Paul
   and pragmatic liberalism, 43
Scalia, Justice Antonin
   and *Romer v. Evans*, 35
Schneewind, J.B.
   and self-governance, 187
Scruton, Roger
   and homosexual intimacy,
      123–124
Self-transformation
   and postmodernism, 179,
      190–194, 205–207, 210,
      213–214, 216
Sen, Amartya, 52, 79–80
Sex drives
   men versus women, 63
Sexual conduct
   and balance of costs and benefits,
      68, 72–73
   other-regarding, 62
   self-regarding, 62
   state regulation of, 34–35, 62,
      195–203
Sexual ethics
   in ancient Greece, 173, 180–184,
      194, 200–201
   and antiessentialism, 174, 176
   and Christian period, 180–185
   and codes of conduct, 180–183
   of lesbians and gay men, 204–217
   and Michel Foucault, 174–185
   specific to lesbians, 204–205
Sexual exclusivity, 13
Sexual intimacy
   heterosexual versus homosexual,
      121–124
Sexual morality, 34–35
   and same-sex marriage, 35

Sexuality
   and essentialist theory, 176
   and social constructionist theory,
      8–10, 176–177
Sexuality Information and Education
      Council of the United States
   and sexual ethics, 204
Shepard, Matthew
   beating death of, 50
Slave/master sexual encounters
   and mutuality, 210–211, 213
Social constructionist theory
   moderate, 9
   and sexuality, 8–10, 176–177
   soft, 8–9
   strict, 9
Social goods
   and communitarianism, 154,
      159–163
Sodomy
   and equation with bestiality, 50
Sodomy laws, 3, 32–33, 50, 63–64,
      96, 129, 196–200
   and majoritarian morality, 32–33
Solidarity
   and pragmatic liberalism, 47, 51,
      53, 55–56
Stanley v. Georgia, 97–98
State coercion
   and moral liberalism, 88
   and recognition of gay
      relationships, 33–34
   and same-sex marriage, 33
Stoljar, Natalie
   and autonomy, 189
Sullivan, Andrew
   and same-sex marriage, 53

Taylor, Charles
   and "morally neutral" naturalists,
      67
Thoreau, Henry David
   and communitarianism, 147
Tribe, Lawrence
   and Georgia's sodomy law, 3
Troxel v. Granville, 98

Universal Declaration of Human
    Rights, 81
Universalism, 8
    versus essentialism in matters of
        sexuality, 8
Universality
    and parenting by lesbians and gay
        men, 163–164, 168
Utah
    and adoption law, 200
Utilitarianism, 43, 65
Utility
    measurable, 73
    and pragmatic liberalism, 43,
        45

Veil of ignorance
    and Rawls's political liberalism,
        18–19
Vermont
    and civil unions, 116, 199–200,
        209
    and gay rights, 53, 116, 129,
        199–200, 209
    and same-sex marriage, 53, 116,
        129
Vocabulary
    and pragmatic liberalism, 46–48,
        58

Walzer, Michael
    and communitarianism, 7, 49,
        139–140, 151–160, 162–163,
        165

and justice, 151–155
    and moral bracketing, 154
    and parenting by lesbians and gay
        men, 136
Wardle, Lynn
    and parenting by lesbians and gay
        men, 133–135, 169–170
    and same-sex marriage, 132
Warner, Michael
    and pleasure, 213
    and state noninterference, 17
West, Cornel
    and pragmatism, 43
West, Robin
    and interracial marriage, 127
    and moral liberalism, 93, 96
Weston, Kath
    and coming out, 145
    and gay community, 146–147
White, Edmund
    and aesthetics, 206
White, Justice Byron
    and *Bowers v. Hardwick*,
        97
Whitman, Walt
    and liberal optimism, 47, 51
Wolfenden Committee Report, 2,
    31
World Wars I and II
    and state regulation of sexual
        conduct, 198

Zablocki v. Redhail, 98